chairs
a history

florence de dampierre chairs: a history

abrams, new york

749.32
D166

0 introduction 6

1 chairs in the ancient world, china & africa 12

2 medieval & renaissance chairs 50

3 country, garden & colonial chairs 78

4 high style: baroque, rococo & neoclassical chairs 148

5 chairs in the nineteenth century 252

6 modern chairs 350

index 420

0
chairs: introduction

Artists throughout history have portrayed Adam and Eve as standing, as if to say that in Paradise before the Fall we stood upright. Standing is in many ways a healthier position than sitting; the body is erect, and the position natural, learned in childhood. Sitting comes later, as an acquired social behavior. Indeed, sitting has been something of a luxury in the panoply of human activity.

Things to sit on were invented for status and comfort. A civilized being sat on a chair, away from the cold, damp floor. As Western civilization evolved, chairs increasingly became a part of life, at first for the moneyed classes, and ultimately, for all. By 1532, the Spanish writer Perez de Chinchon would distinguish his countrymen from the Moors by saying, "We Christians sit at a proper height, not on the ground like animals."

Not everyone has used seats the same way. A Persian friend once vividly recalled his grandmother, the mother of the late Shah of Iran, and her friends seated cross-legged on sofas. When a guest entered the room in their palace in Tehran, the ladies stood up on the sofas to greet them. It must have been quite a picture.

The Bible records that Solomon sat on a magnificent chair, a symbol of his power. During the Middle Ages and later, under the strict etiquette of Louis XIV, chairs functioned as a hierarchical tool. No one expressed this better than Shakespeare:

Is the chair empty? Is the sword unswayed?
Is the King dead? The Empire unpossessed?

Richard III
Act IV, scene iv, 470

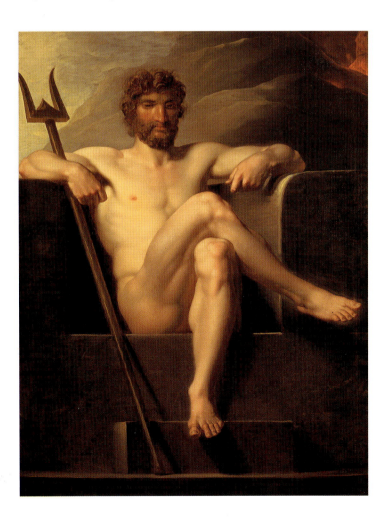

> Heinrich Friedrich Füger (1751–1818), *Poseidon Seated on a Throne*. Oil on canvas. From the Rudolf Nureyev collection. Christie's

Since the end of the eighteenth century, chairs have been equalizers. Offering a chair to a visitor, regardless of his social position, became such an ingrained convention that the last words of Lord Chesterfield on his deathbed in 1777 were "Give Dayrolles a chair," a gesture that secured Chesterfield's reputation as one of the most polite men who ever lived. Yet chairs can represent social disorder as well. A chair lying on its side or upside down in a drawing or painting is a convention to express social upheaval. We can see this illustrated in an ink and chalk drawing by a mid-fifteenth-century Flemish master from the school of Rogier van der Weyden, *Men Shoveling Chairs*. Later, in the late-eighteenth-century etchings of Francisco Goya, *Los Caprichos*, one image represents women carrying chairs on their heads as a symbol of a world gone mad.

Chairs can be surrogates for human beings, from the seat reserved for the prophet Elijah at the Passover seder to the vacant chair representing a faraway soldier in the American Civil War song. In Victorian cemeteries, the armchair was

<
An unusual Russian painted mahogany open armchair, carved in the form of a seated skeleton, with a leathered upholstered slip-seat. The underside of the seat is dated 1838 and inscribed with a note in Russian explaining that the chair was made for a Masonic lodge. From the William A. McCarthy-Cooper collection. Christie's

a magisterial stand-in for the dead. In Eugene Ionesco's play *The Chairs* (1952), chairs are the ultimate symbol of a crowd—empty, absurd, and overwhelming. In the jargon of furniture, the human metaphor continues: Chairs have legs, feet—some with claws—knees, arms, knuckles, and even, occasionally, ears. One of my favorite chairs even has a back carved in the form of a skeleton, standing on human legs.

Physically, a chair is an instrument of both pain and pleasure. It displays our bodies for presentation, showing the best version of our public selves. For portraits of all periods often portray their subjects seated, from the family of Ludovico Gonzaga by Andrea Mantegna (c. 1474); to Madame Vigée-Lebrun's portrait of Otto Nicolas, Prince of Nassau-Sieghen (1789); to Madame Charpentier and her children by Pierre-Auguste Renoir (1877). The chair in a portrait performs many functions; it shapes the body, crops the background, restricts the space that it occupies, and, of course, makes the time pass more comfortably for the sitter.

Comfort in seats seems to have been the major quest of the nineteenth and twentieth centuries.

<
A late-eighteenth-century armchair in the entrance staircase of the Musée Nissim de Camondo, Paris. Photograph by Antoine Bootz

> *Men Shoveling Chairs.* This beautiful drawing by an anonymous Flemish master around 1445 was probably created for the Hôtel de Ville in Brussels. The curious subject may be explained by the common fifteenth-century expression "to mix up stools and chairs," which signified social chaos, since chairs represented important people and stools their inferiors. Carved on the city hall, this image would warn against such an undesirable social situation. The Metropolitan Museum of Art 1975.1 848

Yet, in all its exaltation of industrial efficiency, the Bauhaus School of the early twentieth century gave birth to sleek, handsome, and torturous-looking chairs, the 1925 Wassily Chair by Marcel Breuer and the 1929 Barcelona Chair by Ludwig Mies van der Rohe. Between the World Wars, Scandinavian functionalism could be an almost sinister source of control. The Norwegian chair manufacturer T. M. Grimsrud said of the Finnish architect Alvar Aalto's sanatorium chair that "if the patients were not already sick, then they certainly would be after sitting in one of them."

As a chair brings comfort, it can also take it away. Chairs were favored through the centuries as a means of torture, which, when appropriately outfitted, kept the victim relatively motionless, and at a lower height than the torturer. The most ancient usually were bulky contraptions featuring leather straps and pointed, metallic instruments. More recently, tubular steel and metal project an efficient, antiseptic look, culminating in the ultimate torture chair, the electric chair, where the psychological power of the chair is dramatically absent. The electric chair, being a modern invention, created a supposedly clean and efficient way to die; yet paradoxically it burns the flesh and loosens the bowels of its sitter.

Chairs range from an emblem of social ease to sheer necessity. Going from show-off to shame is another kind of chair, the throne reserved for bodily functions. Initially lacquered, painted, and decorated in the seventeenth and eighteenth centuries as an object of display, it became a shameful appurtenance during the prudish nineteenth century, and was hidden away.

Seating defies linear chronology. Over the centuries, chair styles have come and gone, with elements introduced, then disappearing, only to reemerge at another place and time. The ancient Romans reclined in their seats and Madame Récamier reclined in her chaise longue on the eve of the French Empire, eighteen centuries later. Fashion played a role, too. The hem or width of a skirt has from time to time led to the creation of an armrest, or to its removal.

Materials and fashions change, but the human body and its basic needs and aspirations remain the same, even if body measurements have slightly increased. The mother of all chairs, an Egyptian piece surviving from the fourteenth century B.C.,

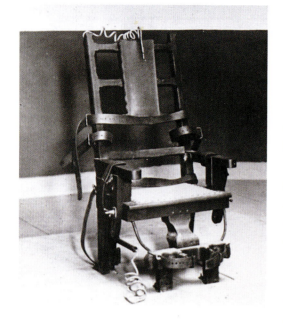

< The electric chair, a method of execution introduced as a clean alternative to hanging. It was first established by the New York legislature on June 4, 1888, as the state's new method of execution. In 1896, Ohio adopted it, and in 1898 Massachusetts followed suit. New Jersey adopted electrocution in 1906, Virginia in 1908, and North Carolina in 1910. Soon after, at least twenty other states were using the electric chair, making it by far the most common means of execution in the modern world.

is remarkably similar to a contemporary chair. Its seat was made of ropes, with legs carved to resemble those of an animal, the feet like the paws of a lion, in order to empower the sitter with the animal's strength and courage. The same lions' paws reappear at the end of the eighteenth century in the chairs by the English furniture makers John Linnell and Thomas Chippendale, and then again a few years later in France, after Napoleon's expedition to Egypt, in chairs by Charles Percier and Pierre-François-Léonard Fontaine.

The refined and elegant *klismos*, developed by the ancient Greeks, lived on for centuries in numerous revivals, from Denmark, England, France, and Russia. The Romans created timeless chairs as well. The field seating of their military officers is echoed in the ubiquitous folding director's chair of today and the Roman magistrate's *sella curulis* is mimicked in Mies van der Rohe's Barcelona Chair.

After the collapse of the Roman Empire, chair design came to a virtual standstill for a thousand years while most people sat (if they were lucky) on stools or benches while their lords or ladies sat on boxlike thrones on a dais. The descendants of these pieces, the campaign chests, were indispensable items of an army officer's kit as late as the Boer War in the late nineteenth century. Educated European and American designers from Augustus Welby Northmore Pugin to Eugène-Emmanuel Viollet-le-Duc and Frank Furness resurrected the throne toward the end of the nineteenth century in a Gothic version of those horrendously uncomfortable chairs.

If the chair had a heyday, it was in Western Europe and, to a lesser extent, in the European colonies, in the seventeenth and eighteenth centuries. Those centuries saw a concentration on refinement, majestically led by the French kings and strictly enforced by the furniture guilds. To this day collectors still sit in those chairs; museums proudly display them; and auction houses orchestrate bidding contests for the best examples. Less fortunate human beings have to content themselves with the purchase of faithful copies.

During the course of the nineteenth century an authoritative style in seats started to disappear and a multiplicity of styles slowly emerged. Many were revivals in the Gothic, Egyptian, or Chinese

v A late-medieval German torture chair. Torture chairs come in a variety of types. Their common feature is that they are covered with spikes in various areas of the seat, thus penetrating the flesh of the victim. Most have a bar at chest height, to immobilize the victim's upper body, and leather straps on the armrests. One of the strengths of this chair lies in the psychological terror it causes, along with real pain. Such chairs were used in Germany, France, and Great Britain until the end of the nineteenth century, and in China until the eighteenth or nineteenth century, often featuring blades on the armrests instead of spikes. Rothenburg ob der Tauber Museum

tastes. Others represented greater creativity, such as the Biedermeier or Victorian styles. On the eccentric fringe were chairs for sexual horseplay, three-legged chairs, reclining chairs with flat arms for drunken colonials to rest their drinks, and nocturnal reading chairs with candlesticks.

In everyday chairs, the abiding theme of the last two centuries was an increasing attraction towards comfort. In the nineteenth century the English clearly had the advantage. Their comfortable chairs were the envy of most Europeans. Following the English lead, the appeal of comfort increased during the course of the twentieth century with its loosening etiquette, manners, and behavior. The discovery of new materials—molded plastic and polystyrene allied with tubular steel—reinforced the existing tendencies. Today's ergonomic chairs, sophisticated in the extreme, with adjusting backs, seats, and headrests designed for the new computer age, seem to be a world apart from their ancestors, and yet their extreme complexity makes it hard to accomplish the goal of total comfort for everyone. For all these innovations, the chair is still an object of unease (a comfortable chair for one person is uncomfortable for someone else), and therefore it is a very personal choice.

If only chairs could talk! One actually did in a witty novella published by Philippe Jullian in 1959, *Memoires d'une Bergère*, the mock-reminiscences of a *bergère*, a particularly elegant French eighteenth-century version of the armchair. Jullian's daring *bergère* leads an adventurous life indeed, traveling from the Versailles of Louis XV into exile and on to a Bohemian existence, and finally to a glorious end. Along the way she meets almost everyone, from Louis XV himself to Talleyrand, Winston Churchill, and even the elusive Greta Garbo. A witness to social interaction since ancient times, the chair seems almost like another character in the human drama. As the poet Alphonse de Lamartine asked:

Objets inanimés, avez-vous donc une âme?
Qui s'attache à notre âme et la force d'aimer?

[*Inanimate object, do you have a soul?*
You, who attach yourself to our hearts and force them to love?]

>
A very rare nineteenth-century Venetian armchair made of Murano glass. Private collection

A chair's possession of a soul—however improbable to us, the firm belief of the Asante people of Africa—would explain its infinite complexity and appeal. Recent auctions solely dedicated to chairs of all ages have attracted enthusiastic collectors; prices of unusual or rare models have skyrocketed; and museums such as the Vitra Design Museum in Weil am Rhein or the Museum of Design in Lisbon display chair collections as a testament to a way of life. Chairs are now starting, at long last, to be recognized as a major design expression. In this book we shall try to explain the political, sociological, philosophical, and fashionable evolution of the chair, with a multitude of anecdotes and legends to illustrate its unique quality and unusual influence on the human spirit. So please, benevolent reader, take a seat and join us on our journey.

1

chairs in the ancient world, china & africa

EGYPT: THE EARLIEST CHAIRS

The earliest seats that survive today were made around 2680 B.C., during the Egyptian Old Kingdom (2686–2181 B.C.). Since Egypt's dry air preserves even delicate materials such as textiles, wood, and papyrus, a surprisingly complete record of Egyptian carpentry can be pieced together from archeological excavation, from which we know that in ancient Egypt design principles were established for many common objects that are still followed today.

The Egyptians believed that every living soul was inhabited by a double, or *Ka*, which could survive after death if the body were preserved in familiar surroundings. Thus, proper burial was essential for happiness in the afterlife. The Egyptians built tombs as houses for eternity, filling them with objects for use after death, including furniture.

Egyptian carpenters were highly skilled at estimating the moisture content of timber. They understood that the aridity of the desert would cause wood to become extremely dry, resulting in splitting and shrinkage, even after a piece had been worked into its final form. Wood was scarce; trees were cultivated for fruit or shade, and only a few indigenous varieties produced usable woods. The very hard acacia was the best, rarest, and most costly; tamarisk and sycamore fig were cheaper. The wood most widely used for fine carpentry was cedar, which had to be imported from Lebanon and Syria. It is not known exactly when cedar was first imported in bulk, but the Palermo Stone, which records the annals of the early kings of Egypt, relates that Snefru, the first king of the Fourth Dynasty (2613–2494 B.C.), "brought forty ships filled with cedar from Lebanon." Egyptian carpenters exploited this excellent timber throughout the Dynastic Period. Much of the funerary furniture in the New Kingdom tomb of Tutankhamun, for example, was of cedar. In addition, box, a hardwood, was imported from

<
A very fine example of an Egyptian chair with a curved, sloping back. Eighteenth Dynasty. British Museum 37339

Anatolia, and ebony was brought from Ethiopia and other regions to the south.

At first woodworking was done with basic hand tools, but by the beginning of the Early Dynastic Period (3050–2686 B.C.), when Upper and Lower Egypt were unified into a single kingdom, more specialized tools were made. The earliest examples of copper saws were discovered by Flinders Petrie at Abydos in 1899–02 and 1921–22, and by Walter B. Emery at Saqqara between the 1930s and 1950s. Emery discovered an enormous cache of woodworking tools, among them straight wooden adze shafts, copper adze blades, and copper saws. There were also copper awls and some small copper engraving tools. Emery dated them to the reign of Djer, who ruled during the First Dynasty (c. 3050 B.C.). By the Fifth Dynasty (c. 2100 B.C.) the shape of the saw had been modified with a handle made to fit the carpenter's hand. In 1888 Petrie discovered a workmen's town dating to the Middle Kingdom (2040–1782 B.C.) at Kahun, where he found tools made of bronze, a major advance over copper. Later, during the New Kingdom (1570–1070 B.C.), carpenters had an extensive tool-kit, including axes, adzes, pull-saws, handsaws, bow-drills, chisels, mallets, and awls.

Egyptian noblemen loved ornamentation, and their chairs raised them above the level of social inferiors such as slaves and farmers, who spent long periods of time squatting on the ground. The first piece of domestic furniture to become common in ancient Egypt was a stool with a rectangular frame. The earliest examples known are depicted on various stelae discovered in the Second Dynasty (c. 2680 B.C.) tombs at Helwan by the Egyptian archaeologist Zaky Y. Saad in 1952. From these images we know that stools with bovine-shaped legs were commonly used during the Second Dynasty. These were followed by a variety of stools, until around 2210 B.C., when the first seats that we would recognize as chairs (stools fitted with backs and, occasionally, with arms) began to appear.

Although stools pre-date chairs, there is an early representation of a royal throne. Narmer, the first king of Egypt, is pictured seated on a canopied chair mounted on a high, stepped dais. Also, in the Second Dynasty tombs at Helwan, a stela of Prince Nisu-hequet shows him seated on a chair with a high back-post and a stretcher below the seat. Since the prince was of royal descent, it seems reasonable to imagine that this chair represents an early throne. It also seems, as we shall see, that chairs or armchairs were widely used as thrones for royalty in Egypt. One of the earliest scholars to excavate in Egypt was the French archaeologist Auguste Mariette (1821–81), who opened the tomb of Hesire, the chief of dentists and physicians in the reign of Djoser (mid-nineteenth century B.C.), discovering eleven panels, five of which portray Hesire, one of which shows him seated on an animal-legged stool with side-poles terminating in papyrus-flower finials.

The ancient Egyptians made a variety of stools, whose quality depended on the rank of their owners. Most were low, with flat seats of woven rushes, which would have been comfortable to the Egyptians, who were accustomed to sitting on the ground or on low seats. Moreover, the average height of an adult Egyptian man of the

>
An Egyptian stool. The seats of stools of this type are formed with a double cove construction of curved wooden slats or woven cords, which pass through holes in the frame. Eighteenth Dynasty. British Museum 37340

Old Kingdom was 1.70 m (approximately 5 feet 7 inches), roughly 40 mm (about 1½ inches) shorter than the average man of today. This difference was reflected in the seat height, the most important measurement used to design a seat. Since suitable wood was scarce, every scrap had to be used with care; for this reason, too, Egyptian stools tended to be small.

The lattice stool was popular with all classes. This type is widely illustrated in Theban tomb paintings and an actual example dating to the New Kingdom can be seen in the British Museum. Round-legged stools were also used, and these have been found in many Theban tombs. The legs were clearly not turned on a lathe, as they show no marks of scraping, are not squared at the shoulder, and have no pivot-hole at the base. Instead, they seem to have been hand-carved and then smoothed with sandstone.

Folding stools were introduced during the Middle Kingdom. Light and convenient to handle when folded, they were ideal for transport. They were formed of frames that turned on metal bolts in an X-configuration, with supports that usually terminated underneath in carved ducks' heads. This design would later be imitated in Greece, Rome, and medieval Europe, an example of the powerful influence Egyptian furniture had on later civilizations. A similar folding stool dating to about 1200 B.C. was found in Jutland (Denmark), which suggests the interesting possibility of cultural interaction between Egypt and Northern Europe.

Folding stools were also made with solid wooden seats shaped and painted to simulate animal skin. A fine example of this type was discovered among the burial goods in the tomb of Tutankhamun by Howard Carter in 1922, a group that included not only this folding stool, but several chairs, as well. These beautiful pieces are little different in style from those used by the middle class, but the quality of their workmanship and the richness of their ornamentation are much more sophisticated.

Cruder, three-legged seats were discovered in the Eleventh Dynasty (c. 2040 B.C.) tomb of Meket-Re at Thebes, which closely resemble the

<
An Egyptian stool with carved legs resembling turned work, with ivory braces and inlays, and the remains of a leather seat. Eighteenth Dynasty. Copyright British Museum 2472

stools now used for milking cows. In the New Kingdom wall paintings at Thebes carpenters are shown seated on such stools. The Egyptians made a great variety of other stools as well, including stools of tied palm branches or woven rushes, low seats with thick cushions for old people, and limestone stools, which were chiseled and polished.

By the Fifth Dynasty (c. 2000 B.C.) the stool had evolved into a seat with elevated sides and a back, a rather uncomfortable early version of the chair. In 1925 George Reisner, an American Egyptologist, discovered the furniture of Queen Hetepheres in a deep shaft close to her son Khufu's pyramid at Giza. Queen Hetepheres was the wife of Snefru, the first king of the Fourth Dynasty. Her armchair, the oldest still extant, is one of the few pieces of furniture to have survived (in part) from the Old Kingdom.

It was unlikely that a chair with a back would be found in an ordinary household until some time in the Middle Kingdom (c. 1930 B.C.). The majority of seats shown in Middle Kingdom reliefs in the Egyptian Museum in Cairo have short back-supports, over which covers or cushions are folded. These chairs have either plain, straight legs or legs fashioned in the form of the front and hind legs of a bull or lion. Also illustrated are a small number of elegant chairs with slender supports shaped like the legs of a gazelle. The

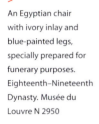

>
An Egyptian chair with ivory inlay and blue-painted legs, specially prepared for funerary purposes. Eighteenth–Nineteenth Dynasty. Musée du Louvre N 2950

surfaces of the chairs illustrated in the stelae often simulate animal skins, suggesting that the chairs were painted in the same way. Although the basic designs of these early chairs are similar to those of modern chairs, Egyptian chair-backs were never joined to the legs, as is typical today; the Egyptian chair was still a stool at heart. Many were very low—only nine or ten inches high—placing the sitter in a partially squatting position, with one knee drawn up.

By the middle of the Eighteenth Dynasty of the New Kingdom, chairs became more common and would have been found in the homes of the wealthy middle class as well as the aristocracy. In this period a type of royal chair appeared, with low arms sloping down from the back and rounded in front. A lion's head was frequently carved over each of the front legs so that, viewed from the side, the owner seems to be sitting on the back of a rather emaciated lion.

Lion paws and heads were common on seats belonging to pharaohs from the Old Kingdom, Middle Kingdom, and New Kingdom. The idea of animal transformation was a very ancient one in Egypt. A fundamental belief of the Egyptian religion was that in the afterlife the dead could assume the form of certain animals at will. Occasionally the legs of the seats were carved to resemble a bull's legs, so that the user might derive some of the bull's strength from them (or, in the case of ivory legs, that of the elephant). Bulls' legs became lions' legs near the end of the Third Dynasty (c. 2613 B.C.), and so were thought to give the sitter the courage and power of the lion, an animal adored for its strength and regal bearing, and identified early in Egyptian history with the sun gods Horus and Ra. From the end of the Third Dynasty the feet of chairs were often shaped like lions' paws, as well.

Thrones were mainly used for ceremonial occasions. Kings and queens, who were considered divine, were the only Egyptians permitted to use armchairs as such. While royal thrones and standard chairs were identical structurally, the quality of their decoration was very different. Royal seats were covered in gold sheets, inlaid with

<
An Elamite lady spinning, from Susa. Stone bas-relief. Musée du Louvre. Photograph: RMN

colored glass or faience, veneered with rare woods, and exquisitely painted and decorated with royal symbols such as the uraeus, or cobra. Decorative elements were often symbolic: lions and sphinxes represented the might of a king, who might also be shown with his bound enemies beneath his feet. Even the colors were symbolic, including gold, the indestructible material of the gods, and the red, blue, and green that represented life and resurrection.

The famous throne of Tutankhamun (Eighteenth Dynasty, 1361–1352 B.C.) is lavishly decorated with gold foil and painted in blue and red. In such seats, faience, colored glass, lapis lazuli, and translucent calcite were often inlaid against a gold background. The front legs featured lions' heads and lion's-paw feet. Less well-known is Tutankhamun's "ceremonial chair," which was decorated with a curious assembly of unrelated motifs, which combine to form a dignified chair of state. The base resembles that of a folding stool, with supports terminating in the carved heads of ducks. The seat is deeply curved, in contrast to the vertical rectangle of its back.

During the Old Kingdom the Egyptians mastered the art of dovetailing and halving joints. The veneering of fine woods over less valuable ones was often practiced; thick veneer was pegged to its support, and thinner veneer was attached with glue. Ivory and gold inlays were used to compensate for the shortage of wood. As incredible as it may seem now, these materials were actually less expensive than wood. Copper nails were used to fasten wood and metal together as early as the First Dynasty (3050 B.C.), and cushions were used as early as the Second Dynasty (2890–2686 B.C.). The early Egyptians also learned how to tan hides using the juice of the acacia fruit and in the New Kingdom they began to make seats of leather, and of woven cords, as well.

Egyptian craftsmen not only created the fundamentals of all seating furniture, they invented rush seats, paw feet, dovetails, inlay, veneer, and folding furniture. Here, at the threshold of history, we find an art powerful and mature, equal to that of any civilization, whose influence began fourteen centuries before Christ and continues to modern times. With the suicide of the last pharaoh, Cleopatra, in 30 B.C., Egypt became a Roman province, and from then on her history was joined to that of the Roman Empire.

GREEK DESIGN: THE STANDARD FOR CENTURIES TO COME

In Greece the history of chairs is difficult to reconstruct, since its line of development was broken at the end of the Mycenaean period, around 1200 B.C. After that, visual evidence of chairs is sparse until the seventh and sixth centuries B.C., when representations of furniture in sculpture and paintings became abundant. The first cultures appeared on the islands and the mainland of Greece early in the third millennium B.C. We know that chairs were in use in this earliest period however, since a few Cycladic statuettes show figures seated in chairs. These chairs present an interesting problem, as they bear no relationship to what we know of Mesopotamian or Egyptian seats of the same period. Thus, it seems likely that people from the mainland moved to the islands by sea and developed their own forms once there.

The Cycladic Islands were isolated, and it was not until the Minoans, who lived on the island of Crete, established a maritime power early in the second millennium that a civilization advanced enough to have genuine luxury appeared in the Aegean. During the Middle Minoan period (c. 1800 B.C.), the Minoans built palaces at Knossos and elsewhere on Crete. These were destroyed around 1700 B.C. by an earthquake, which left no evidence of their furnishings. The English archaeologist Arthur Evans, excavating at Knossos in the late nineteenth century, brought to light the remains of the legendary Palace of Minos, where the influence of the arts of Egypt and the Near East can be clearly seen. Among Evans's discoveries were representations of stools, including one on a clay seal impression that is very similar to the basic Egyptian stool. However, because so little survives from Crete compared to the many representations and actual pieces that we have from the Egyptian Eighteenth Dynasty, comparisons are difficult. Minoan power came to an end when Knossos was destroyed again in about 1400 B.C., and the center of Aegean civilization moved to the Greek mainland. There the Mycenaeans, a Greek-speaking people, were strongly influenced by Minoan culture. Our knowledge of Mycenaean furniture is fragmentary, although written records found at the Mycenaean city of Pylos include descriptions of chairs. While these texts mention chairs made of ebony and inlaid with gold, ivory, or tin, they give few clues to their appearance.

Following the abrupt end of Mycenaean civilization and the burning of its palaces in the twelfth century B.C., there is scant archaeological record of chairs for five hundred years. The eighth century B.C., however, was apparently a transitional period of great importance in the history of furniture. Although records are extremely limited, sculpture and paintings from the late seventh and early sixth centuries B.C. represent seats of very sophisticated design, featuring a number of Egyptian and Near Eastern elements, raising the question of how and when these motifs came to Greece.

< An Attic red-figure *kylix* attributed to the Painter of the Yale Cup. c. 470–450 B.C. The tondo features a youth seated on a stool, enveloped in a cloak with distinctive U-shaped folds. Christie's

> The gravestone of Xanthipos, showing the decedent seated on a *klismos*. 430 B.C. British Museum

<
A chaise longue, or couch, from the Villa Kerylos, a modern reconstruction of an ancient Greek house in Beaulieu-sur-Mer, France. The Greek *kline* combined the uses of the modern bed and sofa, serving not only for sleeping and resting, but also as a seat during meals. One of the most remarkable aspects of the villa is its unique furniture created by the cabinetmaker Bettenfeld from plans drawn up by Pontremoli, always with the Greek spirit in mind. Photograph: Antoine Bootz

>
A folding stool from the Villa Kerylos. This practical, light, and easily portable stool with crossed legs was called in Greek *diphros okladias*. Athenaios (512 B.C.), when describing the Athenians, speaks of slaves carrying such *diphroi* for their masters when they went out. Photograph: Antoine Bootz

Feelings for form and rhythm, precision and clarity, and proportion and order were central to Greek art, and they entered into the shape and ornament of every vessel, painting, piece of furniture, and architectural monument. Greek art was reason made manifest. There was no extravagance of emotion, no singularity of form, no pursuit of novelty through eccentricity. In contrast to what has been found in Egypt, very few pieces of Greek furniture have come down to us, since in Greece furniture was made for the use of everyone, not just the wealthy. We can, however, rely on representations of chairs on vases, funerary stelae, and above all, in literature.

The Greek house was unpretentious and simple, with minimal decoration and few seats. The main types of seats were the backless stool, generally with four perpendicular legs; the folding stool, with crossed legs (either type was called a *diphros*); the bench, which seated several people; the throne, or *thronos*, often with a back and armrests; and a light chair with a curving back called a *klismos*.

In the *Odyssey* (V, 192ff.), Athenaios speaks of the *diphros* as the least important among the seats, compared with the *thronos* and the *klismos*, and

indeed, when Odysseus returns home disguised as a beggar, he is offered a humble *diphros*. Greek paintings represent this chair in many situations. One vase painting, for example, shows a physician seated on a folding stool while he examines a sick boy; in another, a youth about to rub his body with oil lays his mantle on one. Gods and heroes on vases and in reliefs are often shown seated on a *diphros*. Although a *diphros* might be sophisticated—for example, the silver-footed one belonging to the Persian king Xerxes, which the Greeks captured and placed in the Parthenon—it was an ordinary stool used by the great and the lowly alike. It was handy, practical, and light, without back or arm-rails, consisting merely of a rectangular seat, often supported on four turned legs, with a cushion or an animal skin laid on it for comfort.

In Greece, as in Egypt, the variety of stools was considerable. There were folding stools with soft, leather seats; rectangular stools with boxlike seats; three-legged and four-legged stools; and many more. In addition, of course, all sorts of objects, such as rocks, served as seats for poorer people. The stool's height varied, like that of its Egyptian counterpart. Yet, despite the similarities, the Greek stool, like the Greek chair, had a distinct character. Paintings and reliefs depict slaves carrying stools for their masters, often elaborately decorated seats, with either fixed or collapsible legs. The more ancient models were inwardly curving, with animal feet or hoofs, while later versions had plain, straight legs.

Benches, with or without backs, long enough to accommodate more than one person, were also known in Greece. They are mentioned in Greek literature as the seating of choice for those who attended the discourses of Greek philosophers, while the lecturers themselves would occupy a throne or a *klismos*. Greek literature also mentions children at school sitting on benches.

Although early Greek theaters had no permanent seats, theaters of the fourth, third, and second centuries B.C.—for example, those at Epidauros and Delos—have stone seats. The fourth-century theater at Megalopolis features a continuous row of seats with backs, each made of several blocks of stone, with the outer ends terminating in armrests. An inscription states that these benches were dedicated by one Antiochos, who had traveled as an ambassador to the Persian capital at Susa with the Theban general Pelopidas in 367 B.C.

The throne was the stateliest Greek chair, intended for gods, the heroized dead, or important mortals. Thrones were often placed in the temples to the gods, and we can still see pieces of painted pottery depicting both gods and human beings seated on thrones. Like gods and mortals, chairs and thrones were for the most part indistinguishable. The dignity of the throne is described by later Greek writers. In Plato's *Protagoras*, Socrates finds Hippias, the famous Sophist, sitting on a throne while his pupils are seated on benches. The word *thronos* was also synonymous with royal power, as evidenced by Kreon's address to the Theban elders in Sophocles's *Antigone* (lines 189–90): "I know how constant was your reverence for the throne of Laios." Occasionally thrones were used in private homes, as we can see from the scenes of daily life shown in vase-paintings. Thrones, however, were probably only present in wealthy households.

Four types of thrones existed in Ancient Greece: those with animal-paw feet; those with turned legs; those with rectangular legs; and those with solid sides, and a round or rectangular back. Thrones with animal-paw feet were influenced by Egyptian prototypes and seem to have been especially abundant during the sixth century B.C. and the first half of the fifth century B.C. Afterward, this form fell into disuse, appearing only occasionally on monuments. The throne with turned legs appeared very early, as far back as the Minoan period. One example appears on the so-called Harpy Tomb in the British Museum, dated c. 500 B.C. Also found there are two additional thrones, one with legs shaped like those of an animal, and another with rectangular legs, which suggests that all three types were in use in Greece at the same time. The third type of throne, with straight, rectangular legs, is of typically Greek design, originating probably in the second quarter of the sixth century B.C. During the fifth and fourth centuries B.C., thrones were occasionally elaborately decorated with scenes from Greek mythology. The solid-sided throne with a rounded or rectangular back was mainly used for cult and votive purposes, which is why it was often the seat of honor in public places. This throne became popular during the Hellenistic and Roman periods, with few examples existing prior to 500 B.C. One example is the so-called Elgin Throne from Athens, which dates to the fourth century B.C.

The Greeks' most important creation in the history of early furniture was the *klismos*, certainly one of the most graceful chairs ever designed. Combining comfort with simplicity, the *klismos* was a favorite of Classical Greek artists and painters. In the *Iliad* (VIII, 436), Homer says that "Goddesses liked the *klismos*," and describes Hera and Athena as sitting on their golden *klismoi* when they were on Mount Olympus. In the *Odyssey* (IV, 136) Helen sits on a *klismos*, with a footstool for her legs. Numerous representations and variations of the *klismos* have survived on vases and other decorated objects, with women often shown braiding their hair while ensconced in the chair. Typically made from olive, cedar, yew, box, ebony, or citrus wood, and later of bronze, the *klismos* evolved from a simpler type of throne; however, it had plain, undecorated legs rather than the animal paws usually carved on early *thronoi*.

The easy elegance of the *klismos* was typified by its gently splayed legs and curved back-rest, which enclosed the sitter comfortably in its arc. Its smooth curves, in fact, suggest that the technique of steam bending was understood from an early age. In Greek times, the seat's frame was mortised into the legs with tenons or dowels, which can sometimes be seen protruding from the back of the chair. The frame was usually no higher than

> The Elgin Throne, of Hymettan marble. Fourth century B.C. Getty Museum. The throne (from the Greek *thronos*) is the stately chair par excellence, used by gods, the heroized dead, and important people.

the top of the legs and was generally lower. The front of the frame was straight—not curved as has sometimes been thought—and the front legs were broad at the top. The *klismos* was generally without decoration, but there were a few exceptions. In the fifth century B.C., a new type of chair emerged, with either turned or rectangular legs bearing incised patterns topped by rosettes and volutes. The aprons were also carved or painted with mythological scenes. In the prosperous period following the defeat of the Persians in 479 B.C., the *klismos* became the most popular of all Greek chairs, for which reason its form is associated with the Classical period, although its antecedents can be found earlier.

Only a few scant remains of furniture survive from Greece's golden age (500–300 B.C.), but vase paintings show many types of chairs and couches. Couches were sometimes made of bronze or iron, but more commonly they were of wood, and olive woods are specifically mentioned in the *Odyssey* (XXIII, 135ff) and by Pollux (X, 35), quoting Aristophanes. Greek couches were elongated thrones, revealing their Egyptian origin, as do many other forms of Greek furniture. The couch served as both a bed and a seat for reclining during meals, and there are many references to it in ancient literature. Couches are cited several times in the lists of the treasures of the Parthenon ("twelve couches, feet overlaid with silver") and they are also included in the lists of the property of Alcibiades when the state confiscated his property.

Chairs were embellished with inlaid decoration and with silver and ivory feet, but the Greeks (unlike the Egyptian and the Romans) never indulged in the luxury of gold or silver bedsteads. Homer mentions only blankets and rugs when a bed is made up. Fleeces and skins were popular as covers; pillows, often richly decorated, or of silk, perfumed, and of brilliant colors, added to comfort. The couches shown on Greek monuments may be divided into three principal types: with animal legs; with turned legs; and with rectangular legs. All three were later imitated by the Romans.

Although the basic designs of Greek chairs drew heavily on Egyptian examples, the Greeks also developed their own types, such as the *klismos* and the couch, and these would in turn be adapted by the Romans. Seats for people of means were sometimes carved and inlaid with silver, tortoise

>

A *klismos* armchair from the Villa Kerylos. The *klismos* combined comfort with elegant simplicity. In some examples, the back joined the seat at a very oblique angle, so that the sitter could half-recline. In others, the back was almost straight, and a cushion or animal skin was added to modify the angular shape. Photograph: Antoine Bootz

<

A *klismos* chair from the Villa Kerylos. The architecture is modeled after houses on the island of Delos; the patterns of the frescoes and mosaics and the designs of the furniture were inspired directly from antique sources. We owe this masterpiece to Théodore Reinach, an archaeologist, musicologist, and professor at the Collège de France. Photograph: Antoine Bootz

shell, or ivory, and the Romans would imitate this lavishness, as well. Turning, inlaying, carving, painting, encrusting with precious stones, gilding, and steam-bending were all practiced, and construction methods were highly advanced. During the later Classical and Hellenistic periods, Greek chairs were increasingly luxurious, and in these late examples we can begin to see the development of the chairs of Ancient Rome.

ROME: A BLEND OF OLD AND NEW

The Romans admired the Greeks immensely; much of their literature and art was derived from Greek models, and furniture was no exception. In 146 B.C., when Greece finally came under Roman rule, the conquerors adopted even more elements of Greek design than they had earlier. This can be seen in the seats that archaeologists have found in Rome itself, as well as in the examples preserved by the lava and volcanic ash in Herculaneum and Pompeii after the eruption of Mount Vesuvius in 79 A.D.

The remains of Roman domestic interiors suggest a life of solid comfort. Little has been found of the Romans' furniture, since nearly all of it was made of wood and consequently perished, but a few tables, couches, and chairs of marble or bronze survive. To the wealthy Romans, ostentation was more important than comfort or convenience, and they incorporated and enriched forms of furniture from Egypt, Greece, and the Middle East in endless variety to create a luxurious standard of living.

During the life of the Roman statesman and writer Cato (234–149 B.C.), the wealthy classes of Roman society passed with astonishing speed from stoic simplicity to reckless luxury. The patricians and the upper middle class competed in displaying luxuries in their homes and public buildings, spending fortunes on interior decoration. Houses grew larger even as families grew smaller, and furniture became lavish as great sums were paid for couches inlaid with ivory, silver, or gold. Chairs were often inlaid with precious stones and metal. The Roman orator and statesman

< A Roman inlaid iron curule chair, early fourth century A.D. A fine example of a *sella curulis,* a folding chair used by the highest-ranking judicial magistrates of Rome. The iron legs are decorated—in niello and inlays of gold, silver, and red copper—with geometric patterns on the outside and on the inside with scrolling vines. The paw feet are bronze. The crossing joint and the juncture of the legs and the seat are ornamented with silvered bronze relief medallions of lion heads. From the Shelby White and Leon Levy collection

> A detail of the legs of the curule chair shown at left

Cicero allegedly paid 500,000 sesterces for a table of citrus wood, a staggering price at the time.

Designs found throughout the Empire are virtually identical. Examples of furniture carved on monuments in Britain, Gaul, Germany, the Near East, and North Africa all correspond to those discovered in Italy, indicating that a uniform style prevailed throughout the Roman world.

The chief materials used for furniture in Rome, as in Greece, were metal, stone, and wood. The metals used were bronze, copper, and iron, which was the strongest and most durable of the three. The most common stones used to make furniture were marble and limestone, which were especially good for exterior use. Rare woods like citrus and maple were particularly prized. Citrus came from Mauritania and West Africa, and the large demand exhausted the supply, adding further to its popularity. Maple came from Northern Italy. Beech and willow, used for chair frames, were also imported. As in ancient Egypt, wood inlays were much in demand, as were inlays of ivory, precious metals, and tortoiseshell. Inlay on couches, especially, was carried out in various materials, including silver, niello, and copper, contrasting with the bronze frame, or in glass of different colors, sometimes combined with relief ornaments in bone. Pliny the Elder, author of *Natural History,* mentions couches that were gilded or silver-plated, and even some made entirely of gold and silver. None of these have survived. Tortoiseshell veneer on couches is also mentioned by both Pliny and Lucian. Wood veneering, which had been practiced in Egypt and Greece, was particularly developed in Roman times, to the regret of Pliny, who decried the practice as a cheapening of the carpenter's craft.

Throughout the Empire stools were popular, existing in a multiplicity of forms inherited from the Greeks. Several types are illustrated on

Roman monuments. One type derived directly from the *diphros* had four vertical legs and was often so imposing that it was essentially a backless throne. The folding stool with curved, crossed legs seems to have enjoyed both popular and official status. The X-frame folding stool attained special significance as the *sella curulis* used by senators and magistrates, but it was also used on informal occasions, as shown by a relief from Porto, near Ostia, of a woman sitting under a tree. The use of benches in ancient Rome, like the use of stools, mirrored their function in Greece. According to the Roman comedic dramatist Plautus (*Stichus*, II, 36) benches were regarded as seats for the humble. Pliny the Younger, the nephew of Pliny the Elder, himself a Roman official whose letters have provided valuable accounts of life in the first century A.D., records semicircular stone benches in the gardens of private villas, and some benches of this type have been found in the Street of the Tombs in Pompeii.

The Roman throne, or *solium*, existed in two types that evolved directly from the Greek throne. One, with solid sides, became popular in the imperial period for official occasions. The other, with turned or rectangular legs, can be seen on numerous paintings from Pompeii. Larger and heavier than its Greek ancestor, this Roman form strongly influenced thrones of later periods, especially those of bishops in the early Christian church. In fact, some seats found in Italian churches of the thirteenth or fourteenth centuries actually date to the Roman period.

The Roman *cathedra*, a chair with a back, was apparently not nearly as common in Rome as was the *klismos* in Greece during the fifth and fourth centuries B.C., and when it did occur, was a much heavier form. A miniature Roman example of lead now in the British Museum, with its vertical, curving back and straight legs, shows to what extent the beauty of the *klismos* depended on its delicate, sweeping curves. The Latin writers Horace and

<

A Roman metal stool from Pompeii. A number of seats have been found in the excavation of the city destroyed by the eruption of Mount Vesuvius in 79 A.D. Stools like this one were often so substantial that they to qualify as backless thrones. Naples, Museo Nazionale

> A Greek bench from the Villa Kerylos. It is interesting to note the similarity of benches in ancient Greece and Rome. Photograph: Antoine Bootz

>> A Roman bench from Pompeii. Literary sources of the period tell us that benches were considered humble seats in the Roman world, since they offered little in the way of comfort. Naples, Museo Nazionale

> A Roman chaise or couch from Pompeii. Couches were the most costly furniture in Roman private houses, and the name of several Roman couch-makers—Archias, Soterictus, and Beitemus—are even known to us today. Naples, Museo Nazionale

Calpurnius Siculus tell us that the *cathedra* was essentially a woman's chair, as the *klismos* was in Greece. Animal skins and brightly colored pillows were often added, making it one of the most comfortable chairs available. The *cathedra* was also sometimes used as a litter, a favorite means of conveyance for wealthy Romans. Another popular chair was the *bisellium*, a double chair or settee, which often consisted of a wooden frame on turned or carved legs ending in a carved horse's or mule's head.

More prevalent in Rome than in Greece, and eventually serving as the symbol of the decadence of the Roman Empire, the couch, or *lectus*, was a favorite article of furniture in Roman times. In Roman dining rooms it was customary to set three couches at right angles to one another. It seems to have been customary for the "upper" couch to have a headboard, while the "lower" couch had a footboard, and the middle one, neither. Banquets were occasions for private men to savor their accomplishments and show off to their peers. The banquet was apparently as important to the Romans as the salon was to the eighteenth-century French aristocracy, or the court of Versailles to the seventeenth-century nobility. Protocol was strictly observed in the assignment of dining couches around the tables. Without couches there could be no real feast, even among the poor. As much a social gesture as an occasion for eating and drinking, the classical banquet gave rise to a literary genre, the "symposium," in which cultivated men discussed elevated topics. Couches not used for dining seem often to have had both head- and footboards.

Roman couches had the general form of today's beds, with a platform of cushions carried on turned legs, and were often inlaid, painted, or mounted with metal. The most common form was the long couch with turned legs, dating from the Republican and early Imperial periods. The height of the long couch varied depending on its purpose, since couches served family and visitors alike. A pillow resting at one end served as an armrest, as well.

Upholstery was unknown to the Romans, so their seats were made comfortable with pillows, loose covers, and animal skins. The chief materials used in Roman cushions were wool and linen, followed by silk, leather, and skins of all sorts. Expeditions to Africa returned with the pelts of such exotic animals as zebras and leopards, which enriched the décor just as they do today. Fabrics were woven in private houses, an activity that was one of the main occupations for Roman women.

The collapse of the Roman Empire and the subsequent decline of living standards had a major impact on the function and importance of chairs in Europe for centuries to come. The Western world had to wait several centuries before it again saw the creation of seats of the refinement and sophistication of those of the Roman Empire, whose level of extravagance, in fact, had helped bring about its downfall.

BEAUTY AND UTILITY IN ANCIENT CHINA

How and when the chair evolved in China is not clear; in fact, it is not even known for sure how old the Chinese civilization is. We know, from the remains of "Peking man" found in a cave at Chou Kou Tien in 1929 that human beings have lived in China since around 40,000 B.C.; other archaeological remains show that Mongolia was thickly populated as far back as 20,000 B.C. Later discoveries in Hunon and southern Manchuria show that a Neolithic culture was present in those areas only one or two thousand years later, contemporary with the prehistory of Egypt and Sumer.

China has a diverse population including people of various origins, languages, and cultures, which contributes to the confusion regarding the earliest Chinese chairs. We know that the Chinese were the only people in eastern Asia to use chairs before the eighteenth century; however, as with Greece and Rome, actual examples of antique Chinese furniture are scarce. China's violent history of war, fire, flood, and revolution has severely reduced what might have otherwise remained of wooden furniture. What does remain is precise in design and style, and of excellent execution.

The pursuit of wisdom and the passion for beauty are characteristic Chinese ideals, and seat furniture reflects that marriage of beauty and utility. Since the Chinese regarded furniture and seats as utilitarian rather than as high art, few written works exist on the subject. Unlike European cabinetmakers, Chinese craftsmen never

<
A folding stool of *zitan* wood. Seventeenth–eighteenth century. This is the only known example of a folding stool made of this rare hardwood; a few such stools exist made of *huanghuali* wood, but they differ from this *zitan* example in that their horizontal upper members are usually decorated with relief carving. This unique piece is entirely plain. Christie's

> A Chinese painting on glass, c. 1765, of a lady in her study seated on a root armchair, a type of seat associated in China with scholarly and literary tastes. The technique of painting on glass was introduced to China by the Jesuits. Collection Chinese Porcelain Company

v
A folding settee for three made of elmwood and painted red, from Shanxi province. Such double or triple folding seats are part of a tradition of cleverly designed vernacular folding furniture that is easy to transport and store. Peabody Essex Museum

signed or dated their pieces, and kept few records. Moreover, Chinese chair design has changed little over the centuries. A sixteenth-century carpenter's manual, the *Lu Ban Jing*, which is illustrated with numerous woodblock prints, remains the primary written source of information on Chinese furniture.

In China, as in Egypt, tombs provide a major source of information on furniture. Because the Chinese supplied their dead with furniture for the afterlife, actual seats have been found in tombs, including both full-size and miniature models made of bronze, ceramic, or wood; often the tombs contain wall paintings that show the furniture in use.

Archaeological records indicate that the earliest Chinese did not use chairs, but instead knelt on the ground, leaning back on their heels to support their weight. Until the tenth century, kneeling was the most correct and respectable sitting posture, much as it is even today in traditional settings in Japan. Some degree of protection from the cold and damp of the ground was offered by a low couch or mat, on which the sitter would sit very much as he might on the floor.

An autocratic monarchy ensured a lasting and highly regulated system of government that allowed little individualism to take root. Until the end of the tenth century, the Chinese sat on mats or low platforms. Thus, mats may be called the first pieces of seating furniture, not only adding to the comfort of the sitter but also helping to indicate social position. They were woven of straw or rush, often made from reeds and decorated with a silk border. Rules were written for rising from and lowering oneself to the mat.

In early times the wealthy sat on low platforms, a slightly higher platform reflecting greater social status. The earliest examples of such large wooden platforms were discovered at Xinyang in Henan, in the tomb of a fourth-century B.C. ruler of the southern kingdom of Chu. Records from the Han Dynasty (206 B.C.–220 A.D.) indicate that these sitting platforms, called *ta*, were mainly used as honorific seats for high officials and religious dignitaries during ceremonies and sacrificial rites.

The relatively longer low platform was called a *chuang*, and was used as a seat—often ceremonial—in the daytime, and as a bed at night. The evolution to chairs can be dated with some precision to the 200-year period between the middle of the ninth century and the middle of the eleventh. People occasionally sat on elevated seats with their legs hanging during the Eastern Zhou period (770–221 B.C.), but it was only during the Northern Song Dynasty (960–1127) that sitting on a chair at a high table became a common practice, a change that clearly indicates a profound transformation from an older tradition to a more modern one.

What would have caused such a drastic alteration in the daily habits of the Chinese? Height and authority were often related and, as wealth in China increased, the adoption of the chair signaled a new prosperity that had created an entirely new manner of living. The true challenge of the Western chair culture to the Chinese tradition did not take place

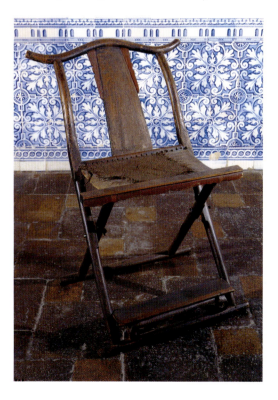

> A Ming dynasty folding chair, once the property of Philip II of Spain (reigned 1556–98). Patrimonio Nacional, Madrid

until the latter part of the third century A.D. By then, the once glorious Han Empire was in chaos and strict Confucianism had given way to the more relaxed Daoism and the newly introduced Buddhism, both of which encouraged intellectual curiosity. In this intellectual climate, the Chinese began to accept and even admire foreign things that had previously been ignored. It was in these circumstances that we see a new era in the Chinese way of sitting and the art of Chinese seats.

Simplicity of design, a lack of ornamentation, and intricate, exposed joinery distinguish Chinese furniture from that of the West. Nails, turning, and glue were never used. The origin of visible joinery, an integral part of the decoration of Chinese furniture, can be traced back to the architecture of ancient temples, the tradition of which has remained virtually unchanged for centuries.

A combination of the miter, the mortise and tenon frame, and the tongue and groove floating panel enabled the dense woods typically used to expand and contract. As a result, Chinese seat furniture was less sensitive to climatic variations than its Western counterpart. This knock-down construction also made the pieces easy to dismantle, a feature well suited for the needs of high officials, who were often traveling.

The oldest Chinese seat, apart from the low platform, was the folding stool, similar to the Western camp stool. Its Chinese name was *hu ch'uang*, meaning "Barbarian bed." It is believed that the *hu ch'uang* was introduced to China in the second century A.D., during the reign of the Han Emperor Lingdi (168–188), who was recorded

<
A rare folding and reclining armchair made of *huanghuali* wood with marble panels. Occasionally called a "drunken lord chair," this type of chair, more than any other Chinese seat, encourages a relaxed posture. Such chairs are sometimes depicted in erotic art. Christie's

to have had a fascination with things foreign. The stool has a unique place among seating furniture in that it requires an infusion of energy on the part of the sitter. The stool is not a seat for relaxation, as the sitter is never given total support. On a stool, one sits in the center in a balanced posture, leaning slightly forward. The folding stool was at that time commonly used by nomadic tribes in the more remote northern and western regions of the country, often for mounting and dismounting horses as well as for sitting.

Folding stools spread throughout China during the subsequent Sui, Jin, and Tang Dynasties, although unlike European seats, these folded from back to front. Easily carried over the shoulder, they quickly became popular for rulers and other dignitaries who were traveling, hunting, or at war. They were also used as garden seats. In China, people often sat on folding stools cross-legged. Later, it became common for sitters to place their legs parallel to the seat's crossed legs, a position that was not used in Europe since there folding seats opened from side to side. The seats of the oldest Chinese stools were often made of parallel tied cords. Later on, for splendid occasions, a stool might be upholstered with fabric, or cushions might be fastened to it by means of cords and tassels. Folding stools were often made in *huanghuali*, a southern Chinese rosewood, and occasionally in other woods, such as *zitan*, a dark, very hard wood from Indochina.

In ancient China, as in Egypt, Greece, and Rome, the folding stool was a prestigious seat and an early symbol of dignity and power. By the late sixth century, models and depictions of stools appeared in tombs of the wealthy, to provide comfort and status in the afterlife. As in most other cultures, stools had many functions, used not only for sitting but to step up to a higher level, or as a small table.

>
A rare round-backed folding armchair in *huanghuali* wood. Sixteenth–seventeenth century. Only a very few chairs of this type made of *huanghuali* have survived. Christie's

A wide variety of stools existed in China. Square and rectangular models were more common than round ones, except in the Ming and Qing Dynasties, which produced a higher number of round stools, as we learn from paintings and woodblocks of those periods. Stools were used by women and men alike. Noble ladies of the Tang Dynasty (618–905) were often depicted sitting on round or square stools, which must have been common. In the Tang Dynasty a stool was considered an ideal seat for a lady, as it displayed the curve of her back, her neck, and her shoulders to best advantage, yet remained a modest manner of seating.

Drum stools have survived in the greatest numbers. Shaped like a Chinese drum, these resembled the more commonly found stone and porcelain garden seats, and were made both from wood and porcelain. Porcelain stools were especially popular for outdoor use and some derivations of them (in Minton Majolica) can be found in England and France in nineteenth-century gazebos and *jardins d'hiver*. Garden stools made of stone were even sturdier, and can be seen today in the North Garden of the Forbidden City in Beijing.

By the Song Dynasty (960–1279), the stool had become commonplace and thus lost its prestige, so the chair replaced it as a dignified seat. At that time, servants and members of the lower class half-squatted on small, rough, and very low stools of unpainted wood. Vendors in Chinese markets today can still be seen using these stools while selling their wares (p. 40).

The traveling folding stool seems to have developed into a form of chair in the Song Dynasty, during the late eleventh to the twelfth century, when a backrest was added to the upper horizontal members of the stool. This was the first attempt to combine the folding stool and the chair into a folding chair, as had happened in the West. From around the late second century A.D. to the beginning of the third century A.D., another type of chair was introduced in China called *sheng chuang*, or woven seat. This was a throne used by Buddhist missionaries on their journeys from Central Asia or India to mainland China. However important the folding stool may have been in the history of the chair's origins, we

> A rare early-eighteenth-century low-backed armchair of *huanghali* wood, of the type known as *meiguiyi*. Overall height: 31½". This small chair is extremely unusual both for the fine quality of its latticework and the detailed carving. Collection Chinese Porcelain Company

< A twentieth-century vernacular bamboo chair, Zhejiang province. Bamboo, which is common in China, is used both for food and for construction of all sorts. Bamboo chairs, being light and made of easily obtained material, have historically been very popular throughout Chinese society. Peabody Essex Museum

cannot ignore the influence of Buddhism on the development of the chair in China. The Buddhist seat referred to as the yokeback chair gave rise to a series of Chinese chairs that were partly responsible for the mania for things Chinese in eighteenth-century Europe. The yokeback seat can be either an armchair or armless, having begun to be accepted by non-Buddhist Chinese, most likely early in the Tang Dynasty (618–906), first by the aristocracy and the bureaucrats, and then by the intellectuals and the wealthy for non-religious functions. By the twelfth century, yokeback chairs were quite common, and they frequently appear in Jin Dynasty (1115–1234) tombs, with ceremonial runners, footstools, and curved yokes. They were also called "lamphanger chairs," as they were considered to be similar in shape to the bamboo wall lamps commonly hung near kitchen stoves. Since they were light, they could be easily carried out to the garden. Footstools might be placed in front to elevate the sitter's feet above the cold and damp of the ground. Paintings and printed book illustrations from ancient China indicate that the placement of a single footstool often distinguished the senior member in a social gathering. The use of a footstool as a mark of status may perhaps be traced to early Buddhist sculpture, in which seated deities are depicted with their feet resting on lotus pods. Nearly all these chairs had a front stretcher designed as a footrest.

<
A nineteenth-century lacquered rootwood armchair. During the late Ming and early Qing periods, the bizarre shapes of rootwood furniture appealed to Chinese literati for use in their studies and gardens as a symbol of a life of refined leisure. Sotheby's

Among extant examples of later yokeback chairs, armchairs are much more common than side chairs. This is most likely due to the fact that the armchair, with its front post and armrests supporting the chair back, has a stronger construction, so more examples have survived through the ages. Yokeback side chairs, however, were the most popular chair type in Chinese daily life, as evidenced by their greater depiction in paintings. The replacement of the yokeback chair with the horseshoe-back armchair and the folding horseshoe-back armchair as the predominant seat in court portraits of Ming and Qing Dynasties manifested a deeper change in the posture of courtly authority. Larger and more imposing than side chairs and enabling the sitter to assume a position of grandeur, armchairs were more prestigious. The use of an armchair as opposed to a side chair, as in old Europe, was a clear prerogative of rank. (Stools and barrel seats were lowest on the scale.) For a personage of real importance a bare armchair was not sufficient; furs or rich fabrics were thrown over it, usually completely covering the chair's framework.

Various kinds of chairs and armchairs emerged simultaneously with other high-backed forms during the Tang (618–906) and Song (960–1279) Dynasties. The round-back style may have been influenced by ancient, curved armrests. Song texts also refer to armrests shaped like baskets and made of bent wood or bamboo,

<
Twentieth-century round stools for women to sit on while selling vegetables in the market. Robert Wilson Collection. Photograph Antoine Bootz

> A seventeenth-century throne chair of *tielimu* wood. Elaborate gilded or lacquered throne chairs were found in temples and halls throughout Imperial China for use by the emperor and empress. Actual examples of these are very rare, their forms only known from paintings. A more simply decorated throne such as this one was probably reserved for the abbot of a monastery. Throne chairs usually resemble a small *chuang,* or platform. Christie's

called the horseshoe armchair in the West due to its U-shape. With its relatively cubic base, the round-back chair mimics in three dimensions the Chinese concept of *tiandi*, or heaven above and earth below, commonly represented in the abstract by a circle surmounting a square.

The cross-legged seat or folding armchair had become so popular by the Ming Dynasty (1368–1644) that it is the only chair listed in the 1436 illustrated children's primer *Xinbian Duixiangsiyan*. Such chairs evolved from the ancient folding stool during the Song Dynasty. During the Ming and early Qing Dynasties, emperors and commoners alike used the folding armchairs a great deal, both for formal and informal occasions. It was often the chair upon which deceased emperors and officials sat in their posthumously painted ancestral portraits. In all gatherings the folding armchair was a status symbol used exclusively by the most important person while others sat on stools or side chairs. Both emperors and empresses used folding armchairs as portable thrones, often paired with a matching footstool, when traveling or relaxing in the garden.

The tendency to simplify, inherent in the Chinese ideals of construction, created lasting models. Certainly the chair, which was used every day and graced the inside of the home, had to be simple, yet despite its simplicity the chair still defined rank and power. The social rules that delineated them were as strict, if not more so, than during the height of the social hierarchy in France in the reign of Louis XIV. Coincidentally, it would be under his reign that the taste for *chinoiseries* would begin in Europe, with the introduction at Versailles of lacquer from the Siamese embassy. From there the fashion would spread across Europe throughout the eighteenth and nineteenth centuries, with Chinese-influenced pavilions and furniture appearing at the Swedish royal residence at Drottningholm, at Sans Souci, the palace of Frederick the Great of Prussia at Potsdam, and in

England, where it culminated in the extravagant Brighton Pavilion around 1820.

Chinese seating furniture influenced European cabinetmakers and designers during the eighteenth and nineteenth centuries, and American furniture designers in the latter part of the nineteenth century. In England around 1760, numerous drawings by Chippendale (in the *Director*) and Edwards and Darly (in the *New Book on Chinese Design*) illustrated the popularity of seats in the Chinese taste and showed China's lasting influence on chair design in England. Twentieth-century chair design draws heavily on Chinese inspiration, and designers such as Charles Rennie Mackintosh around 1910, in Glasgow, and Josef Frank around 1940, in Stockholm, and even contemporaries such as Bonetti and Garouste, in Paris, still borrow from the Chinese style. These examples amply demonstrate how important Chinese furniture-making was, and is, for the development of the chair.

AFRICA: TIMELESS INNOVATION

Westerners became interested in African art at the end of the nineteenth century. At that time interest was focused on masks, carved figures, and small objects; pieces like these profoundly influenced the work of such artists as Vlaminck, Picasso, Derain, Matisse, and Braque, all of whom owned works of African art. More recently, objects of everyday use such as seats have begun to attract interest as well.

Not much is known of the history of African chairs, as most of the early examples have been lost. The oldest recorded African seat came from what is now Nigeria. The only undamaged early example known is in the Museum of Mankind in London, a quartz seat dated from the eleventh to the fifteenth century from Ife, the holy city of the Yoruba people of Nigeria.

African chairs can be separated into two categories: seats for everyday use, and those for ritual, political, or symbolic use; the quality of craftsmanship varies, depending upon the seat's function. Because it is customary in Africa to squat close to the ground, African chairs are often much lower than their European counterparts. The seats of European chairs are generally between fourteen and sixteen inches above the floor; African seats range from three or four inches to about ten inches in height. Made by hand with rudimentary tools, African seats are unique, and often play the role of social arbitrator. In most African cultures, every social group has the right to a type of seat associated with its position in the social hierarchy. In Cameroon, for example, each ruler has his own display throne made, decorated with such symbols of power as leopards, elephants, or snakes. Traditionally, the family of the king of the Kuba people of central Africa was not permitted to sit on the ground; instead they sat on animal skins or chairs. In Zaire, small circular stools with geometrically decorated supports were exclusively used by women.

Archaeological evidence and tradition indicate that stools have embodied spiritual power throughout Africa for centuries. Among some African peoples, for example, the Asante of Ghana, a stool or chair is thought to be the seat of its owner's soul. For the Asante a stool is a central object in spiritual life. Such a seat can only be used by its owner; when unused, it is turned on its side, to prevent someone else from sitting on it and to preserve its inherent spiritual nature. While all stools used by the living are painted white, after the death of their owners they are blackened in a special ceremony, the Adae festival, an honor for one who has died bravely, either in battle or from natural causes. After sacrifices and the pouring of libations over them, the stools are believed to have received the souls of the dead, thereby immortalizing them. Ancestral stool temples, where the blackened stools that once belonged to respected chiefs and priests are housed, are places of communal worship for the Asante. In the nineteenth century, warriors carried the blackened stools into combat, so that the spirits of their ancestors could protect them.

Africans often carry their seats while traveling, using wooden or vegetable fiber handles on the chairs' backs for easier handling. Some chairs are imitations of the white man's seats, used by tribal men only during important meetings, yet not otherwise connected to any traditional rituals. African thrones are made for kings or rulers, serving as emblems of strength that carry magical powers and act as precious links to the past. Their designs vary according to region and tribe. Owing to African trade patterns, there is a stunning variety of African chairs, and it is sometimes difficult to determine exactly where one originated. Thus, for example, the stools of the Mossi people of West Africa are also identified with the neighboring Lobi people; Gurunsi three-legged chairs are similar to Lobi stools; and Asante stools are found among all peoples of the Akan group of Ghana, to which the Asante belong.

The age of an African chair can be difficult to trace, since the techniques of seat construction have not changed much in centuries, and patterns of wear can be the result of either age or extensive use. Whether African chairs come from the dry tropics, from swampy areas, or from forest regions,

>
Wooden stool with kneeling female figure. Zaire, Hemba. Many peoples in Africa trace their ancestors through the maternal line, which explains why the carved figure supporting the seat of a chief's stool is often female. British Museum 1905.6.13.1

the living power of the wood can be sensed. Often the magic power of the carving is increased by the addition of brass or iron tacks (on Asante chairs), glass beads or shells (on the Cameroon chieftain's chair or stool), or animal hair or leather (on backrests from Zaire). On many, the dark, silky sheen of the patina created by years of loving use adds to the innate, living character of the piece.

Owning a seat in Africa is a status symbol, associated not only with an individual's ability to purchase the chair, but also to maintain, clean, and repair it. The size of the seat and the quality of the work invested in it reflect the social status of its owner. While today's wealthy Africans buy and collect European chairs as well, traditional seats are still cherished. In fact, when they achieved political independence, many African societies reevaluated their traditions, emphasizing older forms of seats.

The simplest African seat is the backrest, made from the trunk of a large tree. Derived from the three-legged stool, its equilibrium comes from three supports. No equivalent seats exist anywhere in Europe. Its origin obviously goes back very far in time. Backrests are usually long and wide; reserved for men, their use displays high social rank. The backrests of the peoples of the equatorial forest and of Central Africa feature elaborate carvings.

Stools can vary a good deal. Thousands of different shapes and variations exist, made primarily of wood, yet also of stone, bronze, or ivory. Usually constructed of a single piece of wood, African stools generally have three parts: the foot, or base; the middle; and the seat. The foot and the base are often circular, and occasionally rectangular; the middle is more or less profusely carved, depending on where it was made. The seat

<
Quartz throne. Nigeria, Yoruba. Twelfth–fifteenth century. British Museum 1896.11.22.1

may be round or rectangular, and is often deeply curved for comfort.

Concave rectangular seats are mostly found in three regions of West Africa: the Bijagos Archipelago off the coast of Guinea-Bissau; among the Akan peoples of the Ivory Coast and Ghana; and on the Cameroon coast near the modern city of Duala. The best-known are those of the Asante. The Asante, the dominant people of the Akan group, inhabit the tropical east-central region of southern Ghana. The earliest European record of this area dates from the end of the sixteenth century. The history of the Asante kingdom is difficult to trace, because its records were maintained orally. The greatest Asante hero was the founder of the kingdom, King Osei Tutu, who lived in the late seventeenth and early eighteenth centuries, and increased his territory by annexing a number of neighboring areas. After the reign of King Tutu, the kingdom continued to grow, maintaining a strong trade, mainly in gold dust. The kingdom reached its zenith at the end of the nineteenth century, when it reached inland from the Atlantic coast for almost 375 miles (600 kilometers).

The Golden Stool, or Sika Dwa Kofi ("the golden stool created on Friday"), is woven into Asante history. Miraculously appearing during the reign of King Tutu, it became a symbol of unity among the Asante leaders. Since it was the nation's responsibility to protect the Golden Stool, it was kept hidden and shown publicly only on the most important occasions. Not even the king was permitted to sit on it, nor was it allowed to touch the ground. When it was unveiled, it was placed atop another stool. Sacrificial offerings were made wherever the Asante feared that the Golden Stool might be in danger. In 1900 war broke out with the English when the British governor offered the grave insult of asking to sit on the Golden Stool. The Asante lost the war, but were successful in keeping possession of the stool. In 1920, some roadworkers stole the stool and stripped it of its gold, but it was soon found and the thieves were punished and forced to return it. Stools similar in shape to the Golden Stool were commissioned by chiefs or high-ranking members of Asante society.

> A stool for a woman or child. Zaire, Songyesungu. British Museum 1908.6.22.67

Animal figures carved into the pedestal of a stool often symbolically represent the owner's prestige or rank. For example, the panther and the elephant are believed to convey the great power and authority of a king; the crocodile is a symbol of holiness; and the porcupine is a symbol of the Asante nation. Asante stools can be designed for specific members of society. Stools from Cameroon have bases carved as figures such as leopards or kneeling men. Their distinguishing feature is the lavish and colorful bead and cowrie shell decoration that covers them.

Cylindrical stools may range in type from a simple drum shape to more elaborate forms. One such is the caryatid stool, with human or animal figures supporting the seat. Stools of this type are found in many parts of Africa, including Zaire, Benin, Mali, Nigeria, and Tanzania. Traditionally reserved for chiefs, they embody the idea of the continuity of power. Caryatid figures are usually female, since women are considered the pillars of the family and their presence is thought to bestow wisdom upon the sitter, who is usually a man. If

An Asante stool, Ghana. Like many stools from Central Africa, this example was used as a throne. Collection Alain de Monbrison

the sitter fails to show the figures proper respect, bad luck or illness may result. Often, consecrated white clay is spat at the caryatid's face as an act of veneration. Particularly fine caryatid seats are produced in southeastern Zaire by the Luba and by their neighbors, the Hemba, the Chokwe, and the Zimba.

The figures on the caryatid seats of the Luba and the Songye are generally shown kneeling, while those of the Hemba and the Zimba usually stand. Stools are the most important symbols of Luba kingship, as they are for many African peoples. Not only is the Luba king's palace referred to as his "seat of power" (*kitenta*), sitting is a metaphor for the royal prerogatives. During initiation rites into Mbudye, the secret association responsible for the indoctrination of royal officeholders, rank and title are indicated by the progressive accession to more prestigious forms of seating, beginning with simple mats and proceeding to animal pelts, clay thrones, and finally, to the sculpted, wooden stools of kings and royal spirit mediums. Luba stools, which serve as receptacles for kings' spirits rather than as functional chairs, are such potent emblems that they are often kept secretly in a village different from the home of their owners as a protection against theft. Swathed in white cloth, they are brought out only on special occasions.

A stool shaped loosely like a mushroom and called a *nebala* is found among the Mangbetu of Zaire. These seats made of a single piece of wood are reserved for women, which is rare in Africa, where most stools are for men. For convenience, a leather strap or handle allows the women to carry the *nebala* on their travels. Another woman's stool, similar in shape to the *nebala*, is found among the Yaoure and the Baoule of Ghana. There, women keep their round stools in their huts or in the kitchen. The stools have multiple uses, also playing a role in sacrifices and ceremonies to honor ancestors. A taller, more imposing version of this stool is reserved for chiefs, which allows them to sit at a higher level than the women. The women of Burkina Faso also carry out domestic tasks while seated on small, round stools, assuming a traditional posture: hands on joined knees, feet far apart, and eyes avoiding contact with passersby.

Another simple, circular stool, also carved from a single piece of wood, but not identified with a specific ethnic group, may be seen in markets all over West Africa, used as a stool or as a stand for merchandise. Other stools have a seat

A stool with elephant legs. Ivory Coast, Senougo. Private collection

supported by several legs. Three-legged Lobi stools from Burkina Faso are used by men exclusively, while women use four-legged stools. Contrary to the simplicity of their appearance, Lobi stools are considered sophisticated and important seats, with a centuries-old tradition. Some rare examples bear carvings of human heads and animals; some apparently have even been carried into battle, and their long front legs used as weapons.

While Mongo chiefs in Baringa sit on three-legged stools, their inferiors sit on the floor. Three-legged stools abound in Zaire, where they were often reserved for the nobility during the nineteenth and twentieth centuries. In an engraving of 1871 by the Reverend J. G. Wood, a man of the Bari tribe from the Sudan is depicted carrying his three-legged stool, along with his weapon and his pipe. Tanzanian examples of three-legged stools decorated with brass nails are exhibited at the Royal Museum in Toronto. Sturdy, three-legged stools can also be found in Kenya and Ethiopia. In Kenya, more refined examples are decorated with bronze and copper inlay.

Chairs are rarer than stools in Africa and their designs show a definitive European influence. In 1481, the Portuguese explorer Diogo d'Azambuja established a trading post on the Ivory Coast and simultaneously introduced the chair with armrests. Throughout the centuries the type spread across Africa, becoming an emblem of power and respect owing to its rarity. The Asante created three interesting variations of the armchair, one a copy of the European folding chair bearing the wonderful name of "praying mantis" (*akonkromfi*, in the Twi

> A stool with faces. Zambia. Private collection

language) in reference to the articulated legs of this insect. The *akonkromfi*, which is brought out on joyful occasions, is generally decorated with brass tacks and other metal pieces. Another type of folding chair, the *hwedom*, has high arms and a straight back and is often used as a base for the Golden Stool. The third Asante folding chair, the *asipim*, is without arms, slopes backward, and is richly decorated with brass nails. All three types have leather seats and backs, and thus look similar to Spanish and Portuguese chairs of the fifteenth to seventeenth centuries. The chairs of the Pende of Zaire and the Chokwe from the border of Angola and Zambia also reflect a clear European influence. The oldest of these are usually carved from a single piece of wood, and they sit low on the ground, as do most African seats.

Local African influences created a totally indigenous seat, often decorated with wild animals or carved heads. Chairs of this type made their way to the territory of the Gwere people, where they are particularly small and low with a seating surface between three-and-one-quarter and four inches (eight and ten centimeters) in diameter and a backrest made of a branch bent into the required shape. These small chairs are an important element of Gwere culture. They belong to the older men, who sit on them by day and use them as headrests at night. Before a young girl's circumcision, she asks her grandfather to lend her his chair for the duration of the rite. It is considered a disgrace for a girl not to have a chair for this, for it shows that she has no family. Girls need the chairs in the camp where they are kept separate from the tribe during the period of circumcision, because during this time, they may only kneel.

In Africa as elsewhere, the more elaborate the seat, the greater the authority of the sitter. Whether a stool or an imposing, high-backed seat such as the beaded chairs of Cameroon, splendor elevates a seat to the status of a throne. High-backed seats like those found in Tanzania or

<
An Ethiopian chair of the late nineteenth century. After Portuguese traders made contact with the central African kingdoms in the nineteenth century, some rulers commissioned thrones modeled on European chairs; however, these new thrones featured decorations that were uniquely African. Collection Alain de Monbrison

Ethiopia may have originated as another version of the European-influenced chair. Often created in pairs, with a male and a female version for a king and a queen, these thrones were made of a single piece of wood, and feature exceptional carving. Proverbs refer to the symbolism of the chairs, such as the Ghanian saying, "A king without a throne does not deserve to be obeyed."

Improvisation is widely practiced in Africa; barber chairs have been used as thrones and royal seats have been made of scrap metal. Other seats that have been used as thrones are a *tipoy* (sedan chair), a bench, or, in times past, even the back of a slave, which seems to have once been a favorite seat of power in parts of the continent. Queen Nzingha of Matamba (in present-day Angola), a major figure in sixteenth-century Africa, is depicted in an engraving from 1687 receiving the Portuguese governor in Luanda seated on a slave. Even at the turn of the twentieth century, the kings of the Kuba of Zaire, not being permitted to sit on the ground, sat on an animal skin, on a chair, or if neither were at hand, as we know from photographs, on the back of a slave.

> A large armchair for a chief. Collection of Alain de Monbrison

2
medieval & renaissance chairs

The collapse of the Roman Empire ended the political stability of Europe, with a resulting drop in living standards that had a lasting effect on the function and the importance of furnishings. The Barbarian kingdoms that succeeded the Empire were constantly at war, either with one another or invaders, which led to the development of feudalism. Over the centuries, these wars, together with neglect and decay, took their toll on furnishings of all kinds, so that few examples of medieval chairs have survived from before the fifteenth century.

While the wealthy, stable societies of ancient Greece and Rome produced many types of comfortable chairs, the castles and abbeys of medieval Europe were sparsely furnished. The most common seat was the stool, and it remained so until the seventeenth century. Not until the Renaissance did chairs reappear as a normal piece of furniture even in well-off houses; it took several centuries of social stability to restore the notion of comfort to them.

Throughout the Middle Ages, feudal concepts were ingrained in social behavior. Everyone acknowledged the power of the overlord. He alone sat in a chair, which became the ultimate symbol of feudal rule. In the early Middle Ages, the church emerged as a temporal power, and no distinction was drawn between ecclesiastic and secular seats during the Carolingian (eighth–ninth centuries), Romanesque (tenth–eleventh centuries), or Gothic (eleventh–fourteenth centuries) periods. Chapel furnishings were among the most important objects in a lordly household. Similarly, religious ceremonies and places of worship were part of everyday life to an extent unthinkable today. Lords had their own chapels, and the churchyards were often used for games, wrestling matches, or merchants' displays. The authority of both church and king was expressed by a special seat, which symbolized the power of one individual, whether spiritual or temporal. Throughout the period, chair and throne had much the same meaning.

<<
The throne of Maximian, archbishop of Ravenna from 545 to 556. Sixth century A.D. An almost perfect example of a ruler's chair, this sumptuous Byzantine seat is of wood decorated with carved ivory panels in late-classical style. The panels represent John the Baptist, the four Evangelists, and a variety of scenes from the Old and New Testaments. Museo Nazionale, Ravenna

<
The Throne of Saint Peter, a venerated relic in the Vatican thought to have been the very chair used by Peter as bishop of Rome. In fact, it is a royal throne, made in one of the court workshops of the Carolingian emperor Charles the Bald that flourished between 840 and 866 A.D. It is light and well-proportioned, its wooden frame intended as a support for the ivory decoration. Photographic archive of the Vatican Collection

>
La Lecture (Reading), from a tapestry series depicting scenes of aristocratic life. Loire Valley, fifteenth century. Musée national du Moyen Age (Musée Cluny), Paris. Photograph: RMN. G. Blot/ C. Jean

The author of the Richard II chronicle of 1398 wrote that the king of England sat *En la chayere de justice pour la faire* [on a chair of justice to administer it] to his subjects, thus associating the throne with authority.

An essential feature of a seat of authority was height, which allowed a seated dignitary to be looked up to by all. The preoccupation with height in such seats is an ancient one. According to the Bible, the golden throne of Solomon was raised on six steps, and its influence on medieval symbolism was profound. The importance of the elevated, seated figure is clear in many descriptions and paintings of important ceremonies. The king sat on a chair raised on a high platform, while his subjects stood.

Also associated with Solomon's throne were fourteen lions, twelve on the steps and two on each side; it is no coincidence that numerous seals represent the first Capetian kings of France as seated on high, folding chairs decorated with eagles, dogs, or lions' heads. The use of such devices during the Middle Ages probably continued the same imagery in Roman, Greek, and Egyptian forms. Precious stones, carved ivory, metal, silver, gold, and woods were all used to build and embellish chairs of state. Other important elements in their presentation were the tester, or canopy, and the footstool. These accessories, controlled by rules of hierarchy, proclaimed the power of the lord at many levels of society.

Thrones were also constructed from planks, which were elaborately decorated and carved. The most celebrated surviving example is the throne on which the king or queen of England is still crowned, Saint Edward's Chair in Westminster Abbey, made around 1297–1300 at the command of Edward I (1239–1307) to hold the Stone of Scone, the traditional coronation seat of the kings of Scotland.

Along with the throne, another of the most ancient chairs was the X-shaped stool or chair, with its associations of authority inherited from

<
A twelfth-century chair from Tydal, Norway, of mortise-and-tenon construction. Much of the surface is carved with foliage inhabited by beasts in designs typical of Scandinavian decoration. Oslo University

> The oldest identified chair in Spain, dating to the first half of the fifteenth century. Property of the Enriquez family. Instituto Valencia de Don Juan, Madrid

the Roman senatorial *sella curulis*. This type of chair was practical in a warrior society because of its easy portability. Such a chair was known variously as a *faldistorium, faudesteuil, faudestuef,* or faldstool. Early accounts do not specify that it was a folding chair, however the legs were always crossed in an X. It is tempting to think that the importance of this seat was owed to a special function, and indeed many mentions of it are related to coronations. For example, in the memoirs written in 1316 by Geoffroi de Fleury, the comptroller of Philip V of France (1294–1322), who kept records of royal expenses, we learn that luxurious red velvet fabric and fringes covered the king's now-lost *faudesteuil*, which was delivered for the coronation in Reims on January 9, 1317: *demi aune et demi quartier de veluiau vermeil, pour couvrir le faus d'estuef le Roy . . . aunce et demie de franges, pour ledit faus d'estuef* [half an ell and half a quarter of red velvet to cover the king's chair . . . an ell and a half of fringes for the said chair].

Another, even more ostentatious *faldesteuil* was ordered for the coronation of John the Good (John II) of France on August 22, 1350. It was made by Jehan le Braalier, at a cost of 774 gold *ecus*—an enormous sum at the time—and lavishly decorated with 212 *miniatures* (paintings) on a gold ground. Emeralds, garnets, and rock crystals added to its magnificence. Seats such as this were obviously created for very important events, and their luxury affirmed a king's power.

Pictorial and literary sources suggest that the medieval faldstool was always lavishly executed and costly. The version of the *Song of Roland* that was written down near the end of the eleventh century, for example, relates that at an event in Charlemagne's campaign in the Pyrenees in 777, the emperor sat under a pine tree on a faldstool of solid gold. Charlemagne was a legendary figure in the Middle Ages, and he would naturally be portrayed as seated on a chair of the most precious sort.

Princes and kings carried their faldstools with them when they traveled. Since to survive these trips the chairs had to be handled with care, huge leather boxes, called *bouges*, were built to transport them. The great lords of medieval Europe often had to fight to maintain or increase their power, and as a result they traveled frequently. It was also easier to transport a great household to a new place where food was available than to bring large quantities of provisions to a given location. Folding seats suited these conditions, just as they had those of the early Chinese warlords. In many European countries before the fifteenth century, kings and great lords owned two sets of furniture, one for the summer and one for the winter, both of which they carried with them as they traveled.

Medieval portable chairs were supplied with loose cushions, as similar chairs were in classical times, and in some instances, according to surviving inventories, were even upholstered. Early accounts suggest that the seats of such chairs were usually of leather, even if covered with fabric; indeed, the craftsmen who made such seats were originally saddlers. The accounts of Philip the Bold, duke of Burgundy, for the year 1390 record a "chair for the inner chamber of the Count of Nevers, of wood garnished with cloth and down padding, and a leather case in which the chair may be placed." One seat, called the "Chair of Dagobert," a folding metal armchair variously dated but possibly from the twelfth century, is one extant example of an early X-stool. Although it is traditionally believed to be the seat used by the Frankish kings to receive their vassals' homage, the folding legs, with their lions' heads and paws, are typical of antique work, which suggests that the chair is probably an example of the revival of classical motifs after the time of Charlemagne. Suger, abbot of Saint Denis (1122–51), who in the mid-twelfth century served both Louis V and Louis VI of France as an adviser, apparently added a back and arms to the original folding stool. The abbot's emphasis on the sacred and ceremonial aspects of kingship did much to enhance the image of the French monarchy at the time. Suger understood the symbolic importance of a seat, and how it conferred power on its sitter. Napoleon I was certainly aware of the historic associations of the X-shaped throne, and he made use of it on some official occasions, among them the presentation of the cross of the Legion of Honor in Boulogne August 16, 1804 (see p. 275).

In England, the more important of Henry VIII's richly embroidered chairs were X-shaped,

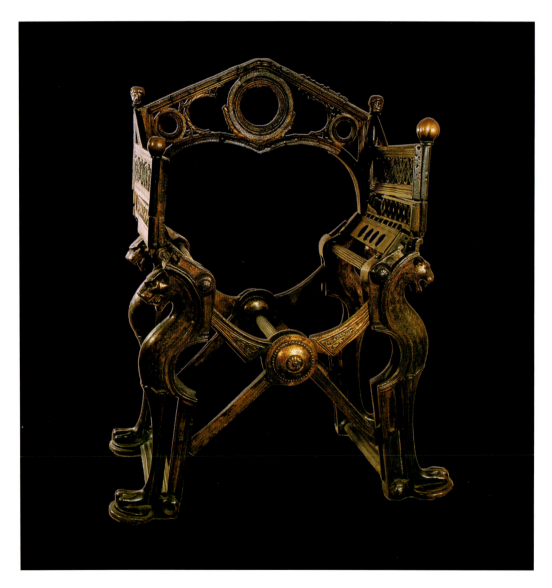

<
The Chair of Dagobert. The legendary King Dagobert (605–39) was the first Merovingian king to rule over a somewhat unified Frankish kingdom. This seat, an outstanding example of early medieval bronze casting, was reworked through the ages to suit the purposes of various French rulers, including Napoleon I (see p. 275). Bibliothèque Nationale de France

as we can see in many portraits of the period. Henry's daughter, Mary I (Bloody Mary), at her marriage to Philip II of Spain on July 1554, was represented by the painter Antonius Mor as seated on a similar chair, said to have been given to her by Pope Julius III. At the end of Henry VIII's reign and early in that of Elizabeth I (1558–1603), a number of X-chairs with "pomells" or finials, of gilt-wood or copper, and others with carved frames, were supplied to the crown by the royal coffer-maker, William Greene. He provided not only the coverings of gold cloth, velvet, and other luxurious fabrics, which were trimmed with fringes and attached to the structure by copper nails, but also the wooden frames. The cost of such chairs was enormous.

Until fairly recently many coronation seats in France and other European countries (but not in England), seem to have had low backs, as shown in engravings by Cochin, Tardieu, and Moreau of the coronations of Louis XV and Louis XVI of France. The low back of the *faudesteuil* allowed it to be used during other events that required easy access to the sitter, such as grooming and hairdressing.

In the beginning of the fifteenth century the *faudesteuil* disappeared in France, only reappearing,

> A rare traveling throne, c. 1620. This curule chair, which can be broken down into separate pieces, is made of wood completely covered with ivory veneer, and decorated with carved fauns' heads. The metal fittings are gilded iron. Following Roman tradition, curule chairs were reserved for high magistrates, the ivory decoration making the seat even more prestigious. Perpitch Collection, Paris

< A carved walnut "Savonarola" chair. Italian, c. 1550. Chateau of Ecouen. Photograph: Antoine Bootz

> A pair of fifteenth-century Spanish armchairs, examples of a category of folding chair with fine inlay produced by Muslim craftsmen in Granada, probably before the Christian conquest of southern Spain in 1492. Such chairs were highly prized, and the Muslim craftsmen who made them continued to work for the Spanish nobility well into the sixteenth century. This chair type was exported to Italy, where it appeared in a number of local variations (see below), although the inlay of the Italian versions was generally much less sophisticated than that of the Spanish examples. Lemmers-Danforth-Sammlung, Wetzlar, Museum der Stadt Wetzlar, acc. no. M8a, b

> A late-fifteenth-century Genoese armchair, similar to the Spanish chairs illustrated above, although the craftsmanship of the Spanish examples is superior. L'Antiquaire & The Connoisseur, Inc.

medieval & renaissance chairs 59

slightly altered, at the end of the century, first in Spain and then in Italy, by way of Sicily. The *jamuga*, or side-saddle chair, was an important development in Spain. This was a Gothic version of the folding, hip-joint chair, the Moorish seat of honor, and the Christians considered it, with its elaborate decoration of inlay in ivory, bone, or boxwood, more important than their own plain *frailero*, or monk's chair. With the coming of the Renaissance, however, the *jamuga* fell from favor. The export of this type of chair to Italy (and not the other way around as was once thought) resulted in a large spectrum of local variations on the folding scissor-frame, including the so-called Dante or Savonarola chair, often less sophisticated than the *jamuga*, and decorated with inferior inlay. The same form would, in turn, be introduced to the French court by Catherine de Médicis in the sixteenth century, and subsequently, to the rest of Europe, but with limited success. The plain Spanish walnut *frailero* used by Christians in the fifteenth century was also collapsible.

In England, where foreign influences took hold more slowly, some X-form armchairs designed by such prominent cabinetmakers as William Kent survived until the end of the eighteenth century. The *faudesteuil* continued its evolution as the French *fauteuil*, or armchair, and was also the ancestor of the *ployant*, the aristocratic, often gilded, folding stool of the eighteenth century. Many versions of this type, now plebeian and inexpensive, survive to this day, one current incarnation being the "director's chair," made of pine and canvas.

As we have seen, chairs either were folding and transportable, or heavy, solid, and stationary. When stationary, in the early Middle Ages, they were often constructed as an extension of the walls of a room. The same principle was followed in churches and monasteries, with abbots' or bishops' thrones, or monks' stalls. In the Romanesque and Gothic periods, another heavy chair appeared, modeled on architecture. This was a chair on a dais with a chest under the seat (*à coffre et à ciel*), or *cathedra*. Numerous inventories mention such seats in bedrooms, placed close to the bed for storage.

As the Renaissance brought a new demand for comfort, the bench, the form (a kind of bench), and the stool were the most common seats. One rudimentary shape was constructed on the model of the milking stool, with a thick, wooden seat

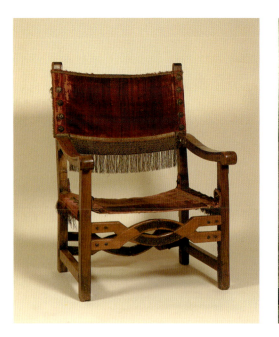

<
A Spanish sixteenth-century metal armchair. Kuegel Collection

<<
A Spanish folding armchair. Second half of the sixteenth century. Spanish Renaissance chairs, like their medieval antecedents, were often foldable. Museo Nacional de Artes Decorativas, Madrid

>
A Spanish *sillon frailero*. Casa y Museo de El Greco, Toledo

v
Seats from the Convent of Santa Clara at Moguer, Spain. Fourteenth century. Museo Diocesano, Moguer (Huelva-España)

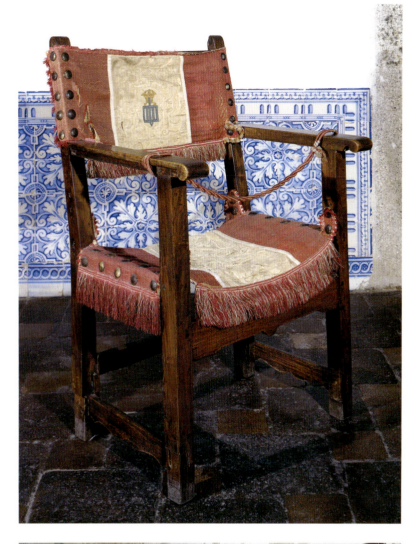

with large holes cut out, into which the legs were fitted. This type stayed the same through the eighteenth century. We shall see examples of it in the next chapter. Benches, forms, and stools were used in hall and chambers alike. The bench was considered superior to the stool, although humbler than the chair. Benches were, however, frequently used by great lords for dining, precedence being conferred by the use of canopies fixed above an honored person. Petruccio Ubaldini, an Italian visitor to England in 1547, was shocked that the future Elizabeth I sat neither under a canopy nor on a chair, but sat instead on a mere bench with a cushion, and so far distant from the head of the table and the king that his canopy did not overhang her.

Chamber benches were often fitted around the walls of a room like church stalls, as were window seats in most parts of Europe. Bankers also sat on benches and kept their valuables inside for safekeeping. People who dealt with money were of lower social position than aristocrats, and benches were associated with their status. During most of the fifteenth and sixteenth centuries in Europe,

the bench, a heavy piece of furniture containing a storage chest, was generally set in front of the fireplace and rarely moved.

The fifteenth century saw the creation of a clever bench called *à tournis*, probably originating in Flanders, which can be found in Burgundian, French, and German illustrations between 1450 and 1525. The back of the seat swiveled so that the sitter could turn his back to the fire while eating, and then turn back to face it afterwards. In England long wooden benches were called forms, and some are said to have been upholstered. They were, we are told, filled with flock to form a slightly convex covering. Students in exclusive "public" schools sat on them and "form" thus became synonymous with one of the classes into which the pupils were divided according to grade, a definition still in use today in English and some American private schools.

In the early medieval hall, benches and settles were the ordinary seats. A settle would have a paneled back and the space between the legs enclosed, to fit closely to the wood paneling. Settles called "Flanders forms" were imported into England

<<
A Gothic silver armchair, the oldest known example of a silver chair, said to have belonged to King Martin the Humane of Aragon (reigned 1395–1410). Barcelona Cathedral

v
The throne of King Martin the Humane of Aragon. Fifteenth century. In 1940 this chair was made into a cult object. Barcelona Cathedral

medieval & renaissance chairs   63

> A medieval ecclesiastical throne. Chateau of Ecouen C1515.nb 91GN53. Photograph: Antoine Bootz

>> An abbot's seat made of oak, with Gothic openwork tracery. During his stay on Majorca with George Sand in 1838, Chopin had this seat moved into the monk's cell they were renting at the Charterhouse of Valldemossa. As Sand wrote later in *Winter in Majorca,* "Finally the sacristan [was] persuaded to move into our cell a large, splendid Gothic chair of carved oak, which was being eaten away by worms and rats in a disused Carthusian chapel." Charterhouse of Valldemossa, Majorca

> A sixteenth-century throne chair. Chateau of Ecouen nb 79 EN1877. Photograph: Antoine Bootz

>> A pine seat from the Convent of Santa Clara de Toro, Zamora, Spain. Museo Nacional de Artes Decorativas, Madrid

< A fifteenth-century Spanish wooden bench or *arquibanco*. The earliest Spanish benches were made for churches and other religious foundations, as part of the wooden wall paneling. This one was made for private use. Such benches were considered comfortable seats at the time. Museo Nacional de Artes Decorativas (inv n 1.612), Madrid

∨ A late-sixteenth-century Italian *cassapanca*. The *cassapanca* is a variant of the box settle, a combined seat and chest. Early versions of the type feature a back and arms of similar height. Generally placed in the middle of a long wall, the imposing structure of the *cassapanca* must have conveyed a monumental impression. Like many examples of the seat, this one features multicolored decoration on a cream ground. Early Italian furniture was often painted rather than carved. L'Antiquaire & The Connoisseur, Inc.

> Konstantin Makovsky (1839–1915), *The Boyar Wedding*. Oil on canvas. In this evocation of seventeenth-century Russian life, the wedding party is shown seated on a *sunduk*, the Russian variant of the *cassapanca*. Hillwood Museum

from the Low Countries in the fifteenth century. John Florio, in his Italian-English dictionary published in 1611, explains that the Italian word *banca* meant any "benches or forms." To a sixteenth-century Englishman, a form was a bench without a back, a distinction the Italians apparently did not make, as we can see from a reference in the Medici inventory of 1553, which mentions *una panca d'albero, con l'appogiato* [a bench of poplar with a back rest]. In many paintings, saints can be seen sitting on a version of a *cassapanca*, a chest with a back, the seat of which encloses a storage space. Such benches were generally in the main living apartment, made comfortable with soft cushions, and might be used as the seat of ceremony for the master of the house.

In Russia before the reign of Peter the Great, benches closely resembling the Italian *cassapanca* were widely used in *terems* (the dwellings of boyars, or nobles) for dining and storage. Such a seat was called a *sunduk*, a word apparently of Tartar origin. In Spain benches (*bancos*), to judge by the number still seen, were used everywhere from the kitchen to the high altar of the cathedral. Most were collapsible. Whether of wood alone or upholstered, the structural principle was the same—the back was hinged to fold down on the seat and the legs were hinged to fold under when the iron braces were released. The back of an all-wood bench was either solid or composed of an arcade supported on spindles. Solid backs were adorned with good hinges, metal plaques, or the crest of a family, city, or monastery. The upholstered benches of Spain were highly prized, with leather or velvet upholstery quilted in lozenges or crescent shapes. The stitching was done with heavy linen thread to form intricate, small-scale garlands scrolled around birds and animals, trophies, urns, masks, and grotesques. The turning was heavier than seen formerly, featuring spirals, balls, and disks in the Flemish style. The wooden portions were heavy, and held together with nails rather than the refined joinery practiced in other countries. Since wood was abundant and inexpensive, cabinetmakers often used thick pieces. The general effect was rather crude.

Through the seventeenth century, household inventories show, benches were widely used all over Europe, particularly for dining. Trestle tables were usually set up at meal time in the main hall

Abraham Bosse (1602–76), *Ladies in Conversation*. Oil on canvas. Bosse specialized in such representations of daily life. RMN ekta89E3910

and immediately dismantled after the meal, since the main hall had many other functions. The benches were pushed against the walls, carried out, or moved as needed. They continued in use as seats for patrons in theaters until 1759 in France, not only in the auditorium, but on the stage itself.

Another sort of stool that was common during the Middle Ages and Renaissance throughout Europe, particularly in Spain and Italy, was the *carreau*, or cushion. *Carreaux* were used as padding for hard seats or as seats by themselves, especially for women, as late as the seventeenth century. Listed in the inventory of the emperor Charles V (reigned 1519–56) are *six carreaux de cuir aux armes d'Aragon*. Cushions were often made of leather, velvet, silk, or needlepoint, often embroidered with the family crest. Cushions, being of Moorish origin, were in fashion at the Spanish court, from which they spread all over Europe. In Italy they became especially fashionable in the time of the Borgias, who were of Spanish origin. When Lucrezia Borgia was married at the Vatican in June 1492, the ladies who followed the bride into the Sala Reale "all found places on the cushions scattered around the platform."

The fifteenth and sixteenth centuries were critical in the development of the seat. In Italy, society became more stable, and as people became more aware of the culture of Roman Antiquity, a more comfortable quality of life emerged a century ahead of the rest of Europe.

As a testament to a new-found comfort and hygiene, the bathroom chair, *chaise percée*, or close stool appeared. This portable latrine, a seat or box containing a chamber pot, was often richly decorated or upholstered with velvet and silk.

The rebirth of Ancient Roman ideals, which had begun to transform Italian literature in the fourteenth century, in the fifteenth century created a new Renaissance style in painting, sculpture, and the decorative arts. Originating in Florence and gradually spreading across Europe, the new style blossomed in the sixteenth century, and eventually superseded the Gothic style. The new style originated in Florence for a number of reasons, among them the city's immense wealth and the patronage of its ruler, Cosimo de' Medici. In 1439 Cosimo was host to a council of Catholic and Greek prelates assembled to discuss the reunion of Eastern and Western Christianity. The Greek prelates brought with them a knowledge of Greek literature and culture, a stimulus to Florentine humanism that made the city the Athens of Italy.

Seats became lighter, their construction more complex and sophisticated. Renaissance chairs were decorated with motifs from classical architecture, including strongly profiled bases and cornices that accentuated their horizontal elements. A lighter, typically Italian piece of seating furniture was born: the *sgabello*, which occurred in many variations. One of the best-known is the *sgabello a tre piedi* (three-footed *sgabello*) belonging to the Strozzi family made about 1491.

The shape of the *sgabello* is derived from a low stool with three legs mounted at an angle, the simplest type of chair that had been popular since the Middle Ages. Its creator, in a stroke of genius, cleverly added a high, thin, architecturally balanced backrest. A *sgabello* might also have four legs, and in some cases, only two very heavy ones, one in front and one in back. Examples from northern Italy were heavier, often rustic, with a broader back with a shaped profile and heavy carving. In Venice, this style of *sgabello* became an elegant object with turned legs. Appearing in France in the mid-sixteenth century under the influence of the queen of France, Catherine de Médicis, *sgabelli* were often made of walnut and were usually supported by two heavy legs in the north Italian style. Their use would continue during the seventeenth century as well.

The French writer Gilles Corrozet (1510–68) explains in his book *Blasons domestiques* that *sgabelli* belonged in all well-furnished bedrooms,

> Pierre Mignard (1612–95), *Louise-Marie de Bourbon ("Mademoiselle de Tours")*. Oil on canvas. The daughter of Louis XIV and the marquise de Montespan is shown seated on a *carreau*, or large cushion. The inventory of Catherine de Médicis, made in 1589 when she arrived at the French court as the bride of Henri II, lists hundreds of magnificent *carreaux*. Later, the seventeenth-century memoirist Françoise de Motteville related that when her mother saw Anne of Austria in 1610 at her wedding to Louis XIII, the new queen was sitting *sur des carreaux à la mode d'Espagne* [on cushions in the Spanish manner]. The fashion for *carreaux* continued well into the century under Louis XIV, as the present painting shows. Versailles et Trianon. Photograph: RMN. Gerard Blot.

along with a dresser, bed, table, and other furnishings [*Chambres garnie d'un buffect, Et d'aultre mesnage parfaict, comme de lict, de banc, de table, de placet, de selle et scabelle, etc.*]. We also learn from the housekeeping records of Henri III of France (1551–89) that

Every Sunday and Thursday, all candelabra have to be lit in the ballroom, musicians have to be summoned, and the chairs for the king and his family have to be brought up, and about twenty other seats, scabelles, *have to be brought as well for the lords and ladies who have to sit.*

Havard, Dictionnaire de l'ameublement

Some *sgabello*-inspired hall chairs found their way to England around 1635, probably introduced by Inigo Jones soon after his return from Italy with Lord Arundel in 1614. Indeed, Italian influence on the design of English chairs was not appreciable before about 1530. Seats of that period made by English craftsmen were, on the whole, inferior to those from the hands of French or German makers. Although a guild of carpenters had been in existence in England since the early fourteenth century and a charter was granted to it about 1475, it is probable that during the fifteenth century very few sophisticated chairs were in private hands, and that the finest seats belonging to the king, the great lords, and the churches were obtained from abroad.

The most important development in the history of the chair during the sixteenth century was the introduction, under Italian influence, of a

>

A rosewood and ebony armchair from the northern Netherlands, c. 1625. This large armchair made of precious tropical woods is an impressive example of an early-seventeenth-century Netherlandish type. The design, with its straight back and rectangular seat, both upholstered, with straight legs braced by stretchers, originated in Spain and was known as a "Spanish chair" in the Netherlands. Rijksmuseum, Amsterdam

<

A portrait attributed to Salomon Mesdach (early seventeenth century) of a gentleman seated in a "Spanish chair," 1620. From the Boudaen Courten Family. Rijksmuseum, Amsterdam

lighter movable chair, the successor of the *sgabello* with or without armrests, called a *chaise à bras*. With the introduction of this form, the chair as a symbol of power began to disappear. The *chaise à bras* is simply a chair with a low back, without a chest under the seat, resting on four relatively simple legs. The age of completely portable furniture that could be moved from room to room as needed had come.

At the same time, there was also a shift in taste taking place throughout Europe, aided by the development of the printing press. Printing affected furniture-makers in many ways. One was through the dissemination of the theoretical texts that laid the foundations of Renaissance classicism, supplemented by engravings of antique objects and motifs and by a knowledge of surviving antique fragments on which these designs were based. Even more precise stylistic guidance was given to furniture-makers by the first printed patterns books. Among the most important of these were by Peter Flotner in Germany, Jacques Androuet du Cerceau I in France, and Hans Vredemann de Vries and Theodore de Bry in the Netherlands.

The purest expressions of Vredemann's style were decorative chairs made in Antwerp about 1600. Antwerp was the home of the late-Renaissance armchair, which was immensely popular in the North. Its influence spread to Cologne, along the shore of the North Sea, and of course, to England during the first part of the seventeenth century. The legs of these chairs are composed of alternating, turned balusters and cubes, the latter connected by rails. The straight backs feature pierced, carved panels, and the seat and the back are often upholstered in leather. Chairs that show the designs of Flotner, du Cerceau, Vredemann, and de Bry are still extant. Their influence, carried by the movement of craftsmen from place to place, had one unfortunate result; that is, it limited the creative freedom

<<
A French Renaissance swivel armchair, from the late sixteenth century. Chateau of Ecouen n88EN9291. Photograph: Antoine Bootz

<
Jacques Androuet du Cerceau (c. 1520–c. 1584), *Design for a Throne Chair*. Print, 1550. Du Cerceau, a French architect and designer, published some very influential engraved designs for furniture, silver, and textiles. In 1550 he issued a set of engraved furniture designs that are one of the first examples of a coherent group of household furniture. The Metropolitan Museum of Art inv 26.50.6

>
An example of a *caquetoire,* a seat typical of late-fifteenth-century France. Many inventories of the time mention these armchairs, intended for women to sit by the fire to chat. The trapezoidal seat was made to accommodate the voluminous skirts of the time. Some *caquetoires* rested on a movable base, which allowed them to swivel (see opposite, left). Louvre inv OA 3120. Photograph: RMN

of individual chair-makers and introduced a stylistic homogeneity throughout Europe.

Another sixteenth-century form was the *caquetoire*, a seat on which women could sit and talk as much as they liked. The name, derived from the French word for chatter, was given to it in allusion to the passion for gossip that is supposed to have popularized it. H. Havard's *Dictionnaire de l'ameublement* (Paris, 1887–90) quotes the publisher Henri Estienne (1528–98) as saying of the women of his generation that "They do not ever seem to be at a loss for words, at least not those who live in Paris, and for this reason the *caquetoire* could be called their perfect seat." [*Il n'y a pas d'apparence qu'elles aient le bec gelé, pour le moins j'en repons pour celles de Paris, qui ne se sont pu tenir d'apeler cacquetoire leurs sièges.*] *Caquetoires* were generally made of walnut, and they exhibited a considerable variety of design. They appeared in France in the sixteenth century as an evolution from the Italian *sgabello*. Nothing like them seems to have been mentioned in any inventory before 1570. The *caquetoire* was a trapezoid-based armchair with high, open armrests, and a high, narrow open back with a central splat, the decorative areas of which were enriched with masks, strapwork, or foliate ornament in the Renaissance style. The elaborate carving of these chairs required a wood soft enough to allow finer and more detailed work than had been possible with the oak so loved earlier. Thus, from 1530 on, walnut began to replace oak as the material for chairs.

The furniture industry grew rapidly in the sixteenth century. One sign of its growth was the fact that turners achieved such importance at this time that they were installed in a special quarter of Paris, which would be the beginning of the future Faubourg Saint-Antoine. Only in the second half of the sixteenth century did the Renaissance style penetrate England and Germany. English and German seats of this period tend to be somewhat crude. The armchairs rest on coarse, square or turned legs and feature high backs, but these may exhibit rich, flat-carved Renaissance ornamentation. The great hall of a fifteenth- or sixteenth-century English manor house would look incomplete without the massive, panel-back chairs that stand against the whitewashed walls, with armor and trophies above and behind them. These chairs seem to have been used solely by

>

A seventeenth-century Italian leather-upholstered chair. Chateau of Ecouen nb88gn 9282. Photograph: Antoine Bootz

<

Abraham Bosse (1602–76). *The Trades: The Apothecary*. Print. The Metropolitan Museum of Art inv. D1392

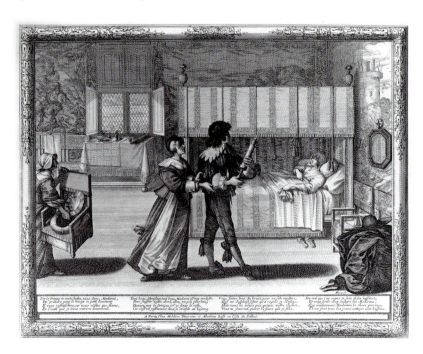

medieval & renaissance chairs

the lord, his wife, and important guests, and then only on ceremonial occasions, as when dining at the high table. For a stranger to have sat in one uninvited would have been a grave insult. A type resembling these armchairs is sometimes called a Shakespeare chair, which has a seat that narrows to the rear, a narrow back, and curved arms.

Another distinctive type of chair introduced to England about the end of the sixteenth century bears a strong resemblance to some fifteenth-century Italian models. This is an oak armchair with a folding frame and a flat back, called a Glastonbury chair. It seems to derive from a chair known from a description and an engraving published in 1866, which was inscribed *Monarchris Glastonie*. The caption of the 1866 engraving reads: "The Abbot's chair, Glastonbury." The type has been extensively faked in modern times.

Although a number of types were in use in England in the second half of the sixteenth century, chairs were still scarce even in large houses. At Hengrave Hall, a Tudor house in East Anglia, in 1603 the Great Chamber contained thirty-two joined stools, but only four chairs. At court, chairs

were still reserved exclusively for the sovereign. When Juan Fernandez de Valasco, Constable of Castile, was entertained by James I at Whitehall in 1604, he wrote that "Their Majesties sat at the head of the table on chairs of brocade with cushions, and at the Queen's side sat the Constable, a little apart, on a tabouret [stool] of brocade with a cushion of the same," the prince being provided with a similar seat.

Another early-seventeenth-century English chair was the three-legged, turned chair, made of oak, ash, or occasionally, yew, which continued to be produced with slight modification until the end of the century. It had a triangular seat intended (one hopes) for a cushion. Similar chairs were probably in Mary Verney's mind when she wrote to Lady Elmes in 1664: "For a drawing room I should have 2 squobs [upholstered stools] and 6 turned woden chairs." In England, turned chairs continued to be popular, especially those with rush seats and high backs formed by three cross-bars. This domestic, country-made furniture would become the American Colonial chair,

<
A seventeenth-century Spanish *sillita de estrado*, a chair used by ladies at court. Museo Nacional de Artes Decorativas, Madrid

Crispijn van de Passe II (c. 1597–1670), *Designs for Chairs*. Engraving, c. 1621. This series is best known from the modified second and third editions of 1642 and 1651. The title, given in four languages, leaves no doubt as to van de Passe's intention, which was to display exemplary pieces of furniture for the connoisseur. All the pieces represented are richly detailed masterpieces, much finer than most examples in daily use. Van de Passe's prints can be compared to earlier series of furniture designs by Jacques Androuet du Cerceau and Hans Vredemann de Vries. The Metropolitan Museum of Art

brought to the New World about 1630 by Puritans during the reign of Charles I.

The chief seat-forms of the southern German Renaissance were four-legged board chairs with carved and pierced backs, revolving chairs with square or semicircular seats and backs with balusters, and folding chairs or stools, with backs and seats upholstered in leather or velvet. As in other European countries, in Germany the armchair with square legs, usually with an upholstered seat and back and a carved apron became popular during the late Renaissance. Toward the end of the sixteenth century, turned legs began to appear. North German Renaissance furniture included typical chairs with four legs—each leg being a small, turned baluster with square pieces linked by rails—and pierced and carved backs. Chairs of this type predominated from the end of the sixteenth century, demonstrating the tenacious adherence to tradition in that part of the world.

The end of the sixteenth century saw many more changes in the evolution of European seating. As the quality of life improved, more people could afford seats, and as techniques and tools developed, the number of small, movable pieces increased. Upholstery became more widespread, and there was an increased use of fringes and brass nails. In England during the reign of Elizabeth I, mere comfort gave way to flamboyant luxury. Later, around 1615–18 under the influence of Inigo Jones, Charles I's surveyor general of works, who had traveled extensively in Italy, elaborate interiors and furniture were created—among them the *sgabello*-inspired chairs mentioned earlier. Upholstery for backs and seats came into widespread use in response to a growing demand for comfort.

The woodwork of the square, upholstered chairs made around 1600 was often covered with damask to match the padded seats and backs. These chairs closely resembled contemporary

A group of five seventeenth-century chairs upholstered in Cordou leather. Chateau of Ecouen nb91gn956. Photograph: Antoine Bootz

Flemish and Dutch examples represented in the engravings of domestic interiors by Abraham Bosse. Many of these chairs were made without arms so that they could accommodate the extravagant dimensions of the farthingale, a large, padded ring that women wore around their hips to give greater volume to their skirts. The French word for the farthingale, *vertugadin*, gave its name in turn to the French version of the armless chair, the *chaise à vertugadin*, a form often mentioned in contemporary French inventories. This chair would be one of the first known modifications of a seat made to accommodate fashion. Many more would occur in the following centuries. The square, upholstered chair was the standard type for its time, and it was also used for dining, in which case it was often covered in leather or turkey-work. As an addition to a suite of farthingale dining-chairs there would often be a "great chaire," a scaled-up version of the same piece, with arms. This was to be the standard form of armchair into the middle of the seventeenth century.

All upholstery techniques, with the exception of a few later inventions such as stitched edges and springing, were developed before 1700. As we shall see in our next chapter, continental craftsmen were the leading innovators of the seventeenth century, and the most notable advances in upholstery comfort were made in Paris toward the end of the century by craftsmen working for the dauphin. When an inventory was drawn up for Cardinal Mazarin in 1653, he had in a bedroom no fewer than fourteen chairs of various kinds, of which two armchairs were entirely covered with velvet nailed to the wooden frame. The inventory also tells us that a great variety of chairs were used on a constant basis in the seventeenth century, a major change from the previous one, when they were still scarce. From the sixteenth century on, chairs began to be upholstered en suite—as a matching set—another interesting development. As the notion of decoration and of creating something pleasing to the eye began to emerge, the chair started to become an intrinsic element

v
An ivory sofa, c. 1640, part of a large set of ivory furniture including armchairs (which mimic the shape of folding chairs), small tables, and a large table, for the household of Prince Johann Mauritz von Nassau-Siegen. Berlin, Brandenburg

A pair of Franco-Flemish baroque walnut armchairs. Christie's

of décor, as it would come to be in the eighteenth century.

Damask, a silk fabric originally from Damascus, which in the twelfth century achieved a world-wide reputation for the quality of its weaving, was the fabric of choice, along with velvet, which was produced from the thirteenth century on in the Italian cities of Lucca, Genoa, and Florence. A more frequent covering for chairs was leather, which was used from the Middle Ages into the seventeenth century. In 1658, for example, the Rector of Claydon in England wrote to Sir Ralph Verney that he "should like very well the painted leather for a suite of chairs and stools."

During the reign of Louis XIII (1610–43) the style of chairs combined influences from a number of countries, including Italy, Spain, and the Low Countries. Indeed, chairs made in the first half of the seventeenth century throughout Europe exhibit many similarities, which reflect the way of life of the rising bourgeois class across the continent. These newly rich men and women displayed their wealth and power in numerous portraits, in which the subject is always represented seated. France's overwhelming impact on chair design was to begin only in 1661, when Louis XIV began to reign after the death of Cardinal Mazarin, the regent of France during his minority. In Chapter 4, we shall examine the reign of this remarkable king, whose influence on all of the decorative arts of Europe—and on the chair in particular—was immense.

3
country, garden & colonial chairs

Wondrous the gods, more wondrous are the men,
More wondrous, wondrous still, the cock and hen,
More wondrous still the table, stool, and chair;
But oh! more wondrous still the charming fair.
                              William Blake, *Imitation of Pope*

The designs of most common chairs came from the servants' quarters of the great houses of seventeenth- and eighteenth-century Europe. The local carpenter would build chairs for the kitchen or maids' rooms, and later would make similar pieces for himself or his fellow workmen. Country chairs are loosely called "country" to emphasize their rural, vernacular, or indigenous origins. They come not from any organized center of production, but represent many individual examples built to satisfy immediate needs. The quintessential quality of country and garden seats is their usefulness; they are meant to be serviceable, not to impress. Their variety is infinite, from the simplest, three-legged milking stool, to the sheep-shearing stool, to the dug-out chair, to the pig bench, to the nursing chair, to name only a few.

In England, Randle Holme remarked in 1649 in his *Academy of Armory*, a monumental manuscript illustrated with woodcuts, that chairs and stools were "made by the turner or the wheele wright," suggesting that seats of stick construction were associated with rural work. The account books of rural joiners reveal just how versatile they were in serving their neighbors' needs. It is important to remember that the making of a "Windsor" chair, for example, was a humble occupation, as was making a milking stool or a dug-out chair: very little skill was involved.

Comfort was second to utility; indeed, comfort is irrelevant to the country chair. Pieces produced in different places are very similar, owing to the continual movement of ideas and

<
An unusual nineteenth-century French country chair in the shape of a sunflower. Collection Philippe Vichot, Paris

workmen even in a time without modern communication. Country chairs are often simple, and while they may be unembellished, they are appreciated for their authenticity, plain lines, and historic value. During the seventeenth, eighteenth, and early nineteenth centuries, seats were handcrafted at home with whatever materials were available, including tree trunks, branches, twigs, boards, horns, and straw. They were also turned out by craftsmen of varying degrees of skill, some adept and imaginative, some mediocre.

The pieces made by village craftsmen or traveling carpenters often imitated models popular in the larger towns, and often the styles that were copied were already out of fashion in the more sophisticated world by the time they reached the countryside. Their features were often combined with other elements, and scaled down to appeal to the taste and budget of the modest customer. Thus, Queen Anne, Chippendale, Louis XV, Louis XVI, and Hepplewhite chairs were translated into homely idioms. Vernacular chairs are generally solidly built of native timber, and show a marked preference for rush or plank seats, and, often, painted finishes.

painted decoration on chairs and stools

In Eastern Europe, painted chairs and stools were a keynote of decoration. As early as 1595 in the region of Hälsingborg, Sweden, and in Bavaria, decorated chairs bore witness to an early tradition. Paint protected the wood and gave pieces a uniform appearance, hid inferior material, and offered an outlet for the painter's creativity. Surfaces might be painted a single color, grained to imitate a finer wood, or given elaborated folk decorations traditional to the area. Painting chairs never became as widespread in England or France as it was in other Northern European countries.

Once the use of background colors was established, green became the most frequently used hue, followed by black, which was particularly favored in Upper Austria. In addition, four others colors—white, blue-gray, brown, and reddish brown—predominate in the color schemes of eighteenth-century country chairs.

Flowers bloomed on many surfaces, and specific floral decorations were identified with particular areas. Roses were much loved in the Alps, and in East Prussia were the only motifs used. The acanthus leaf, so widely seen in ancient Greece and Rome, reappeared in Norway during the eighteenth century on painted chairs. The tulip, both open and closed, was prized in the Tyrol, Switzerland, and Holland, probably as a symbol of the Trinity. Interestingly, religious decorations appeared on chairs toward the end of the seventeenth century, following an earlier tradition. In some regions in the Zillertaler Alps or in the Alpbachtal, for example, floral motifs were frequently joined by animals and birds. In most European countries, where winters were long and cold, the use of brightly decorated chairs seems to reflect a yearning for the warm and bright flowers that come with the summer sun. A colorful chair

>
A nineteenth-century provincial Russian painted throne chair. Sotheby's

near the hearth was an antidote for the freezing winter night, and an outlet for creativity.

Most chair-painters in the Germanic countries, and their counterparts among the Pennsylvania Dutch in America, mixed their colors with skimmed milk and water, which hardened to a platelike surface prone to cracking. With the advent of Neoclassicism in Europe in the mid-eighteenth century, the palette became muted, broadening to include shades of gray, pale green, and blue. In America around the same period, painted furniture became as varied as any in the world, the result of the myriad influences brought to the colonies by various European groups. Thus, American painted chairs show a rich variety of European influences.

After the Revolutionary War Americans continued to copy fashions from England, and a number of chairs in the Queen Anne style survive, both plain-painted and decorated. When the Chippendale style came into favor after

A Spanish painted and parcel-gilt child's chair, c. 1690–1700. L'Antiquaire & The Connoisseur, Inc.

A pair of nineteenth-century Russian painted country children's armchairs. A La Vielle Russie

the middle of the eighteenth century, however, carving became popular, even in the countryside, and most decorative painting on chairs ceased, although plain-painting and woodgraining continued. Of all the imitative techniques, graining was by far the most popular and long-lived, lasting beyond the middle of the nineteenth century. Grains of almost every wood were imitated, and the result, when done well, was both stylish and economical. Graining was carried out with special combs or such improvised tools as feathers, rags, sticks, or even pieces of cork.

Cleanliness was one virtue of the painted chair: it was easier and more hygienic to scrub a painted surface than a polished one, and especially in modest houses, cleanliness was both a virtue and an efficient way to protect against disease. In some Catholic countries and households, the religious calendar dictated periodic redecoration. Tradition demanded, for example, that furniture

> A painted armchair from Skåne province, Sweden, an area that was Danish until the seventeenth century, c. 1831. Painting on chairs was introduced to hide the imperfections of poorer quality wood. Early decoration was usually simple, in the Germanic countries at first consisting of stars and flowers stenciled directly onto the untreated wood. Painted backgrounds became increasingly popular during the late seventeenth century. Nordiska Museum

be repainted before Easter, a task that occupied much of a housewife's time during Holy Week. In some households, chairs were painted twice during the year. For these reasons, most country chairs, regardless of their origin, are painted, or exist in a painted version.

STOOLS, SETTLES, AND BENCHES

Throughout much of history, the floors of rustic dwellings were usually of beaten earth, often covered with straw. This common type of uneven flooring had a number of effects on the way stools and chairs were built.

stools

Since in both Europe and America historically so many people have been poor, stools are more common than any other item of furniture. Stools not only varied in size, from four to eighteen inches in height, but also in the range of functions they were required to fulfill. They were versatile; a larger one might be used as a table. This is demonstrated in Ireland by Andrew M'Kenzie's poetic inventory of 1807 in "The Poor Man's Petition":

Three stools, one larger than the rest
Our table when we have a guest

The three-legged stood was used often, as it still is, for milking all over the world. In some Alpine and Nordic countries and in Ireland, cows were kept inside the house during the winter, separated only from the human inhabitants by a low partition. The "upper end" of the building accommodated the family, while the cows occupied the "lower end." The closeness of the animals generated heat, and made the task of milking easier. This arrangement continued until the end of nineteenth century, and in some parts of the Alps, into the early twentieth. Four-legged stools were also common, and both types were usually made by inserting a wooden wedge into a saw cut made in the top of each leg, once the legs had been pushed into angled holes in the slab seat.

The term "creepie" (or "creepy") was until recently often applied to a three- or four-legged stool in the northern counties of Ireland. The name was already familiar during the first half of the nineteenth century, as a Dublin *Penny Journal* of the period confidently proclaimed, "our own three legged stool, or creepy . . . is evidently the most primitive and ancient form of seating in the world, and which retains its appropriate place in the mud cabin." The term was also used in Scotland in the eighteenth century for a church stool of repentance; it may have migrated to Ireland with the Scottish settlers.

settles and benches

Drafts and wall dampness may account for the popularity of the high-backed settle. In early inventories the terms "settle" and "bench" are used interchangeably, but the distinctive characteristic of the settle is the presence of arms. Settles are also usually attached to the floor. Both settle and bench may have a hinged seat over a storage chest. The word "settle" is of Anglo-Saxon origin, but its shape and function are similar to the Italian *cassapanca* and the Russian *sunduk*. In England, there are still many settles made for inns and farmhouses with eighteenth-century ornaments and molded stiles. Oak settles were occasionally made in that period for use in the open air. At Ham House, outside London, there is a perfectly preserved pair with high, paneled backs and arms boldly carved, in the house's "cloisters," where they have always stood.

The settle could also double as an extra bed near the fire in rural houses, or in those of large families. In Ireland, the practice of having several children sleep together was still widespread in many areas in living memory, for in the winter it

> German milking stools and a Swedish country chair. The three-legged stool was a very common seat. It was simple to make, and its three legs assured that it was stable, even if the pitch of its seat was not so comfortable on an uneven floor. Robert Wilson Collection. Photograph: Antoine Bootz

helped them stay warm. This tradition, which goes back at least as far as the Middle Ages, was also followed in other northern European countries such as Norway, Sweden, and Finland.

Some sat on stones, some sat on blocks,
Some sat on churns, some on wheelstocks;
Some sat on cars, some sat on ladders,
And for shift, some sat on madders . . .
The brisk young sparks, with their kind wenches
Did place themselves on rushy benches . . .
They both on bench of Rushes sat,
Commixt with flags, both wondrous fat
                    W. Moffat, *Hesperi-Neso-Graphia*, 1724

Fireside seats for several people were traditional peasant furnishings. Most surviving examples are made of painted pine or inexpensive wood; however, descriptions from the eighteenth century such as the poem above suggest that a vast variety of materials other than wood were used to allow people to sit near the fire. In England, peat was a common seating material, and in Ireland, benches on either side of the fire were of turf. In times of shortage they could always be used as fuel.

Strictly utilitarian in his outlook, the peasant acquired only such furniture as his needs demanded. Benches and a few chairs satisfied his wants; with upholstery he was scarcely acquainted. In every rustic sitting-room—in Bavaria, the Tyrol, Switzerland, England, and France—the plain wooden bench, sometimes placed along the wall by the table, was the most usual seating at meal time. Benches were also common in taverns, inns, and private dwellings alike for use at the kitchen table. The Provençal poet Frédéric Mistral (1830–1914) recalled an evening with the writer Alphonse Daudet (1840–97) in Arles. The two men came upon a tavern, almost a hovel, near the Rhône, in which they were served a delicious supper. The floor was of beaten earth, the ceiling was blackened by smoke, and they sat upon benches around the table:

Dans une salle basse, dont le sol était couvert d'un corroi de mortier battu, mais dont les murs étaient bien blancs, il y avaient une longue table où l'on voyait assis quinze ou vingt mariniers en train de manger un cabri. . . . Aux poutres du plafond, peint en noir de fumée, étaient pendues des chasses-mouches . . . et, vis-à-vis de ces hommes qui en nous voyant entrer, devinrent silencieux, autour d'une table nous primes place sur des bancs.

[*In a low room whose floor was covered with a layer of mortar but whose walls were quite white, there was a long table where we saw fifteen or twenty sailors seated, eating a young goat. . . . From the beams of the ceiling, blackened with smoke, were hung some fly-swatters . . . and, opposite the men, who fell silent when we entered, we took our places on some benches around a table.*]

La Ribote de Trinquetaille, Frédéric Mistral, 1870

COUNTRY CHAIRS

Historically, chairs evolved from stools. Indeed, in many seventeenth-century English inventories, chairs are termed "back stools." The close association between stool and chair is more obvious with the slab-seated hedge chair of rural Ireland than perhaps anywhere else. The term "hedge chair" stems from the fact that such chairs were made by "hedge carpenters." The hedge carpenter did not serve the same long apprenticeship as a carpenter, and was not as qualified, but he could choose part of a tree for the job to be done and had some relative expertise.

ladder-back chairs

The ladder-back chair, which features several horizontal rails or slats, is found in Dutch interiors as early as the seventeenth century, and some very elaborate versions were made in Venice as early as 1570. Since these were usually rather low-seated chairs, mostly intended for use by women, their backs were proportionately low, with room for only two slats. In later Dutch examples, ladder-back chairs often had four or five slats, and bare, rush seats. The Dutch apparently had a monopoly on the trade in rush-seated chairs in northern Europe in the seventeenth century, for there are

<
A back stool, Lebanon County, Pennsylvania, c. 1750. This type of chair was made in Pennsylvania during the seventeenth and eighteenth centuries using same plank construction with pegged tenon joints, and following the same design, as earlier examples made in Germany. Philadelphia Museum of Art inv 28.10.65

country, garden & colonial chairs 87

> An Irish hedge chair. Since the wood for hedge chairs was often gleaned from hedgerows, the chairs are made of a variety of woods, including elm, ash, sycamore, and whitethorn, unified by brown or red paint. National Museum of Ireland

> An extremely unusual nineteenth-century hand-carved Russian country armchair. Collection Kuegel

<

A nineteenth-century Swedish country side chair. Ronald Brick Collection

>

A dug-out chair. Robert Wilson Collection. Photograph: Antoine Bootz

>

An American fruitwood side chair, made by Charles Robinson of Rochester, N.Y., 1860s. Robinson, Rochester's most prolific chair-maker, worked from the 1830s into the 1880s. Genesee County Museum. Photograph: J. Via

many mentions of "Dutch chairs" or "Dutch rush-seated chairs" in English inventories of the eighteenth century.

Other examples of ladder-back chairs were to be found in Sweden, from the royal castle at Gripsholm, where chairs of this type were provided in the guest rooms. These were comfortable armchairs, sometimes with an upholstered seat. A revival during the twentieth century has made the "Gripsom chair" a household term in Sweden. Earlier documents refer to them by the French word *bergères*, and suggest that they were used by women. Similar rustic armchairs with rush seats and back-splats can be found in the French countryside; in Provence their back-splats are concave.

In Spain and Portugal a similar chair developed, with rush seats, turned uprights, and carved ladder-back rails. Although they seem rustic, they stood in noblemen's houses and were often painted and gilded. They can be identified with the Rousseauesque ideal of communing with nature, and the eighteenth-century infatuation with the simplicity of dairies, garden rooms, and grottoes. Refined versions of rush-seated ladder-back chairs were to be found in polite surroundings during the seventeenth and eighteenth centuries. In the nineteenth century, they stood in English middle-class homes, and later on, would influence the designers of the Arts and Crafts Movement. Shaker and Pennsylvania Dutch chairs in America are yet other versions of the same type.

kitchen chairs

Kitchen chairs can be found in every European country and in the New World. The term not only refers to the fact that they are used in the kitchen, but also to differentiate them from parlor chairs, which are intended for more sophisticated surroundings, and are therefore of more refined construction and finish.

The common denominator is a robustness of form and a rush seat. The seat may be a simple piece of wood, but rush seats are more frequent. A skilled artisan can make two or three rush seats per day at the most, so the cost of such a seat is fairly high. Today, rush seats are ready-made in China, and can be bought very inexpensively,

competition that presents a threat to the livelihood of local artisans. However, the charm of kitchen chairs lies in their homey quality, which cannot be replaced by modern shortcuts.

carpenter chairs

Carpenter chairs have been made since the early nineteenth century, as an adaptation of the English Regency chair with saber legs. They can be found all over Ireland, especially in areas prosperous enough to support the work of carpenters. Although traditionally used in middle-class parlors, they are still considered country chairs. Some have bare, wooden seats; others have an upholstered drop-in seat. The idea of a "carpenter chair" is a contradiction, since carpenters do not ordinarily build chairs; indeed, chair-making goes against everything they are trained to do. To build a chair, one has to cut each piece of wood obliquely, while a carpenter is trained to cut every piece at a straight angle.

provençal chairs

Provençal chairs, like all regional chairs, have a strongly utilitarian character. Provence developed a refined, distinctive style earlier than any other French province, and in the fifteenth century art and furniture design flourished there under King René. In the eighteenth century, under the influence of the Louis XV style, the Provençal style reached its apogee.

Chairs for every household use were produced in Provence, most with a rustic look. The rush-seated chairs (*cadiero*), the armchair (*fauteuil*), and the settee (*radassie*) were often painted an olive green, gray, or gray-blue and were decorated with hand-painted flowers. There is a large armchair called a *fauteuil de bonnes femmes*, designed for grandmothers, and another with a high back and a low seat called the *chaise de nourrice*, designed for nursing. Yet another chair, the

<
A Provençal armchair. Provençal chairs are made in numerous shapes, all sharing a strong Louis XV influence. Characterized by turned legs, they often feature carved olives or wheat motifs on the back. The woods used include walnut, beech, linden, mulberry, and willow. The seats are woven, either of natural straw or of natural and tinted straw combined in a simple pattern. Often the seats are padded with thin, biscuit-shaped cushions made from colorful *boutis*—printed Provençal cotton—and attached to the seat, back, and arms with straps. Photograph: Christopher Maya

<
French country dining chairs with caned backs and seats in a room setting. Photograph: Christopher Maya

country, garden & colonial chairs   91

>
A Vierlander armchair, Prussia, eighteenth century. Vierlander chairs, made by provincial carpenters, are characterized by their intricate inlay of local woods. Germanisches Nationalmuseum

>>
A carved and painted German bridal chair, c. 1840. Chairs of this type recall Romanesque furniture, and early on attracted the attention of scholars because of the traditional decoration on their usually trapezoidal backrests. This form is found in the lower Rhine, Westphalia, and Schleswig-Holstein. Bridal sets of chairs were also made in Provence and Russia during the nineteenth century, usually with one chair slightly larger than the other for the groom. The initials of the couple were generally painted on the backs, along with the wedding date. Collection Matz and Pribell, Cambridge, Massachusetts

chauffeuse, is designed to sit near the fire, and the armchairs called *fauteuils de mariage* are created as a pair, one slightly larger than the other, for weddings. Some low chairs, called *chaises de fileuse*, were designed for spinning.

The most unusual seat is the *radassie*, or rush-seated banquette for two, three, or more people. It is built as a row of three or four armchairs combined, with an arm at each end and individual seat-backs. The *radassie* was designed for the pleasures of chatting, resting, or napping. Another type of banquette, the *radassière*, which appeared at the end of the eighteenth century, is typical of southern France. This is a vast sofa, covered with a soft mattress and numerous cushions, usually set in an alcove framed by columns. It was probably a modification, under the influence of the Turkish sofa, of the southern French *chambre de parade*, a bedroom where one could receive visitors, which would explain its rather theatrical character. During the hottest hours of the day, visitors could lie down to rest and enjoy the pleasure of the siesta. Of course, suspicious minds attribute other purposes to this type of seat. The word *radasser* means to be lazy, and by association, a woman who is a *radasse* is indolent and, often, of easy virtue.

marriage chairs

Carved and painted bridal chairs are a popular tradition. In Alpine and German-speaking countries, these often have trapezoidal backs ornamented with hearts and flowers. The shape is reminiscent of Romanesque furniture, and the decoration tends to be old-fashioned.

vierlander chairs

These typically German chairs originated in Prussia, which, in the eighteenth and nineteenth centuries, was a rich agricultural area.

stabellen chairs

Stabellen chairs are typical of the Alps, where in the past, farm workers commonly met around a table in a *Stube* (sitting room) and sat on these chairs to take their meals, socialize, or discuss important matters. The chairs, which evolved directly from stools, consist of a flat seat—which may be square, oblong, or slightly fiddle-shaped—into which are set four straight, slender legs. Carved in the center of the back, which is either vertical or gently sloping, is the primary decorative motif, often a conventional design. Apart from the forms already described, *Stabellen* vary according to their locality. In Switzerland and Germany they often have heart-shaped backs.

< A Swiss carved wood chair, mid-nineteenth century. The design and construction of this chair is very close to that of the Pennsylvania back stool. This chair is also a sister to the German *Stabellen* chair, a form of the Italian *sgabello*, which also has a flat seat into which four slender legs are set. Musée des Arts et Traditions Populaires. Photograph: RMN

v A carved bear chair from Brienz, Switzerland. Bear chairs and seats, which first appeared around 1860, are still made to this day. The fact that the black bear is the emblem of Bern canton explains why chairs incorporating bears were made in that part of the world, often similar in shape to the *Stabellen*. Jobain, Switzerland

bear chairs

Bear chairs are typically Swiss—the emblem of the Bern canton is a brown bear—and are not found in adjoining areas such as the Black Forest or Bavaria. Benches, armchairs, and hall chairs of this type were made, as well. Some examples contained a music box beneath the seat, so that when an unsuspecting sitter lowered himself into the seat, music started to play! Although not as well known as the cuckoo clock, this chair is sometimes exported. Bear chairs are manufactured today in Brienz by the Jobain Company, which was founded in 1835. The same company also made elephant chairs in a form similar to the bear chairs, which they exported to India from 1900 to 1930.

pennsylvania dutch chairs

Most German settlers came to America from the Rhenish Palatinate, which included much of the Rhine Valley and adjacent lands from Switzerland to Holland. Called "Pennsylvania Dutch" in America, these people imported their distinctive furniture designs along with their other traditions.

Although most of these immigrants were farmers, there were skilled craftsmen among them, and it is often difficult to distinguish between Dutch and German Colonial chairs made in America and those imported from Holland and Germany during the seventeenth and eighteenth centuries. Constructed with back tenons penetrating the seat, secured with keys underneath, and featuring a pierced heart as a decoration on the back, they look remarkably like *Stabellen*, and like them, were used in the parlor, as people in German-speaking America called the room known as the *Stube* in Europe.

Massive wainscot armchairs, usually made of walnut and reserved for the head of the household, originated in Pennsylvania late in the seventeenth century, following a European tradition going back to the Middle Ages. Later a variety of ladder-back and Windsor chairs made their appearance. There were also arrow-back chairs, so called because their backs were made of shaved, arrow-shaped spindles, and judge chairs. Early examples were made with elaborated turning, carving, and scrollwork, and were sometimes called fiddle-back chairs. The seats, woven of rush or splint, varied from their New England counterparts by the type of turning employed. Chairs were often painted and decorated on a background of green, yellow, or brown paint, and stenciled designs of fruit, flowers, and birds were frequently applied.

Elongated benches abounded throughout Pennsylvania Dutch country during the eighteenth and nineteenth centuries to furnish the churches and meeting-houses that played such an important part in everyday life. Like the chairs, these benches were usually well designed, often decoratively turned, and attractively painted. Among them were formal wainscot settees, produced during the eighteenth century, mostly for churches. Other benches were designed strictly for utility, some with hinged, lidded seats for storage; others had tall, narrow sides to protect the sitter from drafts.

Rockers were also abundant. Designs ranged from massive, copiously carved, and painted examples to less ponderous, slat-back types. Some were simply shaped of solid planks; some featured arrow-back slats and gracefully shaped arms; still others were of bentwood construction. The slab seats were fully contoured and matched to the angle of the back for maximum comfort. In one variation, the rockers were attached parallel to the front and back legs so that the chair rocked sideways. Pennsylvania Dutch chairs tend to be plain, country seats designed to meet the needs of rural people, but their painted motifs and skilled turning gave them distinction.

rocking chairs

Rocking chairs are mounted on pieces of wood with curved undersides so that the sitter may rock backwards and forwards, or, in some instances, sideways. They originated as leisure chairs, which could be found in fashionable spas. In the nineteenth century Europeans of means traveled to spas often, and an active social life developed around them. The chairs were often made of wicker painted white, for cleanliness. The Russian playwright Anton Chekhov often has his characters drinking tea and sitting on rocking chairs made by serfs of indigenous woods, modeled after European examples brought back from their masters' travels.

In Germany, Michael Thonet (1736–1871) designed a particularly elegant rocker of bent wood in 1869. In the early twentieth century, some versions of this chair were made of steel

<
A rocking chair of tin, cane, mica, and wood, c. 1875. This rocking chair was made by the tinsmith T. D. Brown for the celebration of the tenth wedding anniversary of Mr. and Mrs. A. Parker in 1875, as the inscription in the star in the back says. Genesee County Museum. Photograph: J. Via

tubing. The rocking chair became popular in the nineteenth century in America, occurring in many variations, including the Boston rocker and the Salem rocker, both derived from the Windsor chair. The Boston rocker was characterized by a rolled seat, curled (or no) arms, with a spindle back and a wide top slat stenciled with flowers, landscapes, baskets of fruit, or other designs.

Some Europeans were disdainful of rocking chairs. For example, the publication *The Ornamented Chair*, which featured articles by various authors, included one in 1838 by Harriet Martineau, "Retrospect of Western Travel," which reported:

[I]*n these small inns* [*between Stockbridge, Massachusetts and Albany, New York*], *the disagreeable practice of rocking in the chair is seen in its excess. In the inn parlors are three or four rocking chairs in which sit ladies who are vibrating in different directions and at various velocities so as to try to head off a stranger. . . . How this lazy and ungraceful indulgence became general, I cannot imagine; but the nation seems so wedded to it, that I see little chance of its being forsaken.*

By the end of the nineteenth century some clever companies, for example, Angus & Co., were doing a brisk business importing American rockers into England. One model was the ladder-backed rocking chair with turned legs and stretchers and finial back-posts. Sold under the delicious trade name of "Sinclair's American Common Sense Chairs," these were rocking and armchairs with either caned or flat-woven ribbon seats and backs. The importers' advertisement read:

Visitors to the U.S. will recall the luxury of these chairs, which are to be found in every American home, and no family can keep house without them. They are made in a variety of styles, so that anyone's taste can be suited.

The American chair designer George Hunzinger created models in which one could recline and rock at the same time. Later, President John F. Kennedy was recorded in numerous photographs rocking on the porch of his family's compound at Hyannisport. When Sotheby's sold this rocking chair in a celebrated auction, it fetched an astonishing several hundred thousand dollars.

windsor chairs

The American Windsor chair is one of the most exciting native expressions in Colonial furniture. The form was English, named for Windsor Castle, where such chairs were used in the garden as early as 1725. Indeed, the English nobility used Windsor chairs outdoors in the gardens and parks of their country estates, and in small boats, as well. The shape was designed to provide shelter from the wind. According to Daniel Defoe, the Windsor chair "is said also to be Queen Elizabeth's own invention, who, though she delighted in being Abroad in the Air, yet hated to be ruffled with the wind." We shall discuss the origin of the Windsor chair more fully later.

By the late 1750s the English Windsor chair had become popular in inns, taverns, libraries, and meeting facilities. Late-eighteenth-century documents described the chair's use in daily life. Tobias Smollett, while imprisoned in 1759, described Windsor chairs in public houses in his *Adventures of Sir Launcelot Greaves* thus:

[O]*n the Great Northern Road from York to London . . . four travelers were . . . driven for shelter into a little public-house on the side of the highway. . . .* [T]*he kitchen, in which they assembled, was the only room for entertainment in the house, paved with red bricks, remarkably clean, furnished with three or four Windsor chairs.*

In America, Windsor chairs, germinated in Philadelphia during the Queen Anne period, finally came to full bloom in most of the country during and after the Revolution. Thomas Jefferson

An American Windsor armchair, c. 1770–1800, made of poplar, maple, oak, and hickory, and painted brown. The American Windsor chair was primarily an indoor piece, although it was used outdoors on occasion. Early examples were expensive, owing to their intricate turning and handwork. After the American Revolution, the Windsor became the primary seat of the lower classes, although it was still used in upper-class houses, such as that of Thomas Jefferson. Philadelphia Museum of Art

>
An American Windsor armchair, c. 1770–80, made of pine, hickory, and maple, and painted dark green. Philadelphia Museum of Art

kept a number of Windsor chairs in the entrance of Monticello, "all lined up like the regimented troops along the dadoes of the walls," which was the conventional way chairs were arranged in the formal rooms of the great houses of England and France. The Windsor chairs, which Jefferson called "stick chairs," served a dual purpose: they could be used where they were placed, or—as was common with light seats in the great houses of this period—carried where they were needed when there were visitors. Besides their portability, the other appeal of the Windsor chairs was that they were equally suitable for the parlor, the kitchen, or even the garden. It is testament to their versatility to find them in such a refined household as Thomas Jefferson's.

Windsor chairs were made of various woods. The legs were hardwood, usually maple; the contoured seats were of softwoods such as tulip or pine; and springy woods such as hickory were required for the shaped tops and spindles. To hide the differences in the woods, the chairs were painted. In early account books "white chairs" could refer to plain, unfinished chairs that would be painted by the purchaser. Green was the most popular color, perhaps dating from the chairs' original outdoor use, followed by red, blue, yellow, and black. Occasionally combinations such as green and yellow were seen.

A 1763 advertisement for Philadelphia Windsors referred to them as "high back'd, low back'd, and sack backed." These are the three major types of early Windsor, although countless period terms testify to the many combinations available to the inventive Windsor chair-maker. There were back-writing armchairs, bow-back settees, round tops, brace-backs, bamboo, and, of course children's Windsors.

Philadelphia seems to have been the center where Windsor chair-making started in this country. Francis Tumble supplied 114 sack-back Windsor chairs for the State House there between 1776 and 1778 for the use of members of Congress. The export of the chairs from the Quaker city and the movement of craftsmen soon carried the Windsor chair craft throughout the colonies. Connecticut, Rhode Island, and Massachusetts in particular were quick to adapt their own local taste to the making of Windsor chairs. New York City developed the bow chair, the only eighteenth-century Windsor design originating outside Philadelphia. Specialized forms available before the Revolution became more prominent after the war, especially settees and children's seats. The rocking Windsor chair was introduced around 1790. By then Windsor chairs had become truly ubiquitous. For enhanced comfort, they could also be upholstered in colored leathers or fabric. Martha Washington had reddish-brown and yellow needlework cushions for her bow-back Windsor side chairs in the Little Parlor at Mount Vernon.

shaker chairs

One hundred and fifty-four years after the Pilgrims arrived at Plymouth, another religious faction, the "Shakers," also immigrated to America. They were persecuted in England because of their unorthodox beliefs and their eccentric religious practices, which included dancing, during which they shook their bodies to express their jubilation in God, and their celibate, communal life. Led from England by their prophetess, Mother Ann Lee, nine Shakers arrived in New York on August 6, 1774. Soon after, they established their first American commune at Niskeyuna, near Albany. They rapidly converted others to their faith and expanded east to Massachusetts and Connecticut. The key to their success was their dedication to hard work. Living in isolated rural communities, they initially depended on agriculture for support, but soon their chair-making became a successful business. One of the sect's earliest industries, Shaker chair-making represented a distinct departure from conventional designs and methods.

<
A Shaker settee. Shaker seats are above all functional. The chairs and settees were strong, light, and designed to support the human body in a comfortable position. Their chrome yellow, red, or natural finishes gave them a charm that was heightened by the addition of woven seats of many colors. Shaker chairs were made in numerous types and sizes, from the small children's chair to the classic tall ladder-back chair, the best-known and most widely sold piece of Shaker furniture. Philadelphia Museum of Art

Shaker chairs were made with bent back-slats and delicately turned legs with round or pointed finials. Ordinarily the armchair was a rocker with four slats; the side chair (with or without rockers), only three. The frame was usually entirely of maple, grained wood sometimes being employed; later other woods such as birch, cherry, and butternut were used, with cherry sometimes used for the slats.

The Shakers also made dining chairs of similar construction with low backs. These only had one or two curved slats and short back-poles, so they could be tucked under the table after mealtime. Near the middle of the nineteenth century the Shakers invented their tilting-chair device, which was inserted under the ends of the back legs to prevent their slipping or marring the floor when the chair was tilted back against a wall. Shaker slat-back chairs were an aesthetic improvement over other early country chairs, and they were made to fit every need from the shop to the home. They could even be hung on peg racks when the floor was being cleaned.

The Shakers were among the first in America to equip chairs with rockers, designed principally for the comfort of invalids and the aged. At first

>
A Shaker rocking armchair from Mount Lebanon, New York, c. 1775–1825, made of walnut. Early American rockers were made of softwood for the seats and of hardwoods such as hickory, ash, oak, or maple for the legs, arms, and spindles. The Shakers of New Lebanon, New York, even stretched their ingenuity to invent an example that both rocks and swivels! During the nineteenth century, rocking chairs became almost synonymous with American life. From the 1850s on, many were factory-made, often entirely of maple. Philadelphia Museum of Art

Shaker rocking chairs were slim and severe in appearance, but after some modifications in size and structure after 1830, they were regarded as exceptionally comfortable seats. They were gracefully cut in profile in the same manner as the arms or legs of candle stands. Their comfort was no accident: every component was carefully measured to fit the human body. Taking a very modern approach to chair design in their search for functional perfection, Shaker craftsmen experimented with their chairs' proportions until they hit on the right dimensions. Rockers were designed with or without arms; the most popular model had scroll arms with "mushroom post" turnings to top off the protrusions of the front-leg tenons.

Shaker chairs were made in graduated sizes, from seats for tiny children to full-sized adult chairs. Recognizing the superiority of Shaker chairs, people at the time were eager to buy them and the chairs were a commercial success. The Shakers claimed to be pioneers in the chair business. One statement places the first date of manufacture at New Lebanon in the year 1776, but the fact is not documented. Documents dating to 1805 and 1806 show that common chairs were sold for six shillings each; "rockin" chairs were priced at sixteen shillings, and "wagain" chairs (sideways rockers) from twelve to fifteen shillings, moderate prices that contributed to the chairs' popularity.

hitchcock chairs

The Hitchcock chair evolved in the 1820s in America from elements borrowed from both Windsor and fancy chairs. Named after its most ardent popularizer, Lambert Hitchcock, it had turned legs and crest-rail, and was decorated with stenciled designs. Hitchcock may not have invented the chair, but he marked more of them with his name than any other chair-maker. Hitchcock chairs and settees had their greatest popularity in the second quarter of the nineteenth century. Well-made and decorated, they sold for $1.50 each in 1829, less than half the cost of a fancy chair. With varying shapes and designs, and with seats of rush, cane, and plank, these inexpensive, stylish chairs had a wide appeal.

Stencils made of paper were used to decorate the chairs; usually several stencils were used to achieve a single design, each adding to the fineness of details. Fruits, flowers, and leaves appear in endless variety and quality on the backs of Hitchcock chairs, with an occasional lyre, building, or cornucopia.

The turtle-back was very popular; the handsome pierced eagle-back was less common. Even though he was a poor businessman, Lambert Hitchcock was an excellent salesman. One of his best sales devices was the use of the word "'warranted." This early form of guarantee must

<
A very rare eighteenth-century child's highchair. Most regional country chairs existed in children's versions. Even high-style Louis XV and Louis XVI chairs can be found in small sizes. Collection Le Trianon Antique

have impressed the vast number of middle-class owners whom Hitchcock reached so effectively. He even set up his own store in Hartford, Connecticut, in addition to selling wholesale to dealers. In 1834 he advertised a new chair store:

Chairs from the factory of Hitchcock & Alford [Hitchcocksville] comprising a general assortment of Cane, Flag and Wood seats, of the best materials and workmanship, and warranty. Will furnish at short notice, Chair boxed in good shipping order. Has also on hand an elegant assortment of mahogany and curl maple chairs, made after the latest fashions, and a superior article. He will keep low price Chairs from other Manufactories, which he will sell as low as they can be purchased in this market. Also, Curl Maple and Plane Cane Seats. Hitchcock & Co continue to keep at their Establishment in Hitchcocksville a general assortment of Chairs and Cabinet furniture.

Lambert Hitchcock
Hartford, August 25, 1834

The second half of the nineteenth century saw a major change as chairs started to be machine-made throughout the world and the quality declined. By the middle of the century Hitchcock chairs were at least partially machine-made, and sadly, their uniqueness also declined.

school chairs

Egyptians learning to write stretched out on the floor or sat on low stone stools; Roman students sat on benches, and Hebrew students sat up at a table. Schools in the early Middle Ages provided seats and tables for their pupils. In English schools in the early eighteenth century, there were long benches called "forms." Later, desks became the most common type of school furniture.

children's chairs

Antique children's chairs are rare; their use in the home was certainly functional rather than decorative. Surviving examples show that they were made to the same patterns as larger chairs, and doubtless by the same workmen.

Wicker chairs were first made for children, owing to their extraordinary comfort. In seventeenth-century Holland, a woman might

> A convertible rocking chair-cradle, made by Samuel S. May of Boston and patented in 1850, of pine, maple, and ash. The crest rail of the rocking chair can be removed and the seat expanded to form the cradle. Genesee County Museum. Photograph: J. Via

nurse a baby in front of the fire while sitting in a chair called a *bakermat*, which looked like a long wicker basket, often with one side lower than the other to allow for feeding the baby comfortably. There was a smaller version designed for a baby alone, which can be seen in many seventeenth-century Dutch paintings. The people of the Netherlands seem to have attached great importance to children, judging by their paintings and furniture. The highchair was also popular there as early as the sixteenth century. Some examples, on wheels with a pot in the seat and a shelf in the front, called *kakstolle*, can still be seen in doll houses at the Rijksmuseum in Amsterdam. They were often profusely painted with folk motifs and bright colors, and are represented in numerous paintings as well.

Tudor inventories also list chairs made for children. Among the furniture belonging to Robert Sidney, Earl of Leicester, in the Wardrobe at Leicester House in 1588 was "'a little chair for a childe, of carnation and greene clothe and tinsell." The earliest extant English example dates from the first half of the seventeenth century. Children's chairs were—and are—made in two forms, one low, so that a small child can sit in it easily, and the other on high supports to enable an adult to feed and attend to the child without stooping. Highchairs follow the style of their time, for example, the Victoria and Albert Museum in London displays a late-seventeenth-century English highchair in the William and Mary style.

In the twentieth century, with the advent of mechanization, numerous furniture catalogues offered walkers, youth chairs, highchairs, and children's rockers. After World War II, Charles and Ray Eames designed and produced stackable children's chairs made of color-stained birch plywood, one of the first mass-produced peacetime applications of their new technology. However, despite critical acclaim, the children's

<
A child's rocking potty chair, 1760–1800, of plank construction in black walnut, with pegged and nailed joints. The pot is suspended from the seat by its wide rim. Philadelphia Museum of Art

country, garden & colonial chairs

>
A collection of Guatemalan children's chairs. Robert Wilson Collection. Photograph: Antoine Bootz

chairs were a financial disaster. Some companies nowadays specialize in children's furniture, with sofas, upholstered armchairs, lounge chairs, and chaise longues, all miniature versions of grown-up models. They are quite expensive, which makes this a small business.

Children's chairs throughout the centuries have mirrored adult models in style and technique. For example, eighteenth-century children's *bergères* were small replicas of full-size versions, as were Shaker children's chairs of the following century. Only a few survive today. More recently, some designers have broken with tradition by refusing to create a scaled-down version of an adult's chair. In the early 1970s Luigi Colani, who was facetiously referred to as the "Leonardo of plastics," designed the "Zocker chair," which consists of an integrated seat and desk, for children. It offers several sitting positions, including straddling, and thus allows the child to move freely while playing. Moreover, the plastic is easy to clean, and is shock- and scratch-resistant. More recently, in 1996 Beausejour Racine Roberty designed a series of whimsical stools in animal shapes just for children, in order to stimulate the imagination.

twig and branch chairs

Twig chairs were first used in China, where they were embraced by scholars in a tradition going back for centuries. It may be that the interest in *chinoiserie* in eighteenth-century England contributed to the development of rustic taste in Europe. In 1765, Robert Manwaring produced *The Cabinet and Chair Maker's Real Friend and Companion*, of which a quarter of the plates represent "Rural chairs for Summer houses or Rural garden seats." The details given are instructive to understand the chairs' construction:

[T]*he chairs may be made with the limbs of Yew or Apple trees, as Nature produces them, but the stuff should be very dry and well seasoned; after the bark is peeled clean off, shute for your pitches the nearest pieces you can match for the shape of the back, fore feet and elbows; if you choose to have strait rails, you may extend the small boughs over them, fastening them with screws where it is necessary, the bottoms let down with a rabbett; some of them are usually painted in various colours.*

One major impetus for rustic design was the rise of the great landscape gardens with their picturesque gazebos and follies, for which chairs had to be made in naturalistic forms. Another source of inspiration was the philosophy of Jean Jacques Rousseau, with its concept of man as a "natural savage," and its great love of nature. In *Emile* Rousseau wrote: "Men are not made to be crowded together in anthills, but scattered over the earth to till it. . . . Send your children out to renew themselves; send them to regain in the open field the strength lost in the foul air of our crowded cities."

A love of nature was shared by the German poet Goethe and by other Romantic writers and artists throughout Europe, so it was not surprising that a taste for "natural" furniture should arise. In the Victorian era, the taste for rustic effects was so enthusiastic that the appearance of wood was imitated in other materials, such as ceramic or cast iron.

Inevitably, the question of taste arose. In 1853 Charles Rennie Mackintosh addressed the question of garden furniture in his *Book of the Garden*, stating that "Rustic seats should be confined to rustic scenery, and the seat for a lawn . . . ought to be of comparatively simple and architectural form." However, rustic chairs of all sorts kept creeping in. Although Mackintosh complained about breaches of good taste, he obviously was not taken too seriously.

Little is known about his rustic work. As Mackintosh said, the craft required a knack that

<
A gigantic German armchair carved from a single elm tree trunk, dating to the end of the sixteenth century. Collection Charles Ratton and Guy Ladrière, Paris

country, garden & colonial chairs 105

>

A design for a twig chair, published as plate 66 in *A New Book of Chinese Design* (1754) by Edwards and Darly. This English pattern book includes a number of designs for rustic furniture. The Metropolitan Museum of Art

>>

A colored drawing of a twig armchair by Emilio Terry, c. 1938. Twig chairs were either made directly from the roots and branches of trees, usually with the bark intact, or they were made of beech and then carved and painted to resemble natural trunks and branches. Another form that took the process of turning a tree into furniture even more literally was a chair made by actually hollowing out a tree trunk.

>

The trade card of John Stubbs (1790–1803), depicting examples of rustic and garden furniture. A hoop-back Windsor chair appears in the top left-hand corner, a ladder-back rush-seated chair on the extreme right. British Museum

had nothing to do with education or training.

It is next to useless to employ a carpenter; they work too much by square and rule, and from habit give their work too much the appearance of art. All rustic work is best done by an intelligent laborer who has a natural talent for these things.

He also suggested that the chairs be made during wintertime, because then workmen

can put together the material picked up from time to time during their usual occupations in the woods and forest . . . curious excrescences found on the old trees, and the natural bent branches.

This manner of manufacture is probably the reason we have so little written information on how twig chairs were made.

In America, the nineteenth-century desire for an escape to the country and the fascination with camps and ranches encouraged the making of large numbers of rustic chairs. When these began to appear about 1840, their style was derived from English types and practices developed during the last half of the eighteenth century. An occasional rustic chair might become a symbolic relic. One such was the Charter Oak Chair constructed in 1857. These were made by skilled and unskilled artisans alike. The Gypsies also created twig chairs of willow, with straight arms and legs of peeled branches and loop backs. These are often called pole chairs.

Twentieth-century America saw the creation of factory-made rustic chairs, inspired by the early hickory pieces made by craftsmen in the Southern states. Among the first and the largest manufacturer was the Old Hickory Chair Company of Martinsville, Indiana. The company's chairs were crafted from hickory saplings, which were easy

<
An unusual Alexandre Noll armchair carved from a single piece of wood. One can just imagine the size of the tree! Collection Delorenzo, New York

<
A set of nineteenth-century furniture, comprising a bench, two chairs, and a table, carved to look as if they were made from roots. These were probably made to be shown in one of the "curiosity cabinets" popular at the time in Russia and elsewhere in Northern Europe. Perpitch Collection, Paris

country, garden & colonial chairs

> A Thomas Molesworth burled fir and Chimayo wool settee. Molesworth's style, which crossed a Western look with the Adirondack style, was imbued with a feeling of Western romance. Like Frank Lloyd Wright and Gustav Stickley, Molesworth saw chairs as a means to create a unified architectural mood. They are the equivalent, in furniture, of a tall tale. Photograph: Christie's

> A Thomas Molesworth room. Photograph: Christie's

to bend, with the bark still in place. They were then chemically treated to kill insects and either left with a natural finish or given a coat of varnish. In a 1904 catalogue, such a chair, called the Andrew Jackson, was offered for $2.75. Twig chairs also became popular at the beginning of the twentieth century with the newly rich, who built massive camps in the Adirondacks, the Rocky Mountains, and the Pacific Northwest to enjoy nature in privacy.

Thomas Molesworth, an American furniture-maker from the 1930s to the 1950s, was the "Buffalo Bill" of cowboy chairs. Born in 1890, Molesworth was one of the most innovative furniture designers and decorators of the twentieth century. He spent more than thirty years developing a rustic Western look for dude ranches, private clubs, guest lodges, and private homes, as well. He designed a Wyoming ranch for the publisher Moses Annenberg, a den for President Eisenhower in Gettysburg, and chairs for Tom Yawkee, the owner of the Boston Red Sox, and for assorted Rockefellers. Gumps and Abercrombie and Fitch marketed his products. His trademarks are honey-colored wood, fir and pine burls, vibrantly colored leather upholstery, Chimayo Indian weaving, and brass tacks.

horn, antler, and animal chairs

The Greeks and Romans considered the stag sacred to the hunting goddess Artemis (Diana), and deer are represented as drawing her chariot. In his *Metamorphoses* Ovid presented the deer as afflicted with melancholy, the incurable disease of the lover. The ancient Gauls wore metal helmets adorned with antlers to endow them with power in battle; and to many peoples, from Europeans and Middle Easterners of the Middle Ages to Natives Americans, the deer was a symbol of fertility and longevity. Even today many Chinese still consider the stag horn an aphrodisiac.

In the fifteenth century in Germany, stag horns were made into chandeliers, called *Kronleuchter*,

<<
A buffalo horn chair. In late nineteenth-century America bison horns were used to make chairs and sofas. Wenzel Friedrich, an Austrian immigrant, started a successful manufactory in Texas, creating rocking chairs, extra-large armchairs, easy chairs, and large sofas, which won him numerous gold medals at shows such as the Southern Exposition in Louisville, Kentucky, in 1886. These seats seems to have been particularly popular in saloons and bordellos in the Wild West, the South, and Texas. *House Beautiful*. Photograph: Alexandre Bailhache

<
A nineteenth-century Russian elk antler chair. Furniture made of antlers or even stuffed bears were often seen in Russian country houses, as many writers report. Collection Luther, New York

however, the use of horns as chair parts is more recent. Sheraton's *Cabinet Dictionary* of 1803 showed an adjustable hunting chair, the legs of which were fashioned from single antlers. It was described as "a temporary resting place for one that is fatigued, as hunters generally are." Around 1820 in Austria, the cabinetmaking shop of the Biedermeier designer Josef Danhauser was making a wide variety of horn and antler chairs, sofas, and armchairs. During the middle of the nineteenth century, H. F. C. Rampendahl of Hamburg specialized in seats made with antlers. Hamburg seems to have been the main center for such seats at that time. Queen Victoria's consort, the German Prince Albert, kept a suite of such furniture—probably by Rampendahl—in the Horn Room at Osborne House on the Isle of Wright. Other examples of horn furniture were made by Yetley and by Silber & Fleming of London.

In "Animal Furniture," an article that appeared in the *Strand Magazine* in 1896, William G. Fitzgerald described and illustrated several uses

>
A deer leg chair, by Robert Wilson. Set designer Wilson has devised unusual chairs to create a maximum impact in some of his productions. Photograph: Antoine Bootz

for real animals in the furnishings favored by travelers and empire-builders. One of these was a porter's chair modeled from a young Ceylon elephant by Rowland Ward "in a perfectly natural position but adapted for the use of a hall porter." Another was a tub-backed armchair covered by a tiger skin with the head and paws "so arranged as to give the impression that the terrible animal is about to spring." The author also mentioned chairs "supported by the four legs of a rhinoceros or zebra, or a favorite horse." He went on to write,

But without doubt the most original "animal" chair I ever beheld was that which belongs to that mighty Nimrod, Mr. J. Gardiner Muir of Hillcrest, Market Harborough. This chair is made from a baby giraffe, which with its mother, was shot by Mr. Gardiner Muir near the Kiboko River in British East Africa. The design is by Rowland Ward, of Piccadilly.

From Théophile Gautier's *Voyage in Russia*, we learn that seats made of stuffed bears were seen often there in country houses. Gautier describes "a sofa contrived from a giant polar bear and little brown bears made into stools."

grotto chairs

Grotto chairs are similar to garden chairs, except that they are never designed to be used outside. In the sixteenth century, grottoes were designed as garden retreats, and adorned with interesting rock formations, fountains, seashells, and often, matching furniture. Late in the century Queen Catherine de Médicis of France commissioned the artist Bernard Palissy to design such a grotto for her. In the eighteenth century the Grotto de Thétis at Versailles was famed all over Europe. In England, Thomas Chippendale was among the first artists recorded to design a grotto chair, which he illustrated in the third edition of his 1762 *Directory*.

In an ironic twist, aristocrats and rich bourgeois of the eighteenth and nineteenth centuries felt the need to escape the realities of their lives into a make-believe world. Part of this impulse was a pretense of simplicity, and part was pure eccentricity, as in the case of the "mad" king Ludwig II of Bavaria. At his Linderhoff castle in 1870, Ludwig built a Venus Grotto filled with a phantasmagoria of his own creation. This room, inspired both by Capri's Blue Grotto and the Venus Grotto where Tannhäuser drank the cup of oblivion, was built of canvas, cast iron, and cement in imitation of a rocky cavern, with chairs made of coral and a gilded, mussel-shell throne.

The rococo period abounded with whimsical creations, and many grotto chairs were designed during the eighteenth century, as Chippendale's drawings show. Few have survived, however. Most grotto chairs today are of nineteenth-century make; their construction is often rudimentary, diametrically opposite to the skill that marks eighteenth-century work. Wooden pegs are usually absent, and often close examination reveals that the components were finished by machine rather than by hand.

Grotto chairs often incorporate scallop shells, sea horses, dolphins, crabs, tritons, sea dragons,

<
A giraffe stool, c. 1895, signed Rowland Ward. In the late Victorian period, not only skins and horns, but entire stuffed animals were used to make some very odd chairs indeed. Rowland Ward, Ltd., which made this stool, specialized in pieces made from African trophies such as giraffes, elephants, and lions. Collection Maroum Saloum, Paris

> An eagle armchair, c. 1840, said to be from a Florentine palace. The origins of this remarkable chair are a mystery. While most zoomorphic furniture, which incorporates griffins, sphinxes, and other animals, was inspired by classical prototypes, this chair stands completely outside that tradition. Wholly formed as an eagle, it seems to be a unique and extraordinary example of early-nineteenth-century Romantic historicism, presumably deriving its inspiration from early medieval art. In the Louvre there is an ancient porphyry vase from the treasury of the cathedral of Saint Denis mounted in the twelfth century with silver eagle's head, wings, and legs of a markedly similar character and form to those on this chair. Carlton Hobbs Collection, London

<<
A nineteenth-century Venetian grotto chair in the shape of a crab. Grotto chairs were specifically conceived to sit in make-believe grottoes or pagodas. All sorts of shellfish were used to convey the fanciful feeling. Collection Ariane Dandois, Paris

<
The same crab-form chair, closed to form a stool. Collection Ariane Dandois, Paris

<<
A nineteenth-century Venetian shell-form grotto chair, painted and parcel-gilt. Christie's

<
A nineteenth-century Venetian grotto chair in the form of a lobster. Christie's

>
A German "Venus" armchair, c. 1800. The mahogany and parcel-gilt Venus armchair, with a back carved as a scallop shell, appears to have no close parallel, although a design in J. A. Dusch's *Gothische Andicke vor Tapetzierer und Shreinner* (Augsburg, c. 1800) does bear some similarities. The sophisticated bolted construction of the chair, which can be dismantled, echoes the techniques of the Roentgen workshops at Neuwield in northern Germany. It is thought that Roentgen adopted this type of construction to facilitate transport on the road trips to St. Petersburg and Paris, to which he exported some of his furniture. The chair's dramatic form and elaborate decoration recalls the style of chairs produced for the Russian court at the time. Both Russians and Germans were partial to these refined and fantastic chairs, which seemed at home not only in grotto rooms, but also in the curiosity cabinets that were all the rage in the late eighteenth century in the two countries. Carlton Hobbs Collection, London

and any other marine animals, real or imaginary. Many seats are painted in a silvery gesso that distinctly relates them to Venice, where a Signor Pauly had begun to manufacture this type of seat around 1880. Another Venetian manufacturer of grotto chairs was Remi, who signed his pieces with a metal tag saying "Remi & Ci." Two popular chair models, the *confidant* and the rocking chair, were invented after 1800. The rocking chair became very popular in America during the nineteenth century.

The S-shaped *confidant*, or *tête-à-tête*, a typically nineteenth-century creation, was manufactured in fairly large quantities. Many people used them in their winter gardens, which were highly fashionable during the Victorian era.

Recently, interest in grotto chairs has revived. They are making their way back, not only outside the house, but inside as well, their originality and whimsy appealing to today's sense of decoration.

campaign chairs

War has always been a great stimulus to invention. Generals, kings, and emperors have needed comfort in the heart of battle in order to function at their fullest. Between 1804 and 1814 Napoleon spent a total of three years and three months on campaign. He lived in his own tent furnished with a beechwood folding chair with a red morocco leather seat and two tabourets for his aides-de-camp, in addition to bedroom furniture. In the same period, the duke of Wellington was also equipped with sophisticated campaign chairs, stools, and a bed.

Folding chairs are also associated with ships. Admiral Nelson used folding mahogany chairs on board the *Victory*, the hinged seats upholstered with split cane. The exact provenance of his furnishings is difficult to unravel, since the makers of eighteenth-century naval furniture are almost as elusive as the pieces themselves. Pieces made around 1800 are relatively rare today, perhaps because of their transient nature and constant use. Chairs of that period usually consisted of sling seats on a wooden or steel adjustable frame. However, earlier examples are still in existence. An iron folding armchair made during the second half of the sixteenth century and known as the chair of Gustav Vasa, king of Sweden (1523–60) demonstrates the existence of campaign chairs in that period, and it brings to mind the folding metal armchair said to have belonged to the ninth-century king Dagobert (see p. 56).

As noted earlier, the early *faudesteuil* was in fact a campaign chair, influenced by the Roman folding stool, which was often made of metal, and the early Chinese folding warlord's stool. Since the power of the rulers of Antiquity and the Middle Ages stemmed from their military success, it seems logical that their chairs should have been modified campaign seats. Russia also had a tradition of folding steel chairs, which were made mainly in

<
A group of convertible pieces, including two folding chairs, a folding rocking chair, and a folding cot-chair. Christie's

the town of Tula, a center of armor-making near Moscow. Gradually, in addition to military and hunting weapons, the masters at Tula began to make furniture and other objects in elaborate wrought ironwork, so that by the 1730s they were making metal folding armchairs, combining polished and blue steel with brass incrustation. A single piece might be decorated with as many as six different metals: steel, copper, brass, bronze, silver, and gold. The complex and difficult process of manufacturing such pieces made them particularly precious, and they were sold for roughly 1,000 times the monthly wage of an ordinary workman of the time. Naturally, only the imperial family or members of the aristocracy could afford such chairs.

In England, when peace was restored after 1815, overseas travel to the colonies resumed and there was an increased demand for furniture that could be packed and folded easily. Several firms competed in manufacturing campaign chairs. Thomas Butler and Morgan & Sanders specialized in traveling Regency pieces, which can be identified by their brass name-plates. Ross & Co. of Dublin was a Victorian maker supplying officers in the Indian army, many of whom came from Ireland, with pieces bearing stamped brass or ivory plaques. William Pocock was also primarily a nineteenth-century maker of traveling chairs. In his biography of Richard Monckton Milnes, later Lord Houghton, James Pope-Hennessy records Milnes's preparation, in his inimitable British manner, for a trip up the Nile in 1842:

"List of luxuries to take up the Nile," Milnes wrote out in his scrabby handwriting at the top of a blank page of a notebook. The luxuries included recipes for making everything that can be made of mutton, pigeons, chicken, eggs, and rice, some extra panes of glass in case those in the cabin broke, a pair of black spectacles, a draught-board, a stuffed pack-saddle, chisels for removing hieroglyphics from temple walls, and a small camp-stool for a boy to carry behind you when you go out walking, there being no stones or places to sit and rest on.

Monckton Milnes, *The Years of Promise,* 1949

Folding military armchairs also appeared in the patent records during the American Civil War. General Grant and his staff were photographed by Mathew Brady sitting on folding metal armchairs at City Point, Virginia, during the summer of 1864. The development of campaign chairs paralleled the rise of patented chairs in Europe and America. In 1861 the inventor Peter J. Hardy patented a reclining armchair hinged so that it could be folded into a "small compass" for transport. Hardy attempted to cover every possibility with his invention. As he wrote, "the chair was designed especially for camp use, though it will be found remarkably comfortable and convenient in any house."

In nineteenth-century America, camp-chairs were made for middle-class people, whereas in

> A convertible table-chair-desk. Initially an oval table with cabriole legs on casters, when the top is folded back and the brass fittings are unlocked, a leather-upholstered chair may be pulled out to face the other half of the piece, now a writing desk. A small brass label on the chair reads: "Hedges/Patent/April 4, 1854." Genesee County Museum. Photograph: J. Via

Europe they were produced chiefly for aristocrats and high-ranking military officers. As a result, European models tend to be more elegant than American ones, the most sophisticated of these being the late-eighteenth-century Russian metal armchairs from the Tula factory.

Fabric covering also was essential in some of the new inventions. For example, in 1861, a Rochester, New York, inventor used "three frames pivoted together on which a canvas is stretched" for his combination camp-bed and chair. Later, the inventor of a combined walking-stick, billiard-cue, and camp-stool used a "cloth web," on which

the person who uses the device sits astride . . . the joint resting on the ground, and balances himself with his feet, making it a very comfortable support at a base-ball, cricket, or shooting match, which will be duly appreciated after an hour standing.

A very similar chair, often with a leather seat, was used by the English gentry for shooting. It was manufactured by the rival English companies Purdey and Holland & Holland. Later in the century, inventors endeavored to make the chair more comfortable by providing a back-rest, for which purpose all sorts of combinations were created. For example, in 1886 Gustav Tietze of San Francisco invented a camp chair that had a back-support hinged to a central leg with a recess to hold two extra front legs. The entire frame could be folded up and fit within the canvas portion of the chair.

Campaign chairs have not lost their appeal in the modern world. The Hardoy chair produced in 1938 and used by the Italian army in North Africa in 1942–43, in which four wooden crosses connected by joints formed a foldable frame over which canvas was stretched for the seat and back-rest, was modeled after a folding English chair patented in 1877. Since the chair could be folded compactly for easy transport, it became popular for travel, and well-known owners such as Thomas Edison and Theodore Roosevelt soon made it famous. From 1905 to the present it has been sold in nearly unaltered form by the American folding and camping furniture producer Gold Metal, Inc. Its popular name is the "butterfly chair," and it is the most copied chair design in recent history. The same model was also produced by Knoll.

<
An unusual three-seated campaign stool, c. 2004. Collection Hermès

The designer Eileen Gray is associated with a campaign chair with a stitched leather seat and leather strap arms. The supporting wood poles can be neatly bundled together and carried. The familiar "director's chair" is yet another modern version of the campaign chair. Such talented designers as Jean Michel Frank created a version in 1933 with a black leather back and armrests.

Country chairs suffered greatly in the advance of technology during the twentieth century. As increasing difficulties in rural living left farmers with little time and money to build furniture, they crafted their benches, stools, and chairs quickly, with little ornamentation. But of course, the charm of country chairs lies precisely in their homemade feeling and individuality. Thus the machine age has robbed country chairs of their most priceless qualities. The only charming ones today are those that have preserved their uniqueness, and which are still made by hand.

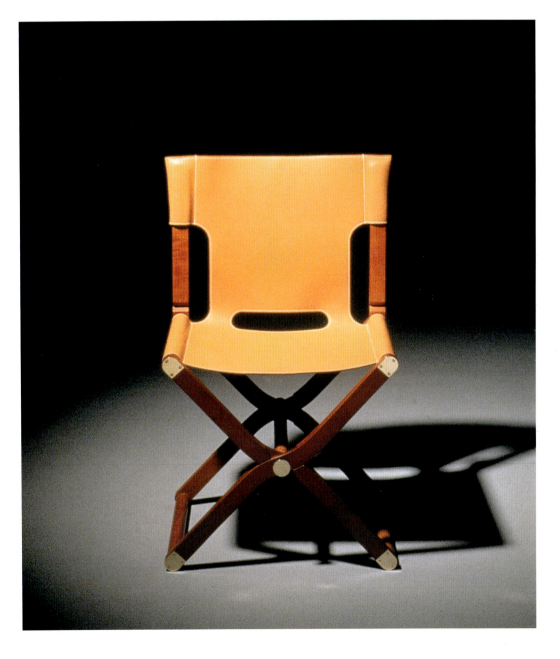

>
A pearwood and leather folding campaign armchair, by Hermès. Recently the French firm of Hermès launched a line with the theme of "Elegance in Movement," with seats designed to combine comfort and utility for travel. The line includes both armchairs and chaise longues. Collection Hermès

GARDEN CHAIRS

Italian Renaissance gardens incorporated classically styled stone benches, but garden chairs were rare in Europe before the sixteenth century, and none have survived from before that time. In the early sixteenth century chairs of any kind were scarce and usually heavy, so it seems unlikely that chairs made specifically for the garden existed then. The formal gardens of Louis XIV at Versailles featured stationary stone benches, and some of the earliest known garden seats are recorded there, as well. A Versailles inventory of 1700 lists *Vingt chaises roulantes de damas rouge cramoise* [twenty roulettes in red damask]. The king took his last meal sitting in his roulette, and almost died in it.

Since all of Europe imitated the fashions of the French court in the seventeenth and eighteenth centuries, it is not surprising that we find similar chairs in England soon after they are recorded at Versailles. Indeed a wheeled garden chair, also called a *roulette*, but in the Windsor style, can be found in a letter dated August 1724 written by Sir John Perceval to his brother-in-law. Describing a tour through Buckinghamshire, he wrote:

The wood consists of tall beech trees and thick underwood, at least 30 foot high. The narrow, winding walks and paths cut in it are innumerable; a woman in full health cannot walk them all, for which reason my wife was carry'd in a Windsor chair like those in Versailles, by which she lost nothing worth seeing.

It must have been a similar garden chair as well that the Englishman William Beckford mentioned in his journal of a trip to Portugal on August 15, 1787:

Mr. Verdeuil, tired of sauntering about the verandas, proposed a ride to a neighbouring village where there was a fair. He and D. Pedro mounted their horses and preceded the Marquis and me in a garden chair drawn by a most resolute mule.

Portugal had very close ties to England owing to their trade, and Portuguese seats of the time followed the English fashion.

Early English Windsor chairs, which were primarily garden seats, were often painted green or left unpainted so that they would weather to a deep, natural color. The English landscape garden, which was fashionable throughout Europe during the second half of the eighteenth century, blended ideas borrowed from Dutch, French, and Italian design. Since these gardens were intended as loosely organized, naturalistic landscapes, their owners desired to move around freely and to change seating locations according to their mood, the time of day, or the season.

In England, garden chairs began to be made of wood and iron to withstand the elements and to be easily movable. Summerhouses and temples, in which people dined out of doors, were often elaborate, solidly built structures that demanded chairs of sophisticated design. Wooden benches, cane chairs, rustic wood chairs, and later, cast-iron armchairs were designed by William Halfpenny, Chippendale, Manwaring, and Georges Jacob,

< An etching by Edwards and Darly, c. 1754, showing a garden chair made of roots. By the second half of the nineteenth century, rustic chairs had begun to appear in public places such as parks, resorts, hotels, and even religious campgrounds. These were crafted from an assortment of woods, including hickory, spruce, elm, ash, birch, laurel, apple, cedar, and willow. Most were made with natural branches. The Metropolitan Museum of Art

country, garden & colonial chairs 119

> A painting by Pierre Denis Martin showing Louis XIV in 1713 being pushed in a *roulette*, or wheeled garden chair, near the Apollo Basin and the Grand Canal at Versailles. The marquis de Dangeau (1638–1729) wrote in his memoirs that the Sun King used such a chair as early as 1689. The chair allowed the king, who loved his magnificent gardens but was plagued by gout later in life, to enjoy the outdoors without pain. Versailles. Photograph: RMN

> A drawing by Jacques Rigaud of a lord and lady being carried in a garden in Windsor chairs. The Metropolitan Museum of Art

> A set of eight English chairs and a table for Kew Gardens, near London, c. 1760. This suite, reportedly made for the use of the dowager princess of Wales, was executed in mahogany in the "rustic" Chinese taste. The style was particularly associated with pavilions during the 1750s and '60s, during a great vogue for Anglo-Chinese gardens. The quality of the work on these pieces is extraordinarily high. Collection Carlton Hobbs, London

among others. Unfortunately, very few examples have survived.

The newspaper *Avant Coureur* of September 7, 1761, describes Parisian gardens with shovel-shaped seats called *pelles à cul* [shovels for the hindquarters]. In the third edition of Thomas Chippendale's *Directory* (1762), a seat and two chairs are illustrated, with the recommendation that they be used in arbors, summerhouses, and grottoes.

In the early nineteenth century, new materials brought into use by the Industrial Revolution allowed garden seats that could stand up to foul weather to be made for the first time. Previously, garden seats had been stone benches fixed to the ground, or wooden seats that could be brought outside when weather permitted. The chairs that emerged with the machine age were of wicker, metal, and later, plastic. One new material for garden chairs was cast iron, which could withstand dramatic extremes of weather. The taste for garden furniture in this new material first developed in Prussia.

> One of the highly original designs for garden benches by Edwards and Darly, from their *New Book on Garden Design*, published in 1754. According to the preface, the book was "calculated to improve the present taste"— a phrase used by Chippendale in the preface to his book, as well. The Metropolitan Museum of Art

>
A folding garden chair made by Georges Jacob for the comte de Provence (later Louis XVIII), c. 1786, for his Pavilion at Versailles. Collection Philippe Vichot, Paris

v
The handwritten tag reads: "For the garden of Monsieur's Pavilion at Versailles." Collection Philippe Vichot, Paris

v
The chair shown folded, then opened. This chair was intended to remain outdoors when folded. The back is covered with heavy canvas, the feet are protected with metal fittings, and the hinges are heavy-duty; the design is nevertheless elegant and refined. Collection Philippe Vichot, Paris

<
A painting by Jean Baptiste Charpentier showing the duc de Penthièvre (1725–93) and his daughter, the future duchess of Orléans, on a bench in a garden. Versailles. Photograph: RMN

<
A watercolor view of the park at the Chateau de Malmaison and Bois Préau, by Auguste Garneray (1785–1824). In the foreground is a country bench. Photograph: RMN. Arnaudet

country, garden & colonial chairs 123

cast-iron chairs

Wrought-iron seats have a long history, from the Roman curule chair, to the medieval *faudesteuil*, to the Napoleonic campaign chair, to the Russian metal chairs from Tula. These seats where always one-of-a-kind, usually folding, often associated with the power of a warlord. Cast iron was a nineteenth-century innovation. A new technology introduced coke-processed iron, which became liquid more easily and was therefore easier to pour into molds. Now chairs, cast in molds of compressed sand, could be made in vast quantities. The fact that so many could be produced at a time changed their use totally. Although cast iron seems to have been developed in England, it is not known for certain whether the first pieces of cast-iron furniture were made there.

The first cast-iron chairs were designed and made in Prussia by the architect Karl Friedrich Schinkel (1781–1841), and then spread throughout Europe and America. Like most Neoclassical artists, Schinkel had traveled in Italy, and had been greatly impressed by the antiquities there. His earliest design for a bench, dated 1825, was an exceedingly simple structure ornamented with French Empire motifs, and was based on bronze and stone stools found at Herculaneum and

\> A cast-iron armchair, after a design by Karl Friedrich Schinkel, c. 1840. Schinkel was the first designer to create seats in cast iron. Staatliche Museen zu Berlin

124 country, garden & colonial chairs

<
An armchair from the Luxembourg Gardens in Paris. Although stone benches were a fixture in formal French gardens, in the eighteenth century a visitor to the gardens of the Palais Royal in Paris could rent a simple chair made of straw for the modest sum of one sol. In the nineteenth century these straw seats were replaced by metal chairs like this one. Robert Wilson Collection. Photograph: Antoine Bootz

<
A nineteenth-century metal garden stool in the antique manner. Collection Philippe Vichot, Paris

A drawing of cast-iron chairs and armchairs. Cast iron, both economical and practical, was the "high-tech" material of its day, and seats in this material are a testament to an era when the goal of uniting art and industry was achieved. Many variations of these seats can still be found in parks and gardens throughout the world. The Metropolitan Museum of Art

Pompeii. Most of Schinkel's seats continued in the same vein, incorporating decorative elements such as cloven hooves, rams' heads, and palmettes. After Napoleon's final defeat in 1815, Berlin, like so many cities in Germany, underwent a great building boom, with Schinkel designing a number of new palaces for the Prussian royal family, as well as benches for the surrounding parks and gardens. Schinkel was careful to coordinate the interior seating—which he had also designed—with the exterior benches.

By 1830, cast-iron garden seats were being produced outside of Germany, including in England and the United States. As the century wore on, foundries became numerous all over Europe and in America, and designs for cast-iron chairs were created at these factories, seemingly without the involvement of artists. Chairs in the Gothic style were particularly favored, and they were produced in Germany, England, the Netherlands, and France. Some Gothic-style settees and chairs also appeared on the American market. In Boston, New York, Baltimore, Dayton, and Utica, New York, at least fifteen foundries produced a similar model in the style.

Another popular model was the rustic settee, which replicated in iron a grouping of oak branches tied together. Although not very comfortable, this model was an extraordinary success, as comfort never seems to have been a priority for garden chairs. One was not supposed to spend a great length of time sitting in them, so their appearance was their most important feature. The design of the "rustic settee" fitted perfectly with the worship of nature so prevalent in the late nineteenth century, which was the inspiration for several models with vines, grapes, and leaves.

straw and wicker chairs

Wicker chairs as we know them became popular at the turn of the twentieth century, for porches, patios, and winter gardens. The production of well-designed wicker chairs began in Vienna and quickly spread to other European countries. Innovative manufacturing techniques allowed the art of making them to become commercially feasible. Changes in lifestyle made wicker furnishings fashionable, and the fact that they were sanitary, weather-resistant, and lightweight increased their appeal.

The term "wicker" encompasses willow, cane, rattan, and reed furniture. Willow, which is highly flexible, has been used to weave chairs since ancient times. According to Pliny the Elder, the Romans twisted together osier wands to make ropes for chair seats and for reclining chairs. Willow came originally from willow shrubs and trees in the wet lowlands of Europe; later it was imported from the West Indies, South Africa, Madagascar, and Indonesia. The blond willow twigs called osiers are the best variety for use in chair-making.

Cane, by contrast, was regarded as a new material for chair-making by Europeans in the late nineteenth and early twentieth centuries. Cane is a by-product of rattan, produced from the bark removed from the rattan plant. Cane was brought to England by the British East India Company from the Malay Peninsula about 1664 specifically for weaving the backs and seats of chairs. It fell into disuse about 1700, and then became fashionable again in the mid-eighteenth century. At the beginning of the twentieth century, many fine English and German chairs were made totally of cane. Rattan, or *Calamus rotang*, is a climbing vine native to the forests of the Malay Archipelago and coastal Southeast Asia, which grows to 600 feet in length. It is strong, water-resistant, can be bent without breaking, and has a natural high-gloss finish, all of which make it ideal for outdoor chairs. It would become the basis of a large and complex American industry founded by Cyrus Wakefield. However, its one drawback is that it does not take stain or paint as well as other types of wicker, such as willow. Reed is also a by-product of rattan. It is cut from the central core of the plant after the bark has been removed. Reed came into use in the 1850s, superseding rattan as the most common material for wicker.

Straw-weaving is an ancient craft; many traditional farm and domestic articles were made of straw, including baskets, chairs, mattresses, cradles, and beds. Peasants as early as the Middle Ages slept on straw, and straw beds are said to have been widely used by all classes of society until the eighteenth century. The 1678 inventory of the possessions of Oxford University lists "One great straw chayre," and many examples remain in England even today. The earliest securely dated one, owned by Edward Jenner (1749–1823), the pioneer of smallpox vaccination, belongs to the Museum of the History of Science at Oxford.

< A nineteenth-century French wicker chair. These were favorite seats for the indoor *jardins d'hiver* (winter gardens) that were fashionable at the time. Collection Madeleine Casteing

> A wicker armchair from a large parlor suite by Heywood Brothers and Company. The Heywood brothers started producing wicker furniture in a shed next to their father's Massachusetts farmhouse in 1826, an enterprise that grew into one of the largest wicker furniture manufacturing companies in the country by mid-century. Seats like this one were designed for indoor garden rooms, which were much in fashion in the late nineteenth century. 1990.41.1.4. Philadelphia Museum

Straw chairs, like winged and hooded chairs, were used to create a warm place for older people and nursing mothers. Similarly, tub chairs with a canopy of willow, or "owsiers," were used in several English and Irish counties by the sick and infirm until the end of the nineteenth century. As mentioned earlier, the *bakermat*, a long basket seat with a low back made of woven willow was in use in seventeenth-century Holland for mothers to nurse their babies before a fire. According to H. Havard's *Dictionnaire de l'ameublement*, straw chairs in France in this period were an Italian import. In the eighteenth century, Madame du Deffand, whose brilliant salon was frequented by Voltaire, called them *la façon de Pise* in one of her letters to Horace Walpole.

In the early nineteenth century, wicker chairs evolved from being either a one-of-a-kind farmer's handcraft piece or an exotic Oriental import to a popular indoor and outdoor seat in both Europe and America. This began when the Austro-Hungarian government sponsored basket-weaving and willow work as a winter occupation in agricultural areas of the Empire, with instructors trained at the Imperial School in Vienna. Soon wicker chairs became fashionable, and the industry, supported by government subsidies, flourished. Over time Austrian wicker chairs became more austere and less comfortable, and so cushioned seats were added for ease of sitting and to give the chairs a less stark appearance.

During the late 1890s, an outburst of creativity centered in the Austrian capital was channeled partly into cooperative ventures among artists, architects, designers, and local craftsmen, with an eye to making inexpensive items for everyday use. Leading members of this movement, called the Vienna Secession, created chairs in willow, cane, and bentwood.

Interestingly, ornate chair designs in wicker first appeared in America, where the Oriental mystique of rattan, cane, and reed, led to the use of an array of Far-Eastern motifs in wicker furniture, including arches, arabesques, diaper patterns, fans, stars, and sunbursts. The Wakefield Rattan Company in Boston is the best-known American manufactory. It merged with its rival, Heywood Brothers, in 1897 to become the largest wicker company in the world. Heywood-Wakefield created endless seats featuring elaborate woven scrollwork, stick-and-ball, double-twisting, and caned backs.

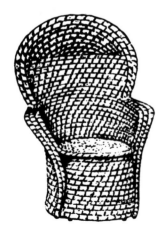

< A drawing of Irish plaited-straw seats. A seat of this type, shaped as a circular pad and stuffed with more straw, was known as a boss. Such seats were used indoors all over Ireland within living memory, especially as fireside seats. National Museum of Ireland

> A design for a star chair, 1938, by Emilio Terry. Born in Cuba, Terry lived in Paris, where he moved in the social circle of Coco Chanel, Jean Cocteau, and Christian Bérard. His designs were highly influential between the two World Wars. Sotheby's

>> A design for an ostrich feather chair, 1938, by Emilio Terry. Unfortunately, very few of Terry's designs were actually made into chairs. Sotheby's

In England, people were content for a long time with their native woven basket chairs, which had been developed during the Middle Ages. In the seventeenth century, John Donne, for example, in his "Elegie I" refers to a typically English basket chair:

Nor when he swolne and pamper'd with great fare,
Sit downe, and snorts, cag'd in his basket chaire

Around the turn of the twentieth century, the English manufacturers Albert and Charles Crampton of Dryad Works struck a middle ground between the ornate Victorian wicker of America and the austere Austrian product. Dryad's chairs were made of willow and featured a sturdy, nail-and-tack-free construction. Their strength and comfort made them the seat of choice in cruise ships, trains, cars, and airplanes at the beginning of the twentieth century. One of wicker's greatest moments was its presence in the airplane seat that carried Charles Lindbergh across the Atlantic in 1927 in the *Spirit of St Louis*.

Such wicker armchairs and stools were designed with great success by Richard Riemerschmid for the breakfast room of the Kaiser Suite on the ocean liner *Kronprinzessin Cecilie* in 1904. In reports of the finished scheme, Riemerschmid's breakfast room was singled out for special mention: "There is a very personal romance in the mood of this small room, which none of the other designers of the first-class cabin has been able to match."

After World War I, the cost of raw materials and labor increased tremendously, which led to the development and creation of the Lloyd's loom chair in 1917. Marshall B. Lloyd, the owner of the Lloyd Manufacturing Company in Michigan, devised a labor-saving loom that mass-produced tightly woven man-made fiber in large sheets. The savings in labor and material helped keep wicker chairs affordable for a large number of customers. However, by the 1930s, most wicker chairs were machine made with man-made fiber, a development that brought an end to elaborate wicker chairs. The nineteenth-century machine

Adirondack wooden reclining armchairs, the American public's favorite sturdy armchair since the First World War. Robert Wilson Collection. Photograph: Antoine Bootz

era had created a well-designed wicker chair and had made it commercially viable. The chairs were omnipresent, not only in gardens, on porches, and in living rooms and bedrooms, but also on trains, airplanes, and boats. Paradoxically, their extreme popularity killed them. In the mid-twentieth century, to meet growing demand and keep the chairs affordable, manufacturers lowered the standards of quality, changed the raw materials, and used less interesting designs. As a result, interest in wicker chairs diminished, and the elaborate, comfortable wicker chairs of the previous century became a thing of the past.

adirondack and westport chairs

The demand for sturdy outdoor furnishings in America was strong before and after World War I as a growing middle class became enamored of fresh air. The size of the country and the relatively inexpensive cost of land allowed the development of summer camps of all sorts, where affordable chairs were needed for porches and lawns. The Adirondack chair, with its angular design and slatted seat and back, became a favorite.

Slat construction enabled local craftsmen to make an inexpensive lawn chair by nailing together pieces of scrap wood, and such chairs are still made today. They can even be bought from popular catalogues such as those of L. L. Bean, and they are considered an icon of the suburban and country home. Their provenance, however, remains a mystery, and there is no proof that they originated in the Adirondacks. The Westport chair, which features a similar design, is constructed of boards rather than slats, is heavier, and is of ampler proportions. Almost certainly, it is an older type than the Adirondack chair. Its original fabrication seems to have been in the small village of Westport, New York, on Lake Champlain, where it was manufactured from 1904 to about 1930. These chairs, unfortunately, were more expensive and harder to produce than the Adirondack and for this reason were less popular.

hickory chairs

Another sturdy American seat is the hickory chair, which met a demand for chairs in summer places throughout the country. Simple and functional, these chairs were constructed from hickory poles, which were boiled and bent into shape on patented metal frames. When dried, these pieces were fitted together into a remarkable variety of seats, armchairs, side chairs, rockers, settees, and swings. Sometimes the rougher outer bark was left on the poles, and sometimes it was removed to expose the inner bark. Seats were woven from the inner bark, a task mostly performed by women and children.

Several companies manufactured such chairs, the most popular being the Old Hickory Chair Company, which operated in Martinsville, Indiana, from 1898 to 1920. All the company's products were tagged to differentiate them from the imitations. Old Hickory's largest competitor was the Rustic Hickory Furniture Company in La Porte, Indiana. Another was Indiana Hickory Furniture. The popularity of the hickory chair was due both to its sturdiness and to its earnest character. In a time deeply influenced by the Arts and Crafts Movement, this quality was strongly appealing and in keeping with the fashion of the time.

bentwood chairs

Many varieties of bentwood chairs were made in America. Examples produced by the Old Hickory Chair Company were considered fancy. The company produced three models: a chair, a rocker, and a settee, all made of second-growth hickory, which limited the number of orders that the company could accept in a given season. Another bentwood chair often found in Amish homes was the "heka schtool," *heka* meaning "underbrush," and *schtool* a dialect word for the German *stuhl*, or chair. The Amish chair is quite comfortable and according to some written accounts, anyone with a supply of smooth hickory saplings could easily make one.

Another type, which comes from Florida, is called the "Florida cypress chair." Made of cypress, cedar, and sometimes slippery elm, all of these chairs have a similar look. Traditionally used outside, they are said to have originated with Native Americans, who were talented weavers. They are sought-after today for porches, lawns, and gardens.

chairs in various new media

Technological progress in the twentieth century helped create some new materials, shapes, and forms of seats for the garden. However, not all the new ventures were successful. In the 1930s, Jacques André, a French architect and his partner, Jean Prouvé, produced a prototype for a garden chair made of perforated sheet metal and acrylic glass. Unfortunately, the metal resisted weatherproofing, and the acrylic glass was heavy, so no manufacturer wanted to produce the chairs. Later, Willy Guhl, a pioneer of industrial design in Switzerland, designed a weatherproof beach chair of fibrated concrete. The design was minimalist,

> A carved stone garden chair in Provence, surrounded by lavender. Photograph: Oberto Gilli

country, garden & colonial chairs   133

\>
A folding reclining chair by Pierre Emile Legrain (1889–1929). In 1923 Legrain established a workshop producing chairs inspired by Cubism and African art. Legrain loved lacquer surfaces, as this chair shows. Collection Delorenzo, New York

<
Metal "twig" chairs. These whimsical chairs without seats were designed by Robert Wilson, who has a special love for chairs. Metals of every sort have been used endlessly by modern designers. Robert Wilson Collection. Photograph: Antoine Bootz

\>
A nineteenth-century iron reclining chair, made to be used outside. Robert Wilson Collection. Photograph: Antoine Bootz

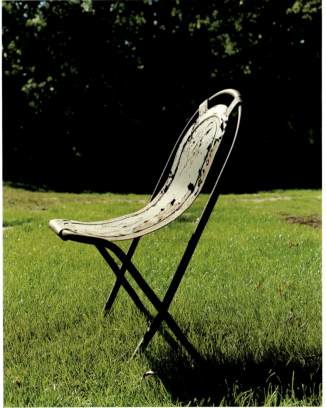

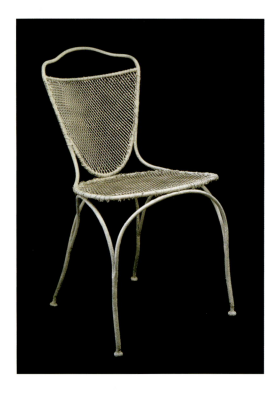

resembling an abstract sculpture, and thus suited its period perfectly. When the leisure culture of the postwar era gave rise to a need for inexpensive, practical outdoor seating, the design became popular. However, by the end of the seventies the discovery that fibrated concrete contained asbestos, a carcinogen, brought an end to this design.

Another new model was the indoor-outdoor reclining armchair, designed by Charles and Ray Eames in 1958. This chair resulted from a complaint by the architects Alexander Girard and Eero Saarinen that there were no good-looking terrace or garden chairs, which they needed for a job they had just completed. In response, Charles Eames designed a chair made of fabric stretched across an aluminum frame. He chose a double T-beam configuration for its stability and the synthetic fiber Saran for the fabric. Unfortunately, the fabric soon rotted when it was left outside, so the first

A white-painted metal garden chair by Alberto and Diego Giacometti, from a rare set made for Jean Michel Frank, c. 1935. Collection Galerie Jacques de Vos, Paris

A white-painted metal garden bench, from the same set as the chair shown above, by Alberto and Diego Giacometti. Collection Galerie Jacques de Vos, Paris

country, garden & colonial chairs   135

\> A very unusual garden bench prototype by Jean Prouvé (1901–1984). In 1923, Prouvé opened his own workshop and a year later was designing and producing modern steel chairs. This prototype, shown without its wooden slats, dates to c. 1924. Galerie de Beyrie, New York

v The same bench with its wooden slats in place on the metal frame. Galerie de Beyrie, New York

mass-produced aluminum chairs are now used only indoors.

Despite a few failures, the new materials of the twentieth century gave birth to some very successful chairs. One example is the Blow Chair, first made in the 1930s of plastic or polyvinyl chloride (PVC). The first inflatable chair successfully mass-produced in Italy, it became an icon of 1960s popular culture. It could be used inside or out, and even in swimming pools—another modern invention.

Many contemporary designers wanted to create an all-plastic outdoor chair, and they developed a number of models. One, the Bofinger Chair, first made in 1964, was an ideal seat for public places. It was light (less than nine pounds), stable, weatherproof, and easy to care for, and millions of plastic garden chairs have duplicated it in numerous variations. Another, the Louis 20 (poking fun at French "Louis" chairs), integrated a body of polypropylene (a type of plastic) with aluminum rear legs. Designed by Philippe Starck to be used indoors or outdoors, the Louis 20 is inexpensive, easy to move, and can be stacked or easily dismantled into recyclable elements.

The designer Diego Giacometti had most of his furniture cast in bronze, unlike more industrial manufacturers, who used iron. However, for some of his large-scale productions, such as several dozen chairs for the outdoor cafe at the Maeght Foundation in Saint Paul de Vence, Giacometti used wrought-iron for practical and economical reasons. Armand André Rateau used bronze to make his extraordinary chairs inspired by antique examples for the Blumenthal indoor swimming pool in New York. These chairs are light, with backs and seats made of patinated bronze in the shape of fishes and shells. The Landi Chair, the official outdoor seat of the Swiss National Exhibition of 1939, was made of aluminum, which not only represented progress and modernity, but

<
A lounge chair.
Collection Hermès

<
A metal and canvas garden lounge chair.
Collection Gansevoort Gallery, New York

was also considered a "Swiss metal." Aluminum was one of Switzerland's most important exports, and it could only be produced using great quantities of electricity, readily available through the country's many hydroelectric power plants. The Landi Chair, which created something of a sensation when it was exhibited, consisted of a perforated steel seat resting on a wire base. It was light (three kilos—less than seven pounds), weatherproof, and reasonably comfortable. Marketed internationally in the 1950s, it was widely acclaimed for its strength and durability.

Wood was also widely used for garden chairs in the twentieth century, especially for deck chairs, which were highly popular. Contemporary designers who were not trying to be modern simply for the sake of modernity and understood that many of the best chairs had evolved from earlier types created some celebrated deck chairs. Examples are Le Corbusier's 1929 cowboy "chaise lounge"; Kaare Klint's 1933 deck chair; and the 1927 Legrain folding and reclining chaise longue.

Eero Saarinen complained of the lack of good-looking garden chairs designed in the twentieth century. Indeed, severe forms do not often work well in gardens, and perhaps for this reason, virtually no contemporary designer has created a successful garden chair. The most pleasing examples are interpretations of nineteenth-century models. Perhaps modern designers take themselves too seriously and lack the imagination for such a relaxed, whimsical form. Moreover, twentieth-century materials such as plastic and aluminum often look out of place in a garden, where cast iron and wood seem more at home. Since gardens are an environment where the imagination can run wild, whimsical chairs look wonderful in them; and since garden chairs are not required to be comfortable, any design is allowed, providing that it is weatherproof and pleases the eye. Perhaps the make-believe world of our ancestors and their fantasy seats are the perfect antidote for the harsh and boring realities of modern life.

>
A print showing Hernan Cortés seated on a folding stool to accept the surrender of Cuahtemoc. The Metropolitan Museum of Art

COLONIAL CHAIRS OUTSIDE OF THE UNITED STATES

The European colonies in Indonesia, Sri Lanka, India, Mexico, and South America produced a number of chair types. Although these colonial models took their inspiration in shape and design from the chairs of their mother countries, they were executed in the colonies from local woods and other materials and were often carved by native craftsmen.

The history of colonial chairs begins in the sixteenth century, after skilled artisans followed the early settlers, and chairs had come into general use in Europe. Early adventurers had little need for sophisticated chairs, and any decorative chairs that they brought with them were mainly for ceremonial use, following the habit of the medieval lords. Thus, these chairs were either imposing, thronelike seats, or of the folding, *faudesteuil* type.

Native rulers sat on thrones or state seats, which often were decorated with precious stones or inlaid with gold or silver, a lavishness that depended on the natural resources of the country. The Dutch governor Van Rhee presented a throne

and a footstool to King Vimala Dharma Suriya II of Sri Lanka in 1693. This curious piece blended ideas from the Orient and the Occident; its most prominent feature was the two golden lions or sphinxes that formed its arms. The exquisite decorations of the throne—gold sheeting covered with precious stones—were undoubtedly the handiwork of Sinhalese goldsmiths. The footstool, however, was of European design, handsomely decorated in the local manner with a molding of cut crystal, beneath which were flowers studded with amethysts.

Although we tend to think of animals on seats as simply decorative, their presence together with flowers has a symbolic meaning on the thrones found in Indian temples. According to the art historian Jeannine Auboyer, "The animal symbolism . . . makes of the throne a veritable distillation of the tangible universe." Similarly, winged heads and cherubs were also used as decorations on ordinary chairs in Europe during the sixteenth and seventeenth centuries. Also, mirroring the European use, at about the time the Dutch were becoming established in Indonesia, what generally did service for chairs in Sri Lanka was a stool that the Sinhalese still call a *bankuva*—from the Portuguese word for stool. The *bankuva* was a notable feature of the veranda, or *stoep*, of older

<
A Mexican print of c. 1854, showing a birthing chair. The Metropolitan Museum of Art

town houses on the island, and it can be found even today in older houses there.

The Roman Catholic Church was an important cultural influence in the New World, bringing in skilled carpenters to build splendid churches. Church chairs, choir stalls, and benches received considerable attention and set the pattern for domestic chairs. Among the finest choir stalls were those built for the Monastery of San Francisco in Lima, Peru. The present church, founded by Fray Francisco de la Cruz in 1535, was begun in 1546, and consecrated in 1673. The carving is of Renaissance design with seat panels in the Plateresque style, a manner derived from the filigree workmanship of Spanish silver. Plateresque and Mudéjar (Moorish-style) designs, popular on sixteenth-century colonial chairs, were inspired by the decorative motifs of Andalusia, since Seville and Cádiz were the port cities in direct contact with the New World. During the seventeenth century, Renaissance designs continued in use.

The woods most commonly used for ecclesiastical and domestic chairs were mahogany and cedar. In Spanish colonial centers, artisans were organized into groups patterned after the trade guilds of the mother country. On August 30, 1568, ordinances for carpenters and sculptors were issued by the city of Mexico. A man who wished to be examined in the art of carving was required to make a writing desk with base, a French-type chair, an inlaid hip-joint chair, a turned field bed, and a table. Disobedience of any of the many ordinances was punishable by fines and imprisonment. On April 7, 1589, it was stipulated that the rules concerning the test of skill did not apply to Indians and that Spaniards might not buy chairs or objects made by natives for resale.

Chairs in eighteenth-century Mexico reflected a strong Chinese influence, not only because of the importation of goods from the East, but because a number of Chinese and Philippine artisans were employed in Mexican workshops. In Brazil during

> A pair of late-eighteenth-century Portuguese colonial hardwood low seats japanned in brown and gold. Christie's

the same period, there were strong French and Portuguese influences in chair design. Although many fine pieces made in Brazil compare favorably with Portuguese palace chairs, a tendency toward heaviness and exaggeration of proportion may usually be seen. In spite of this heaviness, which was partly due to the use of American hardwoods, there is an originality to eighteenth-century Spanish and Portuguese colonial chairs that was lost in later years, when cabinetmakers fashioned exact copies of European pieces.

About the time that Spain was exploring and colonizing the West Indies, Portugal began her colonial expansion in the East. Six years after the voyage of Columbus, Vasco da Gama rounded the Cape of Good Hope in 1497 and reached the southwest coast of India. Trading posts and settlements were established along this coast during the sixteenth century to create a Portuguese monopoly of trade with the East Indies, Ceylon (Sri Lanka), Madagascar, and China.

Although the Portuguese dominated trade with the Far East in the sixteenth century, they soon had competitors. In 1600, English investors founded the East India Company; two years later, several Dutch companies assembled an immense pool of capital to form the United East India Company. During the first hundred

<
A colonial bamboo folding chair. Christie's

country, garden & colonial chairs 141

> A Dutch Colonial chair from Indonesia or Sri Lanka, of ebony and ebonized wood with ivory inlays, probably made for the Dutch East India Company c. 1680–1720. In 1602, two years after the founding of the English East India Company, several Dutch companies united to form the immensely powerful United East India Company. One of its chief exports was Far Eastern furniture, which was highly sought after. Getty Museum

years of the Dutch company's existence, its vast wealth allowed it to dominate trade with the Far East and to spread Dutch influence throughout the Orient. As the company's employees were transferred to various distant stations, their possessions, including furniture, were moved from one outpost to another. Some of these Far Eastern colonies were simultaneously occupied by other European powers, for example Ceylon, where both the Portuguese and the Dutch had trading posts. Moreover, native craftsmen of many ethnic backgrounds working in or nearby these stations also migrated from one to another, each carrying with him his own craft traditions. Thus, it is often difficult to identify the origin of colonial chairs made in the Far East.

In 1646 ebony is mentioned for the first time as a wood for chairs in Batavian (Dutch Indonesian) inventories. After 1720 the number of ebony chairs mentioned in these descriptions dwindles rapidly, and by 1750, the only ebony chair mentioned is the church chair. These chairs were intended for women to sit on during church services, while the men sat in pews. Usually, they were the ladies' personal property, brought with them to church and taken home after the service. J. W. Heydt records this custom in both Indonesia and Ceylon:

The women . . . sit on chairs, and have them borne thither by slaves, and when Church is over, they are brought back home. Each one is intent, not just on having a beautiful Chair, unless it be also furnished with an imposing cushion.

Early versions of ebony twist-turned chairs with seats of woven cane first appeared in the

>
A pair of nineteenth-century Anglo-Indian polychrome-decorated ivory armchairs, probably created for a maharajah. Christie's

<
A pair of mid-nineteenth-century Anglo-Indian silver side chairs. The form of the chair, especially its saber legs, is characteristically English, although the wooden frame is covered in silver. Christie's

descriptions of Batavian notaries in the early 1660s, and were the first examples of caned seats to arrive in Europe. In England and the Netherlands, rattan was much used for seats and backs from after 1660 up to about 1700. In France this technique enjoyed a second zenith in the second and third quarters of the eighteenth century. Caning was initially introduced to the East Indies by Chinese traders, as it was particularly suitable to the hardwoods there, and was a technique easily adapted to mass production. Rattan, however, remained popular in the East up to the nineteenth century. Its use is characteristic of Dutch Colonial chairs.

A distinction can be made between low-relief- and high-relief-carved chairs, which helps to determine the age of colonial seats. Earlier pieces (made between 1650 and 1680) were almost always carved in low relief. By 1690, however, this style was superseded by high-relief carving until the 1720s. Chairs and settees in high relief are rarely carved on the front and back; those that are belong to their own particular group found throughout the entire territory of the Dutch East India Company, each of which is characterized by its own specific floral motif. The choice of floral motifs is often attributed to Dutch influence. The Dutch, as customers for textiles painted with floral designs such as chintz, decided which floral motifs should be used on the basis of the demand in Europe or Asia. To ascertain these tastes, samples of textiles were sent to the Netherlands and to the various company stations throughout Asia.

One popular type of chair that remained in vogue among Dutch officials in Indonesia and Sri Lanka from the seventeenth to the nineteenth centuries is commonly called a "burgomaster chair." It is also known as a "king's chair" or "shaving chair," and is distinguished by its six legs and rounded back. Such a shape was unknown in Europe, although during the Ming Dynasty (1368–1644) in China, a hexagonal armchair was in use. In Indian miniatures some hexagonal thrones are depicted and the epic *Mahabharata* describes similar thrones being used by various kings. However, the legs and rails of the burgomaster chair are of a purely European shape. Sometimes the seat and back can be rotated on the base, which is a clue that this sort of chair was used for several purposes. It is an extremely comfortable seat.

The quality of the wood (often satinwood) and the carving shows that the burgomaster chair was usually a show piece. In Indonesia most of the burgomaster chairs are lacquered red, and one example from India is finished entirely with ivory. Ivory chairs in all shapes were mainly purchased by rich Indian princes or maharajahs. As in Indonesia, European influence appears to have been spreading, but ivory chairs exercised a great attraction for influential Europeans of that period. The first governor-general of India, Warren Hastings, had ivory chairs sent to England. After the English conquest of Seringapatam (Mysore) in 1799, they seized a great number of pieces of ivory furniture that had formerly been the property of Tipu Sultan and of his father, Haider Ali, as booty.

The high-backed Queen Anne chair, named for the English queen who ruled from 1702 to 1714, was adopted in Spain, Portugal, and the Netherlands as the new English fashion, and thence extended its influence to Indonesia and Sri Lanka, where direct Chinese influence also had its effect. In Batavia these chairs, dating mainly from the second and third quarter of the eighteenth century, were called "English chairs," and look eerily similar to their English counterparts. The typical Chinese splat, which is carried through to the seat, is seen quite often on chairs in Indonesia from the beginning of the eighteenth century, and also on the English Queen Anne chair. People in England were keener than the Dutch to surround themselves with everything that came from "India," and styles and influences traveled back and forth. In Indonesia chairs from the second quarter of the eighteenth century and later were made mainly from teak, amboyna wood, and Indian blackwood. Jackwood, coromandel,

>
An Indian Ivory throne chair, c. 1840, veneered on each side with plaques of ivory with brass studding and decorated with incised penwork. This extraordinary chair was probably made on eastern India's northern Coromandel Coast. The tradition of Indian incised ivory, examples of which are rare today, began in coastal Orissa. The more plentiful and better known ivory goods produced further south at Vizagapatam were derived from the Orissan craft. Collection Mallett at Bourdon House, London

<
Glass chairs made for the Indian market, manufactured by Osler. Photograph: D. Massey

<<
A glass chair made by Baccarat, a company founded near Lunéville, France, in 1765. The chairs have a metal skeleton, around which the glass is poured.

<
A glass stool by Baccarat

>
A nineteenth-century Ottoman chair with mother-of-pearl inlay. Private collection

colander, and nedun were the principal woods used for chairs in Sri Lanka. In the early eighteenth century, the Indies-chair style disappeared simultaneously with the wane of ebony and kaliatur furniture and the European influence then overrode all others.

The liquidation of the Dutch East India Company in 1795 marked a change in the direction of European cultural influence, which became so pervasive that the character of Dutch Indies society was affected, and with it chair-making. The rulers were the first to be influenced by European culture, and later new ideas from Europe reached the lesser nobility and well-to-do commoners. English influence prevailed in the nineteenth century and led to the creation of the Raffles chair, named after Sir Thomas Stamford Raffles, who administered Java from 1811 to 1816 as lieutenant governor. It is argued that this designation is not correct because it is assigned to a chair of Sheraton type, but the Raffles chair is now so well known by that name that the appellation has stuck. The many examples of Raffles chairs suggests that they were manufactured on a large scale, and the valuations assigned to them in inventories show that they were cheap. A completely new sort of chair introduced in the second half of the nineteenth century was the rocking chair, which must have been produced in large quantities in that period. Many can be see in old photographs, standing on the porches of houses.

Another veranda armchair, the *krossie gobang*, found both in India and Indonesia, was inspired by the Chinese rest-chair or drunken-lord chair. This reclining armchair had an armrest in which space has been left for a bottle. The facilities provided by this chair were well-suited to a tropical climate and a milieu where drinking was almost the only way of passing time, as one can see from this verse, often sung by Indonesian children:

Hujan datang;   [*The rain has come;*
kambing lari;   *the goat ran away;*
Belanda mabuck;   *the Dutchman's drunk*
delapan hari   *for eight days at a time*]

So, once again, chairs were changing to follow the preoccupations of their time and to adapt themselves to the current fashion.

4
high style: baroque, rococo & neoclassical chairs

LOUIS XIV (1643–1715): BAROQUE

The belief in the divine right of kings produced in seventeenth-century Europe one of the most rigidly structured societies in history: France under Louis XIV. Four days after his father's death, the four-and-one-half-year-old king was addressed by the Judge-Advocate General before the Parliament of Paris in the following words: "Your majesty's seat represents for us the throne of the living God.... The orders of the kingdom render unto you honor and respect as to a visible divinity." This view of his own importance was to shape the king's life.

Louis's identification with the sun and the Roman god Apollo brought the theory of divine right to a quasi-religious stage. The rituals of his court—his *levée*, a rising-from-bed ceremony held every morning; his royal audiences; his meals, which were almost invariably taken in public; his entertainments; and finally his *coucher*, a going-to-bed ceremony at the end of the day—became central events of public life, each ruled by an inflexible ceremonial etiquette.

In 1664 Louis's court numbered 600, including the royal family, the higher nobility, foreign envoys, and servants. Eventually this number grew to 10,000. To be invited to court became a devouring passion for many; even to be there for a day was worth a lifetime of saving. There were quarrels for precedence at table or in attending the king or queen, and fierce competition for favors. To keep this mob of beribboned egos in order, a hierarchy of seating was devised, and strictly enforced.

> A painting by Claude-Guy Halle (1652–1736) showing an embassy from the Doge of Genoa to Louis XIV, held in the Galerie des Glaces (Hall of Mirrors) at Versailles, May 15, 1685. The king's silver throne and other silver furniture in the gallery can be seen clearly. The Princess Palatine, the king's sister in law, wrote in a letter dated December 6, 1682, on the completion of the hall, "There are silver benches and chairs in the gallery." Such furnishings, a luxury that only a king could afford, were considered the necessary stage-properties for the daily performance of kingship. Versailles. Photograph: RMN. G. Blot/C. Jean

< An engraving by Jean Bérain of 1686, showing the Hall of Mirrors at Versailles with the king's silver throne and other silver furnishings brought in from the throne room to receive an embassy from Siam. Bibliothèque Nationale

When the court was installed at Versailles in 1682, an article published in the *Mercure Galant* noted that the seats in the Galerie des Glaces, the Salon de la Guerre, and the Chambre du Roi were almost exclusively of silver. Around 1689, some twenty tons of this furniture were melted down to finance the War of the Grand Alliance.

The chairs and stools (*ployants* and *pliants*) that stood in rows along the walls at Versailles represented royal control, and, as the French court was emulated throughout Europe, this arrangement was followed almost everywhere. The extremes of formality to which this led—in France, and in every country open to French influence, climaxing in the German princely courts of the eighteenth century—must be appreciated to understand how baroque chairs came to be made.

The magnificence of the French court lay partly in the furnishings of the royal apartments, and partly in the splendor of the king himself. This ideal of opulence originated partly in the tastes of Cardinal Mazarin, the powerful First Minister during most of the king's minority. Mazarin encouraged foreign craftsmen to settle in France, and was said to have "constrained most of the nations of the Earth to contribute to the decoration" of his private library, the Galerie Mazarine. Moreover, the ties between France and the Netherlands, and France and Florence, cemented by two French queens of Florentine origin, Catherine and Marie de Médicis, were also instrumental in the development of the baroque style.

Never before had the decorative arts been used so extensively for the propaganda of power. Louis's purpose was twofold: to establish his own power and to undercut that of the aristocracy. He took a keen interest in the furnishings of Versailles, lavishing enormous sums on them, and insisting on seeing wax models for all the more important seats. His minister, Jean-Baptiste Colbert, was largely responsible for founding the Manufacture des Gobelins in 1663 (later, in 1667, the Manufacture Royale des Meubles de la Couronne), devoted exclusively to providing furnishings for the Crown.

Under the direction of Charles Le Brun, such masters at the Manufacture Royale as Jean and

Daniel Marot, Jean Bérain, Antoine Le Pautre, and André Charles Boulle created designs for furnishings, including thrones and other seats. Although these men came from several countries, including France, Italy, Flanders, and the Netherlands, the pieces they produced were in an identifiably French baroque style, a robust manner originating in the forms of the Jesuit architecture of Italy. Chairs were large, masculine for all their lavish decoration, and completely symmetrical. Carving was rich and plentiful in forms drawn from nature and mythology—dolphins, griffins, masks, satyrs—to express the period's love of allegory.

Louis XIV understood the power of a throne to embody kingship, and his throne was majestic indeed. A similar throne had been made in Stockholm by Abraham Drentwett for Queen Christina of Sweden in 1650. Another forerunner was the silver throne of Alexis I of Russia (reigned 1645–76). We have a description of this throne, written by one of an embassy of Englishmen who traveled to Russia in 1664 to thank the tsar for his support of Charles II during his exile. The Englishmen were deeply impressed:

The tsar like a sparkling sun darted forth most sumptuous rays, being most magnificently placed upon his throne . . . of massy silver gilt, wrought curiously on top with several works and pyramids; and being seven or eight steps higher than the floor, it rendered the person of the Prince transcendently majestic.

Louis XIV seats were influenced by many foreign sources, and they in turn influenced the baroque chairs of every other European country. Significantly, after 1690, when the king's power was well established, the royal throne was less lavish. The Inventory of the Crown's Furnishings describes it as follows: *Un grand fauteuil de bois, taille de plusieurs ornemens et argenté, pour servir de trone au Roy lorsqu'il donne ses audiences aux ambassadeurs; ledit fauteuil garny de velours enrichy de broderie d'or et d'argent* [A large wooden armchair, carved and silvered, to be used by the king as a throne when he receives ambassadors; the said armchair upholstered in velvet, embroidered with gold and silvered decorations].

The inventory describes a number of chairs covered with embroidered silk or velvet in various royal residences. Another important feature was the Canopy of State—also found in England, Italy, and Sweden—which seems to have developed from the medieval canopies under which lords sat in raised armchairs to receive requests and administer justice. As the chair and canopy became symbols of state, obeisance had to be made to them, occupied or not.

There were strict rules for the proportions of canopies for each rank: the backcloth of a king's canopy, for instance, reached the ground; a duke's would be shorter, and a count's shorter still. Louis XIV laid great stress on protocol and frowned on or even punished the offenders when anyone at dinner was seated above his rank. The etiquette of seating was part of his philosophy of royalty. The range of chairs was, in order of importance, the armchair, the chair with back, the

<
A silver throne, c. 1650.
Sweden, Royal Collection

joint stool, the folding stool, the hassock, or *carreau*, with gold gimp for a lady of title, and finally, the *carreau* with silk edging for the bourgeois. In the king's presence most people had to remain standing. Permission to use a stool—the only seat allowed in his presence—was a coveted honor. Only with the king's express permission might his own brother sit at table with him, and then only on a stool. The only other men who could sit in the king's presence (again, only on stools), were the king's children and grandchildren. Princes of the Blood and dukes had to stand.

In the queen's apartment, ladies in waiting, wives of generals, and ladies of title (but not duchesses) had to sit on cushions (*carreaux*), although the duc de Saint-Simon wrote in his *Mémoires* that they *preferaient d'être debout à s'asseoir si bas* [prefer to stand rather than to sit so low]. The *Mémoires* of Saint-Simon, and the letters of Madame de Sévigné, the Princess Palatine, and Voltaire are full of anecdotes related to the hierarchy of seating at court and to the jealousy that the use of an armchair, side chair, or stool might create. Voltaire wrote in his *Dictionnaire philosophique* that

Le fauteuil à bras, la chaise à dos, le tabouret ont été pendant plusieurs siècles d'importants objects de politiques et d'illustres sujets de querelles. . . . Devaient-on s'asseoir, dans une certaine chambre, sur une chaise ou un tabouret; ou bien ne pas s'asseoir? Voilà ce qui intriguait toute une cour.

>
A silver and gold armchair, Augsburg, c. 1675. Kunstgewerbemuseum, Staatliche Museen zu Berlin

high style: baroque, rococo & neoclassical chairs   155

>
A room in Rudolf Nureyev's apartment at the Dakota apartment house in New York, showing an English chair of the James II period. Christie's

<
A Louis XIV walnut armchair, c. 1660–80, with its original upholstery

>
An armchair from a suite belonging to the Maréchal d'Effiat, c. 1660. The upholstery is original. Musée de Cluny. RMN

[*An armchair, a chair with a back, a stool were for many centuries important political objects and serious subjects of dispute. . . . May one sit, in a particular room, on a chair or on a stool, or are we not supposed to sit at all? These were the questions that fascinated a court*].

The Princess Palatine, who was married to Monsieur, the king's brother, wrote in a letter to her brother in 1682 that armchairs were reserved for upper royalty. Lower royalty sat on chairs, and tabourets—large, upholstered footstools—accommodated anyone with permission to sit in the presence of the great.

This hierarchy of seating extended throughout society, its effect rippling through the lives of the aristocracy and the bourgeoisie, in town, country, and abroad. In England, by Charles II's reign, the etiquette of using a tabouret had become extremely strict, and was observed both in private houses and at court. When traveling in England in 1669, Cosimo III, duke of Tuscany, made the gracious concession to his hosts at Wilton and Althorp of providing for them chairs similar to his own, while the rest of the company sat on stools. James, duke of York, observed this same etiquette when he went

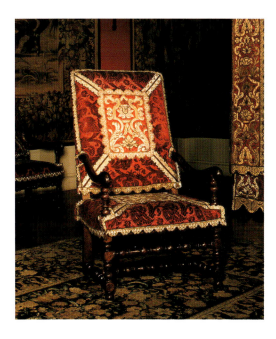

to meet his brother Charles II's intended queen, Catherine of Braganza, on her arrival in England. Upon entering Catherine's cabin, the duke refused the chair placed for him, but, on Catherine's indicating a tabouret, sat down immediately. On an occasion in 1688 the tabouret of Princess Anne was set too near the chair of her sister, Queen Mary; the princess declined to be seated until it had been removed to the correct distance. Similarly, when a young lackey in the service of the French countess d'Escarbagnas brought a chair to a commoner, the countess reprimanded him severely and demanded a stool—the appropriate seat for his social position—with the words *Un pliant, petit animal!* ["A folding stool, stupid!"]

An equally strict etiquette ruled in Spain. According to the seventeenth-century Spanish writer Julio Monreal:

Cushions were only for ladies; men sat on chair or stools according to the rank they held since the chair at this time and even previously was offered only to a person whom one wished to honor for his social position, giving him who was esteemed less, or with whom one was more intimate, a stool.

A special area, called an *estrado,* was reserved for ladies. By extension, a small chair exclusively for women was also called an *estrado,* a usage that continued in Spain until the reign of Philip V in the early eighteenth century. The Spanish writer Maria de Zayas y Sotomayor (1590–1661/69) mentioned the *estrado* in one of her stories: "At the head of the room was a rich *estrado*, with green velvet cushions excessively adorned with silver trimming . . . a throne, seat, and shelter for lovely Lysis."

The Spanish playwright Pedro Calderon de la Barca (1600–81) relates that a first-time visitor to a Spanish house was usually offered the formal chair; on a later visit, he would be offered a stool, and later still, a footstool. This strict code of behavior, combined with the elaborate settings of the baroque age, created a distinction between state rooms, used solely for public display, and private apartments for everyday living, a distinction that reached its fullest expression in the eighteenth century. The baroque "cabinet" was a forerunner of the *petits appartements* so dear to the eighteenth century, and upholstered chairs pioneered a new attempt at comfort. Ultimately, the luxury first contrived for private rooms prevailed, softening the formality of the grander, more public ones, the antechamber and the salon.

Comfort as we know it was invented by the French in the seventeenth century. Versailles inventories are full of drawings, most of them for the dauphin's apartment of 1690, representing wing chairs, canapés *pour se reposer* [for taking a nap], fauteuils with curtains, and day beds, all tufted and cozy-looking. Such furnishings made the dauphin's rooms one of the marvels of the palace.

Sofas were the most important seats introduced during the period. These were supplied by upholsterers, who, toward the end of the seventeenth century, began to supplant the carvers. The upholsterers introduced the taste for brightly colored and comfortable chairs, and some of them became rich and famous. Simon de Lobel, the principal *tapissier* to Louis XIV, was a household name in France around 1680. Upholsterers brought a measure of unification to important rooms long before architects were involved. The notion of upholstery *en suite* (i.e., coordinated) to unify a room developed in the seventeenth century. By the 1640s it must have been com-

<

A Dutch oak hall bench, c. 1700, after a drawing by Daniel Marot (1661–1752). Inventories show that the hall bench or *bank* was almost ubiquitous in well-appointed Dutch houses. They were usually of oak and often painted. Designed to display wealth rather than provide comfort, they commonly featured a coat of arms. Under Marot's influence they were covered with profusions of lavish carving. Chinese Porcelain Company, New York

high style: baroque, rococo & neoclassical chairs   157

>
A drawing by Daniel Marot of chairs and armchairs. Marot played a leading role at the end of the seventeenth century at the Dutch court. The son of an architect and engraver for Louis XIV, he was forced to flee to the Netherlands in 1686 after the revocation of the Edict of Nantes, which had ensured religious tolerance of French Protestants. The Metropolitan Museum of Art

monplace in grand circles to have matching textile furnishings in important rooms. The Ham House inventory of about 1654 shows that several rooms had such furnishings. Lady Maynard's chamber featured "Two great chaires, eight stooles, two cushions . . . of green cloth embroidered with needlework suitable to the bed."

Louis XIV spread French taste abroad through magnificent gifts to foreign monarchs and their ambassadors, such as the state bed and matching suite of chairs and stools that he gave the Swedish count Nils Bielke. Such pieces were intended to display French splendor. As the Louis XIV style was propagated throughout Europe, French artists and craftsmen came into great demand abroad. When, in 1685, Louis revoked the Edict of Nantes, which had granted tolerance for French Protestants, Huguenot artisans, many trained in the Gobelins workshops, poured into England and Holland, giving enormous impetus to the spread of French taste. Foreign princes began to invite French artists to their countries to complete important commissions. One immensely influential émigré was Daniel Marot, a Protestant forced to leave France, where he had been Jean Bérain's best pupil. He became *chef de dessin* for William III of Orange, the stadholder of the Netherlands, and when William became king of England, carried the French taste to that country, as well. The publication in Amsterdam of Marot's engraving in 1702 and 1712 spread his style, and French influence, even further.

French taste was also transmitted through painted genre scenes. The charming views of interiors by Abraham Bosse (1602–76) showing the daily lives of the *haute bourgeoisie* conveyed how the various furnishings went together.

pliants, tabourets, stools, benches, and *carreaux*

The word tabouret suggests a round stool, and from the beginning these stools appear invariably to have been upholstered. Starting at the end of Louis XIII's reign, the *pliant*, a folding stool with an X-shaped frame, began to replace other forms, and under Louis XIV became a hierarchical seat. Inventories mentioned *pliants* and tabourets without much distinction. From about 1650 the *pliant* seems, in France at least, to have superseded other kinds of stools, and was seen in the grandest settings, often upholstered in luxurious fabrics. It spread across Europe during the seventeenth and eighteenth centuries. By the third quarter of the eighteenth century, however, it had fallen out of fashion, and remained in use solely at the French court.

An honor that might be bestowed on a lady at the court of Louis XIV was called *la prise du tabouret* [taking possession of the stool]. At dinner time, the lady who was to be the recipient of this favor was introduced to the king, who then asked her to be seated. Etiquette demanded that she must wait until the king asked her to sit a second time before she "took possession" of the stool, which was in fact not a tabouret, but a *pliant*. Permission to sit in the king's presence was a

major honor, and the expense of gaining it was considerable: approximately 1,540 livres. Widows were known to have refused to remarry to keep their right to it, and young ladies were known to accept old and decrepit husbands if the privilege of a stool came with the proposal!

The memoirist Philippe de Dangeau (1638–1720) wrote that the Grand Dauphin *était toujours sur un tabouret pendant que le Roy etait au bal* [was always on a stool when the king was at a ball]. At Louis XIV's death 1,325 tabourets and *pliants* reserved for high-ranking courtiers were recorded at Versailles. The French royal inventories list several X-frame stools with silver mounts [*garnis d'argent cizelé*], with white embroidered satin and gold fringes, with red damask, red velvet, or lacquered. As many as 466 *pliants* were extremely luxuriously appointed. The others, equally refined, were usually created to match a bed and two armchairs in a specific room. In a suite of furniture, the number of armchairs rarely exceeded two (one each for the king and queen), however, there were numerous stools, depending on the size of the room. The fashion seems to have been the same in England. In the 1654 inventory at Ham House, one bedchamber (now the Museum room) contained "two great chaires, ten folding stooles, two carpets all of clouded satine." In an inventory of the contents of Kimbolton Castle in Cambridgeshire drawn up at the end of the century, stools considerably outnumbered chairs, a proportion that seems to have been followed in the majority of the great houses of Europe.

Occasionally a *pliant* might have a back. On one occasion recounted by the duc de Luynes in his memoirs (VII, 203), the dauphine, pregnant, was uncomfortable sitting for hours on a stool. "The queen ordered that a *pliant* with a small back be made" [*La Reine a donné ordre que l'on fît un pliant avec un petit dos pareil*]. This type of seat was known thereafter as a *dauphine*. Such stools are also mentioned among the furnishings of Charles I at Somerset House in 1649, where there were "twenty-four wooden stooles with backs painted and gilt."

English X-shaped stools were generally upholstered en suite with the chairs, in the French manner. With the exception of those preserved at Knole House, in Kent, almost certainly made for James I and his queen, Anne of Denmark, few upholstered English stools dating from the seventeenth century survive. The royal furniture dispersed after Charles I's execution in 1649 included a large number of stools, covered in almost every case to match the chairs and sold with them.

<
A French *ployant* of gilded wood, from Versailles, c. 1675. Saint Simon wrote of these chairs that *Les duchesses et les Princesses sont assises sur des ployants ou sur des tabourets, car il n'y a point de différence entre ces deux sièges sans dos, ni bras*. [Duchesses and princesses are seated on *ployants* or tabourets, for there is no distinction between these two seats without arms or back]. Madrid, Museo Nacional de Artes Decorativas

In England until about 1685, most stools were produced by joiners. With the restoration of the Stuart monarchy in 1660, walnut and painted beech became fashionable, and stools were made to match a type of bench introduced from the Low Countries. Some of these were of considerable length, like those in oak of the earlier age.

Benches with coats of arms, developed from Renaissance examples, were also common in Spain during the seventeenth century. Some were folding, some upholstered in leather, some of carved wood. Like their Dutch counterparts, they were made more for display than for comfort, and were widely used in mansions, public buildings, and churches. At first church benches stood in sacristies or in private chapels, but later in the eighteenth century they were often arranged in parallel lines in the nave. Bench legs were splayed, turned, or shaped as lyres, their braces made of gracefully scrolled iron.

Seventeenth-century Spanish interiors were luxurious. Describing one, Maria de Zayas y Sotomayor wrote that "The room was fenced in with many green velvet chairs and many little stools for the gentlemen to sit on so that they could enjoy the heat of a silver brazier that diffused perfume. . . ." The accession in 1700 of the Bourbon king Philip V, Louis XIV's grandson, brought Parisian fashions to Madrid, including *pliants*. A beautiful gilded pair, now in the Prado, was a personal gift from Louis to Philip.

Stools existed for many purposes. Randle Holme, in his 1649 *Academy of Armory*, illustrated a low, square stool for nursing. Louis XIV used a stool in his bath (he had, by 1677, six bathrooms at Versailles). Influenced by this French courtly custom, most European aristocrats of the late seventeenth century also had stools in their bathtubs, so that they could sit during their ablutions. In Britain, the duchess of Lauderdale had her "bathing tubb & little stoole within it." Stools are mentioned in the Ham House and Dyrham Park inventories, and other English inventories are full of references to "buffet stooles," presumably for use at dining tables, near which there would usually be a buffet. Another stool associated with dining tables was called *escabelle* in France. Antoine de Furtière's *Dictionary*, published in 1690, mentions that *l'escabelle ne servait guère qu'à la table* [the *escabelle* was only used at the table]. Molière, in his play *L'Avare*, describes *une table à douze piliers turnés . . . garnie par le dessous de six escabelles* [a table with twelve turned legs . . . with six *escabelles* underneath]. The play was first performed in 1669, and considering Harpagon's character, the furniture was slightly out of fashion at that time.

As chairs and comfortable seats multiplied during the eighteenth century, the fashion for stools diminished. Despite the hierarchic significance of the X-shaped stool, the desire for comfort gradually made it obsolete, splendid or not. The *Journal de Verdun* in November 1720 printed the following charade about the tabouret:

Utile et méprisé, on me voit chez les grands
Où souvent je ne sers qu'aux bourgeois, aux enfants
Mais dans un certain lieu, je suis tant de requête
Qu'à pouvoir m'obtenir les dames se font fête.

[*Useful and despised, you can see me in the company of the great*
Where I only assist bourgeois, and children
But elsewhere I am in such demand
That when women obtain me, I am celebrated]

> A pair of Louis XIV tabourets. Christie's

Cushions can be easily moved about. In Spain, the superposition of the Iberian and the Islamic cultures resulted in some people's sitting on the floor and others on chairs. The sixteenth-century Spanish writer Perez de Chinchon once wrote that "Muslims sit on the ground like animals," which he later rephrased as "They sit on the ground like women." And indeed, Spanish women did sit on cushions on the floor, Arab-style, until the seventeenth century. The expression *tomar la almohadilla* [to take a cushion] signified a lady's permission to be seated in the queen's presence, an honor that later made its way to Italy and France. Since seating cushions were square, in France they were called *carreaux* [squares]. There are many references to *carreaux* in descriptions of high-society life during the seventeenth century. Louis XIV maintained nine richly decorated boats from various countries on the canal at Versailles, all equipped with luxurious cushions, with colors matching those of the boats.

Saint-Simon recounted many anecdotes relating to *carreaux*, the trim and fabric of which depended on the owner's social station: gold gimp for ladies of title, silk edging for the bourgeois. Grand beds were often provided with a couple of *carreaux* as part of their accompanying seats, and examples can be found at Ham House and Knole. Gédeon Tallemant des Réaux (1619–92), in his memoir, *Historiettes*, recalled Madame de Maintenon, Louis XIV's second, morganatic wife, lying *sur des carreaux dans sa ruelle du lit avec un peu de colique* [on some *carreaux* on her bed with colic].

Carreaux were also used for kneeling at mass. It was as great an honor for a duke or duchess to be allowed to use a *carreau* in church as it was for them to use a tabouret at court. High-ranking ecclesiastics had the same privilege. A scandal erupted in 1717 during a memorial mass for Louis XIV when the attending bishops stormed out of the cathedral of Saint-Denis when they were refused the use of *carreaux*! Today the *carreau* is no longer a seat, although it lives on as a cushion.

fauteuils, armchairs, and other chairs

Originally the term *fauteuil* referred to any important-looking armchair, or to a chair with arms and back. Eventually it came to mean a fully upholstered armchair. The Louis XIV fauteuil perfectly expresses its time. Created for men who wanted to appear taller in their high red heels and imposing wigs, it stands high, is wide enough for two, and has an exceedingly high back. Its scale and the sumptuousness of its carving and upholstery made it imposing. Such were the fauteuils used at the wedding that same year of Louis XIV and Marie-Thérèse of Spain, which were upholstered in blue velvet embroidered with fleurs-de-lys. The heavy carving of the wood was influenced by Italian chairs. Indeed, the Italian baroque style foreshadows that of Louis XIV and later echoes it.

In Italy, extravagant armchairs were not only made by sculptors, they were thought of as

>

An armchair of the type know as a *fauteuil à la reine*, c. 1710, with its original leather upholstery. Musée du Louvre. RMN

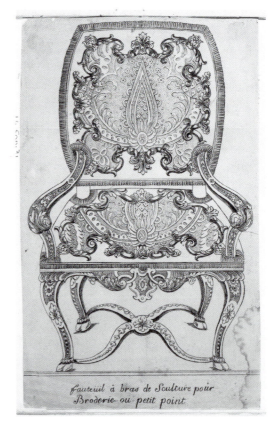

<

A print showing a design for chair upholstery, c. 1700, by Paul Androuet du Cerceau (c. 1630–1710). At the time, the value of a seat's upholstery was far greater than that of the wooden seat itself.

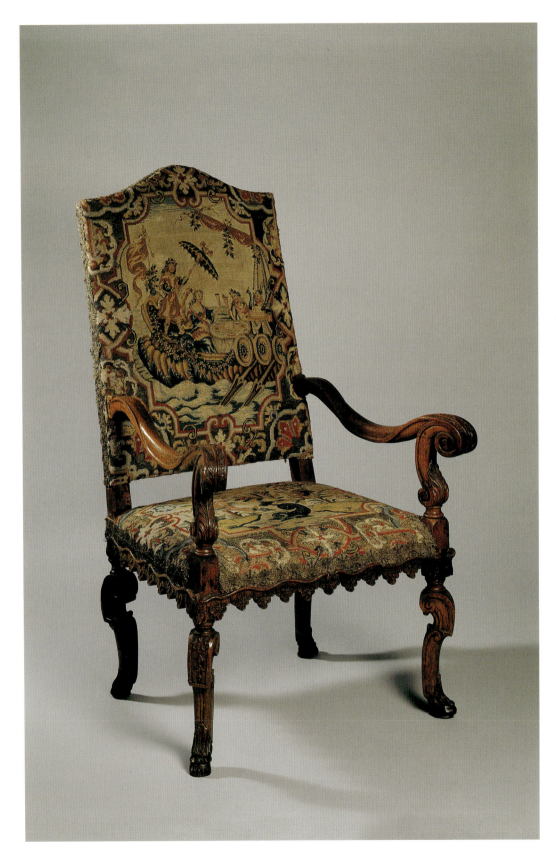

<
A walnut *poltrona* (armchair) from the Piedmont region of northern Italy, with tapestry upholstery. L'Antiquaire & The Connoisseur, Inc.

high style: baroque, rococo & neoclassical chairs   163

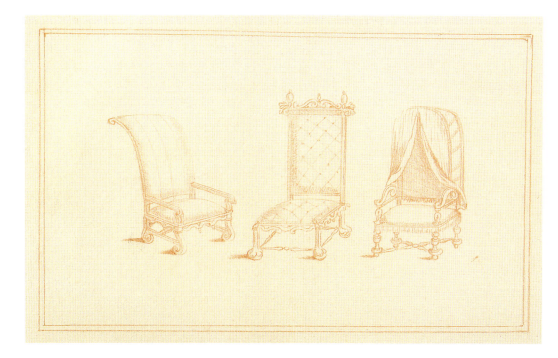

>
A drawing for the dauphin's apartment at Versailles showing armchairs, one with a curtain to protect against drafts. From an eighteenth-century album, *Décoration intérieure et jardins de Versailles*. RMN. Gerard Blot

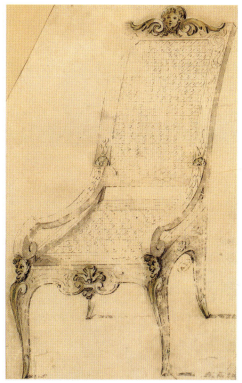

>
André-Charles Boulle was the first great French *ébéniste* and the most celebrated of Louis XIV furniture-makers. Boulle's work perfectly embodied his period's taste for grand style. His name is associated with a type of ornate tortoiseshell and brass marquetry. Collection Gismondi, Paris

>>
A drawing of a chair by André-Charles Boulle. Musée des Arts Décoratifs, Paris

< An English George I (1714–27) gilt hall chair. Christie's

high style: baroque, rococo & neoclassical chairs   165

> A Spanish black and gilt side chair. Caning was a favorite feature of late-seventeenth-century tall-backed chairs, which usually had a heavily carved crest and central splat. This typically baroque chair, of a type that originally appeared in Portugal as the *cadera de sola*, featured turned legs and arms, a scrolled front stretcher, and a high, shaped back. It became popular in Spain, the Netherlands, England, and Germany. Eventually, it acquired carved shells and garlands in the style of Daniel Marot. Christie's

> An American William and Mary carved maple armchair, from Philadelphia, 1715–20. Christie's

sculpture, as things of beauty rather than comfort. There was a profound distinction between the functional chairs in the living quarters of a palazzo and the massive, ornamented chairs that furnished the *piano nobile*. Pietro Longhi's genre scenes of Venetian life show the plainest leather-seated backstools in the family quarters. Italian state chairs, however, displayed flowing outlines and lavish carving and gilding that made them almost impossible to simplify. Some were carved all over with putti, clouds, and acanthus leaves. The influence of sculpture on Italian baroque chairs was of importance for the spread of the style across Europe. Individual chairs, however, are often meaningless by themselves, as they were usually designed as part of a larger group.

The French fauteuil always has stretchers, H-shaped early on, and later in a serpentine X. The legs are scrolled, flat, or turned balusters. The arms swing into the back in great curves carved with a repertoire of decorative motifs derived from Classical Antiquity: acanthus leaves, fruit, flowers, lions' heads and paws, dolphins, and sea horses. The insignia of the monarchy is frequently used: two interlaced L's (the cipher of Louis XIV), the fleur-de-lys (emblem of the French monarchy), and the sunburst (representing the Sun King himself). Gilding and silvering became more and more fashionable as Louis XIV's reign progressed, and the pursuit of splendor led to the creation of new techniques. André-Charles Boulle designed and executed chairs in the lavish technique that bears his name, a combination of tortoiseshell and brass inlaid in ebony. These were imitated elsewhere, particularly in Augsburg.

European lacquer started to develop at the beginning of the seventeenth century, attaining remarkable excellence under Louis XIV, who installed François Le Moyne and other artists in the Gobelins factory to imitate the Oriental style. The 1677 inventory of Jacques Quiquebeuf, councillor-secretary to the king, records a pair of small lacquered fauteuils: *Deux petits fauteuils de bois noircy façon de la Chine, garny de paille* [Two little fauteuils of black-lacquered wood in the Chinese fashion, with straw seats]. The general inventory of Versailles also lists a suite of furniture in the popular *style de la Chine* in Louis XIV's bedroom. An unusual feature is that there were three armchairs in the room.

The Dutch developed a considerable commerce in lacquered work, and the traffic between them and the English, as well as with the courts of Charles II and Louis XIV, created a vogue for japanned chairs that reached eventually to Spain, Portugal, Sweden, and Denmark. In England, shortly before Queen Anne's accession in 1702, Lord Ferrer's steward records the purchase of "8 very fine Japan chairs at 26 s. each." Green and gold appear to have been the favorite color scheme at the time. Around 1745, red with details in silver and gold seems to have been appreciated, as a set of chairs made by Giles Grendey for the Spanish duke of Infantado bears witness.

In Germany around 1690 Gerhard Dagly decorated some chairs for the elector of Brandenburg, using one of his trademarks, a creamy white ground resembling porcelain. Dagly had been appointed *Kammerkunstler* (director of ornaments) in 1687 to the elector Friedrich Wilhelm and his son, who in 1700 became king of Prussia. Dagly appears only to have decorated furniture and chairs made by others. His work is of extraordinary beauty, largely because of the white background against which he set his Oriental scenes.

Venice also became famous in the late seventeenth and early eighteenth century for its lacquer; the technique of japanning was acquired through Venice's trade with the East. Lacquer offered a way to create opulent chairs without precious materials, particularly appealing after Louis XIV's sumptuary edict of 1689, which consigned silver furnishings to the melting pot.

In the royal inventories made under Louis XIV, 103 fauteuils independent of any suite of furnishings are mentioned, each more magnificent than the last. Most were carved giltwood; three were enhanced with chiseled silver; all were upholstered with damask, embroidered silk, velvet, or needlepoint. Four fauteuils in the dauphin's cabinet were

couverts de tableaux de broderie de point satiné rehaussé d'or et d'argent, représentant les Elements, Saisons, et autres sujets, par des figures et enfants, dans de bordures rondes ou ovales de broderie d'or

[*covered in needlepoint panels enriched with gold and silver, representing the elements, the seasons, and other subjects with figures and children, in round or oval frames made of gold needlepoint*].

The fauteuil that Louis used at Trianon for his dinner was wonderfully carved in wood, gilded, and upholstered *de damas rouge broche d'or à gros fleurons, garni de franges, mollet, et gallon* [in red damask, embossed with gold flowers, finished with fringes, trim, and braid].

Fauteuils were the noblest of all armchairs. As *Nouveau traite de la civilité qui se pratique en France parmi les honnestes gens*, an essay published in 1673, explained, "the fauteuil is the most honorable chair, the chair with back after it, and then, the folding stool." At Versailles the fauteuil became a sort of throne, so that in rooms where the king was expected, only one armchair was present. Saint-Simon noted in his memoirs that if the queen would also be joining the company, two armchairs would be ready, *un pour la Reine . . . l'autre pour le roi; et lorsque le roi doit être seul, on ne laisse qu'un fauteuil dans la pièce* [one for the

<

The armchair of the actor and playwright Molière (Jean-Baptiste Poquelin; 1622–73). According to legend, he died while performing in his play *Le Malade imaginaire* [The Imaginary Invalid] in this very armchair. Robert Wilson Collection. Photograph: Antoine Bootz

queen, the other for the king, and when the king must be alone, there is only one fauteuil left in the room]. At the Spanish court, where etiquette was even stricter, the king was seated on a fauteuil and the queen on a *carreau*.

At Versailles, the use of the fauteuil led to the creation of a special position, *porte-fauteuil*, or chair-porter. The king had four men assigned to this duty, each with an annual salary of 400 livres. Their function was to present the king with an armchair before his dinner and to remove it afterward. Only when another king was present was another armchair brought, as when Charles II of England was in residence. In *l'Etat de France*, a contemporary record kept of events in France, we learn that:

Lorsque le Roy et la Reine d'Angleterre, étant à la cour, mangent avec le Roy à son Grand Couvert, le Roy et la Reine d'Angleterre sont servis comme le Roy et par les mêmes officiers ayant chacun un cadenat et un fauteuil et le Roy donnant la droite chez lui à leurs Majestés britanniques

[When the king and queen of England were at court, they ate dinner with the king and were served by the same officials, each being presented, like him, with cutlery and a fauteuil, the king having their Britannic Majesties at his right].

Aristocrats had special majordomos to present fauteuils to important guests. It was considered terrible manners to move an armchair or to take one by oneself. In his *Historiettes,* Tallemant recalls *un certain Cérisante, qui quand on ne lui en offrait pas, approchait lui même un fauteuil, des dames, par malice, firent clouter tous les fauteuils de leur chambre afin qu'il n'en put prendre*

[a certain Cérisante, who would take an armchair even when it had not been offered, whereupon some ladies for spite had all the chairs in their room nailed to the floor to prevent him from moving them].

In contrast to the practice at court, the bourgeois, who liked armchairs for their comfort, commonly kept a number of them in their salons. Molière had twenty-two. He even died in one, a *fauteuil de commodité* with a *crémaillère*, or adjustable back, while acting in his play *Le Malade imaginaire*.

By 1680 the term *fauteuil de commodité* had come to mean a particularly comfortable chair, often with a movable back, attached candle-holders, and a tablet to support a book or papers. These chairs, which were used by people of means for relaxation, reading, writing letters, or grooming, became a standard part of a luxurious bedroom suite from 1685 on. The French Royal inventory of 1687 lists thirty *grand fauteuils de commodité a crémillière* (chairs with adjustable backs), like the "sleeping chayres" at Ham House, which date to about 1678. According to a letter written by Mme. de Maintenon to M. d'Aubigne dated September 15, 1679, the very practical *fauteuil de commodité* had been perfected by one Father Testu. The dauphin gave Madame de Maintenon a particularly relaxing one when she visited him at his residence at Meudon. In 1708 the duc d'Orleans, who would later become the regent, had a *fauteuil de commodité* in his bedroom at Versailles. Voltaire, following the example of Molière, died in his own beloved *fauteuil de commodité* in 1778.

Drawings of easy chairs, wing chairs, and *fauteuils de commodité* for the dauphin's apartment at Versailles still survive, testifying to the comfort of those quarters. Variations of these chairs, called *fauteuils à oreilles, fauteuils de veille,* and *fauteuils confessionals*, were all geared toward comfort. The sleeping chairs at Ham House, described in an inventory of 1697 as "two sleeping chayres carv'd and guilt frames covered with crimson and gould stuff with gould fringe," were strikingly similar, with ratchets to let down the backs. Today they are still covered in their original upholstery. The evidence afforded by the royal tradesmen's accounts in England indicates that upholstered wing armchairs, which are described as "easie chairs" in contemporary inventories, were introduced after the accession to the throne in 1660 of Charles II, who, returning to England from exile in Flanders, brought with him a number of Continental ideas of elegance and luxury.

In the seventeenth century, Holland had been home to a thriving cabinetmaking industry since the late Middle Ages, when the Amsterdam carpenters' guild had been founded as the Guild of St. Josef. Membership grew in the late sixteenth century, when a number of cabinetmakers moved to Amsterdam from Germany and the Southern Netherlands. In 1578, when Amsterdam's population was 30,000, the guild had 125 members. A century later, when the city's population was more than 200,000, the guild's numbered 600, including fifty chair-makers, with a headquarters, or *Kistemakerspand* (chest-makers' house), with showrooms for the furniture made by its members. Guild regulations during the sixteenth and seventeenth centuries obliged chair-turners to make two pieces, a *Setelstoel* and a *Haarlemsche*, to qualify for membership. Unfortunately, since Dutch chairs were not stamped with makers' marks, we do not know the names of individual artisans.

Late-seventeenth-century Dutch chairs provided the models for English baroque examples. The Dutch also introduced caning to Europe, along with such exotic fabrics as chintz. The 1642 book *Boutique Menuiserie*, by the Dutch designer Crispijn van de Passe, was particularly influential in chair design. It illustrated some simpler chairs, with straight backs, double stretchers, and arms carved with dolphins, models similar to those found around 1680 in France and England. Typical Dutch chairs with shallow scrolls on the front stretchers and back, a design often described in early inventories as "horsebone" decoration, became popular in England as well, around 1670. English makers such as Thomas Roberts (who appears repeatedly in the Royal Wardrobe accounts) varied the standard form with cane backs and seats by introducing figures of cupids and garlands. These, and the slightly later backstool, were ideal for the baroque arrangement of chairs lined up against the walls, where their tall, narrow proportions looked like guards on parade. Charles II had spent a great deal of time at Versailles during his exile, so the French influence is not surprising. Charles also brought with him French, Flemish, and Italian craftsmen, who preferred to work in walnut rather than oak.

As the English court embraced the lavishness of Versailles, a new baroque opulence emerged. Toward the end of Charles's reign much of the carving on English chairs was gilded, silvered, or painted. The upholstery might be silk appliqué, Genoese velvet, or stamped leather; the frames featured large, free curves, spiral turning, double-curved legs, and scrolled feet. New types of chair were also created: wing chairs, easy chairs, day beds, and sofas, and the fashion for fine furniture continued through the reigns of William and Mary, Queen Anne, and the Hanoverian kings.

Caning, adopted from Chinese furniture by Dutch and Portuguese traders and introduced into Europe by the East India Company, became popular in England after the Stuart Restoration. An undated petition presented by a group of cane chair-makers in England states that caning came into use there around 1664, and that it was much prized for its durability, lightness, and cleanliness from dust, worms, and moths. Early references to caning in English inventories are scarce, but the 1679 inventory of Ham House does mention footstools of "Indian cane" with gilt frames in the Queen's Bedroom, and six armchairs with "cane bottoms" in the duke of Lauderdale's dressing room.

English inventories refer to cane chairs as "Dutch chairs" or "Holland chairs." The fashion spread to Germany, where makers of the chairs called themselves *Englische Stuhlmacher*, and to Scandinavia. In Sweden after 1680 Dutch- and English-influenced lacquered chairs with cane

high style: baroque, rococo & neoclassical chairs 169

> A side chair with a cane seat from the Netherlands, c. 1680. Caning first appeared in Europe around 1664. This chair, in a style simpler than the grand manner prevailing at court, is typical of the provincial taste that flourished until the mid-eighteenth century in Europe. Such chairs were often modeled from engravings, after the latest fashions had appeared in Paris. Chateau of Ecouen. Photograph: Antoine Bootz

backs and rush seats became popular, and by 1700 were common.

Apparently the enmity between the Sun King and William of Orange forbade importing Dutch caning into France, so it was not until about 1722, in the reign of Louis XV, that cane seats first appeared at Versailles. However, many *petites chaises de paille* are mentioned in the French Royal Inventories of the time of Louis XIV.

The caned chairs' appeal was their lightness, and they infiltrated Versailles under the pretense that they were more practical for gambling or working. In fact, the chair owed its popularity to its freedom from the court's hierarchy of seating. Toward the end of Louis XIV's reign the *chaise de paille* allowed everyone to sit without embarrassment by court etiquette. Many chairs had *carreaux*, or loose, quilted padding, tied to their backs. Listed in the 1694 inventory of the maréchal d'Humières, then governor of Lille, are *Six fauteuils de paille, avec leur carreaux et dossiers picqués de satin de Bruges* [Six caned armchairs, with their quilted cushions and backs of Bruges satin]. Such seats had been fashionable in theaters since around 1680. Cheaper versions of natural wood were called *chaises à la capucine*.

In England, the joint accession of William of Orange and Mary Stuart to the throne in 1689 brought new influences to bear on chair-makers, increasing the cross-fertilization of ideas among England, the Netherlands, France, and Portugal. Despite the Dutch nationality of William of Orange and his antagonism toward Louis XIV, the stylistic keynote of his reign was French, and his favorite designer, as we have noted, was the French refugee Daniel Marot. Among the new features of the Orange-Stewart chairs, which entered England by way of Holland, were the Spanish foot, spiral and bulbous turning, hoop-back cresting, and arch-scrolled front stretchers. English armchairs at the end of the seventeenth century represent the full-blown baroque style: they resemble Dutch seats, and introduce the cabriolet leg already popular in France through the influence of the Dutch traders who had been in turn partially influenced by the Chinese.

Early-eighteenth-century Russian chairs were also inspired by Anglo-Dutch influence. Peter the Great, who reigned in his own right from 1694, wanted to transform Russia from a medieval country into a modern state. In order to achieve this goal—to learn the secrets of the West; to teach his nobles a more civilized way of life; to bring back to his country qualified engineers, naval officers, shipbuilders, and surgeons; and to open diplomatic contact in Europe—in 1697 and 1698 he undertook the Great Embassy, a visit to Sweden, Germany, the Netherlands, and England.

Since his adolescence, the tsar had admired William of Orange—at the time both stadholder of the Netherlands and king of England—foremost among Western leaders. During the Great Embassy, Peter had the good fortune to meet William, first in Holland and then in England in 1698. The tsar stayed three months in England, living in a large, elegantly furnished house, the pride and joy of the essayist and diarist John Evelyn, provided for him by the English government. When Peter and his entourage left, every chair in the house—more than fifty—had disappeared, apparently into the stove! It was a clear demonstration of the level of civilization among the Russian nobility of the time.

Later, in 1716 and 1717, Peter sent Russian apprentices to England and Holland to learn new techniques from the master cabinetmakers of those countries. Peter paid considerable attention to how these young men were distributed among their new teachers. In June 1717, for example, while taking a cure at Spa, the tsar ordered twenty-four Russian men sent from Amsterdam to London, nine of these to join furniture workshops there. Peter relied on his London agent, Osip Veselovsky, to report on the apprentices' progress, which Veselovsky did in detail. Thus, we know that young men were trained in joinery, house-decoration, and chair-making. Their English masters were paid £80 each for their training, and as much again for their maintenance. On average, the apprentices stayed abroad for five to six years. By 1723–24 some had returned to St. Petersburg and had begun to work. In all, about fifteen men returned as highly qualified master furniture- and chair-makers, with the result that many early-eighteenth-century Russian chairs show a strong English or Dutch influence.

The court of Frederick I of Prussia (1657–1713) was furnished with seats in pure Louis XIV style, and from about 1690 all the European courts imitated the prevailing Parisian manner with a variable time-lag. At about the same, the gracefully curved French cabriolet leg was widely accepted, replacing the spiral-turned legs of earlier in the century. The Elector Maximilian II Emanuel of Bavaria (1662–1726), who spent some years in exile in the Netherlands and France between 1704 and 1707, brought craftsmen from both countries with him when he returned home in 1714. He also took German artists with him to France to be trained, among them François Cuvilliés, who would become a major force in the development of the rococo style in Germany in the second quarter of the eighteenth century.

The baroque style, which suited the Germanic sense of grandeur and decorum very well, came later to Germany than to most other European countries. However, the style reached its most extravagant expression and was abandoned far less quickly there than elsewhere. German seats were strongly influenced by styles from abroad, first from Italy, then from France, England, and the Netherlands. Chairs in southern Germany, in the Palatinate, and in Baden-Baden generally featured bold, Italianate forms, while the English influence came from the court of the duke of Hanover, who became George I of England in 1714. German chairs of the baroque period are similar to English Queen Anne chairs, featuring splat backs, cabriole legs, and in some instances, cane backs and seats.

Before the eighteenth century, Spain and Portugal drew most of their artistic inspiration from the Moors. Then, seats began to achieve a more European look, partly through the use of turning. The X-frame or hip-joint chair of the

<
A Franconian baroque side chair, c. 1750–60. Collection Neidhardt Antiquitäten, Munich

Moors developed into the *sillon frailero*, a sturdy, square armchair with straight back and arms, thick front stretchers, and often, a wide seat. The leather upholstery, usually of calf, was sometimes plain, sometimes worked in geometric patterns. Highly favored was *guadamecil*, an intricately patterned leather originally made by the Moors, with relief designs raised by pressure, often brilliantly colored or embossed with gold or silver.

There were also rectangular armchairs, called "monk chairs," from their use in monasteries. According to inventories, these were found in churches, convents, wealthy private houses, and even barber shops. Sometimes the arms were wide, and supported by curved or scrolled brackets. Although lighter than Renaissance chairs, they otherwise differ little from them. There are two theories explaining the extraordinary width of the arms of some. One is that they were used to balance cups and dishes, taking the place of tables in religious houses; the other is that they were used to support large books when monks read and wrote.

Toward the end of the seventeenth century, when the Louis XIV style had thoroughly impressed itself on the woodwork of Spain, the *sillon frailero* evolved a tall, upholstered back, scrolled or turned legs, and elaborate, serpentine stretchers. While the overall shape of monk chairs was largely maintained, spiral-turned legs and stretchers brought them gradually closer to Louis XIII chairs—albeit long after the fashion for them had passed in France. The Spanish type is more vigorous and more masculine than its French counterpart.

After the Methuen Treaty of 1703, Spanish and Portuguese chairs owed much more to English example, and these in turn were influenced by French chairs. Iberian craftsmen emulated the Queen Anne style, with cabriole legs, splat backs, and slipper, claw, and ball feet. The only difference was that the Iberian chairs exhibited a more exaggerated curve of the back and deeper aprons. A chair that seems to have existed only in seventeenth-century France was a folding chair called a *perroquet*. It had a back with finials that hooked forward, so that it resembled a parakeet. The X-frame was hinged transversely so that the chair folded front-to-back, unlike a *pliant*, which folded side-to-side. *Perroquets* were often used at the dining table, or on campaign, in which case, they were upholstered in leather:

A l'armée, le Roi seul avait un fauteuil, Monseigneur et tout ce qui etait à table avait des sièges à dos, de maroquin noir, qui se pouvait briser, pour les voiturier q'on appeloit des perroquets

[*On campaign, the king alone had an armchair. Monsieur and everyone else at table sat in chairs with backs upholstered in black leather, which could be broken down for travel, and which were called "perroquets"*].

Perroquets were thus versions of the early Chinese warlords' folding chairs and precursors of the campaign chairs of the nineteenth and twentieth centuries. They were also similar to the early Spanish Renaissance folding *sillones fraileros*, which likewise had leather seats.

One seat was reserved for bodily functions. Called variously *chaise percée, chaise d'affaires*, or *garde-robe*, it was, starting at the end of the fifteenth century, the subject of many anecdotes. At Versailles during the reign of Louis XIV, no fewer than two hundred seventy-four *chaises percées* are mentioned in sources. Some were simple, some contained a drawer, and some were shaped like stools. Others were made to resemble a stack of books, which were humorously given such titles as *Voyage aux Pays-Bas* [Trip to the Netherlands], since France was at war with Holland at the time.

The *chaises d'affaires* at Versailles were often magnificent, with upholstery in blue, red, or green damask or red velvet. The king's personal chair was of red velvet with three slipcovers, one in red damask, one in green velvet, and the third in red velvet. It was an honor to be admitted to the king's presence when he was sitting on his *chaise percée*. Nicolas Fouquet (1615–80), Louis XIV's fabulously rich minister of finance, also had two very luxurious *chaises percées* in his bedroom at Vaux-le-Vicomte, made of green velvet with gold and silver fringe. *Chaises percées* were often placed in the bedroom in full view; otherwise, they were located in a small room adjacent to the bedroom, hence the name *garde-robe*.

In the same period, the English were also using rich fabric to upholster their "close stools," as the British called their version of the *chaise percée*. One of these seats, created for William III in 1699, was "Formed with gold lace and gilt nails. Lock and handles gilt worth four pounds and ten shillings for the frame of the close stoole and covering it with damask with two pewter pans." The English soon seem to have adopted a box shape for close stools, and in the early years of the eighteenth century they were no longer covered with fabric.

A close stool from Dunham Massey from about 1710 is veneered with figured burr walnut, cross-banded, and bordered with ebony. But in general in England, practicality always seems to have trumped luxury of effect.

Saint-Simon recalled in his memoirs that while at war, the duc de Vendôme customarily received his generals, dictated his letters, and distributed his orders while sitting on his *chaise percée*. One day, "the duke of Parma having matters to negotiate with M. de Vendôme, sent at first the bishop of Parma, who was shocked beyond measure at being received by the duke seated upon a *chaise percée* and was still more so when the latter stood up and turned around to wipe himself." Later in his reign, Louis XIV reduced some of his public display; however, some of the most refined and luxurious *chaises d'affaires* were created for his successor, Louis XV, in whose reign comfort prevailed over etiquette.

<
A French engraving showing a woman washing while seated on a day bed, c. 1700. Versailles. RMN

day beds, sofas, and canapés

The word "sofa" is of Eastern origin and was first used in France around 1680 to designate a divanlike seat. De Caillères, a witty French writer, described it in 1692 as a kind of day bed in the Turkish manner: *Une espèce de lit de repos à la manière des Turcs*. Saint-Simon thought it necessary to explain precisely what a sofa in Turkey was: "In the East, it was merely the dais or platform on which the Grand Vizier sat cross-legged in his audience hall, the person he was receiving occupying a cushion before him on the floor. To sit on the sofa near the Vizier was a rare and great honor."

The day bed seems to have originated a little earlier than the sofa, around 1625 or 1630, serving as a seat for lords or ladies, usually in the bedchamber. Day beds often had a raised pillow-like end, recalling beds pictured on ancient Greek and Roman antiquities. The French called it *lit de repos* or *lit de jour*, and commonly reclined on it at full length. They did the same on a canapé. Many royal inventories mention *lit de repos en canapé*. Early canapés had a bedlike mattress and seem to have served the same purpose. In 1709, the injured maréchal de Villars, paid the great honor of a visit by Louis XIV, received the king while lying on a canapé and wearing a robe.

Canapés, sofas, and day beds reflected a desire for a more comfortable life. During the seventeenth century, no clear distinction seems to have been made among the "sopha," the *lit de repos*, and the canapé (also called *conopée*). At the beginning of the eighteenth century, however, the distinction between the *lit de repos*, or day bed, and the sofa or canapé became clear. The *lit de repos* is the ancestor of the popular chaise longue of the eighteenth, nineteenth, and twentieth centuries. One of the earliest English accounts of a sofa is dated 1700, when Thomas Roberts

>
A rare Louis XIV gilt-wood *lit de repos*. Collection Perpitch, Paris

<
A drawing of a round-sided canapé for the dauphin's apartment at Versailles. From an eighteenth-century album, *Décoration intérieure et jardins de Versailles*. The inscriptions on these drawings describe such pieces both as "canapés" and as "sophas," so the confusion between the two terms continued for some time. RMN. Gerard Blot

<
A drawing for the dauphin's apartment at Versailles, c. 1680, showing a sleeping chair. From an eighteenth-century album, *Décoration intérieure et jardins de Versailles*. RMN. Gerard Blot

produced "4 large Sophas" for Hampton Court, also charging £3.00 for mending "guilt Chaires and sophas in the long Gallery."

As we have seen, long couches and sophisticated upholsteries were brought to England after the restoration of Charles II. In large houses all over Europe, sets of chairs and stools were generally supplemented by a pair of settees or sofas. The German and Swedish courts followed the French fashion, including the use of sofas, day beds, settees, and canapés. The term "settee" does not seem to have been used before the early eighteenth century. "Settees" are usually less comfortable than "sofas," with more wood and less upholstery. In the eighteenth century, especially during the reign of Louis XV, a multitude of sofas and canapés were made in a variety of shapes, with such exotic names as "ottomane" and "paphose." They were often associated with frivolous and slightly dissipated behavior, as though comfort induced promiscuity.

THE RÉGENCE (1715–23), ROCOCO, AND THE REIGN OF LOUIS XV (1723–74)

When Louis XIV died in 1715, his nephew, Philippe, duke of Orléans, became regent of France during the minority of the new king, the five-year-old Louis XV. However, long before Louis XIV died, a modification of his style had already begun. A softer mood was settling in, abolishing the pompous grandeur of his reign. During the early years of the Régence, as the years of Louis XV's minority are called, the strict forms of the old style were lightened by the introduction of curves, and the massive Louis XIV armchair relaxed into softer outlines and freer ornaments.

With the tyranny of Versailles at an end, the aristocracy thankfully returned to Paris to pursue their own pleasurable lives. Numerous "salons" gathered around such witty women as the marquise de Lambert in Paris and the duchess du Maine at Sceaux, attracting writers, scientists, and other *beaux esprits*. Such gatherings required comfortable, movable, informal armchairs. Etiquette lost some of its appeal, particularly since the regent himself, bored and irritated by the endless quarrels over precedence at court, hated ceremony.

During the Régence, Paris became the center of European culture; it was the time of Watteau, the young Voltaire, the plays of Marivaux, and the precepts of Montesquieu. City life became informal, intimate, sensuous, and luxurious, as elegance, poise, wit, brilliant conversation, and charm were cultivated at a level unknown elsewhere. The rococo style originated in Paris, with the desire for an intimate, pleasing way of living in reaction to the solemnity of the baroque. Its first, exclusively French, phase is known as the Régence style, a term that loosely describes the transition from the ponderous style of Louis XIV to the lighter, more feminine manner of Louis XV. It embodied an extravagantly free naturalism,

A painting showing a council of state presided over by the duke of Orléans and the cardinal de Fleury during the Régence, as the minority of Louis XV was called. Châteaux de Versailles et de Trianon. Photograph: RMN. Gerard Blot

based on curved, irregular forms. The craze for *chinoiseries* and other exotic motifs was reflected in the ornamental character of the Régence and Louis XV styles. Also favored were rocks (*rocailles*), shells (*coquilles*), birds, and flowers, all of which were translated into carved ornaments for seats and wood paneling. The term *rocaille* was mockingly converted to "rococo" after the style's popularity waned, when it was considered frivolous for having ignored the example of Classical Antiquity.

The best-known rococo designers were Nicolas Pineau (1684–1734) and Juste-Aurèle Meissonier (1693–1750). Pineau began his career in Russia, designing *boiseries*—ornamental woodwork—for Peter the Great's cabinet in his country palace at Peterhof. Pineau returned from Russia in 1727 and soon became one of the most fashionable designers in Paris. A number of his drawings for chairs survive, in which he introduced asymmetrical scrollwork and *rocailles*. Later, Meissonier's designs carried the tendency toward asymmetry even further. Meissonier, who had been born in Turin, was also an architect, painter, and silversmith. In his lively style of extreme, twisted curves known as the *goût pittoresque*, he created interiors and furniture for patrons as far away as Portugal and Poland. After his death, his ideas quickly fell into disfavor, but they provided the point of departure for many foreign artists and craftsmen, including François de Cuvilliés in Munich, the Hoppenhaupt brothers in Berlin, Haberman in Augsburg, Piffetti in Turin, Rastrelli at Tsarskoje Selo, Rehn and Masreliez in Stockholm, Locke and Thomas Chippendale in London, and Randolph and Affleck in Philadelphia. These designers reworked

<
A Louis XV carved beechwood armchair, upholstered in Savonnerie tapestry, c. 1725–30. Musée Nissim de Camondo, Paris. Photograph: Antoine Bootz

> A wide, upholstered armchair of the type known as a *marquise*, made to accommodate the voluminous dresses of c. 1760–65, signed by Nicolas Heurtaut (1720–71). Heurtaut was a great chair-maker who was registered as a *maître* in 1755. Examples of his seats can be seen at the Metropolitan Museum of Art and the Louvre. This piece formerly belonged to Greta Garbo. Collection French and Co., New York

> A rare eighteenth-century folding campaign armchair. Bill Blass Collection

<
A Dutch burr walnut armchair, c. 1735. Commercial, political, and social relations between England and the Netherlands in the late seventeenth century led to a continuous exchange of ideas between them. Although at first most innovations in chair design were introduced by the Dutch to England, by the early eighteenth century the Dutch began to incorporate English features into their chairs, such as the high, hollow backs, broad, pierced splats, and the angles at which the front legs are set, as seen here. Chinese Porcelain Company, New York

> A pair of Portuguese armchairs, c. 1745. The English trade with Portugal led to a strong English influence in Portuguese chairs. The high, hollow backs and broad, pierced splats are typical of English style and are remarkably similar to those of the Dutch armchair, itself influenced by the English. Chinese Porcelain Company, New York

Meissonier's motifs in a series of elegant variations adapted to indigenous taste, which made them widely popular.

The Germanic countries adopted the rococo style for most of their eighteenth century furniture, and it continued in the shapes of German seats long after the classical motifs of the Louis XVI style had been accepted. In Italy, the rococo spirit flourished early in the century. Indeed, many features of the mature rococo found in Meissonier's engravings of the 1730s originated in Italy. Thus, there is no clear division in Italy between the baroque and the rococo. The designs of Italian seats of this period are often exaggerated, although their theatrical effects are charming. Venice, still a center of wealth and prestige, led in the production of sophisticated seats, most of which were painted and lacquered.

The rococo style in its more fanciful forms was unsuited to the sober taste of English patrons and craftsmen. However, the English derivation of *rocailles*, in spite of this difference in temperament, dominated English chair design for nearly two decades. The carver and gilder Matthias Locke and his collaborator, Henry Copland, were producing chair designs as early as the mid-1740s. These men were responsible for many of the chair drawings in Chippendale's *Gentleman and Cabinet-Maker's Director* (first published in 1754), in which the rococo style is combined with excursions into the Chinese and Gothic tastes. All the foreign elements that had flowed into England during the previous hundred years were finally fused into a distinctive national style, and seats became truly English at last.

With the power of the Netherlands waning in the early eighteenth century and Flanders virtually a French province after 1700, an adaptation of the French style of Louis XV dominated Dutch and Flemish chairs. In Russia, many chairs for palaces were imported from Paris, as they were in Denmark and Sweden. The skill of the Russian carvers was considerable, their imaginations vivid. They had no difficulty executing lavish rococo designs. Swedish and Danish craftsmen were sent to study in Paris, and their seats look very French, combining Parisian techniques with an admirable restraint.

Throughout most of the eighteenth century, Sweden enjoyed a close relationship with France, and the Swedish court and aristocracy spoke and wrote in French. During the reign of Adolph Frederick (reigned 1751–71) and his queen Louisa Ulrica, sister of Frederick the Great of Prussia, French influence was at its zenith. The two thrones made by Adrien Masreliez for the coronation replicate exactly that of Louis XV, which, though destroyed during the Revolution of 1789, was described by the duke de Luynes in his memoirs, noted on May 30, 1743:

Le Roi a fait changer, il y a trois jours, le meuble de son grand appartment. . . . Dans la chambre du throne on a mis un throne neuf, dessous un dais en baldaquin, qui est riche et de bon goût.

[*The king had the furniture of his grand apartment changed three days ago. . . . In the throne room a new throne has been installed, on a rich and tasteful dais with a baldachin*].

Masreliez followed the custom of the time when designing an exceptional seat: he first made a model of the throne in wood and wax to be approved by his royal clients. The dais for Adolph Frederick and Louisa Ulrica's thrones was also after the French model, and was executed by a Frenchman, Pierre Duru, who lived in Stockholm. The fauteuils in the audience room were after French models as well, as were the stools (*ployants*), which were made from a model by another Frenchman, Jean Gaspar Caillon. Although the upholstery was of tapestry made in Stockholm, its decorative motifs were inspired by La Fontaine's fables.

The craze for rococo spread to the Spanish court, as well. French influence came to Spain with the accession of Philip V (1683–1746), grandson of Louis XIV, in 1700. The rococo's early phase, with designs featuring rocks, shells, and foliage, became as popular at the Spanish court as at Paris. However, the seats there were usually executed with less craftsmanship.

The search for comfort, beauty, and luxury led to the invention of many new forms of seats. Carved sofas of all shapes were created to match delicately painted paneling; the skills of the craftsmen throughout Europe improved, resulting in seats of light construction, elegance, and whimsical design.

fauteuils, armchairs, and side chairs

In the epicurean society of the Régence, comfort was all-important, an interest that the seats of the period reflect. Philippe d'Orléans had lived long enough at court to understand the importance of the royal image in impressing both the people at home and the powers abroad. He established himself in Paris at the Palais Royal, which he had inherited from his father in 1701, and which he had had restored by Gilles Marie Oppenord. The first redecorated room was Philippe's bedchamber, which contained a canopied bed covered in crimson silk fringed with gold, eight armchairs upholstered to match, several stools, and a large, pink plush armchair for the toilette. In the Cabinet de Travail stood a magnificent desk, and next to it—for the fulfillment of his more carnal desires—a chaise longue in carved, gilded wood.

Although the regent viewed court etiquette as a distasteful obligation, he did not succeed in abolishing it entirely. His wife, the duchess of Orléans, who shared his lack of enthusiasm for court life, spent hours reclining on a gold-embroidered canapé in her white and gold salon, admiring her collection of *chinoiseries*. Madame, the regent's mother, still a stickler for the rules, complained that "It is pure laziness that keeps Mme. d'Orléans from dining with us; if she eats with me she must

>
A French painted walnut *fauteuil de bureau*, upholstered in leather, c. 1750. This unusual chair features armrests with hidden compartments that can be opened out. Musée Nissim de Camondo, Paris. Photograph: Antoine Bootz

>>
The *fauteuil de bureau*, with its armrest compartments open. Musée Nissim de Camondo, Paris. Photograph: Antoine Bootz

content herself with a stool, whereas when she eats in her rooms with her son and her favorites, she lies on a canapé or sits in an armchair." In choosing comfort and avoiding the company of her strict mother-in-law, the duchess of Orléans was following the spirit of the time.

The Régence armchair is characterized by cabriolet legs ending in *pieds de biche*, or doe's feet. Although it projects a sense of movement toward the legs, it has a more balanced seat than chairs in the Louis XIV style, and its vertical lines are curved to flow evenly into the horizontal of the apron. The typical curve is re-curved like a crossbow; the back is lower than that of earlier seats and is more curved, to follow the shape of the body and to avoid interference with the elaborate coiffures of the time. One can day-dream or sleep in a Régence armchair.

The frames of chairs became more visible, allowing them to be richly carved. Stretchers to brace the legs tended to disappear, however they still persisted with the *fauteuil en confessional*, or *bergère*, after 1725. The *bergère* is an extraordinarily comfortable chair; its upholstered back envelops the seat, which is fitted with a thick down cushion. A description of the *bergère* dating to the first quarter of the eighteenth century from the Archives Nationales illustrates this feature:

Façon de deux bergères . . . les dossiers garnis en pleins, les bourlets de la plate-forme piqués a l'anglaise, avec leurs carreaux en coutil et plume, couverts de damas ver . . .

[*Two bergères . . . the backs upholstered, the seat cushion with stitches in the English style, with cushions in ticking and feathers, covered in green damask . . .*].

The fun-loving society of the Régence indulged in endless card games, which led to the creation of the *voyeuse*. This was a variant of the *bergère* with a flat back surmounted by a rail that allowed an observer to lean over the sitter from behind and watch the game. The *voyelle* is an armless version of this chair, usually made for men to sit astride, using the front rail as a support for their crossed arms. Alas, neither of these seats survived the century. Early in the eighteenth century, a similar English chair was introduced for use in

182 high style: baroque, rococo & neoclassical chairs

> An eighteenth-century *fauteuil de malade*, or invalid's chair. Didier Aaron Collection, Paris

libraries. The reader sat with his back to the front of the chair and rested his arm on the crest-rail in a position like that of the sitter in the *voyelle*. Such chairs were also used by spectators at cock fights.

Shortly before the coronation of Louis XV, the court moved back to Versailles, the regent occupying quarters on the ground floor that had once been those of Louis XIV's son, the dauphin. On December 1, 1723, the regent was sitting by the fireplace of his drawing room, in an armchair of red leather. Feeling depressed, he asked the duchess de Falaris, his favorite of the moment, to come and gossip a bit. She had no sooner started on a story when to her horror, the regent suddenly fell forward. He had died instantly of a massive stroke in his armchair, after ruling France for eight years.

After the regent's death, the court of the thirteen-year-old Louis XV remained at Versailles. It took another seven years to erase the vestiges of the pomp of the court of Louis XIV, rococo curves and light, cheerful colors replacing many of the old forms. Never before had furniture been so exquisite. In keeping with the fashion of the

> A Venetian procession chair, decorated with *arte povera*, c. 1770. Collection Trianon Antiques. Photograph: Ogden Gigli

Régence, comfort, convenience, and elegance were prized above grandeur. The era of the sophisticated *petits appartements* had begun.

In keeping with the new spirit, rooms were smaller and more intimate, and chairs increasingly fitted to feminine contours rather than to majesty. Louis XV seats enfold the sitter in curves adapted to the body, and in order to accommodate those curves, the stretchers connecting the legs of the chairs, which had lingered on to the end of the Régence, were dispensed with around 1725. For still greater comfort, upholstered arm-pads appeared. Most chairs were painted, gilded, or silvered. The use of silver, which reached the height of its popularity in the 1730s, was soon abandoned in France, as oxidization of the silver spoiled the intended effect.

Architectural chairs, made to stand against wall paneling, with straight, often oval-shaped backs and low seats, were called *à la reine*. The inventory of Mlle. Desmare, a famous actress, mentions for the first time in 1746 two chairs *à la Reine couvertes de velours rouges et bleus* [*à la reine* upholstered in red and blue velvet]. The term fell out of use after 1780. The *fauteuil en cabriolet*, a smaller and lighter chair with a curved back, became popular after 1740, the result of the search for comfort and the rococo aesthetic. Other smaller, movable chairs included the popular armless chair, designed for voluminous skirts, and the *fauteuil canné*. The Dutch, who had brought caning to Europe during the seventeenth century, were responsible for its introduction at Versailles around 1729. Caned armchairs were appreciated for their cooling comfort. In the Louis XV's household inventory, four luxurious, sculpted cane armchairs can be found with their cushions in lemon-colored leather:

Quatre fauteuils de canné et bois de hetre vernis, à dossiers cintrez et sculptez ornez d'une campanne de sculpture autour du siège, les accostoirs aussy sculptez par les bouts, et garnis de maroquin citron, clouez de cloux argente.

[*Four varnished beechwood and caned fauteuils with curved and carved backs decorated with carving around the seat, the ends of the armrests carved as well, and upholstered in lemon-colored morocco, nailed with silver studs*].

Madame de Pompadour, Louis XV's favorite and a major patron of the arts, ordered in 1756 for her beloved chateau de Belleville *un petit fauteuil à contours sculpté garnis en canne fine*. [A small sculpted armchair, fitted with fine cane.] Every room in her chateau was a masterpiece of decor. Paintings by Boucher were fitted into the *boiseries* over the doors. Jacques Veerbeckt, the greatest sculptor of *boiseries*, carved the paneling, while the Aubusson and Gobelins manufactories provided tapestries and carpets. The fact that Madame de Pompadour ordered caned chairs for such a refined setting shows that they were fashionable indeed. Caned chairs were used extensively as dressing table chairs, with loose cushions of lemon or red morocco.

The *ébéniste* Etienne Meunier was a specialist in making *fauteuils de bureau*. An especially beautiful example of his work is a caned one of rosewood and palisander marquetry—rare in French chairs—signed and dated 1750, now in the Rijskmuseum in Amsterdam. An accomplished maker of veneered and inlaid chairs combining the

>

A Louis XV *duchesse brisée*. In France a chaise longue with a rounded back is called a *duchesse*. If the foot is surrounded on three sides by a low, curving rail, it is said to be *en bateau*; if it is made in two or three sections, each of which may be used separately as a seat, it is called a *duchesse brisée*. Musée Nissim de Camondo, Paris. Photograph: Antoine Bootz

<

A rare French musician's armchair, 1755. L'Antiquaire & The Connoisseur, Inc.

high style: baroque, rococo & neoclassical chairs 187

> A Louis XV *bergère* or *fauteuil à oreilles* ("with ears"). Musée Nissim de Camondo, Paris. Photograph: Antoine Bootz

< A *canapé à joues* ("with cheeks"), c. 1770–75. With its ample forms—still Louis XV—and its remarkable carved ornamentation of classical inspiration, it is somewhat reminiscent of the work of Foliot or Delanois. Unfortunately it lacks any mark that might establish its origin. Beech, carved and gilt. Musée Nissim de Camondo, Paris. Photograph: Antoine Bootz

Louis XV style with that of Thomas Chippendale was Abraham Roentgen (1711–93), the talented son of a Saxon cabinetmaker. After working in England for eight years and then in Holland in about 1750, he opened a workshop in Germany, at Neuwied on the Rhine. He excelled at marquetry, creating elaborate chairs blending English, Dutch, and French influences.

Bergères continued to be appreciated for their comfort. One cozy version, the *bergère en confessional*, features wings on each side called *joues à oreilles* for greater comfort and privacy. Sometimes the seat was made of straw—like one used by the nanny of the king's younger son, the duc de Bourgogne—with cushions, made of soft leather. Madame Victoire, another one of Louis XV's children, claimed that her love for the comfort of her *bergère* forbade her to follow her older sister into a convent. Madame Campan in her memoirs related that Madame Victoire, pointing to her *bergère*, had remarked, *Voilà un fauteuil qui me perd!* ["This is a chair responsible for my ruin!"] Fauteuils could be the ruin of women in other ways, too. In the novel *Faublas*, the narrator describes a house

of ill repute, with a mechanical fauteuil in one room. This invention consisted of a seat in which a woman could be strapped with her legs spread, and then easily raped.

Il n'a rien de remarquable que cet infernal fauteuil: une malheureuse qu'on y jette se trouve renversée sure le dos, ses bras restent ouverts, ses jambes s'écartent mollement, et on la viole sans qu'elle puisse opposer la moindre résistance.

[*There was nothing remarkable except this infernal fauteuil: a luckless woman flung into it found herself turned over on her back, her arms open, her legs pinned gently apart, so that she could be raped without being able to offer the least resistance.*]

Such chairs were apparently actually advertised; in 1780 they were mentioned in a magazine, *Almanac sous verre*, which described them as "very clean"! The marquis de Sade, in his novel *Justine*, included chairs in numerous pornographic episodes. Chairs seem to have been very handy for that particular brand of gymnastics:

When I was in the state they wished, they drew up their chairs, which were provided with protruding armrests; thus a narrow space between the chairs was left and into it I was deposited; and thus they were able to study me at their leisure: while regarded my fore end, the other mused upon my behind. . . . Their state called for more substantial pleasures; the impudicious creatures rose and made me mount upon a large chair, my forearms leaning upon its back, my knee propped up upon its arms and my behind arched so that it was prominently thrust toward them.

Catherine the Great of Russia was said to have possessed carved chairs portraying various sexual acts and organs, but since there is no real evidence to support this story, these chairs are probably another aspect of the legend of depravity that surrounded the empress, along with her supposed equine lovers. Pornographic chairs most certainly did exist, however, and the eighteenth

high style: baroque, rococo & neoclassical chairs

<
One of a pair of Louis XV gilt-wood *fauteuils à la reine*, by Jean Gourdin, known as Père Gourdin, after a design attributed to Nicolas and Dominique Pineau, c. 1715. When vast hoop skirts came into fashion, the arm rests of chairs had to be set back to make room for them. Inventories only began to reflect this change on a large scale in the 1720s. Collection I. Goldsmith. Christie's

>
A detail of the armchair. Jean Gourdin was appointed *maître menuisier* in 1714 and opened a shop on the rue de Cléry in Paris, where most of the chair-makers had their businesses. His clientele included the marquis de Bercy and the duchesse de Mazarin. After his two sons, Jean Baptiste and Michel, became *maîtres* in 1748 and 1752, he began to stamp his oeuvre *Père Gourdin*. Private collection

century, a period of extravagant licentiousness, gave birth to them. Once created, their usage persisted. It was impossible to put this genie back in its bottle.

Bathroom chairs, or *chaises d'affaires*, became even more luxurious in the reign of Louis XV than they had been previously. One of Louis XV's *garde-meubles* (another name for this type) was of black lacquer in the Chinese taste:

Une chaise d'affaires, fond de vernis noir et aventurine du Japon, à la Chinoise, le dedans du couvercle et la lunette de lac rouge, le bourrelet de velours vert, ladite chaise haute de dix neuf pouces sur quinze de large et dix neuf de profondeur

[*A chaise d'affaires, finished in black lacquer and Japanese aventurine in the Chinese style, the seat and cover of which are finished in red lacquer, with a cushion of green velvet, the said chair being nineteen inches high, fifteen wide, and nineteen deep*].

The emperor Charles VII (Karl Albrecht of Bavaria; 1697–1745) also had a very refined *chaise percée* in the Chinese style, in blue on a white ground, at the Amalienburg Palace, near Munich. Among the women of her time, Madame de Pompadour seems to have been the owner of several of the most luxurious *chaises percées*, featuring gilt bronze mounts and marquetry in rare woods. One of these, delivered in 1753, cost a small fortune:

Une chaise percée à dossier, plaqué en bois de rose à fleurs, garnie de ronze d'or moulu qui coutait 1650 livres

[*A chaise percée with a back, inlaid in rosewood with flowers, embellished with ormolu, which cost 1650 livres*].

Later in the century, however, comfort replaced luxury; Louis XV's favorite *chaise percée* in later life was a no-nonsense model in oak, with a sink and faucets in the English manner.

After 1730 a great range of chairs appeared, with new names such as *marquise*, *duchesse*,

turquoise, *veilleuse*, *athénienne*, and *fauteuil volant*. The strict regulations of the guild helped assure their quality. Guild regulation divided the furniture craft between *menuiserie* (joinery and chair-making) and *ébénisterie* (cabinetmaking and veneering). By legislation in 1744 and 1751, makers were obliged to sign their works with an approved stamp. The corporation of *menuisiers* and *ébénistes* included not only the two principal crafts but all related trades as well. Regulations ordered that the *menuisier* could only make the frame of the chair, which then went to the carver, gilder, or painter, and finally to the upholsterer. The role of *menuisier* was primary; it was he who was permitted to build the chair, choose the carver, and decide its finish. It was also he who dealt with the upholsterer and who was allowed to sell the finished chair. Among the exceptional Louis XV seats were *bergères* signed by such masters as Michel Cresson, *fauteuils en cabriolet* and *à chassis* by Nicolas-Quinibert Foliot, a *bergère en cabriolet* by Louis Delanois, a *petite chaise à la Reine* by Tilliard, and a *fauteuil à la Reine* by Nicolas

Heurtaut. Heurtaut had the unusual distinction of being both a carver and a *menuisier*. The quality of his seats was unparalleled.

The peerless beauty of Louis XV chairs was imitated all over Europe, especially in Germany, and the French artistic domination of that region, which had begun in the late seventeenth century, continued throughout the rococo period. Parisian fashions in furniture, interior decoration, dress, and literature prevailed in German society, and French was the language spoken at most of the German courts. On November 24, 1750, during a visit to Berlin, Voltaire wrote: "I find myself here in France; no one speaks anything but French; German is only for soldiers and horses; it is needed only on the road." From the end of the seventeenth century, well-bred Germans were sent on their version of the Grand Tour, known as the "Knight's Tour," which included visits to England, Holland, Spain, and Italy, but particularly to France.

Germany was the least nationalistic of European countries in the eighteenth century because there was no united German state. Instead, there were more than 600 German states, loosely bound together as the Holy Roman Empire. There were sixty-three ecclesiastical principalities of differing sizes, nine electorates, and fifty-one free cities, each with its sovereign prince and its own court, each in a different stage of economic and cultural development. Although the guild, or *Handwerk*, for chair-makers had been established during the Middle Ages, the regulations for a *Stulmacher* were regional. The prospective chair-maker had to create a "masterpiece," the form and dimensions of which were prescribed to the smallest detail. Because this model remained constant for decades, it was often old-fashioned, and its use

<
A sofa by Michel Cresson, from the Château d'Abondant, c. 1747–50. The unusual shape of the backrest reflects the fact that the piece was carved to fit the wood paneling of the room. Musée du Louvre. RMN

high style: baroque, rococo & neoclassical chairs 191

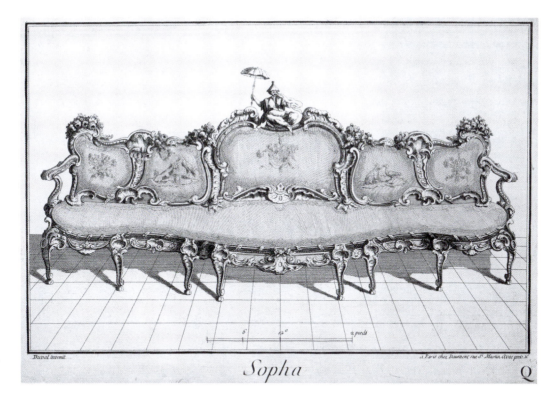

> An etching of a sofa by Jean-Charles Delafosse (1734–91), whose ornamental designs for chairs were highly influential and contributed to the dissemination of the *goût antique* just as the Louis XVI style was coming into fashion. The Metropolitan Museum of Art

> A beechwood sofa with original pink and white paint, possibly German. It is interesting to note its similarities to the etching by Delafosse shown above. It also recalls drawings by the German rococo decorator and furniture-designer Johann Michael Hoppenhaupt (1709–69). L'Antiquaire & The Connoisseur, Inc.

explains why new styles took so long to penetrate Germany, and why, when finally adopted, they survived longer than anywhere else.

The most delicate German rococo style developed in Bavaria, where the elector Maximilian Emanuel had his palace in Munich, the Residenz, and his country palace, the Nymphenburg, just outside the city. The character of Bavarian rococo was established early by the architect and designer François de Cuvilliés (1695–1768). Born in Flanders, Cuvilliés had come to Bavaria as a court dwarf to the elector, who recognized his talent and sent him to study under Blondel in Paris from 1720 to 1724. He became court architect in Munich in 1725. His interiors in the Residenz (1729–37; partly destroyed) and the Amalienburg pavilion in the park at Nymphenburg (1734–39), have a sparkling, whimsical delicacy hardly equaled elsewhere.

<
A north German armchair in the French manner, c. 1755–60, by Abraham Roentgen (1711–93), father of the German cabinetmaker David Roentgen (1743–1807). This exceptional armchair is closely related to similar pieces Abraham made around 1755 for the count of Wied and members of the Schönborn family. Today these pieces are preserved in the castles at Neuwied and Pommersfelden. This armchair is a document par excellence for the dominant French and English influence on eighteenth-century German furniture. Private collection

>
A detail of the armchair shown at left. Private collection

From 1738 until his death, Cuvilliés published a series of engraved designs for ornament, interiors, and seats even lighter and more fantastic than those of his French contemporaries. His designs had a great influence in France and England as well as Germany, notably on Johann Michael Hoppenhaupt, who worked in Berlin for Frederick the Great.

The rococo came late to Prussia. Friedrich Wilhelm I (reigned 1713–40), had little time or taste for the arts, but his son and successor, Frederick the Great (Friedrich II; reigned 1740–86), embarked on a great building program. A Francophile and friend of Voltaire with a taste for poetry, philosophy, music, and art, Frederick transformed his dowdy palaces into models of Frenchified elegance. In 1740 the *goût pittoresque*, the most fanciful phase of the rococo, was at the height of its popularity, and it was in this style that Frederick's palaces were decorated. Until 1746, his architect was Georg von Knobelsdorff, who with the carver and furniture-maker Johann August Nahl established the character of the Frederican rococo. Nahl's style was more vivacious and fanciful than that of any French rococo designer, his chairs abounding in bold, projecting curves and florid, carved details. In 1745 building began on Frederick's summer retreat, Sans Souci, just outside the Potsdam gates. Completed in 1747, Sans Souci was a relatively simple, one-story palace built to Frederick's own plans, which were contrary to Knobelsdorff's ideas. This led to a serious quarrel, and Johann Michael Hoppenhaupt succeeded Nahl as a "Directeur des ornaments." The palace was exquisitely decorated. The courtier and diarist Count Ernst von Lehndorff rhapsodized that "The house, the garden, the furniture, the statues, in short, everything is enchanting and delightful."

Hoppenhaupt was responsible for the interior decoration not only of Sans Souci, but also of the Berlin Schloss, the Potsdam Stadtschloss (both now destroyed), and the Neues Palais at Potsdam. He retired from royal service in 1750, and between

1751 and 1755 published numerous designs for furniture and ornaments. His seat designs are among the most accomplished of the rococo period. Stylistically they derive from the designs of Cuvilliés, some drawings of sofas being eerily similar. Hoppenhaupt's style, however, is more distant from French prototypes, with more curves and fanciful decorations. His seats, enhanced with extravagant cherubs and strangely shaped leaves are, however, well balanced. Hoppenhaupt's influence on German chair design runs very deep, and his style persisted in Germany longer than in other countries.

Frederick the Great had such conservative taste that the style of his furniture hardly changed during the course of his reign. Ailing in June 1786, he was visited by his minister Ewald von Hertzberg, who later wrote that he was "much swollen . . . with dropsy; he could not move without assistance from a chair in which he rested day and night." On August 16, the king awakened only with difficulty. At midnight, sinking in his chair, he murmured, *La montagne est passée, nous irons mieux* [We have crossed the mountain; things will go better now].

In the early morning of August 17, 1786, he died in his favorite armchair, which is still at Sans Souci. It is a heavy, winged *bergère*, painted a yellowish color, after a design created by Hoppenhaupt almost thirty years before.

Of the southern German courts, one of the wealthiest was that of the prince-bishops of Würzburg. Much of the furniture of their Residenz, begun in 1719 by the architect Balthasar Neumann, was designed by the sculptor Franz Anton von Schlott. In 1757, Adam Friedrich von Seinsheim was elected prince-bishop of Würzburg; subsequently he was also elected prince-bishop of Bamberg, which made him one of the most powerful princes in southern Germany. He divided his time between his palaces at Würzburg and Bamberg, and his three summer castles Veitshochheim, Werneck, and Seehof. Some carved chairs and settees at Würzburg recall the engravings of Johann Michael Hoppenhaupt, while at Bamberg the carved seats show the influence of the sculptor Ferdinand Tietz.

Preferring the country to the city, Seinsheim spent several months a year at Seehof, embellishing the castle and park. A unique set of eight rococo seats—two corner settees, a pair of armchairs, and four side chairs—survives from the Franckenstein pavilion at Seehof, featuring off-white trelliswork and carved, gilt, and painted foliage on the inner backs. These pieces recall engravings by Hoppenhaupt for a garden room with matching wall decorations and seats. They also demonstrate the magnificence and imagination of German rococo seats toward the third quarter of the eighteenth century. Bayreuth seats were also very exuberant, characterized by unrestricted use of naturalistic motifs such as foliage, flowers, reeds, and even birds. One example in the rooms at the Neues Schloss in Bayreuth was furnished with a settee *confidante*, its gilt frame decorated with brightly colored flowers. Another room in the palace had four chairs with yellow frames carved with green

> A gilded rococo armchair from Hamburg. Most German princes followed the court style of Versailles, and often sent their furniture-makers to be trained in France. Early rococo chairs in Germany were therefore based on the *goût pittoresque* of Blondel, Pineau, and Meissonier. In the important German states regional variations quickly developed under the influence of court artists and craftsmen. Among the great centers were Munich, Würzburg, Bayreuth, and Bamberg. Saxony and, later, Prussia were also very active.

< An Italian gilt-wood side chair, Rome, c. 1760. L'Antiquaire & The Connoisseur, Inc.

196 high style: baroque, rococo & neoclassical chairs

foliage. These, too, are very much in the spirit of Hoppenhaupt's engravings.

The furniture of Saxony, by contrast, tended to more traditional forms, and showed some English influence. A notable exception to this rule was the taste of elector Augustus II the Strong (reigned 1694–1733; also intermittently king of Poland), who had a preference for *chinoiseries*. After his death in 1733, his son and successor, Friedrich Augustus II (also Augustus III of Poland, 1733–63), had inventories made of his various residences. In the Wasserpalais and Bergpalais inventories, numerous heavy oak chairs are mentioned. In the great room of the Wasserpalais, there were twenty-seven splat-back chairs—a far remove indeed from the vivacious curves of Hoppenhaupt!

In the eighteenth century, Italy, like Germany, was made up of many small states, and it was politically unstable. Austria had annexed Milan and Mantua. Genoa had been cut off from the greater part of her territories. With the death of the last Farnese prince, a Bourbon now ruled Parma and the house of Habsburg-Lorraine governed Florence. Thus, the only independent states of any importance were the Republic of Venice and the papacy, centered in Rome. The Venetians, with their love of festivity and elegance, were perhaps the first Italians to imitate the court of Louis XV, but all of Italy soon followed, adopting the language and fashions of the French court, building furniture and chairs inspired by French models. Venice became a center for high-living Europeans, and the fashion for small, intimate apartments quickly won approval. Created for these spaces, the delicate, painted Venetian chairs and benches (*panchette*), with their bright lacquer and whimsical decorations, are the most easily recognizable of Italian chairs.

In the Papal States, noble families lived in splendid palaces that required carved and gilded chairs. Records of craftsmen are nonexistent, for Italian chair-makers were not required to stamp or sign their pieces. In Piedmont and Naples, palaces were built to rival Versailles. Piedmont was an independent duchy of increasing power and influence. When its duke Vittorio Amadeo II assumed the title of king in 1713, he embarked on a building program befitting his new title. He enlisted the help of the noted architect Filippo Juvarra, who, in turn, employed one of the few Italian craftsmen to deserve the title of *ébéniste*, Pietro Piffetti. The two collaborated on an elaborate prie-dieu for the queen's use in the Palazzo Reale in Turin, a piece inlaid with ivory and mother of pearl, following an elaborate pattern that may owe something to the engraved ornaments of Nicolas Pineau. Piffetti's extravagant style—inspired by the French rococo, yet distinctly Italian—is characterized by opulent inlays of rare woods.

Duchess Louise Elizabeth of Parma, Louis XV's eldest daughter, hoping to re-create the taste of her childhood, commissioned armchairs in France for the royal palace from the workshop of the *menuisier* Nicolas Quinibert Foliot. Foliot carved the chairs in pieces, which were then shipped to Parma for assembly. The Italian craftsmen who put them together also gilded them and attached the upholstery. The chairs are superb, a testament to the quality of Italian *menuisiers*.

Although there are many regional differences, certain common features characterize Italian rococo chairs. The Italian carvers were immensely skilled; in fact, in Italy there was little distinction between carvers and sculptors. Seats were elaborately carved, even when their shapes were relatively restrained. Prie-dieux were a favorite form, the more elaborate ones being made for chapels, while simpler versions were used in bedrooms. Italian rococo chairs often had removable upholstered backs and seats, which gave them a rather bulky appearance. Italian versions of Louis XV chairs tend to be uncomfortable, with upright and rather awkward lines. There was also a distinction between the gilded or painted formal chairs for the *piano nobile*, and the unpainted walnut or cherry seats in private quarters.

<
A Genoese armchair, c. 1740–60, painted light blue and parcel-gilt. L'Antiquaire & The Connoisseur, Inc.

<
A Venetian chair, parcel-gilt and polychromed on a cream ground, c. 1750. L'Antiquaire & The Connoisseur, Inc.

high style: baroque, rococo & neoclassical chairs 199

<
A Spanish rococo armchair from the reign of Charles III, with metallic marquetry in the style of Boulle. Palacio Real. Patrimonio Nacional, Madrid

>
A late-eighteenth-century Spanish rococo armchair. Patrimonio Nacional, Madrid

>
The Portrait Hall at the Catherine Palace, St. Petersburg. The sofa was designed c. 1750 by the Italian architect Bartolomeo Rastrelli (1700–71), who became the leading architect at the court of the Empress Elizabeth.

To improve the quality of Spanish workmanship, Charles III (reigned 1759–88), a great-grandson of Louis XIV, established a royal furniture workshop modeled after the Gobelins in Paris. Spanish rococo chairs can usually be distinguished from French chairs by their prodigal use of wood, old structural methods, and certain details of carving. In Sweden, Nicodemus Tessin the younger, the king's superintendent of buildings, dreamed of creating a royal furniture workshop in Stockholm. In 1718 he wrote to his son, Carl Gustaf, while on his way to Paris "to find some carvers, sculptors, and ornamentalists." He had to wait until 1748, when the talented Adrien Masreliez (1717–1806) of Grenoble became the sculptor and ornamentalist in charge of building the Stockholm Castle. Masreliez was responsible for much of the rococo decoration in Sweden, including the design of a great many chairs between 1748 and 1776 in the Louis XV style.

When Peter the Great visited the Gobelins factory in Paris in 1717 he was particularly interested in the organization of its large workforce. Among the diplomatic gifts that the tsar took back to Russia was a suite of Gobelins tapestries for upholstery. He also visited the workshop of André-Charles Boulle, then at the height of his importance, where he "acquired designs." During the 1740s, the palaces of St. Petersburg were supervised by Bartolomeo Rastrelli, the son of Peter's principal sculptor, who had studied in Italy and France. Most of the seats at the Catherine Palace were designed by him in an Italianate spirit, with an abundance of carving and gilding.

Peter's daughter, Elizabeth Petrovna (reigned 1741–62), imported most of her furniture from France, and during her reign Russia was strongly influenced by the French rococo, the Russian nobility enthusiastically importing French chairs for their palaces. In 1758 agents of one Count Vorontzov purchased a number of pieces in France for his palace, including beds, armchairs, fauteuils, and upholstery material. At the end of the 1740s, the first French trading houses were established in Russia, offering goods shipped from Rouen and Le Havre. In 1746, Russians spent some 37,940 rubles on French furniture.

While still a grand-duchess, Catherine the Great (reigned 1762–96) had already acquired chairs, *bergères*, and fauteuils for her apartments in the Oranienbaum and Winter Palaces. She wrote that the court was so ill-furnished that the same "mirrors, beds, chairs [and] tables that were usually used in the Winter Palace followed us when we traveled to the Summer Palace, then Peterhof, and then Moscow."

The Russian chair-making industry was initiated by the carpenters and carvers who had been ordered by the tsar to build boats at Okhta in 1721. The men began to make chairs during the winter months, their business gradually growing until in 1750 it was an enterprise of considerable volume. In 1742, the empress Elizabeth issued a succession of decrees demanding that officials seek out the master craftsmen who had been sent overseas for training. Thus, workshops of trained artisans capable of creating sophisticated seats sprang up in Russia.

In England, where there were no guilds to supervise the level of craftsmanship, the standards demanded by patrons and the competitive spirit among the chair-makers themselves served equally well. By the middle of the eighteenth century, the character of English chairs had become distinct from that of the rest of Europe. Rococo influence came slowly, and the idiosyncrasies of individual designers and makers were always present. There was no real baroque tradition in England comparable to the courtly styles of Europe, so when the rococo did appear, it was a decorative novelty, not a logical development of an existing style.

Rococo design was taught in London at the Academy of St. Martin's Lane. One of its chief teachers from 1732 to 1745 was the French engraver Hubert Gravelot (1699–1772). He belonged to a group of artists, decorators, and chair-makers enamored with the rococo style that frequented Old Slaughter's Coffee House in Saint Martin's Lane. This was an artists' and chair-makers' neighborhood; Thomas Chippendale lived across the street. For this reason, English rococo is often called the Saint Martin's Lane style.

The best of the English designers at the time was undoubtedly the carver Matthias Locke (1724–69), who played a leading role in introducing the French rococo to England, publishing in 1740 *A New Drawing Book of Ornaments*, one of the first collections of *rocaille* motifs to appear in England. He also was a contributor to Chippendale's book. By 1754, when Chippendale published *The*

<<
An English George II walnut library armchair, c. 1750. Christie's

<
A George II mahogany master armchair, c. 1750–55, corresponding to a French chair pattern illustrated in Thomas Chippendale's *Gentleman and Cabinet-Maker's Director*, 1754 (pl. xix). Ceremonial chairs were produced for civic corporations, clubs, learned societies, Masonic lodges, and livery companies, a tradition that began in the Middle Ages and proliferated during the eighteenth and nineteenth centuries. These oversized chairs were used by a master, or presiding official, and were typically emblazoned with the organization's coat of arms or appropriate emblem. Christie's

high style: baroque, rococo & neoclassical chairs 201

>
One of a set of fourteen English George III dining chairs by Thomas Chippendale (1718–79). Christie's

Gentleman and Cabinet-Maker's Director, the style was fully mature. In the November 1738 *London* magazine, a writer complained that "the ridiculous imitation of the French taste has now become the Epidemical distemper of this kingdom." Sixteen years later the chairs in Chippendale's *Director* show this influence, but although some of the plates present free adaptations of contemporary French chairs, the divided aims of the period and its craving for novelty are expressed by excursions into the Chinese and Gothic tastes.

France was exposed before England to the influence of *chinoiseries*. The charming, elegant, light-hearted rococo style lent itself perfectly to exotic treatment. The earliest examples of rococo *chinoiseries* appear to have been produced by Jean-Antoine Watteau (1684–1721), who, around 1719, painted a series of *figures chinoises et tartars* for the *cabinet du roi* in the Château de La Muette, which, though destroyed in the mid-eighteenth century, is known from prints. A group of superb *chinoiseries* were created by Christophe Huet (1701–79) shortly after 1747 for Mme. de Pompadour at the Château des Champs. Other artists provided *chinoiserie* designs for engravers, among them Jean Baptiste Pillement (1728–1808), whose prints were published in London as well as Paris, influencing the design of *chinoiseries* all over Europe. They were copied in marquetry by French and German *ébénistes* and painted on chairs and sofas. However, nearly all of Louis XV's large-scale *chinoiseries*, including garden kiosks and complete interiors, have been lost. The fact that the French seldom permitted their taste for *chinoiseries* to

<

An American chair after a design by Thomas Chippendale. These chairs represent the highest achievement of Philadelphia chair-making and give us a picture of the height of fashion in America in 1770. John Cadwalader (1742–86), for whom they were made, was a man out to impress. The chairs have been traced back to Benjamin Randolph, an eighteenth-century Philadelphia cabinet-maker. The English influence in chair design was well established, so American rococo chairs were based on English models. The similarity between the two is sometimes so close that it is hard to distinguish an American chair from an English one. Philadelphia Museum of Art

>
An armchair belonging to the Cadwalader family, c. 1770, carved by Thomas Chippendale. Christie's

v
A portrait by Charles Wilson Peale of Lambert Cadwalader, John Cadwalader's brother, leaning on the back of a chair similar to the one shown at left. Philadelphia Museum of Art

A design in watercolor for a Chinese-style armchair, by John Linnell. As we can see, the original color scheme intended for this chair was dominated by red and blue rather than the black and gold of the executed chair (seen here at right). Designing such chairs was John Linnell's major responsibility when he first came to work as a designer in the firm of his father, William Linnell, one of the first cabinetmakers to give concrete expression to the new vogue for *chinoiserie*. Victoria & Albert Museum, London

This chair comes from a set of eight forming part of the famous suite of japanned furniture supplied by William and John Linnell to the fourth duke of Beaufort (1709–56) for the Chinese Bedroom at Badminton House, Gloucestershire. Victoria & Albert Museum, London

influence forms and construction is perhaps attributable to the regulations of the guild. In any case, they produced very few seats comparable to "Chinese Chippendale" chairs, with the exception of a few pieces intended for garden buildings.

The Chinese influence was everywhere in French literature. Even Voltaire joined in the craze, striking a more serious note with his play *Orphelin de la Chine*. In England, a popular French comedy called *Arlequin doctor chinois*, translated into English, played in London in 1720 and was such a hit that it continued to be performed until 1755. It was not long before chairs reflected the new trend.

The English satirist James Cawthorn noted in his poem "Of Taste" in 1756:

For Mand'rin is the only man of taste . . .
Of late, 'tis true quite sick of Rome and Greece
We fetch our models from the wise Chinese;
European artists are too cool and chaste,
On ev'ry shelf a Joss divinely stares,
Nymphs laid on chintzes sprawl upon our chairs;
While o'er our cabinets Confucius nods
Midst porcelain elephants and china gods.

Sometimes the Chinese taste was combined with the Gothic. As another writer in the *World* noted in 1754, "It has not escaped your notice how much of late we are improved in architecture; not merely by the adoption of what we call Chinese, nor by the restoration of what we call Gothic, but a happy mixture of both." Indeed, William Halfpenny published designs for garden seats and pavilions "partly in the Chinese taste," the other part being Gothic.

The Gothicism of Chippendale's chairs was limited to details such as cusps and tracery. For chairs in the Gothic and Chinese styles, square, straight legs with small block feet were usually favored, while a tapered leg with a pierced and molded foot was sometimes used. The Gothic influence was typically English, the seal of fashion being stamped on the revival by Horace Walpole at his house, Strawberry Hill (1750–70), where he took an archaeological approach in the surface decoration, but showed little understanding of Gothic structure. The Gothic revival style, being so typically British, was particularly suited to hall chairs, a seat indigenous to England. By contrast, the Chinese taste spread freely in many European countries.

Antonio Rinaldi, who came to Russia from Italy in 1752 to work for Catherine the Great, between 1762 and 1768 designed the Chinese Pavilion at the Oranienbaum Palace near St. Petersburg, whose decor draws on both *chinoiseries* and European styles. In other parts of Europe, whole rooms were decorated in the Chinese taste, the most spectacular being those in the palaces at Capodimonte in Italy and Aranjuez in Spain. In the Italian theater, the vogue for Chinese-inspired plays and operas was no less strong than in France or England. It is probably no coincidence that the most notable Italian *chinoiseries* were first performed in Venice. It was also in the Serene Republic that japanned furniture was produced as early as the late seventeenth century, although no examples are known to survive from that period. Among the most attractive specimens dating from the 1750s is a complete suite of chairs,

> A German side chair in the Chinese style. Museum für Kunsthandwerk

now in the Ca' Rezzonico in Venice, of bottle-green lacquer exuberantly painted with Chinese festival scenes in gilt.

The so-called Japanese Palace erected in Dresden for Augustus the Strong between 1715 and 1717 was one of the largest, earliest, and best-known examples of German eighteenth-century *chinoiserie*. The building owed its fame to its contents rather than to its architecture: much of the furniture is lacquer, with chairs in scarlet and gold. In Munich in about 1734 the elector Karl Albrecht of Bavaria commissioned François de Cuvilliés to build the Amalienburg pavilion in the park at Nymphenburg. In this exquisite building, perhaps the greatest masterpiece of the rococo style, *chinoiserie* plays a small but significant part. Two of the smaller rooms, the *Hundekammer* with its dog kennels and the *Retirade*, which housed the elector's *chaise percée*, are painted with *chinoiseries* in blue on a white ground by Pascalin Moretti. Frederick the Great built a *chinoiserie* tea house on the grounds of Sans Souci, with a guest bedroom in the style.

The vogue for *chinoiserie* chairs persisted in Germany throughout the rococo period. Most were lacquered. Frederick's sister, Queen Ulrika of Sweden, received the Chinese Pavilion at Drottningholm Castle as a birthday present from her husband in 1753. In the porcelain room there was a suite of Chinese-style rococo green and gold lacquer chairs, which are similar to a well-known set made in England around 1740 by Giles Grendey for the Spanish duke of Infantado. The coloring differs: Grendey's chairs are red with gold and silver decorations, while the Swedish chairs are stiffer, with backs less curved. Despite those differences, the similarities of the seats are remarkable. They demonstrate how influential English chair-making had become.

London chairs were second in quality only to the French examples. Chippendale was largely responsible for the spreading of English influence in chair design. Before the publication of Chippendale's *Director* in 1754, chair-makers in England had been mainly dependent on their own ideas, working without engraved designs.

<<
The coronation chair of Queen Caroline of England, c. 1727. Christie's

<
An armchair from an English George II (1727–60) suite, decorated with eagle heads. Christie's

high style: baroque, rococo & neoclassical chairs 207

> A pair of George I burr walnut and parcel-gilt chairs, c. 1720. Christie's

> An exceptionally fine pair of English George II (1683–1760) oil-gilt walnut side chairs. Christie's

Darly's New Book of Chinese, Gothic and Modern Chairs (1752), a mere pamphlet, was the only earlier work that aimed to provide assistance to the trade. Chippendale's *Director* for the first time supplied a variety of patterns that powerfully influenced contemporary design, and the long and distinguished list of subscribers to the book's first edition is astonishing. None of the rival publications inspired by the *Director* achieves its comprehensiveness and few approach the quality of its design and engraving. Robert Manwaring's book of chairs (1765), *The Cabinet and Chair Maker's Real Friend and Companion or, the whole system of Chair-Making made plain and easy*, was used in America, but appeared too late to influence the rococo style in England. Other talented and accomplished chair-designers and makers, such as William Linnell and his son or nephew John, who left a large number of seat and sofa drawings, contributed to the radiance of English rococo abroad.

Although Chippendale's name is synonymous with English rococo furniture, his work after 1764 is actually Neoclassical, and these pieces are, if anything, even finer than his earlier work. Later, John Linnell also created an original Classical Revival style. A sepia wash sketch in his portfolio of drawings, now in the Victoria and Albert Museum in London, inscribed "Lord Scarsdale's sofa at Kedleston in Derbyshire" represents a marvelous sofa carved with mermen, with interlaced dolphins forming the support. The Kedleston sofa is one of a set of four that recall the magnificence of the type that the multitalented William Kent (1686–1748) had designed during the previous decade.

Many seats by both Kent and Linnell feature decoration of intertwined palm branches, a favorite motif in France. The engraver Cochin had written a few years earlier that to suppress these branches would "deprive our decorators of their last resource." The dolphin was also revived on a few of the finest upholstered armchairs in the rococo style. The progress toward lighter, more elegant designs with rhythmical lines is clearly seen in the upholstered chairs made between 1740 and 1765. Chippendale's drawings for French armchairs are of that type, with characteristic curved arms and scrolled feet.

After visiting Hardwick House in the summer of 1757, Miss Caroline Girle expatiated on the "substantialness" of the furniture and continues there:

If anyone was to compare three or four hundred years hence a chair from the drawing room of Queen Elizabeth's days and the light French ones of George II, it would never be possible to suppose them to belong to the same race of people, as the one is altogether gigantic and other quite Lilliputian.

Dining chairs are perhaps the most characteristic seats of the period. Dining rooms were rare in France and England before 1750, when dining tables and chairs were made to be easily brought together and then removed, for dinner guests might be incalculably numerous.

The chair most conveniently described as "Chippendale" (since many designs are illustrated in the *Director*) has a crest-rail shaped like a bow in sharp angles, and a back-splat of delicate tracery that required the strength of mahogany. Mahogany, a strong wood imported from Central America and the West Indies, superseded walnut as the most common wood for chairs when the import taxes on it were dropped in 1733. The use of mahogany for chairs remained an English specialty until the late eighteenth century, when it spread to France, and then, with the Empire style, to the rest of Europe. Chippendale illustrated a large number of chairs, explaining that more or less carving could be applied at will, an option useful to Americans makers. Although the claw and ball foot survived into the 1750s, Chippendale only illustrated the more fashionable rococo or French scrolled feet. The *Director* was so popular that it was republished in 1755 and again, with

> A detail of the headboard of the day bed shown below, with the engraved inscription *George/Augustus/Frederick/Natus 12 August/1762*. Private collection

additional plates in 1762. Chippendale was widely imitated, particularly in Holland, Scandinavia, Portugal, Spain, and the Americas. In Denmark, English chairs were so popular that in 1747 the government prohibited their importation. The Danes appreciated the economical lines of the English seats, however, so by the 1760s light chairs based on Chippendale designs were made locally, usually of painted or lacquered pine. In Holland chairs kept to the old-fashioned Anglo-Dutch forms, with hooped backs and cabriole legs. By then, the power of the Netherlands was diminishing, and, as a result, so was the Dutch influence on chair design.

Portugal prospered in the early eighteenth century under John V. After the disastrous Lisbon earthquake of 1755, the demand for furniture grew as the city was rebuilt. During this period great quantities of English chairs were shipped both to Portugal and to Spain, as the export records in the Public Record Office in London show. The Portuguese trade somewhat exceeded the Spanish, perhaps because relations between England and Portugal were friendly, and also because there was a colony of English settlers in Oporto engaged in the port wine trade. Portuguese chairs soon followed Chippendale designs, as well. These were finely carved in rosewood (imported from Portuguese Brazil) with lively sprays of acanthus on the backs and cabriole legs.

After France, England was the most important foreign influence on Spanish chair-makers, who copied Queen Anne, early Georgian, and later, Chippendale designs based on French rococo patterns, often with added Chinese or Gothic elements. The English chairs destined for Spain

> A chaise longue with a wax portrait of the infant Prince of Wales (later George IV), London, 1762. This highly important piece of royal silver furniture represents in miniature an eccentric day bed design of the third quarter of the eighteenth century. Its classical decoration is one of the earliest surviving examples of the Greek taste in England. It was given by the prince's doting mother, Queen Charlotte, to George III in 1762, but kept by her later. Private collection

210 high style: baroque, rococo & neoclassical chairs

<
An American carved armchair. Philadelphia, 1760–80. Christie's

<
An eighteenth-century American upholstered armchair. Philadelphia Museum of Art

> An American easy chair attributed to Thomas Affleck, c. 1770. Philadelphia Museum of Art

differed from those made for the home market in that they nearly always had cane seats—doubtless owing to the Spanish heat—an unusual feature in English chairs. Many were painted or lacquered, often in crimson, to hide the wood, which commonly was beech rather than the more expensive mahogany used in England. English-style chairs made in Spain usually had stretchers, either from habit or because the local chair-makers doubted the strength of the fragile-looking cabriole legs.

Surprisingly, Russia also embraced English chair designs, in addition to the French and Italian fashions, as we shall see in the next chapter. Catherine the Great preferred English and German chair models to the French, however in ceremonial settings, following the fashion of the time, she had seats created that were inspired by the French taste. In Germany, Hanover, allied to the English crown, was the principal source of English influence. After 1750 a simplified form of the English Chippendale chair was made there.

The American colonies became so prosperous during the eighteenth century that they were able to defy British taxes, openly rebel, and finally gain their independence in 1783. The Americans built their civilization upon what they remembered, brought with them, or learned through illustrated books from abroad. As the century progressed, the number of English chairs imported to America diminished as talented local makers, following Chippendale's patterns, made seats that were easier to find and cheaper to buy than imports. American makers also followed the publications of the Manwaring and Ince and Mayhew pattern books, and the lack of a guild or other regulatory system helped the industry to develop.

A pair of George III gilt-wood open armchairs by Thomas Chippendale. Christie's

The Chippendale period in America runs from 1760 almost to the end of the century. In Philadelphia, rococo ornaments were known as the "new French style," despite the fact that they came from England and were, by the late eighteenth century, far from new! The Philadelphia maker Benjamin Randolph (active 1762–85), who carried dispatches for General Washington, became an outstanding exponent of the American Chippendale style, with an elaborate trade card engraved in the style of Saint Martin's Lane. Among Randolph's mahogany chairs are some of the best pieces of American furniture. His style was more fanciful than that of his contemporary, Thomas Affleck (1740–95), who had immigrated to Philadelphia from Scotland in 1763.

Philadelphia was undoubtedly the most prolific center in the middle colonies, although chairs were also made in the North to be traded for corn and tobacco grown in the South. New England chairs were less florid than those of Philadelphia, reflecting the Puritan tradition. Philadelphia also tended to retain the Queen Anne style, particularly in dining chairs with hoop backs, shaped splats, and cabriole legs with webbed feet. Not much is known of chair-makers in the South, though many were, apparently, slaves. There are slight variations in the chairs made in the middle colonies and New England regions. A diamond-shaped back splat set behind a large scroll loop was characteristic of the New York area; New England chairs often had an addition of turned stretchers; and Gothic tracery was popular in Philadelphia before the Revolution.

stools, *pliants*, and benches

In the eighteenth century, the two forms of stools, the tabouret and the *pliant*, seemed formal in this period of relaxed manners, and so they were made in smaller quantities and used less often. Their main raison d'être was to satisfy court etiquette. *Pliants*, as one observer noted,

ne servent plus que chez le Roi ou chez les grands Princes et les Ambassadeurs et généralement tous ceux qui sont obligés de garder l'etiquette

[are only used by the king, princes of the blood, or ambassadors, that is, people who are obliged to observe the rules of etiquette].

An iron wall still separated duchesses from other ladies, for they alone were entitled to the honor of sitting on a tabouret in the presence of their majesties. This tradition, begun at Versailles almost a century before, was still very much alive at all the European courts, despite the more carefree atmosphere of the era. Louis XV kept some *pliants*, which were painted red and gold, in the Galerie des Glaces at Versailles. The empress Maria Theresa of Austria had similar stools painted in the same colors for the gallery of her palace at Schoenbrunn. Most stools had feet carved to resemble those of a doe (*pieds de biche*). Some were also used as small dog houses. Madame de Pompadour had such a stool in her bedroom at the Château de Saint Hubert, upholstered in damask, a perfect mockery of court etiquette.

In England after the middle of the century, stools do not seem to have been made in great numbers. However, they were still plentiful in large houses, often from a considerably earlier date. The only stools illustrated at the time were dressing stools and window stools. Ince and Mayhew show designs for "Lady's dressing stools," with elaborately carved, scrolled legs. They also showed "French stools" made "for recesses of windows," much in demand for large Georgian houses. They were probably called "French" because such window stools were popular in France at the time.

In Germany, seat etiquette was as strictly imposed as it was during the previous century. In relation to German court etiquette, F. Karl von Mauser noted in his book *Court Law*, published in Frankfurt in 1754–55:

Nowadays several kinds of chairs and seats exist at Court. First the canapé, which can be used for more than one person. Second, the armchair or fauteuil. Third, the chair without arms or chaise à bras. Fourth, the simple side chair with arms, or chaise à dos. *Fifth, the tabouret, or small stool without back. The more important the room is, the more important the chairs have to be. In the entrance you will only find a simple side chair or* chaise à dos, *never a fauteuil, and the canapé is the most important of all. When ladies and gentlemen come together, the ladies are the only ones supposed to sit on the canapé.*

Later on, Mauser described a ceremonial table following the rule of protocol:

The Emperor [Leopold I] and the empress had armchairs; the duchess of Hanover [mother of the queen] had a side chair; the cardinal of Cologne and Crimani, the Apostolic Nuncio, the Spanish, Venetian, and Savoyard ambassadors had a wooden banquette with red velvet upholstery. However, the upholstery was not stuffed with horsehair like the duchess of Hanover's chair.

Benches and banquettes were still used during the eighteenth century, mostly in galleries and halls. In Venice, small painted benches or *panchette* were set in the halls of palazzos. Elsewhere, the reception rooms and bedrooms of great houses were generally furnished with comfortable day beds and settees. However at Seehof, an estate belonging to the prince-bishop Adam Friedrich von Seinsheim, an inventory dated 1775 mentions benches in the dining room. The use of benches in such refined settings seems to have been most unusual at the time, almost a throwback to the medieval era.

sofas and canapés

Thus first necessity invented stools
Convenience next suggested elbow-chairs
And luxury the accomplish'd Sofa last
                    William Cowper (1731–1800)

"Today," wrote Voltaire, "social behavior is easier than in the past . . . ladies can be seen reading on sofas or day beds without causing embarrassment to their friends and acquaintances." The eighteenth century was the apogee of the sofa or canapé, which was well suited to an era dominated by pleasure, luxury, and frivolity. Early in the rococo period, Oppenordt and Meissonier had designed elaborately curved sofas to match wall paneling. In Germany, Cuvillies and Hoppenhaupt outdid them, creating models with even more extravagant curves, and seemingly endless scrolls. As Mauser explained in *Court Law*, canapés were for ladies to sit on, since the shapes of these seats allowed the sitters to strike graceful poses.

In the reign of Louis XV a number of new types of canapé appeared, bearing names such as *canapé à medaillon*, *canapé en gondole*, and *canapé en corbeille à joues* as the search for comfort stimulated the creation of new models. A smaller type was called a *marquise*; a larger one with two additional seats on each end was called a *confident*. Versions of the *confident* were also developed by English designers, most notably Hepplewhite, in 1788.

A chaise longue was called a *duchesse en bateau*, and if in two or three parts, it was then called a *duchesse brisée*. The *ottomane*, created in 1729, started as a *lit d'alcove* and developed into a sofa with a back curved in a half circle. By the end of the eighteenth century it was the favorite

> A French beechwood carved and gilt *canapé à joues*, c. 1770–75. Musée Nissim de Camondo, Paris. Photograph: Antoine Bootz

< A *fauteuil à la reine*, c. 1768, in the transitional style the marked the movement from the Louis XV to the Louis XVI manner. This armchair, from a suite of *meublants*, meaning that the pieces were intended to be placed against a wall. This suite was made to order for the duchess d'Anville by Nicolas Heurtaut, one of the most active proponents of the return to classicism. His transition-period pieces are remarkable, as this armchair shows. The upholstery is original, from the Gobelins factory. Musée du Louvre OA10290.10296. Photograph: RMN.

seat of its time. It also led to the creation of the *veilleuse*, which was built on an oval plan with one end higher than the other. Italy had its own special sofa, the *ventaglio*, or fan-shape, the arms of which inclined outward at a 45-degree angle.

Apparently even Catherine the Great of Russia received her ambassadors while lying on a vast sofa. In the eighteenth century, often sofas and canapés alike featured mattresses and cushions to make the seat more comfortable, and in some instances they were still used as beds. Roubo gave the following explanation about the difference between sofas and canapés: *Les sophas, ne different des canapés qu'en ce que leurs accotoirs sont pleins comme ceux des bergères* [Sofas differ from canapés in that their armrests are full, like those of *bergères*]. However, that hardly seems to qualify as a real difference between them.

The first room that was redecorated for the young Louis XV in 1718 included two superb sofas *de damas jaune, chamarre de galons d'argent, avec ornements et feuilles de broderie d'argent* [of yellow damask, trim in silver with silver ornaments and leaves].

>

A Louis XV gilt-wood *canapé à confident* attributed to Nicolas-Quinibert Foliot (1706–76). Foliot was elected a master *menuisier* in 1729 and later supplied seat furniture to both the crown and the court. Canapés played a large part during the endless conversations that helped to fill the long, vacant hours at court.

<

A detail of the end of the canapé shown opposite. The legs of this piece are a little less curved than in earlier examples, a step in the direction of the Louis XVI style. Christie's

This refined indolence was also indulged in by English society. In England Manwaring, in his *Cabinet and Chair Maker's Real Friend and Companion*, gives two designs for what he calls "Grand French Settee Chairs," that is, settees with open-work backs formed of large carved acanthus scrolls, which he describes as "magnificent and superb." This type of seat usually combined the functions of settee and couch. From about 1740 in England the influence of contemporary French taste became increasingly apparent in the design of upholstered settees and sofas, rococo ornament gradually supplanting the massive decoration of the early Georgian period. The arms became higher and formed a continuation of the undulating back, a fashion based on Louis XV canapés. Furthermore, Chippendale's indebtedness to French design is apparent in the third edition of the *Director* (1762), to which he added several plates of sofas not previously included. One, for a "Grand Apartment," is a more extravagant version of a design by Meissonier. However, straight legs are illustrated, too, a prelude to the new fashion starting to creep in. Chippendale wrote, "[I]f gilt with burnished gold, the whole will have a notable Appearance." He also often recommended the combination of mahogany and gilt, and noted that "when made large, they have a Bolster or Pillow at each End and Cushions at the Back, which may be laid down occasionally and form a Mattress," as with French sofas.

Chippendale also illustrated a chaise longue with padded back, which, he wrote, the French called *Péché mortel*—Mortal Sin. To fulfill the demands of the libertine, comfort mattered immensely, and sofas provided it.

LOUIS XVI (1774–92)

Although Louis XVI became king of France in 1774 after the death of his grandfather, Louis XV, his namesake style had begun to emerge in the 1750s and was fully developed by the time of his accession to the throne. In other countries, naming a style after the king would have little justification, since most kings had almost no influence on furniture styles. In France, however, the crown was the largest patron of furniture-makers, and the king's taste was law. Moreover, that taste was enormously influential abroad, since most European countries followed the French lead in furniture styles.

Early Neoclassicism began as a reaction to rococo frivolity, and perhaps in a nostalgic yearning for the grandeur of Louis XIV. Classical Antiquity was imitated to create a style more rational and noble than the rococo. Neoclassicism originated concurrently, but apparently independently, in France and in England, and most of its notable manifestations in chair design originated in these two countries or under their influence. In England, the first stirrings of the style can be dated from the return of Robert Adam from Italy in 1758, but there is no such convenient date in the history of French furniture, although the cultivated Madame de Pompadour and her brother, the marquis de Marigny, are often credited with playing an important part in the creation of the style. In any case, ancient architectural forms became the basis of chair design as they had in the Renaissance. Change came slowly; for a long time old and new styles existed concurrently and interpenetrated one another.

Neoclassicism is often associated with the excavation of the buried cities of Herculaneum (from 1738) and Pompeii (from 1749), the sudden revelations setting off a new spark. In Rome, a somewhat independent version of the style, much bolder than either the English or the French version, began to emerge in the late 1760s. Here the presiding genius was Giovanni Battista Piranesi, through his engraved views of ancient Rome, as well as his furniture designs. It became a must for cultivated gentlemen, regardless of their country of origin, to visit Italy, and from the middle of the second decade of the eighteenth century many traveled there on the Grand Tour.

From 1719 onward, when Bernard de Montfaucon's *Antiquité expliquée* first appeared, many publications on classical Antiquity were published in England, France, and Italy. In Germany also, an interest developed through the writings of Johann Joachim Winckelmann, such as his 1754 *Gedanken über die Nachahmung der Griechischen Werke*. Winckelmann lived in Rome as secretary to Cardinal Albani, but his books, published in Germany, helped usher in the Neoclassical movement.

The marquis de Marigny, France's future Minister of Culture and Madame de Pompadour's younger brother, was also sent on a Grand Tour of Italy in 1749, an important journey in the evolution of the French taste. Although the Louis XV style was still in its ascendancy, Marigny's attention was particularly drawn to the study of Antiquities, for his traveling companions, Soufflot and Cochin, were among the chief opponents of the rococo. His other traveling companion was his tutor, the Abbé Jean Bernard Le Blanc, who had published essays on English literature. Marigny and Le Blanc's spirited discussions about English life and manners created in the young man a long-standing interest in England. Marigny, who during his active career as the Directeur des Bâtiments du Roi was the principal figure in royal support of the arts in France, contributed to the French mania for English seats—some versions of which were beautifully executed by Georges Jacob—in the 1770s and 1780s.

Cross-influences between England and France in chair design are illustrated in numerous anecdotes. For example, the French architect and Neoclassical designer François-Joseph Belanger

> A set of two Louis XVI side chairs with back decorated with carved musical instruments. Kuegel Collection, Paris

visited England in 1766–67 at the invitation of Lord Shelburne, for whom he would design, ten years later, the gallery at Lansdowne House in London. On that journey, Belanger met William Chambers and Robert Adam, the influence of whose work is noticeable on the design and furnishings of Bagatelle, the chateau in the Bois de Boulogne that Belanger created for Louis XVI's luxury-loving brother, the comte d'Artois. Adam was very familiar with French chair designs. He had numerous contacts with Neoclassical French artists and designers such as Clérisseau, and was in close touch with the Paris furniture trade. Numerous tapestries were woven at the Gobelins factory to upholster seats in the houses he decorated for his clients. He also enlisted the help of Italian artists such as Pergolesi and Zucchi.

American chair-makers such as Stephen Badlam were directly inspired by English models and pattern books, while the influence of Robert Adam was carried by the Scottish architect Charles Cameron to St. Petersburg. French influence on chair designs was predominant in Germany and Italy, where French engraved designs by Delafosse, Lalonde, Neufforge, and others were widely diffused. In Sweden, the style later called "Gustavian" was influenced equally by French and English models.

fauteuils, armchairs, and other chairs

In character and function, Louis XVI seats were essentially the same as Louis XV examples. As early as 1760, a style called *à la grecque* appeared, starting a craze. Diderot and Grimm are known to have said in 1763:

Tout se fait aujourd'hui à la grecque, la décoration des bâtiments, les meubles, les étoffes . . . tout est à Paris à la grecque.

[Everything is in the Greek style, the decoration of buildings, furniture, fabrics . . . everything in Paris is in the Greek style].

This new manner already exhibited all the characteristics of the Louis XVI style, however, with

220 high style: baroque, rococo & neoclassical chairs

<
A *voyeuse*, or conversation chair, delivered in 1789 for the *salon turc* of Madame Elizabeth, Louis XVI's daughter, at Montreil, by Jean-Baptiste-Claude Sené (1748–1803). Musée Nissim de Camondo, Paris

>
An armchair, c. 1780, signed by Jean-Baptiste-Claude Sené (1748–1803), registered as a master in 1769. Sené became the chief purveyor to the royal household in 1785. He was the major beneficiary of the very large commissions given out on the eve of the Revolution for the furnishing of the royal apartments in the chateaux of Saint-Cloud, Fontainebleau, and Compiègne. Sené also worked for private clients, as is attested by this seat, which is part of a larger ensemble including a sofa, two *bergères*, and eight armchairs. Musée Nissim de Camondo, Paris. Photograph: Antoine Bootz

> French armchairs, c. 1780, signed by Georges Jacob and upholstered with Aubusson tapestry, formerly in the Richard Wallace collection. Jacob was undoubtedly the most original (and the most famous) Parisian *menuisier* of the Louis XVI period. Musée Nissim de Camondo, Paris. Photograph: Antoine Bootz

>> A leather-upholstered desk armchair signed *Nadal*. Jean-René Nadal (Nadal l'Ainé), who was registered as a master in 1756, was especially noted for his seating furniture in the transitional style. Yet, this surprising desk armchair shows practically no trace of Louis XV mannerisms. It bears the mark *CDT*, recently identified as being that of the household of the comte d'Artois, the younger brother of Louis XVI. It was delivered in 1775 to the prince's private apartments at Versailles. Musée Nissim de Camondo, Paris. Photograph: Antoine Bootz

 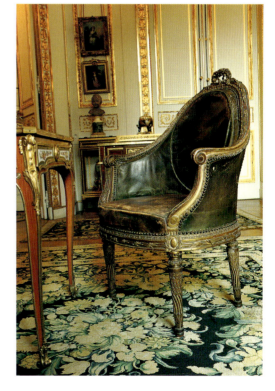

< A pair of Louis XVI armchairs *en gondola*, signed *Bauve*, made for the theater at Versailles. Christie's

chairs more than with veneered furniture, makers and designers clung tenaciously to the Louis XV style, making compromises between it and the new one and thus creating a transitional style. In 1772, Roubo, in his book *Art du Menuisier*, championed both Louis XV and Louis XVI seats, calling them both *à la mode*. A year later, in 1793, Just-François Boucher, the son of the painter, published a book of ornaments that designated the first of these as "ancient" and the second, "modern."

By 1774 the Neoclassical style in seats had almost completely triumphed in fashionable circles, encouraged by such architects as Jean-Charles Delafosse (1734–91), who published numerous chair engravings, among which there is a set of seats in rather heavy *à la grecque* style, with much use of laurel pendants and thick, ropey swags. The Flemish designer Jean François Neufforge (1714–91) was the first in France to publish engravings of Neoclassical chairs, solid, rectilinear, with bold and sometimes Egyptian motifs. Others, such as Richard de Lalonde, whose *Cahiers d'Ameublement* of 1780 presented many designs for chairs in a highly refined Louis XVI style with a liberal use of Roman fasces and helmets as ornamentation. Belanger, who with his brother-in-law, Jean Démosthène Dugourc, played a leading role in developing the *style étrusque*, contributed to the diversity of the Louis XVI style.

The Louis XVI seat could not improve on the comfort of the Louis XV seat, but it did present great variety and originality. Seats might be horseshoe shaped (*en cul de four*); chairs or fauteuils were *à la reine* (straight-backed); a *chaise au dauphin* sported an oval back supported by—what else?—dolphins. A chair with a circular seat and a back featuring an oval medallion bore the name *à la d'Artois*. Backs might be square, rectangular, or even *en chapeau* (hat-shaped). Delafosse designed a series of seats with highly inventive names: the extremely comfortable *convalescente*; the open *obligéante*; the cozy *boudoir*; a kind of rocking chair called a *berceuse*; and so on. The *voyeuse*, created under Louis XV, was still popular among the spectators at cards; however, the legs were now straight instead of cabriolet. Sheraton offered a

> A chair for Queen Marie Antoinette delivered in 1787 for her bedroom at Trianon, signed *Jacob*. RMN

>> A chair from a set of armchair and chair made for the comte d'Artois, c. 1777, for his *cabinet turc*, signed *Jacob*. Musée du Louvre 0A9986-9992. RMN

similar seat that he called the "conversation chair," made with a wide, deep seat narrowing at its junction with the back. The occupant sat with his legs across the seat, facing the back and resting his arms on a padded top rail. The conversation chair, wrote Sheraton, "is particularly adapted for this kind of idle position as I venture to call it."

Other proponents of the new style were the influential *marchands-tapissiers*, who sold ready-made furniture, especially seats. At a time when rooms were usually decorated in a coordinated style, these entrepreneurs were of some importance in that many *menuisiers*, Louis Delanois, for example, sold more chairs to the *marchands-tapissiers* than to private clients. The *marchands-tapissiers* were themselves craftsmen, most being upholsterers. A new style was good for business, creating more demand.

Before 1780 few efforts were made to imitate the real seats of Greece and Rome. Soon after that date, however, there was a movement toward a more purely classical ideal. One reason for this was economic, another was aesthetic, and another social. The full force of Rousseau's appeal for a return to a simpler, less sophisticated mode of life was widely felt. The new manner, known as the *style étrusque*, had originated in England, as the creation of Robert Adam. The "Etruscan" taste rapidly crossed the English Channel, and a severe and classical set of seating furniture, made of mahogany (a new development in French seats, the use of the wood being also derived from

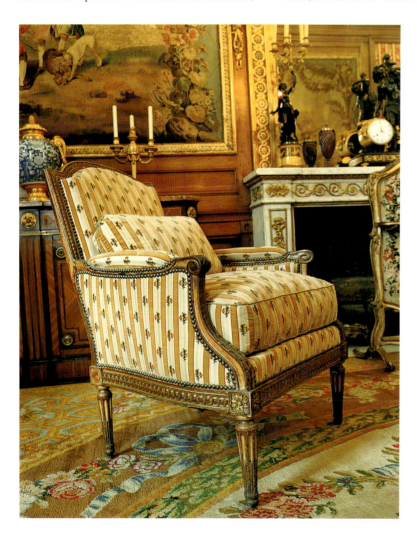

<
A carved and gilt walnut *bergère*, or easy chair, c. 1780, signed by Claude Chevigny, a Parisian master, in 1768. Musée Nissim de Camondo, Paris. Photograph: Antoine Bootz

English influence) and executed by Georges Jacob for the queen's dairy at Rambouillet, illustrated it perfectly. It was designed by the painter Hubert Robert, known as "Robert des Ruines" on account of his love of depicting the remains of Classical Antiquity in his landscape paintings. Such seats were the logical consequence of the antiquarian approach that had underlain Neoclassicism from its beginning, the Louis XVI style being merely its first stage in France, and therefore the beginning of Neoclassical seats in Europe.

Two types of seats still existed throughout Europe: *sièges meublants*, which always stood against the wall, and *sièges courants*, which were placed toward the center of the room and could be moved about at will. The frames were of carved wood, and might be gilded, painted, or polished, the last finish becoming noticeably more popular in grander establishments toward the end of the eighteenth century. These chairs were generally made of beech (for its lightness) or walnut, but pine and occasionally lime wood were sometimes found. Walnut was preferred if the frame was not to be gilded, for its close grain took an admirable polish. The simpler look was in keeping with the Rousseauesque approach toward simplicity. Toward the end of the Louis XVI period chairs were occasionally made of solid mahogany, following the contemporary English practice. When such chairs were upholstered *en crin natté* (of braided horsehair), they were called *chaises à l'anglaise*. Veneered chairs, rare in France, were more popular in Germanic countries.

French chairs were constructed in separate parts, which were assembled by mortise and tenon joints and strengthened by wooden plugs usually inserted without glue. They were remarkably solid, and the frames of most were so well designed that the joints loosen less readily with time and wear than those of contemporary English chairs. Miniature wax models of chairs intended for the use of the royal family were sometimes prepared in advance for approval, and are mentioned often in the royal inventories, although few survive. One extant example now in Sweden represents the coronation throne of King Adolphus Frederick (reigned 1751–71), dated 1751. It is similar to a throne belonging to Louis XV, destroyed during the Revolution. Another example is a model of a chair for Marie Antoinette, now in a private collection. Such models were necessary when a chair of a new, original, or expensive design was concerned. A simpler approval process involved the submission in advance of the details of the carving, either in plaster or wood. When the chair frame had been carved and assembled, the decorative carving was carried out by an independent craftsman. The fluting was partially filled in or cannulated, the filling ending in a small vase or a torch effect. Delicately carved arrows, lyres, swans, urns, wreathes, and festoons were adapted from Greco-Roman sources. If gilding was required, it was carried out by a *peintre-doreur*, another independent craftsman. Gilding was the most common treatment during the eighteenth century, and it was usually done by the process known as water- or leaf-gilding, which allowed great subtlety of finish, including contrasts between burnished and matte areas. Occasionally, oil gilding was used. Coat after coat of gesso was applied and carefully rubbed down before the gold itself was finally laid on. On rare occasions (more often under Louis XV), chair frames were silvered by a similar

> An eighteenth-century dog's chair. Collection Trianon Antiques

process, though silver had a tendency to tarnish, even when it was protected from the air with a coat of colorless varnish.

Color played an important part in eighteenth-century decoration and chair-frames were frequently painted rather than gilded. Sometimes painting and gilding were combined. *Dorure rechampi en blanc* (gilded moldings against a white background) was a favorite treatment for Louis XVI chair-frames. Single colors, notably blue, but also lilac, yellow, and green were used, and sometimes polychromatic effects were adopted. The various parts of the frames carved with floral or foliated motifs were painted in natural colors. Various techniques were used to produce these colors, mostly varieties of lacquer or varnish, but occasionally particularly delicate effects were obtained by painting in watercolor and coating with clear varnish. Unhappily, many of these colors have disappeared today, destroyed by re-gilding or by coverings of black paint as a gesture of mourning after the Revolution and the death of Louis XVI.

Georges Jacob (1739–1814), perhaps the most famous chair-maker of the time, became a *maître menuisier* in 1765 and by the 1780s had established himself as one of the leading chair-makers of Paris. The outline of the Louis XVI chair and richly carved classical ornament owe much to him. He was also among the first in France to use ungilded mahogany for chairs. He introduced the saber leg, and shortly before the Revolution began

> A French armchair from a set of six attributed to Georges Jacob, c. 1795. Jacob was the first *menuisier* to introduce both chairs with open backs and the use of mahogany to France. Collection Carlton Hobbs, London

< A chair from a suite made for the dairy at the chateau of Rambouillet for Marie Antoinette, c. 1787, by Georges Jacob after designs by Hubert Robert inspired by bronze furniture discovered at Herculaneum. Versailles. RMN

making lyre-backed chairs, presumably inspired by English models, as was his use of mahogany. He made pieces for several foreign clients, supplying chairs through the *marchand-mercier* Daguerre, who supplied pieces for both Carlton House and Woburn Abbey, for George IV of England and the Duke of Bedford.

With the rise of the *style étrusque* in the early 1780s, English taste exercised a marked influence in France. Sebastien Mercier, in his *Tableau de Paris*, tilts at Parisian Anglomania:

Les marchands mettent sur leurs enseignes "Magasins Anglais." Les limmonadiers, sur les vitres de leur cafés, annoncent "le punch" en langue anglaise.

[Merchants inscribe "English Shop" on their signs; lemonade-sellers offer "punch" in English on the windows of their cafes].

At about this time French chairs of mahogany with pierced splats or lyre backs in the English manner were first made and mahogany dining tables called *tables à l'anglaise* began to break

An English George III (1760–1809) gilt-wood open armchair, attributed to François Hervé. Hervé was a *cabriolet*, or French chair-maker who worked for George, Prince of Wales, at Carlton House (1783–89), supplying more than £3,000 worth of furniture under the direction of Henry Holland (1746–1806). Christie's

down the longstanding French custom of dining from trestle tables covered with a cloth. French Anglomania was fair turnabout after the massive French influence in England around 1740, and French taste continued to play an important role in England in the decade before the French Revolution, just as the French rococo had influenced Chippendale's designs earlier.

It was easier for the English to slip comfortably into the Neoclassical mode than it was for their European contemporaries. They had a continuing tradition of Italian inspiration, reinforced by the Grand Tour. It is not surprising, therefore, to find similarities between the seats of William Kent (1684–1748) and Robert Adam (1728–92), even though twenty or thirty years separated them. Robert Adam introduced decoration to please the elegant and artificial society of his day, which he called "the parade of life." His seats are ceremonial rather than domestic. Adam was such a leader of the Neoclassical style that soon after his return from Italy in 1758 he had revolutionized the interiors of England. In the words of his 1792 obituary in *The Gentleman's Magazine*, "His fertile genius was not confined to the decoration of buildings, but had been dispersed into almost every branch of manufacture."

Although Adam's chairs were specially designed for each client, his drawings for them were widely diffused by his published works. How generally his designs were copied can be judged by an observation in the last part of his book *Works in Architecture*, which came out in 1773 and 1779. One of the plates is captioned: "Pieces of furniture which were first invented for particular persons, but are since brought into general use." Adam's aim was, in his own words, "to transfuse the beautiful spirit of antiquity with novelty and variety." He usually succeeded, and the best chair-makers of the time collaborated with him. Thomas Chippendale is known to have made a suite of early Neoclassical armchairs after Adam's design

> An pair of English Neoclassical marquetry armchairs with oval backs, by John Linnell, c. 1780. These are the most ambitious adaptations of marquetry to chair construction of their generation. French and Company, New York

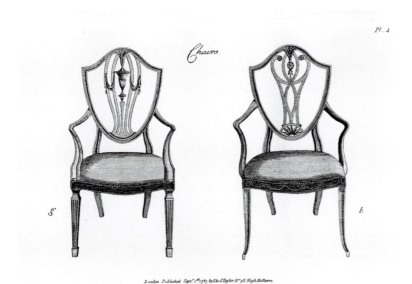

An engraving after a drawing by the cabinet-maker and designer George Hepplewhite from pl. 4 in his book, *The Cabinet Maker and Upholsterer's Guide*. The book was published two years after Hepplewhite's death in 1786. The Metropolitan Museum of Art

for Sir Laurence Dundas in London. Similarly, John Linnell made two elbow chairs for the Eating Room at Osterley Park after a drawing by Adam now in the Soane Museum in London.

As Horace Walpole commented after a visit to Osterley Park in 1773, "The chairs are taken from antique lyres and make charming harmony." Indeed, Adam intended his rooms to present a unified and harmonious aspect, with all elements and components interrelating in the French manner. His chairs were either gilt or painted white with gilt molding, and were thus close to French models. For dining chairs he used mahogany, and occasionally these were in the Etruscan style that he had invented, black-japanned with terracotta and Etruscan ornaments, and polished and varnished cane seats. Although he adopted the repertoire of classical ornament to a variety of uses—the lyre as a device for a chair-back, for instance—surprisingly few of his pieces are of genuine classical form.

The London cabinetmaker George Hepplewhite (d. 1786) was not well known until the posthumous publication of his *Cabinet-Maker and Upholsterer's Guide* in 1788. This comprehensive book, whose influence was to be as great as that of Chippendale's *Director*, epitomized the Neoclassical style of 1780–85 and made Hepplewhite a household name, as famous as that of Sheraton, with whom he is often paired. The designs in the book tend to be conservative. Some illustrations for bedroom chairs hark back to Chippendale's plates; a number exhibit the serpentine curves of the 1760s; and some even include cabriolet legs, suggesting the Louis XV style. However, the *Guide* was thoroughly practical, including some three hundred designs engraved on 126 plates, all preceded by this brief direction regarding proportions, materials, and finish:

The general dimension and proportion of chairs are as follows: Width in front 20 inches, depth of seat 17 inches, height of the seat frame 17 inches; total height about 3 feet 1 inch. Other dimensions are frequently adapted according to the size of the room or pleasure of the purchaser. Chairs in general are of mahogany, with the bars and frames sunk in a hollow, or rising in a round projection, with a band or list on the inner and outer edges.

Hepplewhite's book also illustrated Adam's principle of uniting elegance and utility. Owing to its precision, it was widely used as a trade catalogue both in England and abroad, with the result that Hepplewhite-style chairs were often made years after they had gone out of fashion in London, especially in America. One of the novelties of Hepplewhite's design, and a real deviation from French seats, was the use of lighter wood such as satinwood, which was often enhanced with decorations painted directly on it.

The firm of Seddon's made seats similar to Hepplewhite's, as described in a bill dated 1790, and an armchair of this type in satinwood with painted decoration is also at the Victoria and Albert Museum in London. The 1768 London city directory refers to George Seddon as "one of the most eminent cabinet and chair makers in London." Sophie von La Roche, a German traveler, described in her diary a visit she made to Seddon's in 1786, from which we learn that four hundred journeymen were employed, including upholsterers, joiners, carvers, and gilders—as far as is known the largest cabinetmaking business anywhere in the world in this period. Since England did not have the strict guild rules in force in France at the time, it was easier for English

> A painted satinwood armchair attributed to George Seddon (1727–1801), showing many similarities to the drawings by Hepplewhite shown opposite. Christie's

<
An Italian Neoclassical gilt-wood and painted side chair from the Pitti Palace, by Giovacchino Paoli after drawings by Hepplewhite, c. 1797. Collection Matz and Pribell, Cambridge Massachussetts

> Thomas Sheraton (1751–1806), drawing of two drawing-room armchairs. The Metropolitan Museum of Art

> Thomas Sheraton, drawings for chair backs. The Metropolitan Museum of Art

> Thomas Sheraton, a design for a chaise longue. Sheraton gave his name to the last phase of eighteenth-century English furniture. His fame rests entirely on his book of designs, *The Cabinet-Maker and Upholsterer's Drawing-Book*. The Metropolitan Museum of Art

> Thomas Sheraton's trade card, c. 1795. British Museum

chair-makers to have a large operation. However, Seddon did not produce any publications, and his known pieces show very little individuality.

Thomas Sheraton (1751–1806) was the last important English cabinetmaker-designer of the eighteenth century. He gave his name to the last phase of English eighteenth-century furniture, the elegant and sophisticated post-Hepplewhite and pre-Regency phase of the 1790s, during which the rectilinear, Adamesque Neoclassical style reached its apogee. Sheraton's fame rests on his books of designs, especially *The Cabinet-Maker and Upholsterer's Drawing Book*, issued in parts from 1791 to 1794. Like Hepplewhite's book, this was addressed primarily to the trade and its aim was practical, to acquaint cabinet- and chair-makers with the most up-to-date designs. Sheraton appears to have studied Louis XVI seats, which were brought across the English Channel by émigrés fleeing the Revolution. So Sheraton, like Hepplewhite, borrowed from the French, but only from the last phase of the Louis XVI period, and he imparted an unmistakable English character to his adaptations. Part of the appeal of Sheraton's new chair style may have been the fact that his square-back chairs were much less expensive to make than Hepplewhite's shield-back ones. He made free play with antique ornaments of the type used by Adam—urns, paterae, and swags—but without pedantry. He also emphasized the wood's essential quality and favored simple, sometimes severe, outlines, combined with elaborate decoration of great delicacy.

Sheraton distinguished clearly between "Parlour" and "Drawing Room" chairs. "The general style of furnishing a dining parlour," he wrote, "should be substantial and useful things." "Drawing Room" chairs, unlike "Parlour" chairs, which are straight-fronted, are shown with shaped or rounded seats.

Nothing is known of Sheraton's activities as a maker, although his book had a large circulation. Nearly 600 cabinetmakers, joiners, and upholsterers

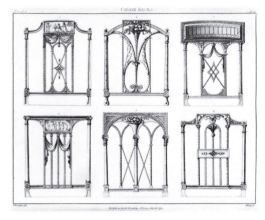

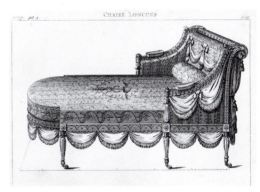

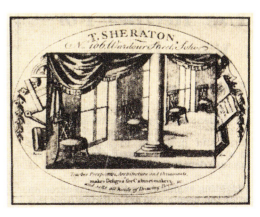

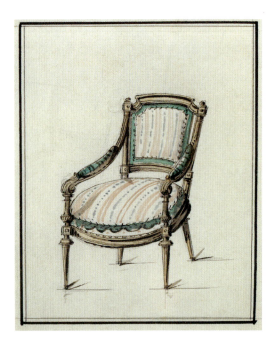

from all parts of England subscribed to it, and it was exploited as a design repertory all over the world. One of the means by which English chair design was spread was the publication of practical, clear books aimed at the trade by men like Chippendale, Hepplewhite, and Sheraton. Their designs were simple, and craftsmen could execute the models presented without being master carvers. In fact, carving was reduced to a minimum, so that the maker of such a chair did not need to be trained for many years in order to execute a decent copy of the illustrated seat.

On the contrary, ornamentists such as Delafosse, Lalonde, or Neufforge designed wonderful seats with exotic names such as "paphouse" or "sultane," but much was left to the imagination of the maker, and they all required skills that only well-trained craftsmen could muster. These designs were useful in France because the guild regulations there in the eighteenth century produced unsurpassed chair-makers and carvers, but the difficult models could not be re-created easily elsewhere. The fact that chair-makers abroad could not put their hands on clear, simple directions for making French chairs was a major obstacle to their imitation. However, exact copies or simplified imitations of Sheraton and Hepplewhite seats could be found almost everywhere.

Both France and England owed a debt to Italy. The Italian architect Giovanni Battista Piranesi (1720–78) published in 1743 his *Prima Parte dell'Architettura e Prospettiva*, the first of many publications to present a theatrical vision of Ancient Rome. Piranesi's prints were to fire the imaginations of architects and chair designers all over the world and create a major impetus to the Neoclassical style. Piranesi was the first designer to use such antique motifs as palmettes, lion monopods, and sphinxes in furniture. He also incorporated Egyptian devices, and some Roman chairs of the late eighteenth century carry decoration drawn from Egyptian Antiquity, anticipating the French *goût Egyptien* by several decades. Piranesi's four-volume *Antichitá Romane* of 1756 also left an impression on the French students of the Academy in Rome and on visiting English architects such as Adam. Piranesi's influence was to be especially important for the development of English furniture of the Regency period, although relatively few chairs were made in Italy under his influence.

◁
A watercolor drawing of an armchair by the French ornamental designer Richard de Lalonde, 1782–86. Several of Lalonde's designs are identifiable with chairs made by Jacob Frères, Séné, Delanois, and others. Such watercolors, which were made to offer clients a variety of selections for the upholstery of their chairs, give us an interesting view of late-eighteenth-century Parisian taste. Collection Trinity Fine Art, London

◁
An Italian carved and gilt armchair, Rome, c. 1783. L'Antiquaire & The Connoisseur, Inc.

high style: baroque, rococo & neoclassical chairs   235

> A rare set of Florentine Louis XVI style gilt-wood armchairs, attributed to Carlo Toussaint. Chinese Porcelain Company, New York

> A pair of Italian Neoclassical armchairs, Rome or Turin, c. 1780. These handsomely designed and carved armchairs represent the best craftsmanship of the Italian Neoclassical period. Chinese Porcelain Company, New York

<

An Italian Neoclassical painted and parcel-gilt side chair, probably Florentine, c. 1790. Similar chairs closely resembling the published designs of Hepplewhite were produced by a number of Florentine chair-makers, notably Carlo Toussaint and Giovacchino Paoli. Both provided chairs to Ferdinand III, grand duke of Tuscany, for the royal apartments at the Pitti Palace at the end of the eighteenth century. Collection Matz and Pribell, Cambridge, Massachusetts

>

A pair of Italian parcel-gilt carved walnut armchairs. These are Neapolitan or Sicilian, From the last quarter of the eighteen century. In contrast to the French practice, in which a *menuisier* would make the chair frame and then pass it on to a specialist in carving for embellishment, in Italy chairs were made entirely by carvers. The fine veining of the wood is most unusual, as is the fact that the seat rails have been cut out rather than sawn. The maker of these chairs may have been an Italian working in France, as they show considerable French influence. Collection Jonathan Harris, London

>

A pair of Sicilian armchairs, attributed to Giuseppe Venanzio Marvuglia, c. 1775, from the collection of the prince of Palagonia, Palermo. L' Antiquaire & The Connoisseur, Inc.

The 1770s saw a mingling of rococo and classical ornamentation in Italy. During the mid-1780s, the Sienese architect Agostino Fantastici created seats in Piranesi's spirit that were precursors of the Empire style. In Venice, however, Neoclassicism had barely taken root, while in Rome, Genoa, and other centers, French influence was still reflected in chair design with the pattern books of Hepplewhite and Sheraton also playing their part since there was no Italian equivalent. Indeed, simplified versions of Hepplewhite, Sheraton, and even Chippendale chairs were seen throughout Italy.

The Neoclassical style was also slow to find favor in Germany. Court furniture-makers in Potsdam and Berlin were still working in the rococo style well into the 1770s. The first Neoclassical designs for furniture were not published in Germany until about 1780 by Franz Heissig of Augsburg. In Weimar, the *Journal des Luxus und der Moden*, established in 1787, finally published designs for classical chairs based on English and French prototypes. The Louis XVI style was never favored in Germany; by the time it

<
A German brass-mounted mahogany fauteuil, c. 1780, by David Roentgen (1743–1807). Roentgen, Abraham Roentgen's son, was the greatest German furniture-maker, the most successful of all eighteenth-century makers, and the first to establish a furniture industry on an international scale. Christie's

was accepted there, the Empire style was already spreading from France and soon superseded the German adaptation of Louis XVI.

In Spain a strong French influence created by the country's Bourbon royalty led to the popularity of Louis XV chairs until the 1770s, several decades after the style was out of fashion in France. In 1799, only too happy to escape the political turmoil after the French Revolution, Jean Démosthène Dugourc, one of the leading designers of the late Louis XVI style and the principal architect of the *style étrusque* in France, was appointed architect to the Spanish court, for which he designed some exceptional Neoclassical seats. However, in the last decade of the eighteenth century, English pattern books were to lead to elongated versions of Chippendale and Sheraton chairs. The English influence was even more marked in Portugal.

The journal of the Englishman William Bedford written in Portugal in 1787 tells us that ample sofas, covered with chintz, furnished his living quarters. We also learn of a very unusual

<
A carved and gilt side chair from Turin, c.1780. L'Antiquaire & The Connoisseur, Inc.

>
A Spanish Neoclassical side chair, made for the bedroom of the Queen Maria Luisa. Patrimonio Nacional, Madrid

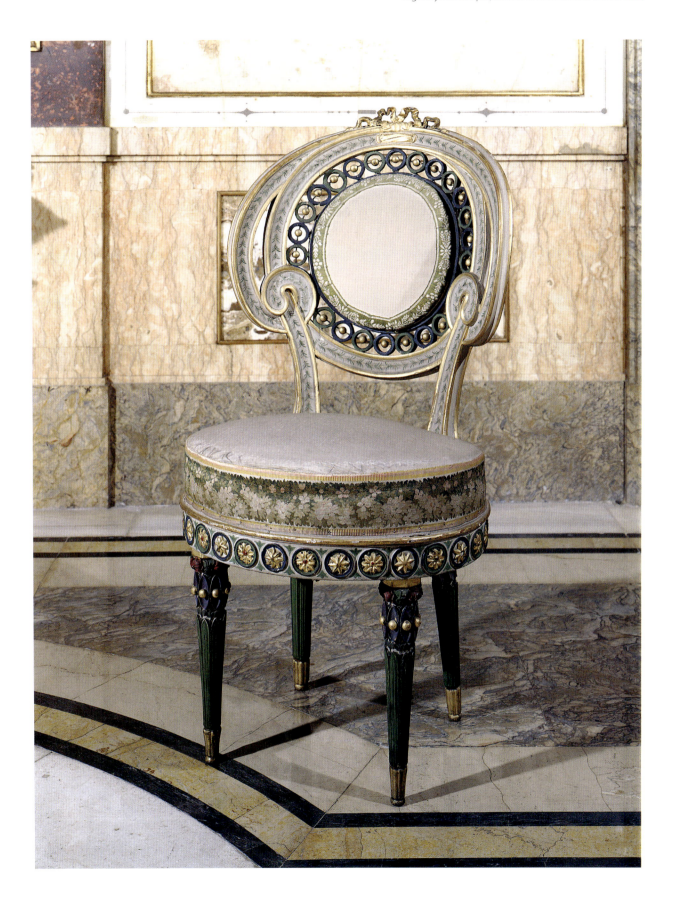

sitting habit in that country, in his entry of October 17, 1787:

D. Pedro & the Grand Prior conducted us into a snug boudoir that looks into the Great Pavilion whose gay & fantastic scenery appeared to infinite advantage by the light of innumerable tapers reflected on all sides from lustres of glittering crystal. The little Infanta D. Carlota was perched on a sofa in a conversation with the Marchioness & D. Henriqueta, who in the true oriental fashion had placed themselves cross-legged on the floor. A troop of Maids of Honor commanded by the Countess sat in the same posture at a little distance.

Thus we learn that the oriental manner of sitting cross-legged had persisted in Portugal, despite the strong English influence, as late as the end of the eighteenth century, even in refined circles. Portugal was probably the only European country where this habit persisted for so long. By the 1780s the custom had long disappeared in Spain, and it had never existed in the Nordic countries.

The classical taste came to Sweden and Denmark early, since both countries enjoyed a strong French influence and employed excellent French architects and craftsmen. The French architect Nicolas Henri Jardin designed, as early as 1760, the dining room of Count von Moltke at Amalienborg in the Neoclassical style. Jardin's work was so appreciated that he was asked to

<
An etching from Goya's *Los Caprichos* series (pl. 26), showing "Chairs on the Head," c. 1799. Wearing chairs on the head meant a world gone mad. The Metropolitan Museum of Art

redecorate the Banquet Hall at Christiansborg in preparation for the wedding of the future King Christian VII. Jardin continued to carry out royal commissions in the Louis XVI style until his dismissal in 1770.

In the late 1780s the English mode dominated Danish chair style. Painted in light colors, with straight lines and often a shield back, chairs were produced following the designs of Hepplewhite and Sheraton, whose pattern books met with the same enthusiasm in Denmark as elsewhere. High import duties and the readily available drawings encouraged the growth of the local chair market, and by the beginning of the nineteenth century Danish chair-makers were making excellent chairs in the English manner.

The Neoclassical style flowered in Sweden, patronized by the ambitious young Gustav III (reigned 1771–92). The finest Swedish architects of the time were Carl Fredrik Adelcrantz and Jean Eric Rehn, and the Gustavian style that they created was considerably influenced by the French *goût grecque*. Many chairs of the period are similar to contemporary Louis XVI work, although some models are derived from English pattern books. Gustavian shield-back chairs are based on Hepplewhite's designs, and further English influence, based on the ladder-back chair, can be seen in the well-known "Gripsholm chair," made for the courtiers' rooms. At the end of the eighteenth century, English and French chairs were so popular in Holland that in 1771 the Amsterdam guild forbade the importation of chairs made outside the Netherlands. All seats had to be branded with the mark of the Amsterdam Joseph Guild, with the letters *J* and *G* flanking the arms of Amsterdam.

Throughout the reign of Catherine the Great (1762–1796), the Russian throne was synonymous

r of Danish
el-gilt oak arm-
s. Christie's

with splendor. Catherine had invited the Italian architect Giacomo Quarenghi to work in Russia, and soon after his arrival in 1779, he was appointed court architect, a post he retained under Catherine's successors, Paul I and Alexander I. Quarenghi designed interiors, furniture, and chairs for the Winter Palace and Peterhof in the Neoclassical style. Charles Cameron, a Scottish architect, came to St. Petersburg in 1779, as well. At Tsarskoje Selo, he was given carte blanche to realize the classical ideals he had formulated after years of studying the art of Ancient Greece and Rome. Some of Catherine's impressions of his work at Tsarskoje Selo survive. On June 22, 1781, for example, she wrote to Baron Grimm:

I have an architect here named Kameron ... the man has a fertile brain. ... So far only two rooms have been furnished, and people rush to see them because they have never before seen anything like them. I admit that I have not grown tired of looking at them for the last nine weeks; they are pleasing to the eye.

Catherine was hard-working and immensely practical. As her secretary Adrian Gribovskii wrote, "She came into the bedroom at ten o'clock and sat on a side chair upholstered in silk in front of a curved table. A similar table and chair for her secretary faced her." A side chair was an appropriate seat for the empress's work; an armchair would have been more comfortable, but at these times she wanted to attend to business. Not much is known of the organization of the chair-makers' guild in Russia, but one master was likely responsible for the carpentry and carving while another saw to the gilding. Russian carvers, who probably learned their craft from Italian workmen, used an abundance of Neoclassical motifs such as urns, pine cones, garlands of flowers interlaced with rams' or lions' heads, and Egyptian sphinxes mixed with festooned roses. The sheer exuberance of the decoration, combined with different colors of gold and bright shades of turquoise, violet-blue,

or orange, created audacious models unlike anything in the West. However, despite the abundance of designs derived from French and Italian prototypes, Catherine clearly preferred English models, as did many Russians. At the end of the eighteenth century, advertisements for English mahogany chairs were published regularly in the St. Petersburg *Register*. The issue of March 11, 1776, ran an announcement that "on the 2-D line of Vassiljevskij Island, at the last house, all kinds of English furniture such as . . . chairs are sold; their price is low." Moreover, as Anthony Cross has pointed out, "Four English shops existed in

<

The formal drawing room at the Catherine Palace, St. Petersburg. Beginning in 1779, the Scottish architect Charles Cameron (1740–1812), an admirer of all things Antique, was entrusted with refurbishing the palace's interior. The armchairs he designed for the room are a testament to his taste. He created a suite of gilded armchairs upholstered in the same white silk with delicately painted blue flowers that was used to cover the wall. The Neoclassical chairs were designed as an integral part of the room in the French manner, with straight, fluted legs and seats shaped in the Louis XVI style. The backs, however, with their sophisticated carving of acanthus leaves and rams' heads, are totally original.

<

The magnificent throne room of Tsar Paul I (1797), designed by Vincenzo Brenna in what was previously the private library of Count Orlov at Gatchina, featured an ornate throne.

St. Petersburg in 1791, selling all kinds of furniture and chairs."

Interest in French design was also strong. Jean Démosthène Dugourc wrote in his autobiography that Catherine's son Paul I, while still a grand duke in 1782, had invited him to relocate in St. Petersburg. Dugourc declined at first, but after the Revolution accepted a similar offer from Spain, where he created marvelous Neoclassical seats.

In America, chair-makers primarily followed the English pattern books, partly because of their English heritage, partly because doing so was easy. Beginnings of the Neoclassical style in America were evident in 1774 during the Continental Congress. The taste of men like Washington and Jefferson was more advanced than that of most of their countrymen, and they were aware that their houses and furnishings would have wide influence. Gouverneur Morris, a delegate from New York, advised Washington that it was important "to fix the taste of our country properly . . . [and] your example will go far." After the Revolutionary War, the importation of seats from England to the United States increased during the Federal period. By 1788, when the Constitution was adopted, Hepplewhite's *The Cabinet-Maker and Upholsterer's Guide* and Thomas Shearer's *The London Cabinet-Maker's Book of Prices* had been published, and shortly afterward Sheraton brought out his book of designs. All three books were widely used in America as sources of patterns for chair-makers, who sometimes copied a model exactly, and sometimes gave it an individual or regional interpretation. The great variety of lightweight side chairs that survive from Federal America is a gauge of their popularity. It is interesting that American chair-makers tended to keep far closer to the original design books than their European counterparts, who rarely copied them precisely.

The apprentice system in America was supervised not only by the guild concerned but also by the local authorities. By the end of the eighteenth century, the period of apprenticeship had become considerably shorter than the seven years established in the late seventeenth century. The demand for seats was increasing, and so, therefore, was the need for journeymen. However, there was no separate guild to supervise each category as in Paris. One craftsman could make chairs and cabinets, carve wood, and gild if he wished to, a freedom that facilitated the creation of large workshops in Philadelphia, New York, and Newport, Rhode Island. Few Americans stamped their work, although the stamp of Stephen Badlam (1751–1815) can be found on chairs in the Henry Francis Du Pont Winterthur Museum in Delaware and the Metropolitan Museum in New York.

One popular chair in America was the so-called lolling chair. In 1778 an Englishman complained about the advance of indolence in *The Gentleman's Magazine*, describing scornfully the "two-armed machine adapted to the indulgent purpose of lolling, and so unwieldy as only to be conveyed, to the great endangerment of the carper, from one part of the room to the other

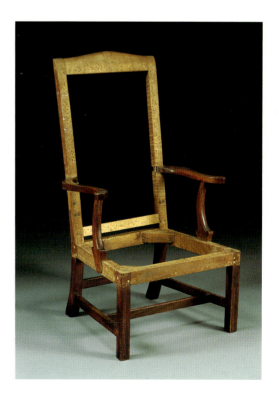

> A Chippendale lolling chair, c. 1760–80. The term "lolling chair" refers to an eighteenth-century English armchair with an upholstered seat and back, the seat generally low and shallow, the back high. In America such a chair is often called a "Martha Washington chair." Christie's

An American armchair from the Marie Antoinette drawing room suite. The armchair is part of a famous set that originally belonged to Edward Shippen Burd of Philadelphia. A large sofa and twelve armchairs still survive from the set, which is a rare example of sophisticated American painted furniture in the Louis XVI style. So close is the design to French chairs of the period that when the suite was sold in 1921 it was identified as French. Philadelphia Museum of Art

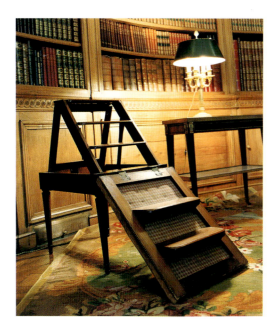

A convertable stool opened to form a set of library steps. Musée Nissim de Camondo. Photograph: Antoine Bootz

upon wheels." Chairs of this general form had been made in France and England during the early and mid-eighteenth century, some versions being called *fauteuils de commodité*. By the 1760s, the popularity of this form had waned in Europe, but in the United States it had developed its own peculiar characteristics, emphasizing a tall back and slim, tapering arms and legs.

Political and cultural ties between France and America strengthened during the Federal Period. The American political elite was well-disposed toward France, both because many of the ideas underlying the American Revolution had their origins in French philosophy, and because they remembered that without the timely appearance of the French fleet, the battle of Yorktown would not have been won. Moreover, many important American leaders had enjoyed long sojourns in France, which they remembered with affection and admiration. John Adams, Benjamin Franklin, Thomas Jefferson, George Washington, and James Monroe all purchased Neoclassical French seats, Jefferson shipping home eighty-six crates of effects from Paris when he returned to America in 1789. A few pieces survive at Monticello, including a pair of Louis XVI looking-glasses and some relatively simple fauteuils or upholstered easy chairs.

Philadelphia became a haven for French émigrés, whose presence stimulated a vogue for gilded and painted chairs in the Louis XVI style, encouraged by the import of royal furniture after the collapse of the old regime. American chair-makers who had to compete with immigrant craftsmen and imported seats were quick to adapt. Before the start of the nineteenth century, Neoclassical taste had become the reigning fashion of the new American democracy. Some craftsmen made seats in the French fashion, some of which were such good imitations of Louis XVI chairs that they could pass for French. Other makers followed the design books of Sheraton and Hepplewhite. In any case, Neoclassical chairs were adopted so universally because of their unique association with

their era. Fashion in dress required tall hats and tightly fitting clothes, and the precise and carefully proportioned Neoclassical seats corresponded well to their restrained order. The character of the Federal period was summed up by William Bentley, a diarist from Salem, Massachusetts, who, after visiting the residence of Oak Hill, furnished by Elizabeth Derby West, wrote that she "never violates the chastity of correct taste."

stools

At the end of the eighteenth century, stools were going out of style. Sebastien Mercier, in his *Tableau de Paris* (IV, 72), wrote that *Il n'y a plus de tabourets que chez le Roi et la Reine, les metteurs en œuvre et les cordonniers* [Today the only stools to be found are in the king and queen's apartments, builders' workrooms, and shoemakers' shops]. Indeed, the inventory of property at Versailles in 1792 does list in Marie Antoinette's bedroom *douze ployants sculptés et dorés, couverts de brocard, ornés de franges de trios pouces à tête et guirlandes* [twelve folding stools carved and gilded, upholstered in brocade, enhanced with fringes], and twelve in Louis XVI's bedroom, as well. Only

A Roman Neoclassical painted and parcel-gilt banquette, c. 1770. Banquettes of this design without a seat back are typical of the best Roman palace seat furniture of the eighteenth century.

a few years earlier, Roubo, in his treatise "The Art of Menuiserie" (1768–72), had noted that *pliants* (folding stools) had become old-fashioned: *Fort en usage le siècle dernier, tant pour les grands que pour les particuliers, mais ces sortes de sièges sont peu commodes; on leur a preferé les tabourets* [In frequent use during the last century, as much for aristocrats as for common people; however these seats are not practical, the tabouret has superseded them]. Clearly, the folding stool was not a favorite during the last part of the eighteenth century, an era that loved comfort too much to tolerate such a hierarchical seat. Fashion at the time was against the privilege represented by the *pliant*, so the stool itself was unpopular. At the same time, the gout stool, designed for resting the feet of one afflicted with the complaint, was a common item in genteel households. Hepplewhite's 1788 *Guide* illustrated such a stool, "the construction of which, by being so easily raised or lowered at either end, is particularly useful to the afflicted." Boswell wrote that when he called on Mr. Pitt in February 1766, he found him "in black clothes, with white nightcap and foot all wrapped up in flannel, and on a gout-stool."

Another favorite backless seat was the banquette. Delafosse designed one with full arms, which he called "l'Italienne." In the great drawing rooms of houses built and furnished by Robert Adam, a formal and stately effect was obtained by long stools arranged against the walls, while in the deep window recesses others with curved ends, frequently caned, were often placed. Such stools do not seem to have been popular in France at the time; the only fashionable tabourets were made to fit into corners.

Hepplewhite illustrates several stools in his 1778 *Guide*, with both tapered and cabriolet legs. The caption states that the frame "may be of mahogany or japanned, as most agreeable, or to match the suite of chairs, and of consequence should have the same coverings." Sheraton illustrated none in his *Drawing Book* (1791–94), and in the *Dictionary* (1803) omits the heading of "stool" altogether. The only stool that he shows is a "corridor stool," which, the text explains, is for "persons waiting," which should be long and narrow, to agree with their situation. Stools had become unimportant indeed; no significant development in their design occurred before about 1800.

sofas

Sofas and canapés were extremely popular in the reign of Louis XV, and even more so under Louis XVI. The taste for sofas seems to have been inversely proportional to the lack of enthusiasm for stools. The variety of canapés was endless, including pieces described as *en gondole, en corbeille*, and *tête à tête*. The *confident*, a large canapé with two additional seats on each end, continued in use, with straight legs in the Neoclassical style. Hepplewhite illustrated a "confidante" in his *Guide*, stating that a living room was not complete without one. He recommended that it be about nine feet long, also noting that one could remove the two ends, which could be used as *bergères*. In 1779 Robert Adam designed one for Sir Abraham Hume, the ends being apparently irremovable.

The chaise longue, or *duchesse*, continued in use, either in one piece or *brisée* (broken) into two or three parts. Titled ladies were accustomed to spend their time in languorous ease on *duchesses*, and Mlle. Bertin, Marie Antoinette's dress-maker, went so far as to receive her famous customers lolling on one. This refined indolence was also indulged in by English society. Lady Louisa Stuart, writing in 1783, reports that when a lady of her acquaintance visited the duchess of Argyll, she found her "lolling in her usual nonchalant manner upon a settee and beating the devil's tattoo with one leg over the other." Mme. Vigée-Lebrun in her memoirs recalled her life in exile in St. Petersburg around 1795. She went out in society often and thoroughly enjoyed herself, finding "all the urbanity, all the grace of French company." She also noted that "All apartments are furnished with long, broad divans for men and women to sit on. I became so used to them that I could not sit on a chair." Comfort was of primary importance in Russia, so the sofa or divan was widely adopted.

> A watercolor drawing of a "Sofa à l'Athénienne," by Richard de Lalonde. Collection Trinity Fine Art, London

Sheraton explains that although the term "duchess" was derived from the French *duchesse*, "what we call a duchess is very different from theirs." In the *Drawing Book* he illustrates an example intended to serve three distinct purposes. It may be used as a bed, as two small sofas, or, when the ends are connected, "to rest or loll upon after dinner." English duchesses, although fashionable for some years, have rarely survived. Evidently their several parts were often put to separate use and were later dispersed.

Duchesses, canapés, and sofas generally were part of a large set, and had their place in state and reception rooms. However, the sofa was often associated with the boudoir, and thus appeared in salacious jokes, such as this epigram about Cardinal de Rohan:

On voit dans ce portrait la perle des prélats / Il brille également au Parnasse, à Cythère. / Il serait assez mal en chaire; / Il est fort bien sur les sophas

[*We see in this portrait the pearl of prelates / He shines equally on Parnassus and Cythera / He would be bad enough in a pulpit / he is especially happy on a sofa*]

For upholstered sofas, Hepplewhite's *Guide* gives four designs, noting that the woodwork "should be either mahogany or japanned in accordance with the chairs; the coverings also must be the same," and pointing out that the dimensions vary according to the size of the room and the pleasure of the purchaser. Hepplewhite also illustrated what he called a "bar back sofa" formed of four connected shield-shaped chair backs, adding that "this kind of sofa is of modern invention," a surprising assertion in view of its long popularity in England. Such a sofa is a typical English and later, American seat.

Sheraton was also content with his earlier designs with slight variations of the Louis XVI upholstered sofa. He recommended two sofas in a drawing room, for the proper furnishing of which "workmen in every nation exert the utmost efforts of their genius." Sofas should be covered with silk or satin and "may have cushions to fill their back, together with bolsters at each end." In his notes on the Prince of Wales's Chinese drawing room, given in the Appendix, Sheraton observed that it contained "an ottoman or a long seat, extending the whole width of the room and returning at each end."

In France at the end of the eighteenth century the ottoman was the rage, the sofa of the fashionable woman. Mercier wrote, *Une jolie femme qui a des vapeurs, ne fait plus autre chose que de se trainer de sa baignoire à sa toilette et de sa toilette à son ottomane* [A lady not feeling well can only move from her bath to her toilet and from her toilet to her ottoman]. The *sultane* and the *turquoise* were exotic variations of the chaise longue. The *paphose* was yet another, very ornate, form of sofa. All these were custom-designed for specific places, as the memoirs of the French chair-maker George Jacob make clear. Their names reflect the period's infatuation with the Orient.

In the latter phase of classical taste, upholstered sofas and canapés became more severe. The square sofa, illustrated by both Hepplewhite and Sheraton, was one of the most popular forms in Federal America.

upholstery

The simplest upholstery is cloth or leather stretched across a rigid framework. This was the form upholstery took in ancient Egypt, Greece, and Rome, although cushions might be added for comfort. In the early Renaissance, leather, prepared by a saddler, was nailed across a chair's frame. Later, padding was sewn together with the covering material, the stitching often forming a pattern. Chairs with such quilting were apparently made in both Spain and Italy before 1600.

True upholstery appeared only at the beginning of the seventeenth century. At first,

>
A painted and parcel-gilt walnut and cherrywood *divano*, or sofa, from the Piedmont region of northern Italy, c. 1780, with plaster decoration, reputedly based on designs by Giuseppe Maria Bonzanigo. From the collection of Count Carlo Francesco II Valpergna di Masino, Viceroy of Sardinia. L'Antiquaire & The Connoisseur, Inc.

straw or feathers might be piled on a seat and a cover nailed over them. Gradually, chair-makers increased the comfort of the padding by making it deeper, by using a better filler such as down or horsehair, or by adding loose cushions. Later, the padding of the seat was laid on a lattice of girth-webbing nailed across the frame, just as it is on many chairs today. The French practice was to lace webs closely to form an unbroken surface, whereas the English preferred an open network.

Springs came into use in the eighteenth century, and with this improvement modern upholstery began. Upholstery was now made to accommodate the human form, and more comfort was achieved using elaborate padding of horsehair, waste silk, and wool. When the *menuisier*, the sculptor, and the *peintre-doreur* had finally completed the frame of a chair or sofa it was handed over to the *tapissier* (upholsterer).

Few antique seats retain their original upholstery, and when they do it is usually heavily worn, so it is hard to imagine the beauty and sophistication of what was originally made. Great pains were taken to see that the material used was appropriate both to the frame and the setting for which it was intended. Even the smallest details such as the braid and the gilded nails with which the upholstery was attached were chosen with the greatest care so as to produce a harmonious effect. Chippendale, in the 1754 *Director*, gives some recommendations about upholstery, and it appears that the smallest details were important to him as well: "These seats look best when stuffed over the Rails, but are most commonly done with brass Nails in one of two Rows and sometimes the nails are done to imitate fret-work. . . ."

Upholsters deserve at least as much credit as the *menuisier* or the sculptor for the finished appearance of a chair. Some *tapissiers* became rich and famous, like Simon de Lobel, the principal upholster to Louis XIV, or Capin, the royal *tapissier* for Louis XVI.

250 high style: baroque, rococo & neoclassical chairs

A *sultane*, signed *Jean Avisse*. Musée Nissim de Camondo, Paris. Photograph: Antoine Bootz

Also in France the influential *marchands-tapissiers* were allowed by the guild to sell seats of all sorts, and it was no doubt an added incentive to produce work of fine quality.

A variety of materials was employed for early upholstery. In Tudor England, cowhide, ornamental leather, plain and embroidered velvet, tapestry, and needlework were all used. Later, especially during the eighteenth century, the variety appears almost endless. Silks patterned and striped, velvets stamped or plain, painted satin, printed cotton, embroidery, damask, leather, horsehair cloth, mohair, and *étoffe pareille à la tapisserie* were all used. Tapestry was employed less than we are led to believe, however, in France a wide range of it existed—Aubusson, Beauvais, or Gobelins. Sometimes pictorial panels woven at the Savonnerie factory were used for upholstery on sofas. Louis XV became very fond of embroidering tapestry himself for chairs.

In the *Director* Chippendale mentioned French chairs and tapestry:

Both the backs and seats must be covered with tapestry or other sort of needlework. Attempts were made from about 1630 onward to produce square edges to seats and backs, but the technique to do so were not mastered until well into the eighteenth century, when this style was sometimes referred to as à tableau.

For square-back chairs the padding of the back was often deep and arranged so that it formed a sharp edge around the back of the chair.

The reverse of the back was generally covered with a material intended to harmonize with that used elsewhere, but not necessarily of the same pattern, and often of inferior quality. Therefore, the backs of *sièges meublants* and sometimes of *sièges courants* were often covered with cotton in checkered patterns. Upholstery was also often enriched with tassels, trims, fringes, and cords. Braid or fringe often masked the bare joints and seams where the material was tacked down to the framework, but fringe was also used purely for decoration. The making of fringes has been described as the "ordinary pastime" of ladies at this period.

Fashion in dress also influenced the upholstering of chairs, particularly about 1720, when space was required for voluminous skirts and hard bolsters became popular on couches, with flat cushions fastened to the back. When not in use, expensively covered chairs would be protected against dust and light by loose covers of a less expensive material, often serge, bay, cotton, and even taffeta. Sometimes this might also be reversed, so that the slip-cover was made of expensive fabric while the cheaper one remained fixed to the seat.

In the mid-nineteenth century, springs became elliptical and elaborate methods were developed to make seats more resilient. Spring upholstery requires a deeper wooden frame, which was best made of hard, non-splitting woods like ash or birch, joined with glued dowels and braced with corner blocks to resist the tension of tied springs. On the bottom the webbing was crisscrossed and stitched together. The springs were arranged over this in rows, stitched down, and tied together. Burlap was placed over them, then a layer each of felt, wadding, and muslin, and finally, the upholstery material. In the nineteenth century, the great diversity of styles, the continued search for comfort, and the development of industry led to the creation of a multiplicity of upholstered seats. Sometimes upholsterers overrode the carvers, and chairs and sofas became bulky. Deep tufting helped hold the filling in place and controlled the shape of the chair.

Upholstery techniques have changed little since the nineteenth century. Although today there are many synthetic fabrics and fillings available, these are not necessarily better than traditional materials. Down, horsehair, and feathers are still the best fillings.

5
chairs in the nineteenth century

PSEUDO-ARCHAEOLOGICAL CHAIRS

With the French Revolution of 1789, the cult of Antiquity became something close to a religion. The Jacobins saw themselves as antique heroes and held up the stoic virtues of Republican Rome as standards of behavior. Likewise, the festivals of the Revolution were staged as antique rituals by the painter Jacques-Louis David (1748–1825) and Neoclassicism became the official artistic style. Even the chairs of the Committee for Public Safety were made on models after the Antique designed by David.

The cult of Antiquity actually originated earlier in the eighteenth century, with the writings of Rousseau, Diderot, Voltaire, Winckelmann, and Goethe. The works of artists such as Piranesi, Hubert Robert, and David expanded on the theme. Toward the middle of the century, interest in the classical world lead to archaeological excavations throughout Italy, and the discoveries made led to the creation or enlargement of antiquities collections as gentlemen from all over Europe competed for the works recovered.

In France, the new style was encouraged by the success of David's *Oath of the Horatii*, exhibited at the Salon of 1785, with its Neo-Pompeian setting and its appeal to Republican sentiments. Louis XVI, sincerely dedicated to reform, and Paris, already stirring with revolution, united in applauding the artist. The imitation of Antiquity was not an end in itself, but a means of creating ideal work of universal validity. The breadth of its appeal can be seen in the work of late-eighteenth- and early-nineteenth-century chair-makers in both Europe and in North America.

The French Revolution frightened most of the European monarchs, who abhorred its ideas of freedom and egalitarianism; when Louis XVI was guillotined January 21, 1793, they feared a similar fate. Catherine the Great of Russia broke off all relations with the French government and urged other European monarchies to form a coalition against France. For a brief moment, French influence in the decorative arts and in chair-making in particular came to an end. However, with the death of Robespierre on July 27, 1794, and the end of the Reign of Terror, France emerged from

<<
A painted and gilt-wood *faudesteuil* (faldstool) from David's studio, one of a group of seats made by Jacob after designs by David and his pupil Moreau. Châteaux de Versailles et de Trianon. Photograph: RMN. Gerard Blot

<
An Etruscan-style seat from the reign of Carlos IV, designed by Jean Démosthène Dugourc. Patrimonio Nacional, Madrid

> A German armchair, c. 1790. This is a truly exceptional chair; its use of gilt-lead mounts is a rare but occasional feature of German furniture, and the sophisticated bolted construction of the beech frame echoes the techniques developed by David Roentgen to facilitate the export of pieces to Paris and St. Petersburg. Collection Carlton Hobbs, London

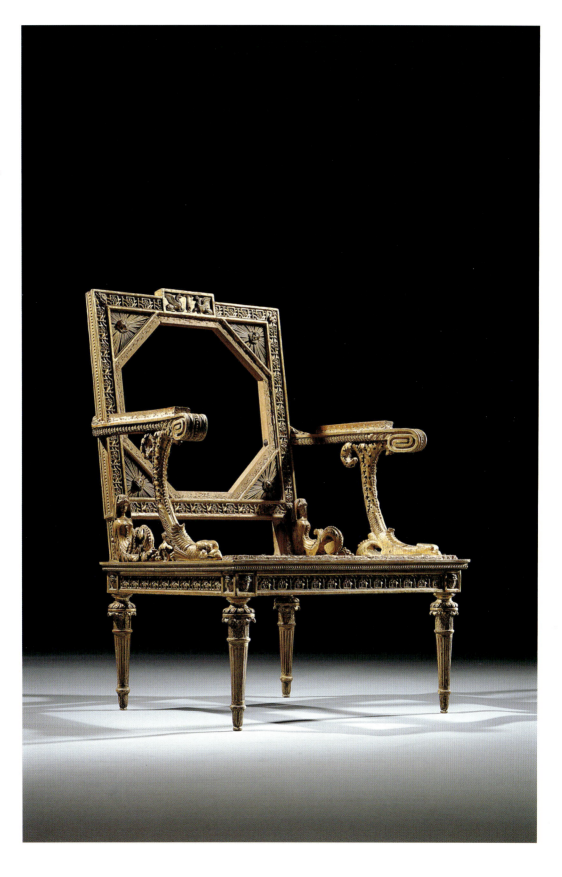

A Madame Récamier chaise longue, attributed to Jacob Frères (1796–1803). Inv 0A 11384 Louvre. Photograph: RMN. Arnaudet

turmoil. With the rise of Napoleon and the Empire style French influence resumed, and with it, the imitation of Antiquity.

Jacques-Louis David, Napoleon's First Painter, introduced the empress Josephine to the designers Charles Percier (1764–1838) and Pierre-François-Léonard Fontaine (1762–1853). This brilliant pair transformed her house, Malmaison, with antique-style chairs and furnishings, establishing the Empire style as a Neoclassical setting for the imperial court. Because the simple forms and applied ornaments were easy to reproduce, aspects of this style became popular throughout Europe for much of the century.

As the Empire style flourished on the Continent, in England the Regency, with its various Greek, Egyptian, Gothic, and Chinese styles, blossomed, opening the door for the archaeological revivals of the nineteenth century. These pseudo-archaeological movements, too eccentric for most of the rising bourgeoisie, were generally patronized by intellectuals, writers, artists, and aristocrats.

> An Italian settee influenced by the excavations at Herculaneum, c. 1810. Private collection

imitation antique chairs and armchairs

Classical chairs were attractive. The Greek *klismos* appealed to the poetic, intellectual, and political sensibility of the time. One of the most graceful chairs in the history of furniture, combining comfort, elegance, and simplicity, it featured a slightly sloping back surmounted by a thick, arched and bent crosspiece, which curved around the sitter's back. The caned or rush seat was covered with a cushion or animal skin for added comfort. The curved legs were slender, sometimes bearing incised patterns and topped by rosettes and volutes. Architects, decorators, and painters at the end of the eighteenth and the beginning of the nineteenth century reproduced these tapering legs and sloping backs in their drawings, leaving the problem of how to actually build the chairs to the chair-makers. The makers either attenuated the curves of the legs or replaced the curved front legs with straight ones. This solution, which had been foreshadowed by eighteenth-century English chair-makers, became the rule: Most neo-antique chairs made in France and later, elsewhere, have straight front legs and curved back legs.

> A *klismos* chair by Nicolai Abraham Abildgaard (1743–1809), the leading Danish Neoclassical painter, designed and made for his own use, c. 1800. Museum of Decorative Art, Copenhagen

< A Danish *klismos* chair painted gray to simulate metal, c. 1810. Bill Blass Collection

< One of a pair of ormolu and patinated bronze *chenets* (andirons) decorated with a *klismos* chair, possibly after a model by Simon-Louis Boizot, Paris, c. 1790. The figure refers to the nuptials of Paris and Helen of Troy. In Book II, the *Iliad* describes Helen as seated on a *klismos* in her bedchamber, lost in thought. Private collection, New York

Several artists, including David, Percier, and Fontaine in France; Thomas Hope (1769–1831) in England; Nicolai Abraham Abildgaard (1743–1809) in Denmark; and Benjamin Latrobe (1764–1820) in America, attempted through the study of antique chairs to create a convincing classicism in harmony with the increasing interest in archaeology, which introduced the French Directoire style. David's paintings of Roman historical subjects were thought to embody correctness where staging was concerned. David commissioned Georges Jacob (1739–1814), the leading chair-maker of the day, to produce models for his vast studio, after designs by himself and his pupil, Moreau.

David also had a day bed of dark mahogany mounted with gilt bronze stars and upholstered with material of Pompeian design, and a *klismos*, a chaise longue, and a light Roman bench, well-known from his portrait of Madame Récamier. Some of these appear in the painter's *Amours*

<
A Russian *klismos* chair, c. 1810, in the library of Bill Blass. Bill Blass Collection

de Paris et Hélène, finished in 1788 for the comte d'Artois, brother of Louis XVI, as well as in such other Neoclassical paintings as T*he Death of Socrates* (1787) and *Lictors Bringing Home to Brutus the Bodies of His Sons* (1789).

The crowds who came to see the *Brutus* at the 1789 Salon hailed it as an expression of the Revolution, and David found himself the artistic mouthpiece of his time. Thereafter, he gave himself to the Revolution in a rare marriage of politics and art. He accepted its principles, illustrated its incidents, organized and adorned its fêtes, and commemorated its martyrs. By 1794 David was elected to the Committee of Public

Two north Italian fruitwood side chairs in the *klismos* style, c. 1810, one decorated with penwork. Christie's

Safety. After Robespierre's fall, however, David was arrested and only released, after three months' imprisonment, on the pleas of his pupils. He retired to the privacy of his studio, but returned to prominence in 1799 with a masterly panorama, *The Rape of the Sabines*. With Napoleon, he enjoyed a new career.

Classical-style chairs were fashionable in France only for about twenty years. Around 1805, the French abandoned them for the Empire style, another twist on the influence of Antiquity. In many European countries neo-antique chairs remained in favor much later in the century, for a multiplicity of reasons. In Denmark, neo-antique chairs emerged under the influence of the painter Nicolai Abildgaard, who, like David, designed chairs for his own use in Greek styles, notably in the *klismos* shape. These were directly copied from Greek ceramic painting, and decorated with painted panels imitating red-figure vases. When Abildgaard chose these antique forms, he was probably trying to do more than create an alternative to the common style of the day. As a professor at the Royal Academy of Art, he was obliged to carry out tasks for the royal family; yet he was an advocate of freedom and equality. His Greek-inspired chairs, like those in France, were an expression of attitudes both artistic and political. This fad quickly spread and became a style. By the 1830s another artist, the sculptor H. E. Freund, created a house that came to be called "Herculaneum in Zealand." It was a serious attempt to transfer the pure style of Antiquity to a northern milieu, and it profoundly influenced the next generation of Danish artists. The painter Thorvald Binderboll (1846–1908), for example, designed, with the artists Constantin Hansen, G. C. Hilker, and Joergen Roed, Greek-inspired chairs for the liberal headmaster of the Borgerdyd School (the school of Civil Virtue), whose social circle included every major Danish artist at the middle of the nineteenth century, as well as the liberal political figures who laid the foundation for the Danish constitution, which was adopted in 1849. It was also in this circle that neo-antique seats were popular.

Neo-antique seats seem to survive longest when they are introduced with a particular ideology rather than as a mere fad. Such was the case in both France and Denmark. In Sweden the chairs were also associated with a quest for liberty. Gustav III, a Francophile who had absorbed the ideas of the Enlightenment, built a pavilion in Neoclassical style at Haga, near Stockholm, as a retreat. The Grand Salon, decorated by the painter Louis Masreliez, who designed all the interiors and much of the furniture, is one of the finest Pompeian interiors in Europe. The sofas and chairs, including *klismos* chairs based on an antique model, were made by the Swedish chairmaker Eric Ohrmark (1747–1813).

Swedes of both middle and upper classes embraced the new liberalism, and everywhere the watchwords were progress, liberty, reason, and science. Gustav III, however, considered these new ideas as a threat to his monarchy. While he busied himself with plans to save Louis XVI, a group of Swedish nobles plotted his assassination. He was shot on March 16, 1792, and died ten days later. The *klismos*-inspired chair, however, lived on in Sweden until the first quarter of the nineteenth century.

In England, chairs in the antique style appear to have been influenced by French examples,

A Danish neo-antique armchair with sphinx supports by H. E. Freund. Museum of Decorative Art, Copenhagen

knowledge of which was transmitted by the architect Henry Holland (1745–1806) and by the designer Thomas Sheraton. The custom among cultivated Englishmen of taking the Grand Tour further exposed them to classical influences, as did the publication of the first volume of the *Antiquities of Athens* by James ("Athenian") Stuart and Nicholas Revett. The publication of Volume I in 1762 seems to have been a starting point of the English Greek Revival. By 1814 four volumes had been published, sparking the interest of a large audience. Thomas Hope, the chief exponent of Neoclassicism in England, wrote in 1807 that the French Revolution "has restored the pure taste of . . . ancient Greek forms for chairs." This antique taste is described by Sir Walter Scott in the *Quarterly Review* in March 1820 as follows:

Our national taste indeed has been changed in almost every particular, from that which was meager, formal, and poor, and has attained, comparatively speaking, a character of richness, variety, and solidity. An ordinary chair in the most ordinary parlour, has now something of an antique cast—something of Grecian massiveness, at once,

A Danish stool in the Herculaneum style by Nicolai Abraham Abildgaard. Museum of Decorative Art, Copenhagen

> A Danish chair decorated with angel faces, c. 1845, by the Danish painter Constantin Hansel (1804–80). Museum of Decorative Art, Copenhagen

v A chair by the Danish architect Gottlieb Bindesboll (1800–1856), c. 1838. Museum of Decorative Art, Copenhagen

and elegance in its forms. That of twenty or thirty years since was mounted on four tapering and tottering legs, resembling four tobacco-pipes; the present supporters of our stools have a curule air, curve outward behind and give a comfortable idea of stability to the weighty aristocrat or ponderous burgess.

Sheraton recorded the change in his later designs for chairs in his *Cabinet Dictionary* (1803). However, in England ancient Greek influence was only one of many exotic stains. Although Grecian symmetry was the professed aim of fashionable designers after 1805, it soon became necessary to make excursions into other, more exciting styles to satisfy public taste. As Loudon wrote in his *Encyclopedia* of 1833:

The principal Styles of Design in Furniture as at present executed in Britain may be reduced to four; viz. the Grecian or modern style which is by far the most prevalent; the Gothic or perpendicular, which imitates the lines and angles of the Tudor Gothic Architecture; the Elizabethan style, which combines the Gothic with the Roman or Italian manner; and the style of the age of Louis XIV, or florid Italian, which is characterized by curved lines and excess of curvilinear ornaments. The first and modern style is by far the most general and the second has been more or less the fashion in Gothic houses from the commencement of the present century since which period the third and fourth are occasionally to be met with, and the demand for them is rather on the increase than otherwise.

Thomas Hope is the perfect illustration of design at this time in England. His influence was far-reaching, especially after the publication of his designs in *Household Furniture and Decoration* in 1807. He had originally designed antique-inspired chairs for his own use to complement his collection of classical and Neoclassical statuary and objets d'art, and he imitated ancient seats as closely as had Jacques-Louis David and Nicolai

<
A late Gustavian Swedish chair by Ephraim Stahl (active Stockholm, 1794–1820/21) in the *klismos* style, c. 1795. Collection Ariane Dandois, Paris

Abildgaard. His Grecian chairs with saber legs and tilted backs were copied directly from Greek vase-painting. However, after the publication of Baron Denon's *Voyage dans la Basse et Haute Egypte*, Hope became interested in Egyptian seats and is best-known for his work in the Egyptian taste. He devoted his last years to the study of Gothic architecture.

Chairs after the antique became known as "Grecian," which became the accepted term for the seats based on Regency patterns produced in the last phase of the Classical tradition. These were particularly fashionable for dining rooms and men's clubs. The architect Philip Hardwick designed some of the best pieces in the style in 1834 for Goldsmiths' Hall, a London club. Hardwick's dining room chairs had leather seats and back-rests, crest-rails decorated with carved palmettes, and saber-form front legs. This handsome, dignified version of the Regency *klismos* is typical of the Grecian taste. Established Regency forms continued into the 1830s and '40s, when straight lines of Grecian chair design gave way to a growing taste for comfortable, rounded forms. This shift ultimately led to the emergence of the Victorian balloon-back chair.

In America, revivals flourished from the first quarter of the nineteenth century, with many chairs based on the Greek *klismos*; Greek-inspired couches were even created in the workshop of Duncan Phyfe as late as 1825. The Greek Revival movement, which had started as a French and English fad, resonated with the new country's ideas of liberty. Serving as Surveyor of Public Buildings in Washington from 1804 to 1812, the architect Benjamin Latrobe expressed the hope, in an 1811 address to the Society of Artists in Philadelphia, that "the days of Greece may be revived in the woods of America, and Philadelphia become the Athens of the Western World." During the Madison era, Latrobe supervised the furnishings of the White House, working closely with Mrs.

>
A pair of English Regency decorated and parcel-gilt *klismos* chairs, c. 1810. Christie's

An American sofa designed by Benjamin Henry Latrobe for William Waln of Philadelphia, of painted and gilded yellow poplar, maple, oak, and white pine with gesso ornaments. Much of the original caning on the seats in this suite survives. The original upholstery was crimson silk damask. Philadelphia Museum of Art

Madison. The chairs were based on the *klismos*, as shown in Thomas Hope's *Household Furniture and Interior Decoration*, published in London in 1807. Greek-inspired seats had a long life in America, abetted by numerous technological advances. Bronze powder was substituted for gold leaf, and later, the appearance of gilt was achieved even more cheaply by heating tin, mercury, ammonia, or sulfur. Around 1815, stencils made their appearance, an American novelty that permitted rapid decoration, and replaced expensive freehand work.

Although Egyptian-influenced furniture preceded the Empire style in France, in America classically-inspired, Empire, and Egyptian-influenced seats all appeared at about the same time. In Prussia and Russia, too, the three styles also appeared simultaneously. As late as 1828, the German architect Karl Friedrich Schinkel (1781–1841), a fervent apostle of pure classicism, was designing antique-inspired chairs for the Prussian palaces, and his contemporary, the architect Leo von Klenze (1784–1864), influenced by Percier and Fontaine, was designing chairs incorporating motifs and forms derived from Greek architecture and decoration. Von Klenze's most famous patron was Ludwig I of Bavaria, who shared his enthusiasm for Antiquity, and who appointed him Supervisor of Court Buildings and later, director of the Building Authorities of Bavaria. Von Klenze also exported his skills to Russia at the end of the 1830s and in the years following. At the invitation of Nicolas I, he created antique-inspired chairs similar to those he had designed in Munich around 1830. Soon after, in 1837, the Russian architect Alexander Brjullov designed a Pompeian dining room for the Winter Palace, with chairs inspired by the Greek *klismos*. The chairs came from the workshop of Peter Gambs (1802–71), oldest son of Heinrich Gambs (1765–1831), a talented cabinetmaker. A pupil of

> An American side chair designed by Latrobe in the *klismos* style, c. 1808. Latrobe, an architect, designer, and "'French engineer," was one of those most responsible for bringing archaeological correctness to the Federal style in late-eighteenth-century America. This set of furniture created for Waln was among the first to exhibit Latrobe's knowledge of classical antiquities. It shows a skillful reinterpretation of the Greek *klismos*, as well as of ancient Roman and Egyptian decorative motifs. Philadelphia Museum of Art

> A painting by Gustave Clarence Rodolphe Boulanger (1824–88) of a Pompeian-style house belonging to Prince Napoleon, c. 1860. Chateaux de Versailles et de Trianon. Photograph: RMN. Arnaudet

> A stool after a drawing by Charles Heathcote Tatham (1772–1842). Tatham, an English architect and designer, was instrumental in creating the Regency style. Bill Blass Collection

> An Eastern European Neo-Pompeian painted armchair, c. 1910, formerly belonging to Princess Zita de Bourbon-Parma, the last empress of Austria. R. Louis Bofferding Collection, New York

Roentgen, Peter Gambs became the cabinetmaker for the court, creating numerous chair styles. Although the antique style was popular in Russia for a time, it was a passing fad among many. Ultimately, the variety of styles and the quest for comfort during the second half of the nineteenth century won out over beauty in Russian chairs.

Classically trained architects and painters were attracted to antique-inspired seats, and variations of such seats returned in the twentieth century, mainly among painters such as Franz von Stuck in Munich, or architects such as Josef Frank in Stockholm. Von Stuck's villa in Munich is a Neoclassical abstraction, where the furniture adapts Pompeian models to the outlines of the Art Nouveau style. The seats are primarily *klismos*-inspired, and the couches are enhanced with inlays and painted decoration. The villa was even awarded a gold medal at the Paris Exhibition of 1900. Like David and Abildgaard before him, von Stuck designed his own seats as part of the creative environment of his art.

The *klismos* was especially favored in the Nordic countries, Central Europe, and America. In Sweden Carl Malmsten produced a *klismos*-inspired chair, as did the Finnish architect Alvar Aalto in his earliest work from the 1920s. Robsjohn-Gibbons was totally influenced by ancient Greek chairs, and in mid-1940s California William Haines created Neoclassical interiors and *klismos*-inspired chairs. As these examples illustrate, the ancient world continues to be a source of inspiration for chairs, even in the modern era.

empire and neo-egyptian chairs

"Soldiers, forty centuries look down upon you," Napoleon proclaimed to his troops, pointing to the pyramids in the distance. Eager to establish his own place in history, he had brought archaeologists and artists on his Egyptian expedition in 1798. Like Louis XIV before him, he understood that grand gestures were an important part of the staging of government. Egyptian-influenced furniture had existed before Napoleon's time, and indeed Egyptian motifs and hieroglyphs were an established part of the vocabulary of the Neoclassical movement. In fact, Jean-Baptiste Claude Sené (1718–1803) had created a set of seats featuring Egyptian heads for Marie Antoinette's bedroom in the chateau of Saint-Cloud shortly before the Revolution. After Napoleon's 1798 expedition, however, pharaonic motifs became almost ubiquitous.

Dominique Vivant, Baron Denon, an antiquarian who had accompanied Napoleon to Egypt, became famous for his book *Voyage dans la Basse et Haute Egypte*, which published engravings of the drawings he had made on the expedition. Denon was to become the head of the state museums and the de facto minister of culture under the emperor, and as such his influence on the Empire style was important. *Voyage* achieved international fame; by 1808 it had been published in England, Germany, and Italy. Following its release, *le goût d'Egypte* enjoyed a new popularity. The English designers Thomas Hope and George Smith both acknowledged their debt to Denon in their rooms and seats in the Egyptian style.

In 1799 Napoleon seized power and began to govern as First Consul, and prosperity came quickly thereafter. After the chaos of the Revolution, the order of Napoleon's rule allowed art and furniture design to flourish as the newly

> A drawing for two chairs by Charles Percier (1764–1868) and Pierre-François-Léonard Fontaine (1726–1853), c. 1801. Percier and Fontaine were largely responsible for creating the Empire style. The Metropolitan Museum of Art

A painting by Innocent-Louis Goubaud (1780–1847) showing the Roman Senate before Napoleon, November 16, 1805, in the throne room at Fontainebleau. Châteaux de Versailles et de Trianon. Photograph: RMN

rich turned their attentions to the arts. Soon, a distinct return to classical forms became apparent. In 1798 Louis-Martin Berthault, a pupil of Charles Percier's, designed a chaise longue and accompanying seats for a lady of fashion, Juliette Récamier. Madame Récamier's apartment was one of the attractions of Paris that all distinguished visitors wanted to see. Her seats, executed by Jacob, were soon imitated by every fashionable chair-maker. Madame Récamier loved these pieces and kept them all her life; most of them now belong to the Louvre Museum.

A committee of artists headed by David in the early years of the nineteenth century proposed an eclectic style based on the imperial forms of ancient Greece, Rome, and Egypt. In response, the architects Pierre François Léonard Fontaine (1762–1853) and Charles Percier (1764–1838) formulated a set of designs in their *Recueil de Décorations Intérieurs* in 1801, where they not only used the term "interior decoration" for the first time but also showed that they had already created the Empire style. All that was needed were the addition of a few motifs such as giant N's in laurel wreaths, eagles, and bees, to make it fully Napoleonic. Later, sphinxes and other Egyptian figures appeared as well. Fontaine and Percier believed in the unity of architecture and interior design, and drew upon Antiquity as their exclusive inspiration. As they wrote, *On se flatterait en vain, de trouver des formes préférables à celles que les ancients nous ont transmisés* [One will try in vain to find forms preferable to those which the Ancients have passed down to us].

One salient feature of Empire chairs is the saber shape of the back legs, a feature that was

> A French Empire mahogany armchair, c. 1810. Empire seats are rectangular, massive, and sumptuous, with rich woods and metal mountings offsetting their rectilinear simplicity. Didier Aaron Collection, Paris

v A French Empire mahogany desk chair, c. 1809. Didier Aaron Collection, Paris

only fully accepted around 1800. True saber-shaped legs, which are curved rather than inclined and slope strongly backward, were introduced about the same time on both sides of the English Channel. Somewhat stagy and highly uncomfortable, Empire chairs were masculine and rigid seats for warriors wearing sabers and tight-fitting pants. The *joie de vivre* of the eighteenth century was gone, and along with it, comfortable chairs. The new seats represented a society that was regaining a sense of discipline after the breakdown of political, religious, and social rules during the Revolution. Napoleon was determined to restore order and stability to morals and manners, which he thought vital to the rebirth of France and to the success of his rule. He railed against immodest dress in society and on the stage, insisted that his ministers marry their mistresses, and forbade card-playing for money at the imperial court. The court became a model of brilliant dress, empty speech, and boring representations. In his words, "a new established government must dazzle and astonish. The moment it ceases to glitter, it falls. Display is to power what ceremony is to religion."

Napoleon insisted on strict protocol for public occasions. Although his wife and mother

were allowed to use armchairs in his presence; all others, including other members of the imperial family, sat on ordinary chairs or stools. Talleyrand, Napoleon's foreign minister, recalled in his memoirs how the First Consul knew how to manage decor and seating to intimidate a visitor. Just before the Luneville peace agreement in 1801, he received the Austrian minister, count Louis de Coblenzl:

Bonaparte himself organized the setting. He sat at a small writing table put in a corner of an antechamber. All the other seats had been removed, except two sofas situated far away from the table. With only one lamp, the Austrian count came in the dimly lit room. Napoleon, standing near his table, sat down and the poor ambassador, confused, had to stand during the whole meeting.

The court at the Tuileries, Madame de Remusat, the empress Josephine's lady of the bedchamber, wrote in her memoirs, resembled a military parade, with the addition of women. The playwright Alexandre Duval further noted that when Napoleon entered a room, everyone, including his wife, rose so promptly that it could only have been

likened to a military maneuver. When Napoleon finished reviewing his guests, he would then watch them dance, with an expression of such boredom that nobody could have had much fun.

Napoleon rivaled Louis XIV in his patronage of art, for, like Louis, he wished to proclaim the glory of France. He kept Percier and Fontaine fully employed until 1814 as architects, pageant masters, interior decorators, and furniture designers, often requiring them to design, redecorate, or refurnish state apartments at great speed. The thrones are like armchairs flanked by winged lions, rosettes, wreathes, and laurel branches, all adapted from the Antique. Throughout the Empire period most chairs had square backs. Those made by the Jacobs with a few exceptions had square or rectangular backs with an equal amount of wood showing on either side. At the end of the Empire period gondola-shaped chairs became increasingly popular in France. Light-weight and easily moved, they were as comfortable as larger chairs and took up far less space, especially in a small room such as a boudoir or a dressing room, where they were first used. In shape and construction gondola-shaped chairs do not differ greatly from desk chairs from before the Revolution. Mahogany, rosewood, and ebony were the rule, with brass or gilt mounts in the forms of swags, festoons, mythological figures,

<
A throne from the painter David's studio, c. 1790. Jacques-Louis David apparently used actual thrones to stage his painting of Napoleon's coronation in 1804. Three examples of these thrones still exist, all made by Georges Jacob. This one features ivory spheres engraved with stars, just as it appears in David's *Portrait of Gaspard Meyer* of 1795/96. The forms of such seats were usually simple, with decorations limited to applied reliefs or figures cast in bronze and gilded. Collection Axel Vervoordt, Antwerp

chairs in the nineteenth century 273

>
David's drawing for the *Coronation of Napoleon*. Union Central des Arts Décoratifs, Paris

>
A drawing by Percier and Fontaine watercolored by Sclick showing Napoleon's throne. Union Central des Arts Décoratifs, Paris

>>
The throne room of Napoleon I, Château de Fontainebleau. Photograph: RMN. Arnaudet/Schormans

<
Painting by Joseph Franque (1774–1833) showing the empress Marie-Louise watching her son, the King of Rome, sleeping on a sofa similar to the throne from David's studio (see p. 272). Châteaux de Versailles et de Trianon. Photograph: RMN. Arnaudet

>
Painting by Philippe Auguste Hennequin (1762–1833) of Napoleon giving the Legion of Honor on August 16, 1804, using the Chair of Dagobert (see p. 56). Châteaux de Versailles et de Trianon. Photograph: RMN. Gerard Blot

and the Napoleonic emblems of the bee, the crown, and the letter N.

The Jacob family played a crucial role in the execution of Empire seats. Famous for his work under the old regime, Georges Jacob survived the Revolution, but like many fine craftsmen, he was almost ruined. Thanks to David, he survived the Terror and even found employment during it. David introduced him to Percier and Fontaine, from whose designs he made the chairs for the Committee of Public Safety. With the fall of Robespierre and the creation of the Directory, opportunities began to open up again for chair-makers. In 1796 Jacob retired and handed over his business to his two sons, Georges and François-Honoré-Georges. In 1800 he returned to help in the large task of furnishing the Consular apartments in the Tuileries. On the death of his son Georges in 1803 he rejoined his other son, with whom he worked under the business name of Jacob-Desmalter (1770–1841; Desmalter was the name of a family property). The firm provided

A chair for the Tuileries Palace theater, c. 1810, by Georges Jacob and his son Jacob-Desmalter, from a large suite of painted and gilt beech chairs. Collection Gismondi, Paris

> A pair of French mahogany and leather armchairs by Jacob-Desmalter, made for the Council of State at the Tuileries Palace. Collection De Rempich, Paris

many of the finest seats for the Napoleonic palaces, mostly working from the designs of Percier and Fontaine. Now that the guild system had been broken by the Revolution, the firm grew to a size unseen in France earlier, employing about 350 workmen, but still maintaining its standards of craftsmanship, unlike other chair-makers of the period. Georges Jacob finally retired in 1813 and died the following year. François-Honoré-Georges, known as Jacob-Desmalter, continued to produce seats in the Empire style until 1825, long after Napoleon's fall from power, passing the business on to his son Georges-Alphonse, who kept it going until 1845.

The influence of Percier and Fontaine remained strong across Europe owing to the wide dissemination of their book, *Recueil de Décoration*, and their many pupils. In Denmark, for example, Gustav Frederick Hetsch, who had studied under Percier and was both a professor at the Academy and a leading decorator, favored the French Empire style. Consequently, the Classical Revival survived in Denmark almost until 1850. Twenty-five years later, the German designer Leo von Klenze was so inspired by Percier and Fontaine that the chairs he created for Ludwig I's Residence in Munich resemble examples that they created for Napoleon. However, unlike Percier and Fontaine, who used Jacob-Desmalter almost exclusively to execute their creations, von Klenze used various workmen, including Melchior Frank and Johann Hans Mayer. A guild survived in Germany at the time, and it exacted the same standards as had the French guild before the Revolution. The German guild was abolished around 1848.

The Empire style was also popularized by a pattern book, *Meubles et Objects de Goût*, published by Pierre Antoine Leboux de la Mésangère (1761–1831) in 1802, as well as by the numerous illustrations he published in fashionable

<
An Austrian Wetzdorf armchair. Collection Carlton Hobbs, London

>
A German side chair by Karl Friedrich Schinkel, c. 1825. Berlin, Staatliche Schlösser und Gärten

magazines. In Prussia, for example, Friedrich-William III openly embraced the Empire style and had the designs of La Mésangère slavishly copied. Karl Friedrich Schinkel, with his work for the Prussian royal palaces inspired by the Antique, created a Neoclassicism strongly influenced by the French style. Born in Neurippen in 1781, Schinkel studied architecture under Friedrich Gill at the age of seventeen and later at the Berlin Academy. In the early 1800s he traveled around Europe, which was then under the irrepressible influence of Napoleon, and was inspired by its strength. Upon his return to Berlin in 1809, he was considered talented enough to design furniture and seats for Queen Luise's rooms in the Charlottenburg Palace. His seats, ultra-modern in their day, were inspired by the Empire style, however they reflected a strong originality as well, foreshadowing the Biedermeier style.

The Empire style spread also in the wake of Napoleon's armies and under the patronage of his many relatives, to Holland (where the emperor's brother Louis was king), to Germany (where his brother Jerome was king of Westphalia), Sweden

>
An armchair design by Karl Friedrich Schinkel, Berlin c. 1828, with re-created upholstery. Staatliche Schlösser und Gärten, Schinkel-Pavilion, Berlin

(where his general Jean-Baptiste Bernadotte was elected crown prince in 1810), Italy (where his sisters Pauline, Elisa, and Caroline were respectively a Borghese princess, grand-duchess of Tuscany, and queen of Naples), and Spain (where his brother Joseph was king). During the reign of Jerome Bonaparte in Westphalia, a French architect and pupil of Percier, Grandjean de Montigny, refurbished the Castle at Kassel and the palace known as Wilhelmshöhe, then temporarily known as Napoleonshöhe. Some of the seats for the magnificent rooms were commissioned from Jacob-Desmalter. Others, in much the same style, were made locally.

In Holland, in 1808 Louis-Napoleon gave orders for the town hall in Amsterdam to be converted into a royal palace and refurbished by Dutch artisans. Most of the seats, in the French Empire style, were provided by the upholsterer Joseph Cuel and again followed the inspiration of Percier and Fontaine. The Napoleonic taste was stamped on Italy so effectively by members of

An Italian armchair with griffin arm-supports, c. 1810. Collection Axel Vervoordt, Antwerp

A detail of the same

the emperor's family that the Italians continued to imitate it long after his fall from power. The Bonapartes had little faith in Italian craftsmanship, a sentiment shared by most of Europe. In 1805, the German dramatist August von Kotzebue described the furniture at the Villa Borghese, the Roman house of Napoleon's sister Pauline, as "magnificent and tasteful, for which circumstances a visitor immediately guesses that it is not an Italian lady who rules here."

The Bonapartes imported most of their chairs from Paris, however they endeavored to train local craftsmen. Elisa Bacciochi, another Bonaparte sister, described as "the second genius of the imperial family," established a manufactory at Lucca under the direction of a Parisian furniture-maker, Jean-Baptiste Youf (1762–1838) when she was created grand-duchess of Tuscany in 1805. Youf provided French Empire seats for her palace at Lucca and for the Palazzo Pitti in Florence, thus playing a part in bringing the Empire style to Italy. Returning to France in 1814, he supplied a very large suite of furniture and 120 chairs for a Norwegian client, disseminating the style even

chairs in the nineteenth century 281

>
A rare early-nineteenth-century Italian Neo-classical painted and parcel-gilt armchair (one of a pair), with dragons. Collection H. M. Luther, Inc., Antiques, New York

>>
An Italian *fauteuil* by Filippo Pelagio Palagi (1775–1860), c. 1808. Palagi, a painter, sculptor, architect, and designer, trained in Rome, where he worked on the redecoration of the Quirinal Palace for Napoleon. Later he settled in Milan, and still later, in Turin. Sotheby's

further. An Italian, Giovanni Socchi, created for Elisa some remarkable seats and desks combined. Though obviously in the Empire style, they are unlike the furniture that was being made in Paris at this time. Socchi's fame rests on these ingenious creations, two of which remain in the Palazzo Pitti, and another of which is at Malmaison. Each of these pieces looks, when closed, like an oval chest of drawers on legs. A portion of the front conceals a chair that may be drawn out. If two handles are pulled forward, the two halves of the top move to either side and a container for pens, pencils, and papers is raised up, converting the piece into a writing-table and chair. After the Restoration of the French monarchy in 1815, no more is heard of Socchi.

Elisa's sister, Caroline Murat, remodeled the royal palaces in Naples so lavishly that when the Bourbons were restored to the kingdom in 1815, one of the young princes is said to have exclaimed to his father as they admired the new elegance of the royal villa at Portici, "Father, if only we had been away for another ten years!" Far from defacing the Napoleonic emblems, the restored Italian princes continued the style of their conqueror after 1815. This choice is particularly reflected in the work of the influential Filippo Pelagio Palagi (1775–1860), who designed the interiors of the royal palace in Turin for King Carlo Alberto starting in 1832, incorporating Empire elements into his magnificent seats, which Palagi strove to make even more sumptuous than Percier and Fontaine had.

Spain, too, embraced the Empire style, even before Joseph Bonaparte became its king. Soon after 1800, Charles IV commissioned Percier and Fontaine to decorate the Platinum Room at the Casita del Labrador at the Palacio Real in Aranjuez. The interior of the room was made in Paris and sent to Spain for assembly on site. Another French designer, Jean Démosthène Dugourc (1749–1825), appeared in Madrid in 1800. Although not much is known of his activity in Spain, he was commissioned by Charles IV shortly before the end of his reign to decorate two rooms at La Moncloa Palace in Madrid. Dugourc may have designed some chairs made in the royal workshop, and indeed seats closely resembling his drawings still belong to the royal collections today. Dugourc spent some twelve years in Spain and must have done a fair amount of work there. The Spaniards adhered to the Empire style until about 1830, when the vogue for Gothic and neo-baroque superseded it. Ferdinand VII (reigned 1813–33), after the defeat of Napoleon, carried on his father's

<

A Roman gilt-wood armchair with silk upholstery from the Fonthill Suite, c. 1800, one of an extensive suite that lined the walls of the Grand Drawing Room at William Beckford's Fonthill Abbey in Wiltshire. Between 1796 and 1818, Beckford and his architect, James Wyatt, created this great Romantic edifice, of which the painter Benjamin West commented, "I am lost in admiration—and feel that I have seen a place raised more by majick or inspiration than the labour of human hands." Collection Carlton Hobbs, London

> An engraving showing the Fonthill Suite in situ, in J. Rutter's *Delineations of Fonthill*, of 1823. The suite was sold as lot 1534–40 on the thirty-second day of the great Fonthill sale that same year, when it was purchased by the third marquess of Londonderry for Wynyard Park, Durham.

project and ordered numerous seats from France, and the Spanish workshops produced a considerable number, as well.

In Sweden, Empire seats preempted all others in aristocratic circles by 1810. After Gustavus IV (reigned 1792–1809) joined the third coalition against France in 1805, Napoleon seized Sweden's last possessions on the Continent, Pomerania and Stralsund. As a result, the Riksdag deposed Gustavus and his childless uncle succeeded him as Charles XIII (1809–18). Without an heir, the Riksdag asked Napoleon to allow one of his ablest marshals, Jean-Baptiste Bernadotte, to accept election as crown prince. Permission was granted, and crown prince Bernadotte took the name of Carl Johan. When he arrived in Sweden in 1810, he was instantly popular, and his coming awakened an interest in everything French. After his succession as Charles XIV in 1818, the Empire style flourished in Sweden, especially when his queen, Desirée, returned in 1823 after a twelve-year absence. Court life was revitalized, and ostentatious furniture was created for the royal palaces. French imperial elegance was further established with the wedding in 1823 of crown prince Oscar to Josephine of Leuchtenberg, the granddaughter of Napoleon's first wife, Josephine de Beauharnais.

Swedish Empire seats were distinctly aristocratic—large-scale, and usually made of gilt wood or dark, polished mahogany, which contrasted strikingly to their gilt-wood or ormolu ornaments and mounts. The only Swedish seats reflecting an English influence were dining room chairs. These had saber legs and rope-carved backs, like the "Trafalgar chairs" made by Thomas Sheraton to celebrate Admiral Nelson's great victory. As in France, suites of furniture for salons were usually made by a single chair-maker to achieve the desired uniformity. The most famous Swedish chair-makers of the Empire period were Lorentz Wilhelm Lundelius (1787–1859) and J.-F. Nordin, who were responsible for most of the seats at

A Russian armchair, c. 1800. After the Revolution of 1789, many French aristocrats and others emigrated to Russia, including the court painter Mme. Vigée-Lebrun, who later wrote: "In respect to social amenity, St. Petersburg left nothing to be desired. One might have believed oneself in Paris, so many French were there for fashionable gatherings." This explains why Russian chairs were inspired by French models. Hillwood Museum

Rosendal. Rosendal, the residence of crown prince Carl Johan, is both the finest example of the Swedish Empire style and the best-preserved house of its time. The seats in the Lantern Room, dating to 1827, were of magnificent gilt-wood in the pure Empire style, some twenty-five years after its French heyday.

The power of Russia grew immensely in the eighteenth century, largely owing to the efforts of Catherine the Great. Madame de Staël, who traveled to St. Petersburg in 1812, struck by the size of the country, wrote that, "There is so much space in Russia that everything is lost in it, even the chateaux, even the population . . ." Catherine's court attained a degree of luxury and refinement second only to Versailles under Louis XV and Louis XVI. The court language was French, and the ideas those of the French aristocracy.

The number of French emigrés led to the creation of the chair style called "Russian Jacob," after the Parisian chair-maker. An extensive use of mahogany, straight lines, and decoration with brass strips or rosettes characterized the period. Most chairs of this type were made by Christian Meyer, who was already working in St. Petersburg by 1782. After 1800, the Russian Empire style also followed French examples. Paul I (1754–1801), Catherine's son, who ascended the throne in 1796, was a great admirer of all things French, and most of the aristocracy shared his enthusiasm. Madame Vigée-Lebrun recalled in her memoirs a visit to the richest resident in Moscow, prince Bezborodko:

When I went to see him, he showed me rooms full of furniture, bought in Paris from the workshops of the famous upholster Daguerre. Most of this furniture had been imitated by his serfs, and it was it impossible to distinguish between copy and original.

Paul I was also a madman terrifying in his changeable tastes and affections. At the beginning of his reign, he loathed Bonaparte, but later he conceived such tenderness for the French hero that he kept his portrait and exhibited it to everyone. During his reign terror became the order of the day, and eventually he was assassinated. After a long struggle, the conspirators in his murder finally managed to strangle him—where else?—in an armchair.

Paul's son, Alexander I, who became tsar on March 24, 1801, was as much loved in Russia as Bonaparte was in France. Like Bonaparte, he had been brought up on the French Enlightenment and tempered his autocracy with liberal ideas. Early in the nineteenth century the Empire style made its appearance in Russia. Three major figures are identified with the Russian Empire style: the architects Andrei Nikiforovich Voronikin (1759–1814) and Carlo Rossi (1775–1849), and the cabinetmaker Heinrich Gambs (1765–1831). Voronikin, probably the illegitimate son of count Stroganov, was educated in France. Upon his return to Russia, he worked on the Stroganov palace, and then refurbished or redecorated numerous rooms at Pavlovsk Palace after a fire in 1803. His seats are highly original, combining antique motifs with great freedom. Voronikhin designed a spectacular set of furnishings for the Greek Hall of gilt and carved wood finished to imitate bronze. One astonishing chair, made for the library desk of the Empress Maria Feodorovna, featured back uprights in the form of cornucopias, designed to hold flowerpots.

Carlo Rossi was born in Naples, the son of an Italian ballerina and—according to legend—Paul I. He began working in Russia in 1808, after numerous travels in Europe. In 1816 he was named Architect to the Court, just at the time when the Empire style was beginning to diversify. In the tradition of Russian and French architects, he designed the interiors of his buildings to the smallest detail. Rossi designed seats for the Winter Palace, the Mikhailovskii Palace, the Anichkov Palace, and Pavlovsk. His chairs are often completely gilded and ornamented with low-relief carving. Toward the end of the first quarter of the nineteenth century, both form and ornamentation in his seats became increasingly light and simple. Sometimes he used smoked birch (a light wood), moving away from the original French Empire style.

Rossi's finest pieces were made in the Gambs workshops. Heinrich Gambs, a pupil of Roentgen, had established himself in St. Petersburg in the late 1780s. His workshop comprised various sections responsible for the different stages of furniture-making. From 1803 many seats coming from his workshops were designed by Voronikhin, and by 1805/06 the partnership of Voronikhin and Gambs had reached its apogee, attaining a standard rarely surpassed.

To sum up the influence of the Empire style in Russia, F. F. Vignel, a high-ranking Russian official, wrote in his memoirs:

Everything was made "à l'antique." Everywhere there were cassolettes [perfume burners] and little tripod tables, curule chairs, sofas and seats with feet and arms in the form of eagles, griffins, and sphinxes. Painted or lacquered and gilded wood and ordinary brass disappeared gradually, while the use of mahogany increased. It was adorned with brilliantly worked bronze figures, lyres, medusa's heads, lions and even rams. All this had arrived by 1805 and, in my opinion, has never been bettered.

As the century advanced, Russian chair-makers increasingly used indigenous woods instead of mahogany. The Empire influence continued with the nomination of August Ricard de Montferrand in 1817 as Architect to His Majesty's Cabinet. As such, he was responsible for interiors in the Winter Palace. Montferrand, who had been a pupil of Percier and Fontaine in Paris, continued their principles of design. However, by the middle of the nineteenth century, a certain looseness, eccentricity, and exaggeration in the Empire designs led to an eclectic neo-baroque style, which borrowed influences randomly from many sources.

In England, too, there was considerable French influence on the Regency's Egyptian revival chair designs, which appeared after Napoleon's expedition to Egypt. This influence incorporated two somewhat conflicting elements. One sprang from the archaeological study of antiquities, an interest that occupied men of taste throughout Western Europe. The other was a popular craze for Egyptian motifs that swept over England after Nelson's victory in the Battle of the Nile on August 1, 1798. The sensational victory ironically contributed to the spreading to England of the Egyptian taste, which had been made fashionable originally by Napoleon, Nelson's great enemy.

The severe classicism of David was echoed in England in a set of chairs that Henry Holland designed for Samuel Whitbread at Southill about 1796, whose saber legs and bold head ornaments recall the second phase of Neoclassicism and the Empire style. These chairs were probably executed by the firm of Marsh & Tatham, which had worked extensively for the Prince of Wales. Charles Heathcote Tatham (1772–1842), the brother of one of the cabinetmaking partners, was a pupil of Henry Holland, the leading architect and furniture-designer in England at the time, who sent him to Rome in 1794. Over the next three years Tatham built up a collection of classical fragments for his master, and supplied him with sketches of Greco-Roman ornaments that he later incorporated into his own chair designs, which were instrumental in the creation of the Regency style. Tatham published these drawings from antiquities that he had seen in Italy in *Etchings of Ancient Ornamental Architecture* (1799). This important publication had further editions in 1803, 1810, and 1836, not to mention a German edition (Weimar, 1805). Tatham later published other works, including *Etchings Representing Fragments of Grecian and Roman Architectural Ornaments* (1806). According to *The Architectural Publication Society's Dictionary of Architecture*, edited by Wyatt Papworth, the influence of Percier and Fontaine in France was paralleled in England by that of Tatham.

>
The Victory Chair, c. 1810, a unique English Regency commemorative armchair made of oak from HMS *Victory*, Lord Nelson's flagship, on whose deck he died. The back, in the shape of a ship's transom, is carved with the royal coat of arms. Collection Mallett, London

French influence on seats remained of great importance in England, despite the fact that the two countries were at war. Moreover, the Prince of Wales had decidedly pro-French sympathies, in direct opposition to his father. From the time he came of age in 1783 until his death in 1830, the Prince of Wales (Prince Regent, 1811–20; George IV 1820–30) was a distinguished and extravagant patron of the arts, and it is from his position as Prince Regent that this period is called the Regency. The variety of styles of the period is a testament to the prince's originality and eclecticism.

As late as 1826 Peter and M. A. Nicholson in their *Practical Cabinet Maker, Upholsterer and Complete Decorator* mentioned the Egyptian style as one of the three styles—with the Greek and Roman—on which contemporary furniture might be based. The new style primarily developed through two talented men, Henry Holland and Thomas Hope. Holland's chair designs reflected the sculptural forms suggested by Tatham, the latter being responsible for the design of the most archaeologically correct seats ever made in England. Hope's designs were popularized in a much less pedantic and much more comfortable way by George Smith. Here the Regency style came close to that of the French Empire, although without the Napoleonic devices.

Hope was a dilettante, a "gentleman of sofas," as Byron called him. In 1807 he published a folio volume, *Household Furniture and Interior Decoration*. This book, which established Hope as an *arbiter elegantiarum*, was satirized bitterly by Sidney Smith in the *Edinburgh Review* in July 1807, Smith arguing that Hope's chairs were "unsuitable for use until the time when aldermen wear armor and take their afternoon naps in Guildhall." Like the French Empire chairs designed by Percier, to which his book paid tribute, Hope's seats are not

>
A pair of English Regency snake chairs. Christie's

<
An English Regency arrow-backed settee. Christie's

chairs in the nineteenth century

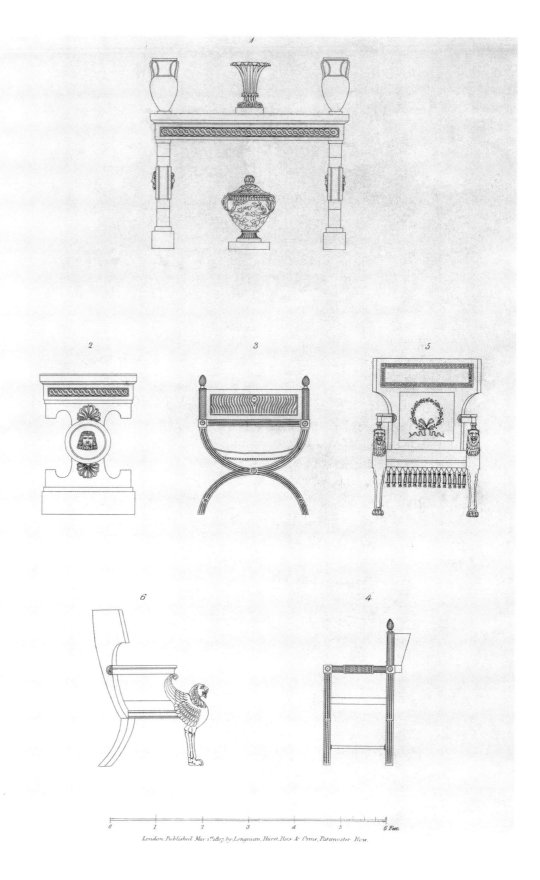

<
An English ebonized beechwood armchair after a design by Thomas Hope (1769–1831), c. 1810. This chair is based on plate 59 (fig. 1) in Hope's book, *Household Furniture and Interior Decoration*, 1807. Its only significant deviation from the original design is that the posts supporting the arms are less elaborate. Excessive severity has been avoided by an extensive use of applied brass decoration and inlay. Collection Carlton Hobbs, London

>
An etching of designs for chairs by Thomas Hope, plate 20 in his book. Hope, an Anglo-Dutch banker, collector, and theorist, published the book to teach good taste. Including a detailed inventory of Hope's London house in Duchess Street, the book had an enormous impact on contemporary fashion and made him the arbiter par excellence of the Regency style. In 1827 John Britton wrote that the book had "not only improved the taste of cabinetmakers and upholsterers, but also that of their employers." Like David in France and Abildgaard in Denmark, Hope often copied the furniture of Antiquity. The Metropolitan Museum of Art

<<
An English Regency convertible library armchair, c. 1810. Christie's

<
A George IV walnut astronomer's chair, formerly in the collection of the eleventh earl of Dalhousie, Scotland. Collection Axel Vervoordt, Antwerp

>
An English armchair, c. 1815, made of oak with its original deep-buttoned maroon leather upholstery, the arms supported by two massive griffins. The griffin, half lion (king of beasts) and half eagle (king of birds), is the most magnificent animal in Greek mythology. Animal supports of this type, which derive from French Empire models, are unusual on English chairs. The furniture of Buckingham Palace includes two gilt council chairs with seated-sphinx supports. Collection Carlton Hobbs, London

comfortable. Yet, two decades after the publication of *Household Furniture*, his influence was still felt. Besides Percier, Hope acknowledged his debt to other sources, notably Bernard de Montfaucon's early-eighteenth-century *L'Antiquité expliquée*, the work of Piranesi, Wilhelm Tischbein's engravings of Greek vases, and Vivant Denon's *Voyage dans la Basse et la Haute Egypte*.

Hope's Egyptian room at Deepdene, his country estate, contained two couches and four matching armchairs painted black and gold, of which one couch and two chairs survive at Buscot Park, Berkshire. They rank as the most important pieces of English furniture in the Egyptian taste owing to the archaeological accuracy of their decoration and their eclecticism. Until Vivant Denon's publication, little was known about Egyptian art, although Egyptian motifs had appeared in architecture, furniture, and chairs for many years. In France they were mainly used as Napoleonic symbols. Hope, however, sought to reproduce the chairs and couches pictured in hieroglyphic paintings and carvings. Maria Edgeworth, a visitor to Deepdene, wrote in 1819 that "There is too much Egyptian ornament, Egyptian hieroglyphical figures, bronze, and gilt, but all hideous." Other visitors must have been more favorably impressed, for the English taste for Egyptians seats was soon well established, partly the result of Nelson's dramatic victory over the French fleet in the Battle of the Nile. James Gillray's famous cartoon of Nelson destroying the "Revolutionary Crocodiles" of the Nile firmly linked crocodiles with Nelson in popular imagery. Later numerous crocodile couches and sofas sprang from the imagination of designers such as Nash for the Brighton Pavilion. The results exhibited a charm and a feeling of fantasy unequaled in other countries.

Chairs were of various kinds, including massive thrones with sides formed of winged sphinxes or lions, armchairs with winged chimerae forming the front legs and arm supports (or in smaller versions, arm supports only), and the celebrated "Trafalgar" type, related to the *klismos*, with concave saber front legs, rounded knees, and scrolled uprights and cresting. This

< A Regency couch by the firm of Gillow. This classic couch form was introduced from France in various media, including mahogany, satinwood, rosewood, or painted and gilt lightwood. The fully developed form has scrolling ends (as here). When made as a pair, the couches featured an armrest on one side stretching half the length. Christie's

> A chaise longue in the Chinese taste similar to those at the Royal Pavilion at Brighton. *Chinoiserie* furniture became popular among the Prince Regent's friends, its light and decorative appearance making it particularly favored for use in bedrooms.

> An English japanned-wood chaise longue in the shape of a dragon, c. 1810. Antique-style couches with animal legs became a stylish element during the Regency in England. In *Household Furniture*, Thomas Hope presented a number of designs for couches in Egyptian taste. The following year, George Smith wrote that such pieces were "admissible in almost every room." Sotheby's

seat was typically English, although, as we have noted, similar designs were also made in Sweden. However, several decorations, such as the double lotus meeting at the intersection of the cross framing of a chair, or the metal bold head, round or star-shaped, which Hope used in running sequence—along a couch rail, for example—were French-inspired and similar to what can be found in some Empire seats. The English Egyptian taste, slightly more whimsical than that of the French Empire, lingered on, owing to its general appeal, despite a chorus of criticism from scholars.

Napoleon's Empire style was soon carried to America, however, the American Empire style, with its Greek and Egyptian lines and elegant proportions, came a few decades after it had penetrated nearly every corner of Europe. Here, too, the designs of Percier and Fontaine were influential. George Smith's book *A Collection of Designs for Household Furniture and Interior Decoration* (London, 1808) played a part as well, but the highly popular American Empire style was less ornate than the French and heavier than the English Regency. Duncan Phyfe (1768–1854), the preeminent chair-maker in this style, worked in New York from 1795 to 1847. He appears to have been too prudent to play the role of an innovator, but surviving pieces bearing his label are of high quality. He used the finest Santo Domingo mahogany and West Indian exporters are said to have called the best wood "Duncan Phyfe logs." Phyfe's classically inspired seats include a curule

chairs in the nineteenth century 295

chair and chairs with lyre-form backs. French Empire taste is represented by wreaths, swans, and Egyptian details on seats.

Other important masters of the period were Michael Allison (d. 1855) and Charles-Honoré Lannuier (1773–1819). The French-born Lannuier advertised himself in the *New-York Evening Post* in 1803 as "a maker of all kinds of furniture . . . in the newest and latest French fashion." His work remained recognizably French in origin though he succeeded in creating what might be called a New York Empire Style of very fine quality, which was considerably lighter than the original French version. However, it was only one trend among many, like the Egyptian-style seats of the Regency period.

A taste for comfort led to the creation of monumental seats. Solid-looking chairs increasingly became the mode for fashionable American design from about 1815 through the rest of the nineteenth century. In short, Napoleon's motive to expand French grandeur through the decorative arts worked beyond his expectations. Moreover, the Empire spirit suited the classicism of this period wonderfully well. Its persistence in most of Europe for more than a generation indicates that it was generally acceptable, even in England. Ironically, the instigator of the style, Napoleon, finished his days without any Empire chairs. Sadly, his last seat on St. Helena, the *fauteuil de malade* in which, dying, he sat when he last left his bed, was designed by an Englishman, the famous Mr. Bullock, and made by an anonymous Chinese carpenter.

The Egyptian taste lived on, especially in England, where originality in seats prevailed. The painter William Holman Hunt, deciding, after a trip to the Nile Valley in 1854, to create some chairs for his own sitting room, had some Egyptian-style seats made after models in the British Museum. Around 1880, the English porcelain manufactory Brown-Westhead, in search of ideas for garden stools, created a kneeling Egyptian woman as a

<
A French Egyptian-Revival armchair. Collection Nicole Mugler, Paris

> A drawing by Gaetano Landi for an English room in the Egyptian style, c. 1810. 62.635.215 The Metropolitan Museum of Art

veranda seat. Around the same time, Liberty and Company commercialized the design of original Egyptian seats in the British Museum in large quantities.

At the beginning of the twentieth century, the discovery of the tomb of Akhenaton sparked more interest in Egyptian seats. The painter Maurice de Vlaminck created some Egyptian-style stools for his house in Chatou, and soon Derain, Matisse, and Picasso shared this interest. The Ballets Russes joined in the Egyptomania and Sonia and Robert Delaunay even designed costumes and sets in the style. In 1922 the discovery of the tomb of Tutankhamen by Howard Carter and the extraordinary number of seats and luxurious objects that were unveiled contributed to the expansion of the Egyptian fad. Copies of the chairs and armchairs that had been discovered sprang up everywhere as the beauty and refinement of the first seats inspired new designs.

empire and neo-egyptian stools

Up to a point, Napoleon attempted to resurrect Louis XIV's etiquette, which is why there are so many stools in his chateaux. However, he relaxed his etiquette for the ladies of his court. In the empress's great drawing room at the Tuileries there were seven large armchairs, thirty-six side chairs, and only five stools. This arrangement did not please the duchess of Angoulême, Louis XVI's daughter, who occupied the empress's quarters after the Bourbon Restoration. In August 1816, she asked at the time of her return that the gilt-wood chairs be replaced with stools, according to the etiquette of her father's day. Two or three X-shaped stools, originally designed by Percier and Fontaine from Roman models, were produced in quantity with only slight variations.

The stool gradually lost its importance as etiquette changed. A century geared toward comfort did not encourage its use, and the stool became mainly a garden seat, or a curiosity.

NEO-GOTHIC CHAIRS

Gothic chairs were briefly popular in England after 1740. Chippendale and Darly had published several designs incorporating Gothic details, and starting in 1747, the elegant Horace Walpole began to decorate his house, Strawberry Hill, in the Gothic style. This first impulse of the Gothic revival lost momentum rapidly, and was confined almost entirely to England. Then, early in the nineteenth century, there was a renewal of the Gothic taste, and chairs in this style became fashionable throughout Europe. As one writer commented in 1813, *Naguère nous ne voulions que de l'Antique, c'est du Gothique qu'il faut maintenant* [Not long ago, all we wanted was the Antique; it is the Gothic that we must have now].

The first pattern book of the nineteenth century to illustrate a comprehensive range of Gothic chair designs was George Smith's *Household Furniture* of 1808. In addition to the "mansions of our Nobility and Gentry" that Smith mentioned as suitable for these designs, Gothic cottages, which became fashionable early in the century stimulated demand for the seats. The trend started in England, and it was the first time that chair designs were intended not for aristocrats, but for the rising class of merchants, bankers, industrialists, and professional men, for whom chair design would be created during the latter part of the century in most of Europe.

Medieval revival corresponded with the rise of Romanticism. In France, the Gothic vogue became widespread, owing partly to the writings of Chateaubriand on the Middle Ages. Gothic-style chairs were said to be in the "Troubadour" style, a name that expresses the nostalgic and poetic influence of the genre. Details derived from flamboyant Gothic churches were applied to chairs; seats with backs decorated with tracery were called *à la cathédrale*. A similar poetic influence came from the novels of Sir Walter Scott, which were translated into various European languages and helped propagate the Gothic taste.

<
A sofa from a suite of Charles X Gothic rosewood seats in the manner of Jacob-Desmalter, c. 1825. Christie's

In Germany it became an article of faith that Gothic influence was purely Germanic, as the Germans were descended from the Goths. In fact, the Neo-Gothic was a popular style among the German Romantics partly as a reaction against French influence. In Italy, the taste was also strongly nationalistic, inspired by Renaissance as well as medieval art, and called the "Dantesque" style. The chairs were X-shaped, and were often upholstered in dark red cut velvet.

Few of the Neo-Gothic chairs of the first quarter of the nineteenth century were even trying for historical correctness. They were often whimsical fantasies created for well-to-do patrons to set in rooms in the Gothic style. The seats tend to be similar all over Europe. Chairs attributed to Franz Jager from the Franzenburg Fabrik near Vienna look very like those made in Paris. Striking similarities can also be noted between English Gothic chairs and seats made by Peter Gambs for "The Cottage" on the height of Peterhof for the empress Alexandra Feodorovna (1798–1860) of Russia.

> A German Gothic side chair designed by Karl Friedrich Schinkel, c. 1835. Berlin, Staatliche Schlösser und Gärten

> A French Gothic armchair *à la cathédrale*, c. 1830, attributed to Veuve Balny the Younger (1832–39). Galerie Camoin, Paris

Born a German princess, the tsarina was not the only royalty infatuated with the Neo-Gothic taste. By the 1820s George IV of England commissioned the firm of Morel and Seddon to create Gothic furnishings for Windsor Castle. A suite of dining chairs made of parcel-gilt rosewood with gilt bronze enrichments is particularly well known. The royal family must have cherished them, for, according to the firm's records in the Royal Archives, forty-eight of these chairs were made, and H. Clifford Smith recorded in 1931 that twenty-four were then in the throne room at Buckingham Palace, brought in from Windsor in 1834.

The dining room and the library, or "cabinet" in France, became the locus classicus of Gothic seats. As early as June 1810 a magazine, the *Repository*, illustrated a Gothic sofa, table, chair, and footstool for the library with the cautionary note that the "articles in this style must fit the general appearance of the house." In March 1827 a writer in the same journal expressed his feelings concerning Gothic chairs in the library in this lyrical passage: "No style can be better adapted for its decoration than that of the Middle Ages, which possesses a sedate and grave character that invites the mind to study and reflection."

By the late 1820s the demand for Gothic seats had only increased. Numerous pattern books followed Smith's, and skilled workmen multiplied. The cost of design was going down. Commercial considerations, rarely far away when stylistic considerations were involved, were noted in the *Repository* in August 1827: "We have so many skillful workers in gothic, that very elaborate pieces of furniture may be made at a moderate price, compared with what it was a few years ago." In addition, talented architects and furniture makers such as Burges and Pugin in England, Bellange and Viollet-le-Duc in France, Schinkel in Germany, Gambs in Russia, and Richardson and Furness in America had each embraced the style in a different manner.

Peter Heinrichovich Gambs (1802–71), the son of Heinrich Gambs, who had been a pupil of Roentgen and a court cabinetmaker, created many seats in the Neo-Gothic style. Among them was a suite made for the St. Petersburg Russian furniture exhibition of 1829, and others for the imperial family and members of the aristocracy. Karl Friedrich Schinkel (1781–1841), probably the most talented German architect and chair-designer, was a true Romantic-Classicist, creating eminently practical, original, and even comfortable Gothic seats. He certainly did not strive for historical correctness, unlike most of his contemporaries in England.

Neo-Gothic chairs had a long life in the German-speaking countries of Central Europe, where it had become fashionable to build country houses in medieval styles or to emphasize the Middle Ages in houses that already existed. After 1880 the taste of most Germans turned more to the Renaissance, with the exception of Ludwig II of Bavaria, who, inspired by Richard Wagner's operas, had an imposing Romanesque castle built at Neuschwanstein in 1883, which featured a Neo-Gothic bedchamber, with seats in the style. In Italy, especially in the north, which came under Germanic influence, a considerable fashion developed for Neo-Gothic seats, and in about 1850, Alessandro Sidoli published a number of engravings of Neo-Gothic seats and other furniture, which continued to be made through the century.

William Burges (1827–81) was the least historically correct English chair-designer of the Gothic period. He designed seats for himself or for the marquis of Bute, which reveal a feeling

v
The Gothic dining room at the Cottage Palace in Alexander Park at Peterhof. Photograph: A La Vieille Russie, New York

A watercolor design for a boudoir in the Gothic style, c. 1836. Musée des Arts Décoratifs, Paris

for fantasy and a delight in the "grotesquerie" of the Middle Ages. His approach differed totally from that of Augustus Welby Northmore Pugin (1812–52), perhaps the greatest propagandist of the Gothic Revival. Although Pugin had supervised the manufacture of the Morel and Seddon chairs for Windsor Castle in the 1820s, a decade later he was speaking of those chairs with disgust, and insisting on archaeological accuracy. His books of designs, notably *Gothic Furniture in the Style of the Fifteenth Century* (1835), called for simplicity and reason. After his conversion to Catholicism in 1835 he published *Contrasts: or, A Parallel between the Noble Edifices of the Fourteenth and Fifteenth Centuries, and of Similar Buildings of the Present Day . . .* , in which he presented his personal creed: Protestant religion and furniture were bad; Catholic religion and furniture—by which Pugin meant Gothic—were good. His preference was for bold, solid, chunky seats like the ones he designed for the Houses of Parliament, made of oak. He wanted to establish a style based on immutable truths and attempted to reproduce the essential qualities and structures, not just the ornaments, of medieval chairs. Pugin was not the only person to despise the earlier Neo-Gothic chairs or to call for a return to the true principles of medieval art. In France, Eugène-Emmanuel Viollet-le-Duc (1814–79) carried on a similar campaign for "a return to healthy ideas." His reconstructed

∨
A pair of English oak sides chair by A.W. Pugin for the House of Lords, c. 1848. Jonathan Harris, London

interiors, however, were too archaeological for French taste and his Neo-Gothic *chaises à la cathédrale* were relatively short-lived in France.

Gothic seats were also made in America, especially in the English fashion. Alexandre Roux, a French cabinetmaker working in New York, made seats in a range of historical styles, successfully trying the Gothic around 1840, and the firm of an American, Joseph Meeks, made a set of walnut chairs in the style for the White House in 1846. However, the Gothic had little connection to America's past, and its popularity did not last long.

In the mid-nineteenth century, there was a reaction against the elaborate Neo-Gothic of Burges and the early Pugin. Bruce Talbert's (1838–81) *Gothic Forms Applied to Furniture* (London, 1867) offered designs of "honest" neo-medieval plank construction for chairs and other furniture, evoking imitations from Stuttgart to New York. The designs of Charles Lock Eastlake (1836–1906) represented a similar frame of mind. By 1877, however, "medieval masquerades" were no longer fashionable in England and Eastlake became better known in America, where his book was published in 1872 and where his name became a household word. Chairs in an "improved" taste were said to be "Eastlaked," however, most of the "Eastlake style" chairs produced in the U.S. were in a rather shoddy Gothic Revival style that rarely answered his call for simplicity, solidity, and sound craftsmanship.

Two architects, Henry Hobson Richardson (1836–86) and Frank Furness (1839–1912), created furnishings designed to fit their buildings in the "modern" or "reformed" Gothic of Eastlake and Talbert. Furness's seats were eclectically designed, as was his architecture, but they hardly embody restraint. Furness, as was common at the time, apparently made a cult of ugliness. According to an 1869 issue of *The Builder*, his designs resulted from competitions where "each man feels that his best chance of distinction is to put forth something more wild and startling than his neighbors have done." There was also a great variety in Richardson's seats, which range from massive oak and mahogany cathedrae to spindle-form benches and chairs not unrelated to the furniture made by William Morris and his circle in their protest against the crudity of industrialism. However, unlike Morris, Richardson realized (as Frank Lloyd Wright would later) that machines could create beauty if directed by artists. His seats embodied the dichotomy of his age, as romantic as the paintings of the Hudson River School and as rational as the new industrialists.

Honesty in the use of materials was one basis of the Arts and Crafts Movement, anticipating the medieval-inspired chairs that William Morris and Dante Gabriel Rossetti designed for their own use around 1856 (see p. 304). Despite their serious lack of comfort in a century more and more geared toward it, Gothic chairs enjoyed a long life. They seem to have struck a nationalist chord in many people, and in Pugin's case, a religious one as well. Indeed, Gothic chairs embody an ancient and reassuring power. The sitter wants to sit upright in a Gothic chair; it would be absurd in fact to slouch in such a seat, which is why these chairs' uncomfortable structure is of no real consequence.

> An American Gothic-Revival armchair, mid-nineteenth century. *House Beautiful*

ARTS AND CRAFTS, AESTHETIC MOVEMENT, AND ROMANTIC NATIONALIST CHAIRS

Although during the later part of the nineteenth century industrial manufacturers of chairs produced pastiches of traditional styles, innovators in both Europe and America were beginning to break free from bourgeois taste. Augustus Pugin, the prime mover in the development of the Gothic style in English chair design, was well aware of the damaging effects of mass production on aesthetics. The influence of his ideas resulted, around 1860, in the emergence of two concomitant approaches to the design of chairs. One of these, the Art Furniture Movement, developed from the Gothicism of the 1840s and 1850s. At the same time, the designer William Morris advocated a return to a medieval ideal of craftsmanship. The Art Furniture Movement gave rise to the Aesthetic Movement, and Morris's ideas produced the Arts and Crafts Movement.

The Art Furniture Movement saw the birth of a new breed of artists, among them the designers Christopher Dresser (1834–1904) and William Godwin (1833–86). Their common link was their love for the arts of Japan. Dresser, unlike Morris, understood and accepted the implications of mechanized production and stressed the importance of design rather than craftsmanship. Trained as a botanist, he was a prolific designer whose work was strongly influenced by Japanese aesthetics after a trip in 1877 to the Empire of the Rising Sun. The few extant examples of his chairs are austere, simple forms, enhanced by fabrics woven in geometrical patterns, which Dresser designed himself.

Edward William Godwin, an architect, was called "the greatest aesthete of them all" by Oscar Wilde, who, like the expatriate American painter James McNeill Whistler, was one of Godwin's patrons. Like Dresser, Godwin had an early appreciation of the functional, architectonic qualities of Japanese design, and his angular pieces mark

<
A very rare William Morris chair prototype, c. 1865. Philip Webb, one of the partners in Morris's firm, designed the famous "Morris chair," a simple piece based on a rush-seated Sussex chair with upholstered arms and a cushioned back and seat. For comfort, the back was adjustable on a hinge at its base. A massively solid chair, it was designed to create a new style, in keeping with Morris's socialist principles. Robert Wilson Collection. Photograph: Antoine Bootz

a radical break with European styles. Godwin designed for a number of firms. Early in his career, he worked on commission at two major houses in Ireland: at Glenbeigh Towers, for Rowland Winn, and at Drotmore Castle (designed and built between 1867 and 1869), for his friend and patron, the third earl of Limerick. At Drotmore, Godwin's chairs were in oiled wainscot oak with natural calf upholstery. Godwin also collaborated with Whistler on William Watt's stand for the 1878 Paris Universal Exhibition. He had designed a "Greek chair" for Watt in 1875, and in 1877 designed a "Jacobean chair" for the firm of Collier & Plunckett of Warwick. His favorite material was ebonized wood, often in square laths of machine-made regularity, which made his chairs suitable for factory production and also allowed them to be widely imitated.

With the publication of Godwin's book *Art Furniture* (London, 1877) and the exhibition of Japanese crafts at the 1876 Philadelphia Centennial, America developed a craze for all things Japanese. The American landscape painter Frederick Edwin Church (1826–1900) built Olana, his "Persian villa" on the Hudson River, which he furnished with seats synthesizing the best from both Eastern and Western cultures. For Church and Godwin, Japanese influence represented an honesty and abstract ornamentation similar to that of medieval seats. At about the same time, the Russian artist Ivan Yakovlevitch Bilibin (1876–1942), another Romantic nationalist, wrote of his indebtedness to Japanese art, and many of his illustrations were directly inspired by Japanese prints.

Godwin's chairs were Anglo-Japanese in name only. Although their simplicity and lightness created a "Japanese" effect, they were unlike anything made in Japan. Moreover, Godwin had no interest in the revival of craftsmanship, in contrast to Morris and his circle. Godwin, in fact, asserted the importance of the designer over the craftsman and, perhaps unwittingly, pointed the way toward the mass-production chairs.

William Morris (1834–96) was a man of seemingly boundless energy and talent, as a designer, craftsman, poet, political theorist, and socialist propagandist. He began as an architect in 1855, in the office of the Gothic-Revival architect G. E. Street, where he met Philip Webb (1831–1915), who would later become one of the most important designers for Morris's own firm. Morris's attempts to furnish the house in Bloomsbury that he shared with Edward Burne-Jones (1833–98) led to the creation of spectacular, medieval-inspired painted chairs, decorated with illustrations of legends such as that of King Arthur or the quest for the Holy Grail. These were large, not likely to be moved, "such as Barbarossa might have sat in." For the base of these chairs, Morris took as his model the stool depicted in Rossetti's pen and ink drawing *Hesterna Rosa* (1850/53). The chairs are a testament to Morris's imagination and to his collaboration with Rossetti and Burne-Jones. At the end of November 1856, Burne-Jones wrote to his father's housekeeper:

Morris is doing rather the magnificent there and is having some intensely medieval furniture made—tables and chairs like incubi and succubi. . . . He and I have painted the back of a chair with figures and inscriptions in gules and vets and azure, and we are all three going to cover a cabinet with pictures . . .

In 1861 Morris founded the firm of Morris, Marshall, Faulkner & Company, which was an immediate success. It moved from modest to large workshops in London, then was reorganized as Morris & Company in 1875. In 1881 the firm moved again, to Merton Abbey in Surrey. Morris died at age 62 in 1896, but the firm survived until 1940.

Morris's philosophy of improvement was not much different from those of other leading Victorian figures. He defined two types of furniture, one being "workaday . . . simple to the last degree," and the other "state furniture . . . as elegant and elaborate as we can [make] with carving or inlaying or painting."

The editor of *The Cabinet Maker and Art Furnisher* in an appreciation published after Morris's death in 1896 wrote that "he blessed and made popular the old Wycombe rush-bottomed chair . . . [which has] crept from the kitchen to the grander apartments." Morris and Co. had made rush-bottom chairs with turned frames of black-stained birch, which were acceptable in aesthetic households during the 1870s and 1880s. Ironically, however, most of their clients were drawn from the aristocracy and the wealthy merchant class. While Morris preached the doctrine of art for everyone, only the very rich could afford his work. Moreover, only the well educated could appreciate his lofty aestheticism. But in a last twist, just after 1900, when the movement came to be regarded as a dead end, Morris's company received the ultimate establishment accolade: it was asked to decorate the British Pavilion at the Paris Exhibition of 1900. By then, however, some of its members had started to succumb to Art Nouveau influence.

The architect and designer Charles Francis Annesley Voysey (1857–1941) began his profession under the influence of William Morris, but soon evolved a personal style of much greater lightness and imagination that would open the way to Art Nouveau. When he exhibited a hooded chair at the Arts and Crafts Exhibition Society in 1896, one anonymous critic wrote: "How curiously old friends get promoted. William Morris brought the rush-seated chair from the kitchen to the drawing-room. Mr. C. F. A. Voysey has carried the hall porter's chair upstairs and so purged it of its grossness that it now may be welcomed in the daintiest of bedrooms."

Simultaneously in many European countries, the Arts and Crafts Movement led to an idealization of folk culture and to a strong nationalistic revival, known as Romantic Nationalism. The Arts

<
A willow armchair by Gustav Stickley. Stickley made his chairs to be "simple, durable, comfortable, and fitted for the place [they were] to occupy and the work [they had] to do." Their forms were based on vernacular plank construction, consisting of solid oak horizontal and vertical members mortised and tenoned together with primitive vigor. Christie's

and Crafts Movement had a long life in America, where it had begun in the 1870s and grew steadily until World War I. The movement in the United States might be called the swan song of the English tradition. The first American Society of Arts and Crafts was founded in Boston in 1897, and the second in Chicago a few months later. The aesthetic influence can be found in three major areas: the Northeast, the Middle West, and the West Coast. A number of designers are associated with the founding of the Boston Arts and Craft Society, the best-known being Elbert Hubbard and Gustav Stickley. In America, the Arts and Crafts ideal produced a domestic idiom in one of its offshoots, the Mission Style. The sources of this style were two: the direct, rather crude work produced in the Spanish missions of the Southwest and English Arts and Crafts pieces. The term "Mission Style" is said to be derived from the functionalist beliefs of the designers, who declared that furniture has a mission: to be used.

> An American bamboo armchair by James Walli with an inset lacquer panel, c. 1886. Museum of Art, Rhode Island School of Design

Gustav Stickley (1858–1942) the leading proponent of the Mission Style, was one of the most important figures in the development of Arts and Crafts chair design in America. Between 1901 and 1916 he edited *The Craftsman*, the magazine that more than any other propagated the ideas of the Arts and Crafts Movement in America. The comfort and convenience of the sitter were enhanced by generous, leather-covered pillows in earth tones with large brass studding and a factory-made spring-supported seat. Although the furniture was machine-produced, Stickley and his fellow designers emphasized the look of hand craftsmanship with mortise-and-tenon construction and exposed pegs at the front of the chairs. Unlike Morris and the English Arts and Crafts designers, Stickley advocated the use of modern tools and machines at his place of business, the Craftsman Workshops in Eastwood, New York. However, he also understood the appeal of handmade details. The quality and character of his chairs quickly attracted other talented chair-makers.

The architect Harvey Ellis (1852–1904) started in 1902 to write for Stickley's magazine and soon began to design chairs for him that display an elegance not usually associated with Stickley's severe forms. Ellis, it is said, made the craftsman movement poetic. He incorporated inlays of contrasting wood, copper, brass, and pewter, which, as he wrote in an article in *The Craftsman*, "contrast well with the gray-brown of the oak." Another American designer, Charles Rohlfs (1853–1936), became famous outside the United States for the high quality and imagination of his chairs, decorating the strong outline of his oak chairs with delicate carving inlays. Elbert Hubbard (1856–1915), a writer and an apostle of aestheticism with long hair and flowing ties, founded a community of craftsmen, the Roycrofters at East Aurora, New York, based on the principles of William Morris. There he created oak benches and chairs in a plebeian version of the Mission Style; his teaching and ideas of community may have influenced Frank Lloyd Wright.

In the eastern United States, the Arts and Crafts ideal faded during the First World War. In the Middle West, however, centered in Chicago, it developed into one of the most significant movements of the twentieth century, the Prairie School. Frank Lloyd Wright (1867–1959) was the Prairie School's chief protagonist, and his ideas set much of its philosophy, which gave great importance to chair design. Wright started designing furniture in his early twenties for his own use. His chairs are angular, often with long, narrow slats. He wrote that "the most satisfactory apartments are those in which most or all of the furniture is built in as a part of the original scheme." All his work was closely related to the Arts and Crafts Movement, however, unlike Morris he was an early advocate of machine-made furnishings. In the machine, he said in a lecture at Hull House, "lies the only future of Arts and Crafts." Nevertheless he was never, apparently, completely satisfied with his chair designs. "My early approach to the chair was something between contempt and desperation," he wrote in *The Natural House*. Later he continued,

We now build well-upholstered benches and seats in our houses, trying to make them all part of the building. But still you must bring in and pull up the casual chair. There are many kinds of 'pull-up' chairs to perch upon lightly. They're easier. They're light. But the big chair wherein you may fold up and go to sleep reading a newspaper . . . is still difficult. I have done the best I could with this 'living room chair,' but, of course, you have to call somebody to help you move it. All my life my legs have been banged up somewhere by the chairs I have designed. But we are accomplishing it now. Someday it will be well done.

In 1904 Wright designed some painted metal office armchairs on swivel bases, and also some wooden frame chairs in which the basic form is reduced to a cube. These pieces were amazingly advanced for their time and were to have great

<
A nineteenth-century Afghan seat known as *la selle de Genghis Khan* (Genghis Khan's saddle), formerly belonging to the decorator Christian Bérard from around 1930 to 1949.

> A pair of Russian Arts and Crafts armchairs with original embossed and polychromed leather upholstery. Collection A La Vieille Russie, New York

influence on later furniture design, through the work of Gerrit Rietveld. Wright's later chairs were increasingly eccentric. For example, he designed circular chairs with segmental arms for a circular-plan house, and polygonal chairs for a hexagonal-plan house. Some of his clients found these so uncomfortable that they disposed of them.

The influence of the British Arts and Crafts Movement on most European countries can hardly be overstated. The damage to aesthetics that industrialization threatened at the turn of the century was a real concern for intellectuals, artists, and chair-designers alike, and the only logical remedy seemed to be a return to indigenous craft traditions, particularly to those of peasant cultures, which were perceived as unspoiled. In Norway, the archaeological excavation of the Viking ships at Tune (1867) and Gokstad (1880) provided a major stimulus for the Viking Revival, also known as "the dragon style." Viking Revival chairs became popular in Sweden and Denmark, and were used to promote the idea of a unified Scandinavia. At the Paris Exhibition of 1900, Westerners became acquainted with the Norwegian, Finnish, and Russian Folk Revival styles and loved them. In the late nineteenth century, two folk art colonies had been created in Russia to revive and improve peasant crafts. The first of these was established in the 1870s at Abramtsevo, near Moscow, by the railroad magnate Savva Mamontov and his wife, Elizaveta. The second was founded in the 1890s at Talashkino, near Smolensk, by the princess Maria Tenisheva. Once more, ironically—as had been the case with the Arts Crafts Movement in England—craft and craft chairs were patronized by aristocrats and rich

merchants. In order for production to be efficient, it had to be organized as an industry, even if only a cottage industry, the very thing that these patrons had initially set out to combat. The similarities of the English and Russian movements do not stop there. Like the chairs of William Morris, Russian crafts chairs were often carved from oak, and when upholstered, were covered with leather, sometimes painted with images from folk tales, as Morris's had been decorated with illustrations of medieval legends.

France seems to have been the one industrialized country in Europe to resist the Arts and Crafts Movement and the Folk Revival, perhaps because France industrialized relatively slowly. French designers, presumably, did not perceive the new machines as a threat. Moreover, throughout their history, French seats were prized for their beauty and luxury, not for their coarseness and simplicity, and so French designers, chair-makers, and *ébénistes* had never been concerned by the mass market, even after the Revolution. The notion of mass consumption started at the end of the nineteenth century in the Anglo-Saxon countries, under the impetus of William Morris. This moment marked the first time since the Middle Ages that France had played no role in an important development in chair design. It was, perhaps, the beginning of the end of French hegemony in the field. France, however, was the birthplace of a very individual style based on still-active traditions, which was also a revolt against the technocracy of the age and which led to the creation of the most uncomfortable seats of the twentieth century: the Art Nouveau style. The seats in this style would lead the way to modern chairs.

ECLECTIC BOURGEOIS: NINETEENTH-CENTURY CHAIRS OF THE MACHINE AGE

"The longer I live," Oscar Wilde once observed, "the more keenly I feel that what whatever was good enough for our fathers is not good enough for us." This remark could have been the motto of the nineteenth century, a time of enormous changes brought on by the Industrial Revolution. Chair design reflected these changes. The machinery and assembly lines that created vast wealth in Europe and America made possible the manufacture of seats in larger quantities, more quickly, and less expensively than ever before. Prosperity also increased demand. After years of war and revolution, people who could do so sought refuge in domestic life—if possible, ensconced in a cozy chair. Middle-class people wanted both to imitate the aristocracy and to show off their new wealth. They also wanted comfort, and their money's worth, as well.

One of the first bourgeois seats created during this period was the Biedermeier chair of Austria and other German-speaking countries. Ironically, the Biedermeier style was the child of the aristocratic French Empire and English Regency styles.

∨

A small, late-nineteenth-century elephant bidet, probably from a bordello, signed *Pascucci, Nice.* Collection Philippe Vichot, Paris

As the rising middle class of Europe began to look back to the days of the French Bourbon kings, they displayed seats that reproduced the "Louis" styles of the *ancien régime*. These new chairs were more comfortable and more lavishly decorated than the originals after which they were modeled; their artistic quality, however, was far below that of the pieces carved by the eighteenth-century masters.

The chairs of the nineteenth century, from the gargantuan Biedermeier sofa to the fussy Victorian papier-mâché nursing chair to the Napoleon III tufted slipper-chair all reflected the middle-class lifestyle, which flourished at most social levels in every European country. The literature of the period also reflected, through the work of such writers as Emile Zola, Gustave Flaubert, Georges-Charles Huysmans, Gabriele D'Annunzio, Edgar Allan Poe, and Oscar Wilde, the importance of the environment. These authors' stories illustrated how chairs situated a character in his milieu or expressed his social position. For example, Oscar Wilde wrote, at the beginning of Chapter Four of *The Picture of Dorian Gray*, "One afternoon a month later, Dorian Gray was reclining in a luxurious armchair in the little library of Lord Henry's house in Mayfair." Edgar Allan Poe, in his "Philosophy of Furniture," published in *Burton's Gentleman's Magazine* in 1840, went further: "It is an evil growing out of our Republican institutions that here a man of large purse has usually a very

> A pair of late-Victorian mahogany settees, upholstered in contemporary Aubusson tapestry in a room in the apartment of the dancer Rudolf Nureyev. Christie's. Photograph: Fritz von der Schulenburg

little soul. . . . The corruption of taste is a portion or a pendant of the dollar manufacture."

Poe was speaking of the way middle-class Americans conceived of decoration in the mid-nineteenth century: the showier a seat was, the worse it became. The only redeeming qualities of chair design at the time were its emphasis on comfort and the omnipresence of upholstered furniture. The love of comfort was made possible by a more relaxed attitude toward etiquette, and comfortable seats further reinforced relaxed postures and positions, eroding the power of etiquette even further. This progression can be partly attributed to a lack of strong political leadership in most European countries. The furniture made in the reign of Louis XIV, for example, had reinforced a hierarchical social structure. Louis XIV would probably have been horrified to learn that the magnificent style he had instigated would be, more than a century after his time, re-created for bourgeois pleasure.

Unlike the styles of earlier centuries, those of the nineteenth century did not evolve in a continuous progression; a new style did not suddenly make existing ones unfashionable. For the first time in the chair's history, many diverse styles flourished together. In fact, all of the major nineteenth-century styles coexisted and co-mingled throughout the century. While all of the pseudo-architectural chair styles from Gothic to Arts and Crafts seem to have been made for use by men in their libraries or clubs, the more comfortable machine-made seats attracted women, who proudly displayed them in their boudoirs or living rooms.

biedermeier chairs

The Biedermeier style emerged in the period following the Napoleonic Wars, around 1814–15, a time of profound political and social upheaval. When the last German princes abandoned Napoleon after the battle of Leipzig, the Empire style fell out of favor, its cool grandeur too pompous for a period of poverty and too aristocratic for an age of liberal ideas. Indeed, despite superficial resemblances, Biedermeier chairs have little in common with Empire seats. The charm, comfort, and lighter forms of Biedermeier are primarily derived from *Zopfstil*, the German variant of the Louis XVI Neoclassical style.

<
A side chair by Josef Danhauser of Vienna, considered the best Biedermeier furniture-maker. The Metropolitan Museum of Art

<<
A Biedermeier armchair. The simplicity and clean lines of the seats combined with their light-colored woods give the chairs a curiously modern appearance. Decorative motifs such as sphinxes, dolphins, and especially, swans, sometimes appeared on Biedermeier seats. Bill Blass Collection

chairs in the nineteenth century 313

> A salon in the apartment of the dancer Rudolf Nureyev featuring a Russian Neoclassical ormolu-mounted Karelian birch settee, c. 1810. This piece is similar to a settee designed by Carlo Rossi (1775–1849) now at the State Hermitage Museum in St. Petersburg. Photograph: Fritz von der Schulenburg. Christie's

> A Biedermeier sofa, c. 1830. Christie's

<
A French Directory shield-back mahogany side chair, early nineteenth century. Collection H. M. Luther, Inc., Antiques, New York

<<
A Russian mahogany armchair, c. 1825. Collection A La Vieille Russie, New York

Biedermeier style was also influenced by English furniture. All eyes had turned to England, the conqueror of Napoleon and the nation whose economic and industrial development was advanced so far beyond that of the Continent. English chairs had long been known in Germany, through the English royal family's connection to the duchy of Hanover and from the engravings of such English chair-makers as Chippendale, Sheraton, and Hepplewhite. Michael Angelo Nicholson's book, *The Practical Cabinet Maker*, published in 1826, also influenced Biedermeier craftsmen. For example, their penchant for sofas with strongly curved armrests, small tapering legs, and a single-viewpoint design was prefigured in Nicholson's book.

Vienna, the center of the Biedermeier style, was an overwhelmingly middle-class city, from which few new artistic impulses emerged. Moreover, people had been traumatized by war, and sought comfort in the warmth of hearth and home. Unlike other German-speaking countries, Austria had not embraced the Empire style—an irony, given that Napoleon's consort, Marie-Louise, was the daughter of the Austrian emperor Francis II.

After Napoleon's defeat, representatives of the great European powers gathered in 1815 to redraw the political map of Europe at the Congress of Vienna, which focused international attention on the city. Many attending ministers passed through the study of the Austrian chancellor, Prince Metternich, whose chairs were in the Biedermeier style, and enormous numbers of seats were made to accommodate the visiting delegations. These people were receptive to the arts and crafts of the Austrian empire, and through them, the style spread.

After years of war, not to mention the oppressive formality of the imperial etiquette, people were longing for the reassurance of simple comfort. The chair-designer Josef Danhauser (1780–1829) personified this new attitude. He had started his factory in 1804 in Vienna, at first

>
A Biedermeier rocking armchair. Didier Aaron Collection, Paris

emulating the designs of Percier and Fontaine. Soon his style changed, becoming more personal, and gradually evolving into Biedermeier. Solidity and comfort became key components of chair design. Many fruitwoods (maple, cherry, apple, and sometimes birch) were used and mixed for maximum effect. As in the French Empire style, the lyre motif was widespread, but it was now used in a new way: The seat's back was shaped like a lyre and curved to create a comfortable support, as in the Greek *klismos*. The legs were also curved for better balance and effect.

The X-shape of the classic folding chair also came back into fashion. Biedermeier designers adopted this ancient type in wood, embracing its form, but not its hierarchical function. These chairs were not made to be folded, since folding chairs were not comfortable. Banquettes, too, became fashionable, since they were easy to use for entertaining during this pleasurable time in Vienna, when the music of the elder Strauss filled the air. The Revolution of 1848, which took place in Paris the same year that Karl Marx published the *Communist Manifesto*, was the death knell of the Biedermeier style. Until then, the German-speaking bourgeois, as well as the Russians, Danes, and Swedes, reveled in their comfortable Biedermeier seats. Each nationality put its own stamp on the style. In Sweden, where the court preferred grand seats in the Empire style, Biedermeier did not catch on until comparatively late. The new fashion was inaugurated not in Stockholm, but in the southern province of Skane, which was close to Denmark and northern Germany, where Biedermeier flourished. Few

<
A Russian birch side chair, c. 1820. Collection A La Vieille Russie, New York

>
A Russian mahogany and gilt armchair and matching side chair, c. 1825. Collection A La Vieille Russie, New York

pieces were signed during this period, and so the makers remain anonymous. In Sweden the style became so popular that it flourished until well after the middle of the nineteenth century, and was then revived again around 1900.

One particularly Swedish feature is the use of blond woods. Birch was the most common, but elm and cherry were used, as well. Ebonized decoration often replaced ormolu and gilt mounts. In Russia, where a version of the Biedermeier style was popular among the aristocracy (in part owing to the fact that the middle class was so small), Karelian birch wood was often used, along with poplar, mahogany, and walnut, and all were often varnished. In 1824, the architect Vasily Stasov (1769–1848) designed a set of walnut armchairs in the Biedermeier style that were made by the cabinetmaker Grosse for the study of Alexander I. Their most distinctive feature was their uprights, each a single piece of wood that stretched from the base of the legs to the top of the back, a form that was widely imitated. Many examples of this design can be found in various palaces, and simpler versions were made in Russia until about 1830.

Traditionally, Hungarians and Czechs looked to Vienna for inspiration. Austria exported its wares to Moravia and Bohemia and also exerted a strong stylistic influence in Italy, especially in Naples and Parma. At the Neapolitan courts of Francesco I and Ferdinand II, the Biedermeier spirit triumphed, as can be seen from the many paintings in the Capodimonte Palace in Naples of family groups of Bourbons, all seated in locally made Biedermeier chairs. In Parma the former French empress Marie-Louise ruled over a small court furnished with Biedermeier seats. She had by then married the count of Neipperg, with whom she lived in middle-class comfort. Indeed, many royal palaces of the time, from Naples to Russia, were steeped in the bourgeois spirit.

louis style chairs, 1820–1900

While Austria, Germany, and Eastern Europe enjoyed their Biedermeier chairs, seats in the styles associated with various French kings appeared in most Western countries from the 1820s to the 1900s. Strangely, the idea of reproducing the grandeur of the French monarchy seems to have originated in England. At first, Louis XIV chairs were chosen for reproduction. Interest in French seats of that period was encouraged by the English aristocracy, many of whom were buying French furniture after Napoleon's defeat. Among these was George IV (reigned 1820–30), who furnished Windsor Castle with chairs in the French style.

Among the early English chairs in the Louis XIV style are the opulent pieces introduced in the 1820s in the drawing room at Tatton Park, Cheshire. During the rebuilding of Belvoir Castle, Leicestershire, around 1825, the principal rooms were also decorated in the Louis XIV style. Shortly thereafter, several houses in London, including York House (1825–26), Londonderry House (1825–28), and Crockford's Club (1827), an infamous gambling house, were decorated in various Louis styles. Even the Waterloo Chamber in Apsley House, the duke of Wellington's London home, was furnished in the Louis XV style.

As the chair style generally known as "Louis Quatorze" gained popularity in England, the baroque forms of the Louis XIV period became more and more confused with the rococo of Louis XV, and increasing use was made of elaborately carved and gilt scrolls, swirls, shells, and feathers. A design for a "Louis Quatorze Room" said to be based on the interiors of Crockford's Club appears in *George Smith's Guide* of 1828, which also presents a chair in extravagant rococo style with the following criticism of the new trend: "As this mansion is solely appreciated to nightly purposes of pleasure, perhaps such a taste may be in unison with the wasteful transfer of property made in such establishments." Despite such criticism, by the mid-forties, neo-rococo seats were being made by virtually every firm in England, although it is often difficult to identify the manufacturers, as few of them signed their products. The firm of William Smee and Sons, in its catalogue of 1840, showed typical mid-nineteenth-century rococo seats with sprung, deep-buttoned upholstery,

<
A painting by Eugène Lami (1800–90) showing a reception for Queen Victoria and Prince Albert at the Château d'Eu, September 3, 1843. Châteaux de Versailles et de Trianon. Photograph: RMN. Gerard Blot

chairs in the nineteenth century 319

> A painting by Antoine Thomas (1791–1834) of Louis XVIII in his invalid chair. Châteaux de Versailles et de Trianon. Photograph: RMN. Arnaudet/Blot

> A painting by Henri Scheffer (1798–1862) of Louis-Philippe in a meeting with his ministers at the home of the comte Mole, August 3, 1838. Châteaux de Versailles et de Trianon. Photograph: RMN. Blot/Jean

which were described as "superior lounge chairs." The firm of Miles and Edwards on Oxford Street made chairs in the neo-rococo style. These companies began to offer their clients decorating services, replacing the architect, because such a loose chair style and the decoration that went with it did not require the trained skill of an astute designer. In fact, these seats, with their curved shapes, scrolls, and volutes, could be executed by indifferent craftsmen and could even be produced successfully by machine. Mechanical carving techniques were developed to answer the demand of the growing market of the well-to-do bourgeoisie, who wanted showy, comfortable, and reasonably priced décor. In the early 1800s, various wood-shaping machines came into use. Around the 1830s, the mechanical circular saw appeared, and around 1840, carving machines were introduced to make Louis-style chairs.

Veneers also became popular. The foreign woods that were generally used for them were more resistant than English woods to worms and their use improved the appearance of a seat greatly. Steam-driven machines for cutting veneers were introduced in the early nineteenth century, and veneers became so common that the word developed a pejorative suggestion of social climbing. Dickens made this reference clear in *The Pickwick Papers* (1836–37), when the old chair exclaims in offense, "That's not the way to address solid Spanish mahogany. Dam'me, you couldn't treat me with less respect if I was veneered."

William IV of England (reigned 1830–37), loved the comfort of enveloping armchairs in the neo-rococo style, although he intensely disliked gilding. In France Louis-Philippe (reigned 1830–48) and his queen, Marie-Amélie, were the incarnation of the bourgeois couple, with tastes to match. During Louis-Philippe's reign, French seats were made in various eclectic styles, and were, above all, comfortable. Large and heavy versions of the Louis XV armchairs were favored, as well

<
An unusual nineteenth-century upholstered armchair, formerly in the house of Christian Dior, Paris. Bill Blass Collection

>
A Napoleon III giltwood *chauffeuse*, a chair for sitting by the fire, c. 1860. R. Louis Bofferding Collection, New York

>>
A Napoleon III upholstered side chair, c. 1865. Collection Madeleine Casteing, Paris

as a seat called the "Voltaire" featuring a high, curved back, named after the famous writer, who, although he did die in a similar chair in 1778, never actually saw this particular type. Besides the high back, other features were added to the Voltaire, such as casters that allowed it to be moved easily, and sometimes, a hilt, carved in the wood of the top rail, for ease of handling. The neo-rococo and various Louis-style chairs were designed to be used in every room, but their principal popularity was in the drawing room or the boudoir, where feminine influence was strongest.

By the middle of the century in England, neo-rococo seats were superseded by a more rectilinear, controlled style recalling Louis XVI. In 1851 in France the Second Empire was established, during which Napoleon III embarked on a series of official building projects in an attempt to re-create some of France's former glory. In the same spirit, Louis styles became popular, the emphasis in seating being toward Louis XV and Louis XVI. The empress Eugénie so admired Marie Antoinette that she ordered the redecoration of the apartments of her own chateau at St.-Cloud in a Neo-Louis XVI style. A number of new chairs in this style, coil-sprung for comfort, were introduced, and some of the original period pieces were enhanced to make them look more sumptuous. Although these seats exemplify the empress's somewhat parvenu taste, Eugénie displayed real originality in instigating the new seating style—along with the crinoline dress, which forever linked the two, since sitting comfortably while wearing such a dress required a low, armless seat. Eugénie was so thoroughly associated with the Neo-Louis XVI style, which prevailed even after she and her husband were deposed and exiled, that it became known as "Louis XVI Impératrice." Once it became popular with the bourgeoisie, a series of new, exceedingly uncomfortable seats was introduced, with such scrolling and carving that it was almost impossible for a sitter to lean against the back. Because of the discomfort of late-nineteenth-century wood-frame pieces (especially those made primarily for display), another type was devised for actual use, the all-upholstered seat, which was often placed in the midst of a room rather than against the wall, a radical break from the eighteenth-century habit.

Toward the middle and end of the nineteenth century, the demand for seats had three distinct tiers. At the upper end of the market was a small, knowledgeable clientele led by the empress Eugénie herself, who admired Marie Antoinette and hoped to downplay her own modest origin. She and other such collectors mixed superior copies of eighteenth-century seats among genuine pieces. Many great collections of French seventeenth- and eighteenth-century furniture were assembled during this period, including those of Prince Demidoff and the duke of Hamilton. Baron Ferdinand de Rothschild used his chairs to furnish the great house that he had built at Waddesdon, near Aylesbury, England, in the late 1880s. Some pieces made by English firms such as Gillow or French firms such as Beurdeley in the early 1900s were such seamless copies of the original models that decades later an expert is needed to determine whether they are genuine eighteenth-century pieces or not. Significantly, Alfred Beurdeley boasted that during 1870, the year of Napoleon III's fall, he had visited the Garde-Meuble (the royal furniture warehouse) and had ordered every piece copied.

At the middle of the market, the desire for comfortable seating ushered in an era of stuffing and padding, which totally distorted the shapes of the chairs, making any resemblance to previous Louis shapes increasingly remote. In some instances, the wooden frame disappeared completely, resulting in a new creation: the all-upholstered seat, which might be covered in velvet, needlepoint, or carpetlike fabric and finished in masses of fringes and tassels. At the lower end of the market, especially in the 1890s,

<
A round ottoman in the Renzo Mongiardino house in Milan. Photograph: Antoine Bootz

seats became increasingly fussy and spindly, which gave them an appearance utterly foreign to their eighteenth-century French prototypes. Industrial development and the search for a less expensive product only accelerated the process. The majority were constructed in dark mahogany with a highly polished surface, and despite being called "Louis," looked not in the least French.

The ultimate abomination in France was the Henry II-style dining room favored by the middle class, a trend that unfortunately lasted until World War I. The so-called Elizabethan style in England was no better. The various Louis styles also enjoyed a fairly wide success in the commercial world. Seats in the Louis XV or XVI style seem to pop up in every grand hotel or on every Atlantic liner, following the example of the Ritz in London. Department stores bearing the description "French salon," also featured the unavoidable Louis XVI-style chair.

The interchange of ideas and influences between France and England in the matter of seats increased. France at the time was the largest single importer of English seating furniture on the Continent, while English firms employed French craftsmen and designs in the "Old French Style" (as any Louis or rococo style was called) were avidly copied. Thomas King published the popular *Modern Style*, along with *French Designs*, in 1833. In the latter book, the plates were advertised as "displaying the French taste for lightness and elegance and showing various descriptions of the present style in Paris."

Other European countries also embraced the Neo-Louis styles enthusiastically; among the German-speaking nations, Austria being the first to do so. The severity of Biedermeier had grown softer through the 1830s, and by the mid-1840s neo-rococo was well established, its quick acceptance eased by the strong tradition of the rococo style in Austria and Germany. The Austrian firm of Karl Leistler won praise for its curvaceous chairs at the Great Exhibition of 1851 in London,

>
A nineteenth-century Viennese side chair. Bill Blass Collection

and had already supplied a large number of seats in the neo-rococo style from 1842 onward for the Liechtenstein Palace in Vienna, as had the Thonet company. Michael Thonet, later famous for his invention of bentwood chairs and the founder of the world-famous Thonet company (see pp. 368–71), made numerous pieces in the most lavish neo-rococo style in the late 1840s and early 1850s. It is also quite obvious to see the resemblance between the convoluted bentwood and the neo-rococo swirls. The success of the Thonet chair during the latter part of the nineteenth century and later, with over fifty million seats sold of just one model before 1930, is an indication of the affection that the Western world held for the rococo style.

Neo-Louis seats came sooner to Prussia than to Bavaria, where they would survive longer. The Green Room in the Berlin Palace, where Queen Elizabeth of Prussia came to live shortly after the coronation of Friedrich Wilhem in 1840, was designed in the neo-rococo style to conform to the authentic rococo character of the palace, which had been enlarged in 1741 by Knoebelsdorff. By the late 1850s and 1860s, neo-rococo enjoyed as much popularity in Germany as anywhere. When Queen Victoria's oldest daughter, Vicky, married prince Friedrich Wilhelm of Prussia in 1858, and the couple moved to their own palace in Berlin, one of Vicky's ladies in waiting complained that the princess had furnished it too much like Osborne House on the Isle of Wright. The princess longed for the comfort favored by her mother, Queen Victoria, which was rare in Germany at the time. When the princess moved into the Neues Palais the following summer, her mother instructed her to have "necessary conveniences" (i.e., toilets) installed there, as well.

English chairs, far more comfortable than German examples, were imported to Germany through the Hanseatic towns, although few were luxurious. German seats were produced in Mainz, in the Grand Duchy of Hessen. Two famous chair manufacturers in that center of the German furniture trade were Anton Bembe and the firm of William Kimbel. After 1835, Kimbel produced three pattern books in numerous installments containing many designs in the neo-rococo style. Then Anthony Kimbel, a member of the same family, set up shop in New York, further expanding the German influence.

Although in Germany, as in most other European countries, the popularity of the neo-Louis styles tended to slacken after 1870, it received an unexpected renewal under the influence of Ludwig II of Bavaria, whose increasing eccentricity drove him to commission several architectural extravaganzas. Ludwig's love of seventeenth- and eighteenth-century France and his longing for days long past led him to begin projects like Herrenchiemsee and Linderhof Palaces. In the island palace on Herrenchiemsee, Ludwig II tried to re-create Versailles in its entire vastness. Although the absolutism of the Bourbon kings could not be realized in the age of constitutional monarchy, Ludwig wanted at least to erect a memorial to the form of government that he admired and to the man who had embodied it. However, the palace was never more than just a fragment of an idea. Only the rooms that played an important role in the court etiquette of Versailles were envisaged, and Herrenchiemsee was never completed.

Linderhof, erected by George Dollmann between 1870 and 1886, was built in the rococo style so as not to compete with Ludwig's Versailles. Madame de Pompadour and, in particular, Marie Antoinette, whom Ludwig admired owing to her unfortunate fate, were to be the main figures. Each of these buildings required suitable seating furniture. Chairs, armchairs, thrones, and sofas were all designed in a riotous elaboration of neo-rococo. At Herrenchiemsee, most of the seats were designed by Julius Hofmann, assisted by Adolf Seder, who worked under Dollmann and succeeded him as architect when Dollmann could not meet his deadlines. Delivery continued during the 1880s, but work stopped in June 1886, when the king was pronounced incurably insane. On June 13, 1886, Ludwig died under mysterious circumstances.

<
An unusual nineteenth-century English armchair. Bill Blass Collection

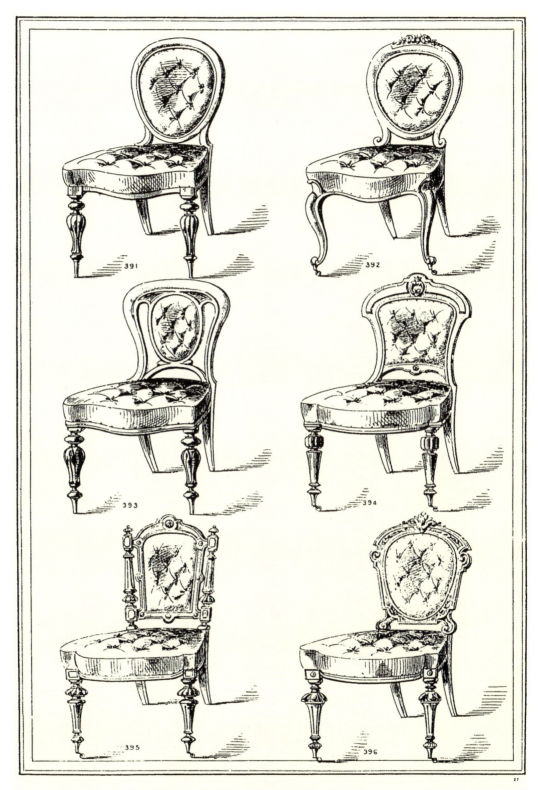

> A page of designs for dining chairs, with upholstered backs, published by J. Lovegrove Holt in *Modern Furniture*, London, c. 1820. The Metropolitan Museum of Art

At Linderhof, the principal supplier of seats seems to have been the Munich firm of Anton Possenbacher, working from designs by Adolf Seder, who played an important role in the development of handcrafts and chair designs in Munich at the time. All delivery took place during the mid-1870s, and no expenses were spared. In the Blue Cabinet, the gilded sofas and chairs were upholstered with coverings of gold-embroidered, figured Lyon silk, matching the walls. In the dining room, the elaborately gilded armchairs and chairs were covered in red embroidered figured Lyon silk, and in the East Gobelins Room the gilded and scrolling armchairs were appropriately upholstered in red Gobelins tapestry. Linderhof was the king's favorite palace, and the only one of his that was completed.

German rococo seats in the eighteenth century had exemplified an extravagance unequaled anywhere else, and building on the strength of this history, German neo-rococo seats continued well into the twentieth century. As late as 1898, the firm of Julius Zweiner was producing rococo-style bedroom furniture for the Royal Palace in Berlin. Trends in Scandinavia and Russia closely followed those in Germany. By the 1850s and 1860s neo-rococo was firmly established, and the popularity of the style was reflected in many Swedish interiors. The founder of Stockholm's Nordiska Museum, Arthur Hazelius, had in his study a rococo sofa and balloon-back chairs similar to those of many bourgeois interiors at mid-century.

Russian drawing rooms of the period were also invaded by seating furniture in the Louis XV style, made of rosewood or partially gilded mahogany, with cabriolet legs, carved, and heavily decorated. The architect Stackensneider provided sketches for neo-rococo seating furniture in the Gilt Drawing Room at the Winter Palace in St. Petersburg in

<
A Russian red-painted *kirstar* chair, c. 1870. Hillwood Museum

>
A French nineteenth-century gilded rope chair. Collection Madeleine Casteing, Paris

1850. This suite was executed by Vasily Bobkov, one of the leading chair manufacturers in St. Petersburg. In 1894, Robert Melzer designed a complete neo-rococo scheme for the private dining room in the Winter Palace. The white-painted seats made by Friedrich Melzer displayed none of the spindliness that was so prevalent at the end of the nineteenth century. Unfortunately, by this time many Russian seats were caricatures of their fabled predecessors, lost in heaviness, elongation, and a total lack of restraint.

Italy, despite its love of Neoclassicism and its infatuation with the Empire and Biedermeier styles, began to develop a taste for neo-rococo seats. Against all logic, Neoclassical and Empire styles became associated with the old monarchy, while Count Camillo Cavour, one of the architects of the unification of Italy in 1861, was known to be surrounded by neo-rococo seats, which thus became associated with a forward-looking attitude. The firm of Ferdinando Pogliani in Milan made many neo-rococo seats with a special Italian twist: curving backs in the Louis XV style were often combined with straight, square legs in the Louis XVI manner.

Seats in a curvilinear neo-rococo style were fairly short-lived in Italy. The middle class and bourgeoisie favored Renaissance-inspired styles and Neoclassical seats, which suggested the great periods of the Italian past. Ironically, neo-rococo seats remained popular among the aristocracy. When the staterooms in the Quirinal Palace in Rome were refurbished for Umberto I at the end of the nineteenth century, the seats were all in the neo-rococo style.

The royal palace at Queluz, Portugal, a small version of Versailles, is a remarkable rococo monument. In the mid-nineteenth century, Pedro IV had a spectacular circular bedroom there, decorated by Manuel da Costa, an admirer

A sheet of French watercolor designs for chairs, by Maison Poirier et Remon, a firm active c. 1862–1900. Musée des Arts Décoratifs, Paris

A Napoleon III upholstered armchair, c. 1860. Collection Nicole Mugler, Paris

of the French rococo. Though sumptuously decorated, the bedroom, like the rest of the palace, was, by Portuguese custom, sparsely furnished. As late as the nineteenth century, furniture and chairs were moved from one palace to another as the royal family traveled. Neo-rococo seats were moved endlessly, always ending up in Queluz, which eventually became the preferred summer residence of the royal household.

The Rococo Revival style was the dominant fashion for seats in America during the mid-Victorian period. Today, the best-known craftsman in the style is John Henry Belter (1804–61), who came to New York from Germany, in 1844, and established himself as a leading furniture-maker. Using iron molds and steam, he developed a technique to bend and laminate rosewood, which allowed the formation of sweeping, curved shapes, which in turn could be elaborately carved. The strength of the laminated wood permitted intricate piercing and carving of leaves, vines, fruit, and flowers, all inspired by the bounty of the American land and the popularity of nature worship. Belter had many imitators, even though he made an effort to protect his laminating and bending process with patents issued at various times between 1847 and 1858.

Belter worked in what was essentially a plywood process, using rosewood either entirely, or for the outer layer, in as few as three and as many as sixteen layers (usually between six and eight), to make a panel less than an inch thick. The panel could be shaped in molds by steam heat and later carved. Belter was thus able to replace the traditional rail-and-stile construction of chairs with molded one-piece backs, which were carved and upholstered. The firms of Alexander Roux, Joseph Meeks and Sons, and Charles Baudouine, among others, also made neo-rococo seats during the 1850s. To avoid infringing on Belter's patent, Baudouine made his chair-backs of two pieces with a center joint. None seems to have achieved the technical virtuosity of Belter's work.

During the American Civil War (1861–65), business was poor for the chair industry, and many small firms closed. Moreover, the sensuousness of the neo-rococo-style seemed inconsonant with the harsh realities of the period, so fashions in chairs turned toward the more rectilinear Louis XVI Impératrice. By the mid-1860s, seats had become simpler and more streamlined, with straighter lines. The preeminent chair-maker of the Louis XVI Impératrice style was the New York-based Leon Marcotte (1848–80), who was of French extraction. His seats followed the general shape of the Louis XVI style, using dark woods and delicately wrought ormolu mounts. The fashion for neo-Louis XVI seats continued into the 1870s, and as the century drew to a close, pieces were made to look increasingly like their original prototypes. Chair-makers in the twentieth century, stimulated by demand, created ever more seats in the Louis styles, and none in the modified neo-Louis. The public wanted more accurate copies, good or bad, of the eighteenth-century models. Some were probably created to fool the gullible; others were just bad copies. As the modern age advanced and contemporary designers created more comfortable and appealing seats, the demand for eighteenth-century reproductions never ceased.

balloon-back chairs

As a counterbalance to heavy "Louis" armchairs, makers in the Victorian era developed a new design, the small, movable balloon-back chair, whose back uprights were merged into the top-rail. The design was based on that of French Louis XV panel-back side chairs, but the upholstery in the back was omitted, and the form was more fluid than that of the French original. This seat could be moved around a drawing room or parlor easily, to allow guests to mingle.

At Osborne House on the Isle of Wight, Queen Victoria shaped European policy in her sitting room while seated next to her beloved Albert in a balloon-back chair. Variations were used in dining rooms, and a lighter, completely round-backed type was used for the bedroom. These open, circular-backed bedroom chairs were sometimes known as Quaker chairs. The English "fly chair" was another light, movable chair, inspired by a French model known as the *chaise volante*, a favorite in drawing rooms and boudoirs. Some balloon-back chairs had turned front legs, a solid mahogany frame for use in the dining room, leather seats, and buttoning. Early Victorian drawing-room balloon-backs were made of rosewood; others, which became equally popular in France, England, and Russia, were in papier-mâché or blackened wood, with lighter decorations and inlays of mother of pearl. Slender bedroom versions were made of walnut.

The variety of *chaises volantes* is endless. Some are painted gold; they may have cabriolet or straight legs. The seats may be upholstered, caned, or buttoned, and they often bear distinctive names, such as "Chiavari," "fly," or "buckle back" (presumably from its resemblance to a belt buckle). All were useful and practical. Chiavari chairs derive their name from the city where they originated, Chiavari, on the Ligurian coast east of Genoa. First made there at the beginning of the nineteenth century, they soon became popular throughout Europe. Chiavari pattern chairs were used when Schinkel furnished Charlottenhof in 1826 for Crown Prince Friedrich Wilhelm of Prussia, who had seen such chairs while visiting the Royal Palace in Naples in 1822. Their combina-

<
A Gathering at the Home of Mme. Brisson, 1893, a painting by Marcel André Bashet (1862–1941). Châteaux de Versailles et de Trianon. Photograph: RMN. Gerard Blot

tion of utility and elegance had wide appeal; similar chairs can be seen in views of rooms furnished for Napoleon III and Eugénie at St.-Cloud and Fontainebleau.

The demand for lighter seats and the attendant problems facing chair designers is evident in a letter that the architect and designer J. B. Papworth received from his client A. Galloway:

I wish you would think of a chair that would be easy to sit in and yet not heavy. Remember, it is a room constantly in use, and it is of the greatest importance that the chair be comfortable. Can't you unite novelty, elegance, and the comfort of a lounging chair? The one shown us at Snell's was neat and pretty, but we have seen many like it and it would not be easy to the back.

The balloon chair in all its variety and its combination of practicality and comfort seems to have been the answer.

papier-mâché chairs

Papier-mâché —literally, "mashed paper"—known in Persia and India in Antiquity, reached France at the beginning of the eighteenth century, where small objects such as boxes and trays were soon made using the technique. These pieces caught the attention of Frederick the Great, who set up a factory to make similar objects in Berlin in 1765. England discovered the medium at the same

> A French papier-mâché nursing chair, ebonized and decorated with mother of pearl, a technique that came into use after 1825. Thin pieces of mother of pearl were laid on the wood and varnished according to a predetermined pattern. After the varnish had dried, acid was applied, and the areas of the mother of pearl that were not varnished were eaten away. The result was an attractive addition to the surface, resembling inlay. The process was used throughout Europe to enliven papier-mâché chairs with birds, butterflies, and flowers. Private collection

time. In 1758 the writer Robert Dossie published instructions for making papier-mâché pieces, but no chairs of papier-mâché were made until Henry Clay of Birmingham revolutionized its manufacture by introducing a heat-resistant variant that was as sturdy as wood. Beginning with trays, Clay soon turned to chairs and other furnishings. The Victorians loved papier-mâché for its cheapness, durability, and above all, its malleability. The vogue for papier-mâché chairs persisted throughout Europe until about 1870. It was most pervasive in England, where the combination of Clay's process and Victorian taste insured continued success.

Jennens and Bettridge, which replaced Clay's firm as the leading factory around Birmingham, created the widely imitated example of mid-Victorian taste, the "Day Dreamer" armchair. It was decorated on the top, we are told,

with two winged thoughts, the one with bird-like pinions, and crowned with roses, representing happy and joyous dreams; the other, with leathern bat-like wings, unpleasant and troublesome ones. Behind is displayed Hope, under the figure of the rising sun. The twisted supports of the back are ornamented with the poppy, hearts-ease, convovulus, and snowdrop, all emblematic of the subject. In front of the seat is a shell, containing the head of a cherub, and on either side of it pleasant and troubled dreams are represented by figures. At the side is seen a figure of Puck lying asleep in a labyrinth of foliage, and holding a branch of poppies in his hand.

This seat, which was exhibited at the Great Exhibition in 1851, was the epitome of the Victorian era, the malleability of papier-mâché allowing the creation of the multiplicity of symbolic figures. Other seats reflected contemporary trends: the chaise longue; the Elizabethan chair with strapwork back; the heavily decorated, Rococo-Revival nursing chair; and the "legere," chair, with balloon back and cabriolet legs.

Chair-backs could be enhanced with painted panels, and various effects in gold and colors

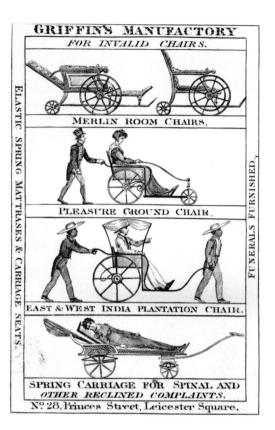

A trade card showing chairs for invalids. The Metropolitan Museum of Art

could be added to the glistening black ground. Intricate seats were often reinforced with metal or wood frames, to make them sturdier. Papier-mâché chairs—brilliant, colorful, reasonably priced, and imaginative—were much loved by the Victorians; their wonderful excess perfectly suited the period.

patent chairs

The protection of new inventions and discoveries by letters patent dates back to Greek Antiquity. From the late Middle Ages to the nineteenth century, rulers offered patents both as a reward and as an inducement to foreign craftsmen to migrate to their countries. The nineteenth century saw an explosion of patents. Among these, new types of chairs made for use by the sick, invalids, or travelers required patent protection. These chairs might incorporate special devices such as adjustable backs or footrests; the seats might be made of a new material; or the piece might be combined with a desk, cradle, or bed. Whatever the combination, patent chairs were designed to meet the new demand for comfort, and interest in their creation was high.

Folding iron chairs and bed-chairs inspired by campaign furniture were made for invalids. Like multipurpose medical, dental, and barber chairs, they were initially made of wood, then metal. In another category was the adjustable-back easy chair, covered with leather and buttoned, made of mahogany, oak, or walnut, and sold as a club, reading-room, or boardroom chair. There were also domestic chairs, often combinations such as bed-chairs, cradle-chairs, or table-chairs, made of fruitwood, oak, or walnut. Finally, practical seats for theaters, planes, cars, trains, buses, and later, for subways, were made of lighter and stronger new materials such as bamboo, metal, tubular steel, or molded plastic.

The English, with their well-developed sense of comfort, were interested in patent chairs early in the nineteenth century. One of the earliest patents recorded in England was Samuel James's 1813 invention of an elegant "Regency sofa or machine for the ease of the invalid and others." William Pocock's 1814 advertisement for "Improvements in Furniture and various Inventions for Invalids" featured a mechanized wheelchair and a reclining chair for the gouty. Although made for invalids, such comfortable chairs found a market with the general public, too. Between 1827 and 1863, no fewer than twenty British patents were granted for various improvements to reclining chairs. These "machines to increase ease and comfort" were based on a system that required the sitter to release a spring in each arm so that it could be drawn forward or backward, adjusting the angle of the back simultaneously. The best known was Robert Daw's recumbent chair, patented in 1827. Each Daw chair bore a paper label that read:

A person while sitting in the Chair may fix the back at any inclination by raising the spring beneath that part of each arm where the hand rests; and while holding up both the springs, draw the arms backward or forward to the desired situation, and having loosed both springs at the same time, the back of the chair will be found perfectly safe to recline against.

The demand for reclining chairs grew, and in 1830 George and John Minter, upholsterers and cabinetmakers of Princess Street in London, received a patent for the manufacture of fully automatic reclining armchairs. In their advertisement they listed five different models, each available in either a mahogany or rosewood frame. Further options included chairs produced with or without wings, optional leg rests, and, in one case, the alternative of "Merlin" wheels and a fall-down footrest. These types of chairs became extremely popular in Victorian interiors; indeed, the Minter chairs were displayed at the Great Exhibition held in London in 1851.

The Minter brothers were not alone. In America, George Hunzinger designed a number of patented folding, reclining, and rocking chairs.

>
An invalid's reclining chair. The Metropolitan Museum of Art

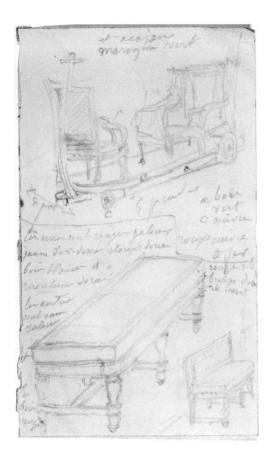

<
A drawing of a mechanical chair designed for Louis Philippe and his queen, Marie-Amélie. Château de Versailles

v
The label of the mechanical chair

In February 1866, he patented a reclining chair mechanism that remained in use for a number of years, based on a ratchet built into the arms, which were linked to pivots on the back rails. By lifting the arm and repositioning the ratchet, one could position the back at various angles. Ingenious reclining and folding armchairs were also devised by American inventors for various modes of public transportation, such as a compact folding seat for train cars that was patented in the late 1890s. Passenger chairs for steamships were developed later, as were airplane seats. The creation of the railroad system encouraged the development of numerous comfortable types. In America, the Annual Report of the Commissioner of Patents indicated that three types of car seats with reversible backs had been patented in 1852 alone. And from 1850 to 1880, various railroad companies fitted their "parlor railway coaches" with Doctor Horton's reclining chairs.

Railroad passengers were not the only ones to receive the attention of the inventors. Patented in 1879 in America, the Harwood patent fiberboard seat was intended solely for chairs. It was supplied either as a part for new chairs or as a replacement for broken cane seats. The seat was prepared from paper pasteboard or leather board, which was then coated with or dipped in dye. The final finish was a coating of gelatin embossed to resemble leather, which, when dry, was varnished with shellac. The introduction of this seat relieved a bottleneck in the production of chairs by permitting the manufacturer to bypass the time-consuming process of caning. It became so popular that Harwood seats were even successfully exported to England.

Another American seat exported to England was invented and patented by George Gardner in May 1872: perforated plywood veneer. Designed as a substitute for cane and for settle or banquet use in its own right, the material was fitted to a wide range of seats "suitable for house, shop, or institution." Chairs fitted with plywood seats were initially sold in England as the "Newest American Novelty."

Theater seats and variations of dentist and medical chairs were created and improved one after the other to fulfill ever-changing demand. However, to be successful in the expanding nineteenth-century patent market, a model had to be clearly distinguished from the competition, which led to exaggerations. In the 1880s, the Boston manufacturer De Bert Hartley produced a "reclining house chair," featuring up to fifty different positions and twenty-five different styles! With the appearance in the twentieth century of such new materials as tubular steel, models were

chairs in the nineteenth century 335

>
Patent opera chairs.
Christie's

>
A folding chair, patented by H. Mahoney, c. 1875. Genesee County Museum

>>
An advertisement for the patented Andrews' Improved Opera Chairs. The Metropolitan Museum of Art

simplified, and solutions to the problem of making a chair respond to the sitter's movements were provided by, among others, Marcel Breuer and Le Corbusier. New materials continued to surface; chairs made of plywood, polished steel, corrugated cardboard, polyurethane, and acrylic resin were patented during the course of the century. A new concern with ergonomics stimulated yet another set of patent seats for the disabled. One example is the Carna Chair, a light folding wheelchair made of titanium, rubber, and aluminum developed by Kazuo Kawaki in 1991.

upholstered chairs and sofas

Suddenly in the doorway I saw an armchair, the big armchair I read in, which went out, swaying. . . . Other chairs followed it, the armchairs of my living room, then the low divans, which dragged themselves along like crocodiles on their short legs; then all my chairs, which bounded like goats, and the footstools, which sprung like rabbits. . . .

If every period has the nightmares it deserves, Guy de Maupassant's description, in his short story "Qui Sait?" of a nightmare involving upholstered furniture offers a revealing look into the mind of the late nineteenth century. Indeed, overstuffed seats seem to have crept all over the living rooms, drawing rooms, studies, and bedrooms of the period. The accession of Queen Victoria to the English throne in 1837, her marriage to Prince Albert in 1840, and the birth of her nine children presented the world a model of domestic fidelity. Victoria's life embodied an ideal of bourgeois virtue that was widely imitated. Indeed, her comparatively rootless childhood drove her into a frenzy of root-growing for the rest of her life. Upon returning from a holiday in 1844, she described her domestic haven:

The children again with us, & such a pleasure & interest! Bertie & Alice are the greatest friends & always playing together. Later we both read to each other. When I read, I sit on the sofa, in the middle of the room, with a small table before it on which stand a lamp & candlestick, Albert sitting in a low armchair, on the opposite side of the table with another small table in front of him on which he usually stands his book. Oh! If I could only exactly describe our dear, happy life together!

Victoria's holidays were often spent in her private houses, Balmoral and Osborne, in which her taste for upholstered seats for the comfort

< A British *borne*, a sofa designed to sit in the middle of a room, and ottomans, plate 3 from Henry Wood's *Designs for Furniture*, London, c. 1840. The Metropolitan Museum of Art

of her many children, relatives, and attendants dominated. As padded seats became a metaphor for familial bliss, the upholstered look became immensely popular. The invention of helical wire springs lowered costs, and as cushioned seats were both more comfortable and less expensive than chairs with lavish carving, they became available to an even larger audience. Indeed, almost no wood was visible on seats planned for comfort, since their construction required only a rough wooden frame. Even carved feet could be dispensed with, since feet were hidden behind the dense fringes that were in fashion at the time. Often the trimmings that completed the bases of these armchairs and sofas were costlier than the fabrics they embellished.

As textile mills were founded throughout Europe and America, wool and cotton fabrics also became more cheaply available. Expensive silks or brocades were not the only fashionable option. Stamped plushes in beautiful patterns and colors became popular, and they were, and looked, comfortable. Serge, jute, *algérienne* (a silk and cotton blend), velvets of all sorts, embroidery on canvas or silk, needlepoint, and oriental carpeting were the new fabrics of choice for the comfortable deep-tufted seats. Bands of wool-work trimmed low easy chairs and ottomans alike. Haircloth, with its hard, smooth surfaces, was admired for several decades despite its unpleasant texture, chiefly by people of limited means, who liked the fact that it was almost indestructible. By the 1870s, however, its lugubrious effect was considered old-fashioned.

Chintz slipcovers and tartans were Queen Victoria's favorite patterns for her private homes at Balmoral and Osborne, the houses most reflecting her taste. The fashion for chintz slipcovers began as a reaction against stuffiness, and by 1876, those who valued simplicity refurbished their drawing rooms with chintz and light paint, a fashion that has continued to this day. The vogue for plaid is also reminiscent of Victoria and Albert, as Lady Augusta Bruce's description of Balmoral attests: "The carpets are Royal Stuart; the curtains, the former lined with red, the same Dress Stuart and a few chintz with a thistle pattern. The chairs and sofas in the drawing room are Dress Stuart poplin."

Fillings, including horsehair, feathers, down, wool, and cotton, became less expensive, owing to the machine revolution. These factors led to the creation of thickly padded and tufted seats offering a satisfactory support to the similarly padded, tufted, fringed, and draped Victoria herself. Some of these pieces were curious departures from the customary concept of seats, but they functioned adequately for their purpose, which was to permit a woman wearing a vast crinoline to sit on them, and when around 1870 the bustle came into fashion, allowing a woman to sit sideways. In this (far from easy) position, she could display not only the full glory of bustle and train, but also the painfully acquired elegance of her tiny waist.

Cushions strewn about were thought to make a room look less stiff. Sofas had their quota of elaborate plump fantasies in needlework, and tall-backed chairs were fitted out with chair bolsters, tightly stuffed sausages swung from cords. More was definitely better. Springs were perfected so that wire-framed shapes remained firm, and a new device, deep tufting, helped hold the increased fillings in place. Europeans became infatuated with the comfort of the Near East, and Turkish corners became the craze. Starting around 1830, many new types of upholstered chairs, sofas, divans, and ottomans with softer and deeper shapes began to appear under this influence, first in France, then in England, and then in other European countries. Far more relaxed postures became permissible for adults. Children were still expected to sit bolt upright, preferably in silence.

The new "lounging" fashion was roundly condemned in *The Art of Conversation*, a short book on manners published in England in 1842, with remarks on fashion and address by one "Captain Orlando Sabertash."

There is a practice getting vogue, almost a sort of fashion, among young gentlemen who wish to impose upon the unwary, by nonchalant airs of affected ease . . . which I must here denounce as a breach of good manners. . . . I mean the practice of lounging in graceless attitudes on sofas and armchairs in the presence of ladies. All these vile and distorted postures must be reserved for the library couch or armchair, and should never be displayed in the society of gentlemen, and still less in that of ladies.

He added that "Lounging is not a foreign vice, though foreigners take up the practice to an extravagant degree when mixing with English society." His remarks suggest how widespread the "lounging" habit was, and how beloved the new comfortable seats were.

Seating etiquette differed greatly from one country to another. When Queen Victoria's oldest daughter, Vicky, the consort of Prussia's crown prince, Friedrich Wilhelm, gave birth to her first son, the future Kaiser Wilhelm II, the Queen was shocked to learn that it was customary in the Prussian royal family for the new mother to observe the child's christening while reclining on a sofa in a recessed room beside the altar. Queen Victoria was incensed at the idea, and sent an outraged letter to her daughter insisting that she promise "never to do so improper and indecorous a thing as to be lying in a dressing gown on a sofa at a christening! . . . [A]s my daughter & an English Princess I expect you will not do it."

In France new varieties of seats were created: the *pouf*, the *causeuse*, the *fumeuse*, the *berceuse*, the *borne*, the *confident*, the *indiscret*, the *crapaud*, the *fauteuil bébé*, the *boudeuse*, the *vis-à-vis*, the *rothschild*, the *douillette*, and the *confortable*, essentially, an English easy chair. The English created variations on the easy chair, as well: the Prince of Wales, the Woolsey, the Smoker, the Spanish, the Jersey, and a high-backed wing chair usually called "a grandfather," adding to the long list already developed in the eighteenth century.

An early appearance of the *pouf* (literally, a puffy shape) is found in the *Bedroom of Comte Charles de Mornay*, a painting by Eugène Delacroix. This kind of sofa spread rapidly through Europe after 1840, and may owe its presence in the bedroom of the comte de Mornay (who was Minister Plenipotentiary in Morocco when the painter traveled there) to the similarity of the ottomans that de Mornay had found in North Africa. The *pouf* had an equal number of detractors and admirers. The first group thought it more annoying than useful and that it took up so much space; the second included the writer Théophile Gautier, who, characterizing the taste of the period, wrote, "What could be more charming than a group of women of different and contrasting beauty seated on a *pouf* at the center of a salon in a billow of guipures and lace, which froths at their feet like the sea at the feet of Venus?" The image that immediately comes to mind is the famous painting by Franz Xavier Winterhalter of *Eugénie among the Ladies of Her Court*. Indeed, the low, armless *pouf* was an ideal seat for women wearing crinolines, as it easily accommodated the amplitude of the skirts. It was comfortable, although, upholstered in bright needlepoint or velvet with ropes and tassels, usually a little too garish to be handsome.

The *borne* was a central island in a room, about two meters in diameter with a middle pillar for a backrest, often featuring a palm tree in its center. The first time this seat is mentioned is in the *Memoirs* of Prince Metternich, who called it simply a round sofa. The *borne* was much larger than the *pouf*, but both were circular. The ottoman, Turkish sofa, or divan (the terms apparently were interchangeable) was a long, low upholstered seat for three or four persons placed in a recess. Some early Victorian ottomans were circular with buttoned upholstery and divided into four wide seats that could carry eight people. The Romantic Movement, inspired by Lord Byron, was probably responsible for the introduction of this oriental

> A page of curved-back upholstered "smoking chairs," published by J. Lovegrove Holt in *Modern Furniture*, London, c. 1820. The Metropolitan Museum of Art

piece to Victorian interiors. Byron's admirers had undoubtedly read of the voluptuously lounging lady in "Don Juan," whose hair

*Fell in long tresses like the weeping willow
Sweeping the marble underneath her chair,
Or rather sofa (for it was all pillow,
A low, soft ottoman).*

The later Victorian ottoman was a square, hexagonal, or circular seat, luxuriously padded and upholstered, and placed in the center of the room. Today the term "ottoman" is still used, although it now denotes an oversized footstool.

The *confortable*, also called a *fauteuil Pompadour*, was a completely upholstered, overstuffed lounge chair, essentially the same as the English spring chair or easy chair. It was usually covered with enormous lace antimacassars. Epitomizing a sentimental approach to design, easy chairs were held in affectionate regard in England, America, and on the Continent. In 1838, Eliza Cook wrote, in "Old Armchair," a poem to her late mother's chair that became famous on both sides of the Atlantic:

*I Love it, I love it; and who shall dare
To chide me for loving that old arm-chair?
I've treasured it long as sainted prize;
I've bedewed it with tears, and embalmed it
  with sighs . . .
Would you learn the spell? A mother sat there
And a sacred thing is that old arm-chair*

The Victorians realized the full meaning of the chair and how an empty seat perfectly symbolized the aching void left by the death of its regular occupant. A multiplicity of seats implied an active social and familial life, which may be why so many different ones were created. Smaller and lighter versions existed for ladies—the *crapaud* (frog), for example, another version of the upholstered lounge chair. It was compact and enveloping, low to the ground, and not very deep, recalling the shape of a frog, hence its name. Its place of

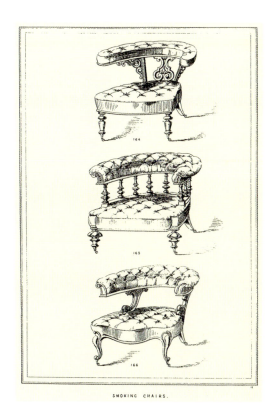

SMOKING CHAIRS.

choice was in the bedroom, near the fireplace. The upholsterer Devilers invented the type in Paris around 1838. A slightly smaller version was called a *fauteuil bébé*. The *boudeuse* was a drawing-room seat incorporating two chairs separated by a central back. The two sitters sat back to back, hence the name, which means "sulker." The Prince of Wales (named for no apparent reason) was also an English lady's chair; the Woolsey was a larger easy chair with a deep, circular seat, inclined arms and back, and shorts legs. The *berceuse* was a French and Italian all-upholstered version of the rocking chair.

The return of the high-backed winged easy chair was welcomed by such writers as Lady Barker, whose 1878 book *The Bedroom and Boudoir* espoused a taste that rejected chairs that were "a mass of padded and cushioned excrescences." In contrast, Lady Barker illustrated a mid-eighteenth-century winged chair, remarking that "If one must have large armchairs in a boudoir, or in a bedroom, here is one which is big enough in all conscience, and yet would go more harmoniously with an old fashioned room than any fat and dumpy modern chair." Indeed, the high-backed, winged easy chair was warmly welcomed around the world during the last decade of the nineteenth century. Owners loved these chairs with their great ears and ample proportions, which offered a sort of halfway house between the bed and the world of active work. They also made an excellent resting place for convalescents. "The most fashionable type of easy chair at the present time is that known as the Fireside or Grandfather," wrote the anonymous author of an article on easy chairs published in *Furniture and Decorations* in October 1897. Similar lounge chairs were found in America, according to Andrew Jackson Downing in *Architecture of Country Houses* (1850). Like Captain Orlando Sabertash, Downing seemed to deplore the effect such seats had on behavior: "Lounge, better adapted for siesta than to promote the grace of dignity of the figure."

Edith Wharton, in her *Decoration of Houses* (1897), mourned the loss of the elegance of eighteenth-century armchairs and *bergères* compared to contemporary upholstered pieces:

The old armchair or bergère is a good example of this combination. The modern upholsterer pads and puffs his seats as though they were to form the furniture of a lunatic's cell—and then, having expanded them to such dimensions that they cannot be moved without effort, perches their dropsical bodies on four little casters. Anyone who compares such an armchair to the eighteenth-century bergère, with its strong tapering legs, its snugly fitting back and cushioned seat must admit that the latter is more convenient and more beautiful.

However, she remarked further that the tall, upholstered armchairs known as "firesides" were so comfortable that they could even be used as dining chairs: "Such chairs could be employed at the head and end of the dining table, where their stately appearance would be peculiarly appropriate, whilst as chimney corner seats they would lose nothing of their usefulness."

The *confident*, also called the *vis-à-vis*, *tête-à-tête*, or, in Italy, the *amorino*, was a popular sofa that seated two. According to one nineteenth-century poet, "two half-moons form the seat, in inverse pose." A similar piece with three seats was called an *indiscret*, presumably an allusion to the romantic triangle so common in nineteenth-century French life and fiction. A still larger version, the companion chair, which could seat six persons, was designed for the center of a drawing room. The *baigneuse* was another comfortable sofa, in a shape vaguely similar to a bathtub, with rounded extremities. The *fumeuse* was similar in shape to the *voyeuse* of the eighteenth century, on which the sitter sat astride. Below the armrest was a shallow box that could hold pipes, cigarettes, and matches. Its English sister, the "smoker chair," often featured a drawer below the seat, which contained a spittoon. Although the spittoon was frowned on as an article of furnishing during the last quarter of the nineteenth century, spitting continued, and the drawer satisfied the Victorian gentleman's exacting standards of comfort, and allowed the ladies to pretend that the habit had passed away. The chair was described in the magazine *Furniture and Decoration* in February 1897 as follows:

Under the seat of an ordinary standard chair, a club divan, or an upright arm-chair, is placed a drawer. This drawer is kept normally closed by means of spiral springs, and is brought forward by means of a cord, terminating in a small button. A pan (which for cleaning purposes is made removable) is contained within the drawer. Thus, when required, the spittoon may be drawn forward, and then released, when it returns to its place automatically.

English makers specialized in practical seats, creating many variations. "Literary machines" were adjustable seats combining a book-rest with a reading seat, a type described in the supplement to the 1846 edition of Loudon's *Encyclopedia* as "by no means elegant in form, but we can assert . . . that it is exceedingly comfortable to sit on; not only the back, but the head being supported by the peculiar form of the upper part of the end." Similar seats were created for members of the Prussian royal family. A leather-covered reclining chair was devised about 1826 as an invalid chair for the ailing king Friedrich Wilhelm, designed by the architect and furniture designer Karl Friedrich Schinkel. He had been inspired by the English Regency chair, which he had seen while in England the same year. Many more seats, which could almost be mistaken for English club chairs, were made thereafter for aristocratic Prussian patrons.

The abundance of seats in the Victorian era is illustrated by the number of parlor games involving chairs. There were many variations of "musical chairs," with such colorful names as "caterpillar," "change the seats," "the king's come," "how do your neighbor?" and "sea and fishes," all requiring numerous chairs.

The best-known comfortable English seat or sofa, upholstered in leather and loved throughout the world for its comfort, was the Chesterfield. Ironically, in its country of origin, it was described by Rosamund Marriott Watson in *The Art of the House*, written in the late 1890s, as an "obese, kindly-hearted couch . . . about as comely as a gigantic pin-cushion and as little convenient in a room of moderate dimension as an elephant." Despite this unflattering comment, Chesterfield sofas and armchairs continued well into the twentieth century and were appreciated for their strength and comfort. The abundance of comfortable sofas seems to have made stools obsolete. When their raison d'être gone, stools were too uncomfortable compared with sofas. The only stools that remained were such practical ones as the footstool and the gout stool. The rest were replaced by various *poufs*, ottomans, and the like, which better fit the new way of life.

The extravagant upholstered pieces that we have discussed here were developed during the Second Empire. By the 1890s they began to hint of the elephantine, both in contour and in their howdahlike trappings. Their days were numbered.

ART NOUVEAU, *JUGENDSTIL*, *SEZESSIONSTIL*, AND GLASGOW SCHOOL CHAIRS

Between 1890 and 1910, Europe saw the development of a style that became known as Art Nouveau. The name is derived from a shop in Paris, La Maison de l'Art Nouveau, founded in 1895 by the dealer Siegfried Bing, which exhibited the work of young, mainly French, designers. As Bing later noted, "At its birth, Art Nouveau . . . was simply the name of an establishment opened as a rallying point for youth keen to show their modern approach. It was only in relation to art as applied to furniture, to ornamentation in all its forms, that the need of a new departure was felt."

The term "Art Nouveau" is used in the English-speaking world, as well as in France and Belgium. In Germany and Scandinavia, the term is *Jugendstil*, after the magazine *Jugend*; in Austria it is *Sezessionstil*; in Catalonia, *Modernista* or *Arte Joven*; in Italy, *Stile Florale* or *Stile Liberty*, after the famous London store of that name. The style varied by region, and it had many sources, incorporating Celtic, Scandinavian, and even Japanese motifs, perhaps reflecting the self-doubt of a society at the brink of modernity. Art Nouveau chairs feature exaggerated, asymmetrical curving lines and tentacular flowers and leaves. Nature was the main source of inspiration, as it had been for William Morris. A premium was put on craftsmanship and originality, and on style before substance.

Belgium was receptive to the new style early on. The architect Henry van de Velde (1863–1957) displayed his enormous originality in a house he built for himself at Uccle, near Brussels, in 1895. The chaste interior with its clean lines and undecorated chairs greatly impressed Siegfried Bing, who commissioned van de Velde to design four complete rooms for his Parisian shop in 1896. This secured van de Velde immediate European recognition—and some abuse, as well. His spare chair designs proved to be an important link among Arts and Crafts, Art Nouveau, and modern industrial design. Van de Velde was strongly influenced by the work of the Scottish designer Charles Rennie Mackintosh, with whom he exhibited on two occasions, and who pulled him closer to modernity. Van de Velde's chairs were painted white, some with upholstery designed by the Belgian Symbolist painter Johann Thorn Prikker (1868–1932), whose work was greatly influenced by Javanese batik design. Thorn Prikker also designed chairs in an insubstantial, spidery style.

Art Nouveau architects and designers as far-flung as Victor Horta and van de Velde in Belgium; Hector Guimard, Louis Majorelle, Eugène Gaillard, and Emile Gallé in France; Charles Rennie Mackintosh in Scotland; Mackay Hugh Baillie Scott on the Isle of Man; H. P. Berlage in Holland; Antonio Gaudí in Spain; and Eliel Saarinen in Finland all designed their own furniture to create environments expressing their visions of modernity. These artists were disgusted, as van de Velde put it, by "the insane follies that furniture-makers of past centuries had piled up in bedrooms and drawing rooms." Yet their creations were often more "insane" than any from the past.

The Belgian architects and designers Victor Horta (1861–1947) and Gustave Serrurier-Bovy (1858–1910), like Henry van de Velde, created their chairs to fit into specific interiors, designing every detail of their houses inside and out, from windows to wood paneling to light fixtures. Most

<
A side chair, c. 1895, by Henry Clement van de Velde (1863–1957). A Belgian architect and designer, van de Velde was one of the most important propagandists of the modern movement. He was also influenced by Morris and Voysey. Collection Barry Friedman, New York

chairs in the nineteenth century

> François Rupert Carabin (1862–1932). *Nude Woman Resting Her Knee on a Chair*. Oil on canvas. Carabin was one of the strangest furniture-makers of his time, a true artist who worked in many media. His seats synthesize sculpture and furniture design, suggesting a subtle but disturbing eroticism. Often a kneeling female nude supports the backrest, while another supports the seat. The image of women projected by these chairs is not the ideal of love and beauty seen generally in Art Nouveau, but one that is disturbingly servile, abject, and even degraded. Photograph: RMN

Art Nouveau chairs were designed as part of such ensembles, as in Horta's own house in Brussels, now a museum. Horta loved petal shapes, drawing his rhythmic, fluid designs from botanical forms that show the influence of both Symbolist art and French eighteenth-century ornamentation. Details of his work were widely imitated by commercial marketers of the Art Nouveau style.

The new style was not accepted in French intellectual circles, however. Edmond de Goncourt, for example, decried the "delirious rantings of ugliness" of the Salon d'Art Nouveau of 1895. Nevertheless, many French designers developed Art Nouveau chairs. Nancy and Paris became the two principal centers of Art Nouveau furniture design, although in neither was a distinct, recognizable style propounded, for most of the artists working in those centers had their own ideas of form. Working at Nancy were Emile Gallé, Louis Majorelle, Eugène Gaillard, and Eugène Vallin. Their work, characterized by rich floral marquetry, was often commercially made. The style of their chairs, as critics have pointed out, is not particularly original, being largely modeled on Louis XV forms, with floral details and an occasional bit of Japonisme, which was introduced to France by Whistler around 1876. However, unlike their Louis XV antecedents, most Art Nouveau seats are extremely uncomfortable.

Emile Gallé (1846–1904), best known today for his art glass, also designed chairs inspired by flowers. His "Aux Ombrelles" piece, created for the 1900 World Exhibition in Paris, with its back in the shape of a flower and a pierced lozenge of carved flowers in the front of the seat, was exceptionally successful and was praised at numerous European exhibitions of the School of Nancy. Louis Majorelle (1859–1926) was the most prolific furniture- and chair-maker of the school, his mechanized workshop producing relatively luxurious seats at prices within the reach of the middle class. The contours of these seats, even the Art Nouveau examples, were based on Louis XV patterns, although he favored mahogany when most of the other Nancy School designers used local fruitwoods in the eighteenth-century tradition.

The designers working for Bing in Paris, including Georges de Feure (1868–1928), Georges Hoentschel (1855–1915), and Eugène Colonna (1862–after 1936) were more eclectic in style than those of the Nancy School. De Feure produced delicate, spidery seats in gilt wood with embroidered velvet upholstery, unfortunately all very uncomfortable-looking. Two highly original French designers were Hector Guimard (1867–1942) and Ruppert Carabin (1862–1932). Guimard designed the Art Nouveau street furniture of Paris, including the entrances to several Métro stations; as a result, the Art Nouveau style in France was sometimes derisively called *le style bouche de Métro*. The elaborate, curving lines of Guimard's finely made seats seem to embody their period, a time often called the Belle Epoque.

Carabin's chairs can be seen as an illustration of the views of their time, in which bordellos, prostitutes, and courtesans were an accepted

<
A ladder-back side chair, c. 1903, designed by Charles Rennie Mackintosh for the Willow Tea Rooms in Glasgow, with its original horsehair woven upholstery on a slip-seat. This is a rare example of the first version of a Mackintosh design, stamped *31* on the back seat stretcher. Mackintosh used chairs as components of a general scheme, in this project to define and break up space. Collection Barry Friedman, New York

part of life. Indeed, in most literature after 1850, romantic love had ceased to exist, while physical love was an obsession of fiction and poetry. Writers such as Gustave Flaubert and Honoré de Balzac represented women not as the angels of earlier fiction but as dangerous seductresses. Nonetheless, the graphic expression of these views appalled most critics of the time, and Carabin's work was declared acceptable, perhaps, for a museum or as a curiosity, but not as furniture for a private home. However, Carabin's symbolism brought him close to the work of Mackintosh and Frank Lloyd Wright, who designed seats considered by many as abstract sculpture, without reference to function.

Charles Rennie Mackintosh (1868–1928), an outstanding Scottish architect and designer, was the leader of the Glasgow School and a preeminent figure in the international Art Nouveau movement. He became known throughout Europe after he won the design competition to build the School of Art in Glasgow. His seats have a curious, virginal quality differentiating them from the robust masculinity of Arts and Crafts chairs and the curvilinear sensuality of French Art Nouveau.

Mackintosh's designs were based on the combination of straight lines and very gentle curves. Some chairs have tall, attenuated backs; others are low, almost cubical. With Mackintosh, the pendulum swung toward modernity.

Mackintosh's work was not well received in Britain, and after about 1905 he was ignored by the British public. On the Continent, however, his work was widely shown. He exhibited in Venice in 1899; in Vienna in 1900; in Turin, Budapest, Munich, and Dresden in 1902; and in Moscow in 1903, at an exhibition organized by Sergei Diaghilev. In 1901, Mackintosh entered a competition called *Haus eines Kunstfreunds* [House for an Art Lover], organized by the journal *Zeitschrift für*

> A high-backed chair of stained oak and rush for the lunchroom of the Argyle Street Tea Rooms in Glasgow, designed in 1897 by Charles Rennie Mackintosh. On the crest is an emblem combining Celtic and Japanese features. Collection Barry Friedman, New York

<
A chair by Joseph Maria Olbrich (1867–1908), c. 1899, for the guest room of the Villa Friedman in Hinterbruhl, near Vienna. Its forms clearly express the artistic ideal of the Vienna Secession movement. Historical Design, New York

Innen Dekoration of Darmstadt. As a result, his work influenced many leading European designers and architects, especially in Austria and Germany. He also became a friend of the Viennese designer Josef Hoffmann, with whom he collaborated on several projects.

Another English architect and designer, Mackay Hugh Baillie Scott (1865–1945), exerted a strong influence in northern Europe, especially in Germany. In 1898, he was commissioned to furnish the interior of the Grand Duke of Hesse's Palace at Darmstadt, one of the focal points of the Art Nouveau movement and the most important commission received by any English designer of this period. In 1899, the grand-duke Ernst Ludwig of Hesse founded, along with the Viennese architect Joseph Maria Olbrich (1867–1908), an artists' colony at Mathildenhohe, a park in Darmstadt. This project was the first major German undertaking to create a community as a *Gesamtkunstwerk*, a term coined by the composer Richard Wagner to mean a unified creation incorporating a number of media, an idea also expounded by the Arts and Crafts Movement. Ernst Ludwig's motivations for his experiment were a mixture of nationalistic, financial, and idealistic concerns. The unification of Germany in 1871 had ignited an interest in Germanic culture, and design was seen as a means to solidify national identity. The grand-duke also hoped to attract attention to Darmstadt as an art center. A grandson of Queen Victoria, he had been exposed to English design, and wanted German artists to profit from English influence.

The grand-duke's art colony made itself known through outside projects, commercial commissions, and exhibitions. It remained active until 1914, and was a visible forum for *Jugendstil*. For the first time between 1890 and 1905 a group of very gifted designers changed the entire direction of chair design in Germany, owing to a combination of business, government, and artistic influences. National self-consciousness was the fuel for this change, and *Qualität* (quality) became its watchword. The idea of a national style echoed the philosophical precepts of Friedrich Nietzsche (1844–1900), the most influential thinker of late-nineteenth-century Germany. Nietzsche called for the establishment of a national culture through unity of thought, will, and aesthetics, and his writing challenged artists to create a new form of design.

In Munich, Herman Obrist (1862–1927); August Endell (1871–1925); Joseph Maria Olbrich, who would later help found the Darmstadt artists' colony, and whose presence there accounted for much of its influence; Richard Riemerschmid (1868–1957); and Peter Behrens (1868–1940) formed a brilliant community, and from 1897 to 1898 established the Vereinigte Werkstätten of Munich and Dresden. The Belgian designer Henry van de Velde also settled in Germany in 1899, in 1904 becoming the director of the Arts School and the School of Arts and Crafts in Weimar. In 1919, he appointed Walter Gropius as his successor at Weimar, and thus was indirectly responsible for the foundation of the Bauhaus School.

Peter Behrens's designs quickly went beyond curvilinear Art Nouveau seats. The new style he introduced is seen in the house he built for himself in Darmstadt in 1901. In the dining room, his light, white-painted chairs, displaying fluid forms and curved, linear elements without the swirling forms of French Art Nouveau, showed the way to the future. Indeed, Behrens and

> A wainscot chair in the sixteenth-century style, c. 1900, by Richard Riemerschmid (1868–1957). Riemerschmid, influenced by the Arts and Crafts Movement, produced simple designs using traditional forms with a modern twist. Collection Barry Friedman, New York

Richard Riemerschmid became the first industrial chair-designers. With their work, well-designed chairs were produced in quantity and sold commercially for the first time. Surviving chairs that Riemerschmid created—for example, for Herman Obrist's house in Darmstadt—were the first made according to ergonomic principles. They clearly demonstrate his ideas of logic, honesty of construction, and above all, a new notion of comfort.

Vienna, the capital of the multiethnic Austro-Hungarian Empire, was a hotbed of art, where many Art Nouveau designers thrived. Otto Wagner, Olbrich's mentor, and Josef Hoffmann, founder of the Vienna Secession in 1899, both worked there. Like his German counterparts, Hoffmann designed chairs guided by an ideal of the unity of architecture, decoration, and furniture, and his stark, functional style was quite unlike the flowery Art Nouveau. His abstraction of form into linear planes, as manifested in his *Sitzmaschine* [machine for sitting] of 1908, would exert a strong influence on twentieth-century design.

In 1903, Mackintosh, together with the Viennese painter Koloman Moser (1868–1918), founded the Wiener Werkstätte, a group of artists and designers who shared a studio, and whose ideal was expressed by Josef Hoffmann in a 1911 lecture: "We want to establish intimate contact among public, designer, and craftsman, and to produce good, simple household utensils. We start from purpose; utility is our first condition." Hoffmann and Moser worked together frequently, and their designs are often similar. In 1903, Moser created seats featuring geometric patterns, which were the forerunners of cubist chairs. His seats are similar to those of the British Arts and Crafts Movement, but, as in England, simplicity and quality required pots of money. Rich sponsors were needed to produce those simple chairs, and the Wiener Werkstätte was plagued with financial problems.

The chair designers in Holland, as in Scandinavia, were influenced equally by the functionalist style of Austria and Germany and by the Art Nouveau of France and Belgium. Hendrikus Petrus Berlage (1856–1934), the Dutch architect who designed the Amsterdam Stock Exchange, created strong, chunky chairs. Being a propagandist for Frank Lloyd Wright, he was undoubtedly influenced by *Jugendstil* and *Sezessionstil*. In turn, he influenced Rietveld and Mies van der Rohe, who was his student.

In Italy, the influence of the French and Belgian Art Nouveau was strong, but not exclusively so. Some designers looked to France,

with its naturalistic floral decorations, and others to the austerity of the Arts and Crafts Movement and the *Jugendstil*. Italy, like Germany, was unified relatively late, in 1860. The new kingdom had before it the daunting task of attaining the economic and cultural level of the more advanced countries of Europe. The Paris fair of 1900 challenged the country's designers to move forward with new styles, or stay hopelessly locked in outmoded traditions. Several designers rose to the challenge. Agostino Lauro, a furniture designer and manufacturer in Turin, created seats in a style close to the French Art Nouveau. Vittorio Valabrega, another furniture manufacturer from Turin, re-created a small salon in the *Stile Florale* that he had originally designed for an exhibition in Turin in 1898, to great acclaim in the press. One writer, noting that the room was the first complete interior in the new style, enthused: "The whole effect is one of lightness, fluency and elegance." Valabrega's seats are a strange mixture of Art Nouveau and Arts and Crafts influence; nonetheless he was awarded a gold medal at the Paris Exhibition of 1900.

Other Italian designers, such as Alberto Issel (1848–1926), created chairs and sofas with angular lines derived from Mackintosh's work, from British Arts and Crafts examples, and from *Jugendstil*. Eugenio Quarti (1867–1929) was at the other end of the spectrum. An exhibitor at the Paris Universal Exhibition of 1900, he showed delicate mahogany chairs, with details in brass, copper, and silver wire, and inlays of mother of pearl. The most original designer of all was without doubt the talented Carlo Bugatti (1856–1940). As one critic at the 1902 exhibition at Turin wrote,

The artist who truly knows how to give an individual imprint to his furniture is C. Bugatti. Not everything that flows from the fantasy of this Milanese artist is beautiful. His work as a whole seems to be a reflection of oriental fantasies. . . . This is why Bugatti, living outside every movement, owing everything to himself, and demanding everything from himself, is nevertheless the exhibitor who most clearly remains stamped in one's memory.

An equally enthusiastic German critic, Georg Fuchs, lauded Bugatti as original, inventive, and "one who could lead Italy out of darkness and confusion." He developed a highly original—and very lavish—style. Blending Middle Eastern fantasy and Japanese naturalism, his pieces feature metal and ivory inlays combined with parchment and enhanced with painted decoration. The general effect was one of strident novelty. He was rewarded at the Turin exhibition of 1902 with a first prize for his original curvilinear seats.

The Catalan architect Antoni Gaudí (1852–1926) was another eccentric Art Nouveau designer. His chairs, designed to accompany his buildings as integral parts of a whole, often comprised thick, eddying scrolls merging into one another, making even the most elaborate products of Majorelle or Gallé seem restrained by comparison. For the Palau Güell, a town house that Gaudí designed in Barcelona around 1885–89, he created, among other exotic seats, a chaise longue on twined metal legs that, as the art historian Henry Russell Hitchcock noted, "offers startling premonitions of that of the mid-twentieth century." For the chapel of Santa Coloma de Cervelló in Barcelona, he designed benches with rough, wooden seats on spidery iron legs. Gaudí's seats are amazingly comfortable, a quality particularly evident in his Casa Calvet office chairs, for which he was determined to reduce the idea of a chair to its essentials. These are a perfect example of successful Art Nouveau chairs, combining British Arts and Crafts ideals of craftsmanship with a body-consciousness characteristic of the twentieth century.

<
The "Cobra" chair by Carlo Bugatti, shown at the 1902 Turin International Exhibition of Decorative Arts in an installation called the "Snail Room," made Bugatti's reputation as a highly eccentric designer. The chair, of decorated calf velum over wood and hammered copper, is signed *Bugatti* on the back in red crayon. Collection Barry Friedman, New York

6
modern chairs

Modern chairs are the product of materials and techniques developed during the last hundred years. Made of laminated wood, steel, rubber, and plastic, they allow the sitter to ride in comfort on suspended steel. They are also the product of a new, hurried, tense lifestyle. Their inspirations vary greatly, reflecting the fashions of the twentieth century.

The sole restriction of modern chair design is the necessity to comply with contemporary machines, thus there are an unprecedented number of designs for which progress is the keynote. Otto Wagner (1841–1918), the *éminence grise* of both the Vienna Secession and the Wiener Werkstätte, stated in an address to the Vienna Academy in 1895, that "All modern forms must reflect the new materials and the new requirement of our time: If they are to meet the needs of modern man, they must express our improved, democratic, clear-thinking selves." Designers had to "civilize technology," in the words of the architect Marcel Breuer (1902–81).

Architects, with their engineering background, were well placed to develop new chairs that were both functional and handsome. Chair design particularly appealed to architects, as it allowed them to express their design philosophies in three dimensions. As Peter Smithson wrote, "[W]hen we design a chair, we make a society and a city in miniature." One can see clearly the sort of society and city envisaged by, for example, the modernist architect Ludwig Mies van der Rohe (1886–1969). His chair designs project an orderly, antiseptic, and efficient world. The fact that architects create "a city in miniature" through chairs has never been truer than in the twentieth century. As Peter Collins points out in *Changing Ideals in Modern Architecture 1750–1950*, it was not until the twentieth century that "The ultimate test of architectural genius became whether or not one could design a new kind of chair." As a result, after World War II, architects and designers were identified with the chairs they created. We think of the Mies chair, the Eames chair, the Breuer tubular seat, or the Le Corbusier chaise longue.

Modern seats are children of the machine age, of the chemist, and the engineer, striving for novelty. They come in many shapes, forms, and materials. Although nineteenth-century industrialization introduced many new materials for chairs, including pâpier-maché, cast iron, and rattan, their shapes varied only slightly. The twentieth century, with its wealth of available materials, opened a radically new dimension to chair design. The machine look created from laminated wood or tubular steel was the foremost style of the period. The handicraft look, a descendant of the Arts and Crafts Movement, also attracted Scandinavian, English, Italian, and French designers. The biomorphic look, with its roots in the Art Nouveau style, appealed to yet another group mostly enamored with rubber and plastic. The glamour look, represented by the Art Deco movement, struck a chord among wealthy collectors. At the opposite end of the spectrum is the utilitarian look, often linked to the machine look.

Ironically, the machine look was best created by handcrafting representations of the industrial process. Mies van der Rohe's Barcelona chair of 1929 is a perfect example; although it appears machine-made, it was originally produced almost entirely by hand. Similarly, the handicraft look is often made by machine. For example, the famous "Peacock" chair designed by Hans Wegner in 1947, inspired by vernaculars forms, was machine-made, with only the finishing done by hand. Similarly, the materials best able to express the abstract essence of nature (for the biomorphic look) are synthetics such as plastic or foam rubber. In modern chair design nothing is what it appears to be, conflict and paradox abound, and appearances are deceiving. Moreover, some of the most technically advanced seats perfectly suited to mass-market production have been aesthetically too avant-garde for popular appeal. Such was the case with the first truly modern chair, Gerrit Rietveld's Red and Blue Chair designed in 1917.

Modern chairs are often drawn in conflicting directions, toward the luxury of glamour or the simplicity of abstraction. The Art Deco style, whose slightly exotic charm combines novelty with nostalgia for an elegant past, embodied the new notion of glamour and found an immediate response from the public. This fashionable style, which supplanted Art Nouveau during the inter-war period (1918–39), co-existed with the Machine Age style of Le Corbusier, Rietveld, the Bauhaus, and De Stijl. However, two new enthusiasms, Cubism and "primitive" art, were important factors in the decline of Art Deco. On the other hand, the reaction to Modernism and the cult of simplicity so alien to the principles of Art Deco were not long in coming. Just as there had been resistance to Art Deco, there were many who found Modernism without charm, so the pendulum swung the other way once again.

Interest in the baroque was reflected in interiors by patrons such as Carlos de Bestigui around 1936. Bestigui had commissioned the Swiss architect Le Corbusier (Charles-Edouard Jeanneret; 1887–1965) to design the interior and the spiral staircase of his Paris apartment, the drawing room of which he then filled—as if in reaction to Le Corbusier's austerity—with rounded, heavily upholstered seats! Surrealism invaded chair design in the shape of Mae West's mouth made into a settee, stools supported by three lifelike acrobats' legs, and even a chair shaped like a lobster. Victoriana reappeared; Dada emerged. Taste in the thirties

>
A Venetian armchair after a design for the Ballets Russes. Private collection

continued to oscillate across a spectrum of styles. For those with "taste but limited incomes" there were birch-wood laminated chairs mass-produced by Finmar Ltd. after models by the Finnish designer Alvar Aalto (1898–1998). The seats were simple and light, in molded plywood shapes at economical prices. On the other hand, French designers such as Jacques Adnet, Andre Arbus, and Marcel Campion continued to cater to an exclusive clientele, carrying on in the tradition of Ruhlmann, but trying out new mediums.

The conflict between function and appearance continues, exacerbated by the wealth of new materials available after World War II. During the war, shortages of goods challenged designers to work with materials that were less scarce. The disruption in trade also shifted the creative center of chair design from Europe to the United States. The first major movement after 1940 was that of Organic Modernism, led by Charles Eames and Eero Saarinen. As Frank Lloyd Wright had predicted, the machine had come to stay in chair design.

The postwar economic boom created an enormous demand for domestic furniture. To meet it, American companies such as Herman Miller and Knoll International created inexpensive, well-designed chairs by Eames or Saarinen for the

<

A pair of ebony side chairs with mother of pearl marquetry, created c. 1920 by Maurice Dufresne (1876–1955), for the David-Weill house in Paris. These are a superb example of the luxury of materials and high quality of workmanship of the Art Deco period. Collection Anne-Sophie Duval, Paris

>

A detail of one leg of the chairs shown opposite, showing the mother-of-pearl inlay

general public. Scandinavian designers followed quickly, creating seats that, in the words of one of their propagandists, "led modest, orderly lives." Italy reentered the furniture world with the pure classicism of a chair designed by Gio Ponti in 1950.

The Scandinavians, particularly the Danes, tried to find a harmonious compromise between futuristic impulse and respect for tradition, creating a Scandinavian style whose influence continued well into the fifties and sixties. By then, slick, pre-war Modernism seemed attractive again. At the same time, rebellious youth claimed a role in the shaping of style with the emergence of pop culture. Italian designers excelled in creating such irreverent plastic seats as the inflatable Blow Chair, and the Sacco (or beanbag) Chair. The new anthropomorphic shapes were often made of foam rubber, Gaetano Pesci being one of the material's most famous proponents. Other new media were introduced by Frank Gehry, who designed a cardboard seat called Easy Edges; and by Shiro Kuramata, who created Miss Blanche, a seat of Plexiglas, and another, made of rib mesh, poetically called "How High the Moon." The

dichotomy of tradition and innovation was still there, however, for example, in Philippe Starck's chair, Louis 20. The title says it all, even in jest. In chair design it is hard to erase a thousand years of civilization. The human body remains the same, and the chair's primary function is to be sat on, whatever the advances in technology.

GLAMOUR-LOOK, ART-DECO, AND CUBIST SEATS

As with many styles before it, Art Deco was not given that name until long after it appeared. The style began primarily in France, with some concurrent instances in England and Italy. One early appearance was in 1909, with Sergei Diaghilev's Ballets Russes and the premieres of *Sheherazade* and *Thamar*, which caused a furor. Contemporary writings abound with descriptions of the astonishing effect these ballets had on their audiences, who were transported by the erotic librettos, sensuous music, choreography, and above all, the brilliant sets and costumes by Leon Bakst. In America Art Deco's main proponent was Donald Desky, the designer of Radio City Music Hall.

The popularity of *Sheherazade* brought on a craze for all things Persian. Large, elaborately decorated cushions piled in heaps were used in lieu of settees, in imitation of those on which Zobeide, the ballet's heroine, reclined. Beyond the exoticism of the Ballets Russes, Art Deco designers also drew inspiration from the forms of nineteenth-century furniture and applied ornament, bringing these influences together and transforming them with characteristic French elegance. In the four years preceding World War I, Paris was the brilliant center of European culture to which artists of all nationalities were attracted. Inspired by the philosophy of the Munich Werkbund, with its aim of bringing together artists, craftsmen, and manufacturers to produce well-designed, inexpensive furniture, several large Parisian department stores

< A pair of bronze armchairs by Armand Albert Rateau, c. 1920, commissioned by Mr. and Mrs. George Blumenthal for the patio of their indoor swimming pool in New York. Collection De Lorenzo, New York

< A rare set of gilded armchairs in the "gondola" shape, c. 1925, by Sue & Mare. The set includes a matching sofa. Collection Vallois, Paris

> An ebony chaise longue signed by Paul Iribe (1883–1935), made 1913–14. Collection Anne-Sophie Duval, Paris

> A *méridienne* (day bed) by Etienne Kohlmann, c. 1936. Collection Olivier Watelet, Paris

∧
A pair of hexagonal coral wood armchairs, c. 1920, by Pierre Charreau. Collection Galerie Jacques De Vos, Paris

<
A Cubist leather armchair by Jacques Emile Ruhlmann. Collection De Lorenzo, New York

> A pair of rare cube armchairs covered in shagreen by Jean Michel Frank (1895–1941), c. 1930. Collection Vallois, Paris

> A pair of armchairs by André Arbus (1903–69), c. 1940. Collection Olivier Watelet, Paris

<<
The iconic director's chair, by Jean Michel Frank. Collection Vallois, Paris

<
Marlene Dietrich on location for *The Garden of Allah* in the desert near Yuma, Arizona, in 1936, seated in a classic director's chair. Private collection

opened specialized departments, under the direction of established designers, to sell contemporary seating. These shops within shops were important in introducing Art Deco to a wider public.

Many Art Deco tendencies coexisted. Seats included comfortable armchairs, sofas, and divans upholstered in colorful silk or brightly printed velvets. Leather was still the fabric of choice for dining chairs and *fauteuils de bureau*, and tapestry, designed by artists such as Raoul Dufy or Robert Delaunay, covered luxurious armchairs created by Ruhlmann, Sue, or Mare. André Mare (1887–1932), a painter, turned his attention to interior decoration in 1910 and after working with the architect Louis Sue (1875–1968) on the decorations to celebrate the end of the war in 1918, with him founded the Compagnie des Arts Français, which became known as Sue and Mare.

Art Deco was dismissed, even in the twenties and thirties, as kitsch, both by admirers of older forms and advocates of Bauhaus design.

Nevertheless, talented designers such as Paul Follot (1877–1947) and Armand Albert Rateau (1882–1938) created highly decorative seats for a select group of clients, including the couturier Jeanne Lanvin and the fashionable duchess of Alba. At the 1925 Paris International Exhibition, which showed work from twenty-one countries (America, Germany, Norway, and Australia being noticeably absent), critics gave high praise to Rateau's subtle blend of new and old. Indeed, the Exhibition was a triumph for the *ensembliers*, or decorators, with seats in the Art Deco style featured in an array of color, comfort, and luxury. Compared with them, the chairs by Charlotte Perriand and Le Corbusier shown in the Pavillon de l'Esprit Nouveau seem cold, a disparity that prefigured the later schism between the "decorative" and the "functional."

Josef Hoffmann's designs for the Austrian Pavilion were not much different from his prewar work. His seats, still showing the influence of

> An armchair by Robert Mallet-Stevens (1886–1945) with its original zebra cover made for Arletty. Private collection, Paris

> A variation on the traditional campaign chair by Jacques Quinet (1918–92), c. 1945. Collection Olivier Watelet, Paris

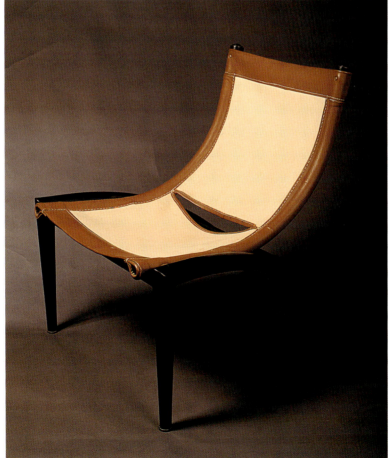

<
A side chair by William Haines. Liz O'Brien Collection, New York

<
An armchair and ottoman by Paul Frankel, c. 1936. Collection Gansewoort, New York

> An armchair by Rudolph Schindler, c. 1934, created for the van Patten residence. Collection Gansewoort, New York

Mackintosh and the Arts and Crafts Movement, were distant indeed from the Art Deco spirit. Different, also, was the Danish Pavilion, which presented a dining room with Neo-Pompeian *klismos* chairs. One most interesting exhibition was the *cabinet de travail* in the Polish Pavilion, featuring Cubist chairs. From 1910 until the late twenties, Cubism, which offered a way to revolt against provincial conventions combining a Post-Impressionist view of the world with a Kafkaesque sense of existential anxiety, was a powerful stylistic force in Eastern Europe, particularly in Czechoslovakia. The influence of Viennese Modernism, Hoffmann, and the Wiener Werkstätte on early Art Deco pieces was also pronounced. A utilitarian object such as a chair became, in the eyes of the Cubists, an excuse for the creation of a work of art, in which functional considerations and ties to production were secondary. Such ideas, almost the opposite of Modernist thinking, were quite similar to those of the Art Deco masters, who were obsessed with quality.

The designer who most impressed both press and public was Jacques Emile Ruhlmann (1879–1933). Ruhlmann's pieces at the 1925 Exhibition were spectacularly luxurious, reflecting his avowed intention to work only for the richest clients, for whom he produced what were probably the best-made and most expensive seats of the time.

In contrast to Ruhlmann's essentially masculine designs, those of André Groult (1884–1967) and Jules Leleu (1883–1961) were feminine, pared-down versions of the Louis XV style. Groult and Leleu created interiors and seats as backgrounds for the elegant women of the time. Groult, who designed a highly praised lady's bedroom for the Paris Exhibition, is best remembered for his use of sharkskin. Leleu, equally if not more admired, was responsible for the exhibition's dining and living

<
A very fine lacquered chair in the African taste by Jean Dunand and Jean Lambert-Rucki, c. 1924, a rare example of African influence on European furniture. Collection Vallois, Paris

>
Two details of the upper leg of the chair shown opposite, showing a lacquered face supporting the seat

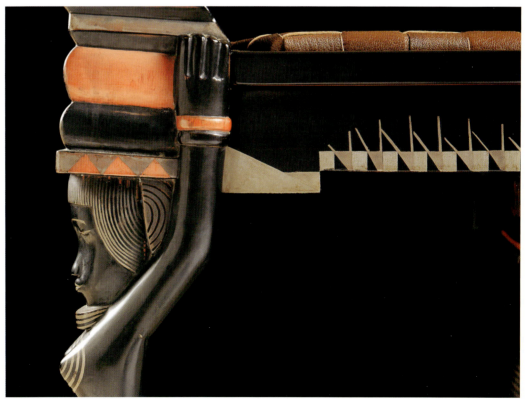

A red lacquer chair, c. 1934, by Jean Dunand. Dunand's seats, usually simple in form, were enhanced with as many as twenty coats of lacquer and often decorated with geometric designs in gold, silver, and inlaid eggshell. Collection De Lorenzo, New York

rooms. He went on to design seats for ocean liners and embassies.

Following the current taste for rich surfaces, Jean Dunand (1877–1942) revived the techniques of Chinese and Japanese lacquer. In addition to his own seats, Dunand lacquered seats for other designers, including Ruhlmann and Legrain, and enlisted other artists to create designs for his finishes, which accounts for the wide range of motifs with which he is associated. Eileen Gray (1879–1977) was also known for her work in lacquer. Irish-born, Gray studied at the Slade School of Art in London before settling in Paris in 1907, where she created sculptural seats derived from the ideas of the De Stijl group.

During the 1920s, a trend inspired by Cubism and African art emerged that would eventually hasten the end of the Art Deco style. Its most distinguished and successful exponents were Pierre Legrain, Marcel Coard, and Eileen Gray. In the mid-twenties, Gray abandoned lacquer and worked with the architect Jean Badovici to create seats that were both functional and eccentric, using such materials as tubular steel and cork, with elements recalling the ceremonial stools of the Asante people of Central Africa. Legrain (1889–1929) was the designer most influenced by African art. His seats are strongly carved, as are many African chairs, and he loved using such unusual materials as open-grained palmwood, lacquer, parchment, and ivory to accentuate the exoticism of his work. Marcel Coard (1889–1929), equally enamored of African art and Cubism, designed one-of-a-kind seats in refined, contrasting materials such as ebony, ivory, lapis lazuli, mother of pearl, and shagreen.

In the meantime, Art Deco was changing. The growing taste for simplicity was seen even in the work of the most expansive decorators. Jean

An armchair by Jean Royère (1902–81), c. 1945. Collection de Beyrie, New York

Michel Frank, working in Paris and California, was among the first of the Parisian designers to abandon rich colors, relying more on the subtle luxury of fine materials in neutral tones of cream, ivory, and beige. His squarelike seats were greatly influenced by Cubism; however, the English designer Arundell Clark in the mid-twenties is reputed to have been the first to introduce a truly square armchair. Frank was also the creator of the famous "mouth" settee, a product of Surrealism derived from Salvador Dali's portrait of Mae West. Art Deco around 1930 seemed to have lost momentum; it was shortly to disappear in favor of two essentially anti-decorative modes, Modernism and the International Style.

MACHINE-LOOK, BENTWOOD, AND LAMINATED WOOD SEATS

Modern seats were developed using three technologies: metallurgy, plastics molding, and lamination. Of these, only lamination retains some memory of traditional material. Lamination started with bent wood, and particularly with the work of Michael Thonet (1796–1871). Starting in 1819, Thonet began to make chairs with steam-bent parts, almost single-handedly bringing chair-making from the realm of handicraft into the industrial age. In the following half-century, he and his successors built the largest chair company the world has ever known, and created an enduring seat type.

Although few chairs created during the nineteenth century appealed to the designers of the twentieth century, Thonet chairs, with their elegance, elasticity, and reduction of labor and material, are an exception. Once a chair had been designed and the required forms made, its individual parts could be mass-produced by unskilled or semi-skilled workmen. The resulting savings allowed Thonet to sell his chairs at prices far below those of chairs made by traditional methods, so that his sturdy, attractive, and well-designed chairs became widely available. Moreover, their originality appealed to talented avant-garde designers. When the architect Adolf Loos designed the interior of the Café Museum in Vienna in 1899, a chair design introduced by Thonet some forty years earlier was one of its major features. Perhaps even more surprising, a chair that Thonet began producing in 1870 was chosen in 1925 by Le Corbusier for the interior of his Pavillon de L'Esprit Nouveau. Le Corbusier recommended Thonet chairs because, he said, "This chair, whose millions of representatives are used on the Continent and in the two Americas, possesses nobility." Thonet's firm is reputed to have sold 30,000,000 chairs of the Café Museum type by 1920, while twenty-six other firms produced roughly 12,000 chairs per day in imitation of Thonet designs by 1900. The models chosen by Loos and Le Corbusier are still being made in large quantities by the same manufacturing process, which Thonet introduced late in the nineteenth century.

Thonet began his experiments in 1830 at his birthplace of Boppard-am-Rhine, Germany, in a one-man cabinetmaking shop that he had operated for eleven years, where he fabricated his first bent chair parts from pieces of laminated veneer. He continued to experiment, and by 1836 had constructed his first bentwood chairs. In 1841, the Austrian chancellor Clemens Metternich, famous for his role at the Congress of Vienna, after coming upon Thonet's bentwood chairs during a trip to Germany, was so impressed that he persuaded the cabinetmaker to move to Vienna, even arranging free transportation for him in a diplomatic carriage. Thus, in 1842 Thonet established himself in Vienna, entering a partnership with the neo-rococo furniture-maker Carl Leistler, with whom he supplied seats (some of bentwood) to Prince Liechtenstein. He did not restrict his work to commissioned furniture, however, but persisted in his original idea of mass production. Although his early models were close to

> A bentwood rocking chair, c. 1880, by Michael Thonet (1796–1871). The first rocking chair that Thonet designed was his "No. 1" model of 1862. Following this, the rocking chair, virtually unknown in Continental Europe, became fashionable there by 1880. Private collection, New York

Biedermeier in style, his later designs were refined and original, their flowing lines sometimes recalling neo-rococo chairs.

Thonet's technique was totally revolutionary. It avoided joints and complex cutting by using parts steam-bent into curved shapes. This technique had long been used in the construction of ships and carriages, but it had never before been used to make chairs. By 1859, when Thonet produced Chair No. 14, he had developed a fully mechanized process of gluing together a number of bent strips to construct a solid member of almost any desired curved shape. The process was remarkably efficient, especially for the time. Since the chairs were undecorated, they could be shipped easily. Chair No. 14 consisted of six parts assembled with only ten screws. Costing about three Austrian shillings (about seventy-five U.S. cents) in the money of the day, it has sold over fifty million copies to date.

In 1850 Thonet created his famous bentwood Chair No. 4, the prototype of the Vienna Café chair, which is still in production. In 1851, he showed some of his chairs in London's Great Exhibition, where they earned the first of the many awards that he would receive at each exhibition he entered. In 1853 he took his five sons into partnership, calling the firm Gebrüder Thonet; that year the firm received an imperial monopoly patent "for the production of chairs and table legs made of bentwood" until 1869. The International Exhibitions in Munich in 1854 and Paris in 1855 increased the market for bentwood seats. Thonet's huge catalogue presented seats for every use, from babies' high chairs, rocking chairs, lounge chairs, all sorts of folding chairs, theater seats, and garden chairs in no less than twenty-six different varieties. The diversity can be explained by the fact that, starting in 1860, the firm had introduced its first rocking chair, swivel office chairs, and children's

chairs. Moreover, almost all of the side chairs began to be offered with accompanying armchairs and settees. By 1871, the year of Michael Thonet's death, Gebrüder Thonet had established sales rooms throughout Europe, and in New York and Chicago, and employed a staff of around 35,000.

When Gebrüder Thonet's imperial patent expired in 1869, other companies began competing for a share of the market. With production under control, Thonet continued to experiment with new methods of constructing chairs. Among the most surprising forms that grew out of these experiments were those that were produced by carefully cutting, bending, and laminating large wooden sheets. Unfortunately, while these chairs were light, graceful, and sturdy, they could not be mass-produced economically at first.

During the first decade of the twentieth century, Thonet and one of its main competitors, Kohn, shifted from in-house designers to architects to design their seats, engaging many of the leading figures associated with the Wiener

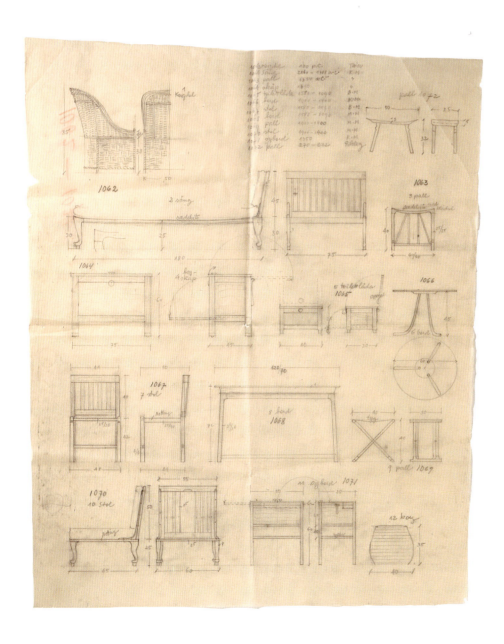

^
Alvar Aalto lounge chair "No. 43," c. 1936, of bent laminated wood with a solid birch frame and textile webbing. Collection Barry Friedman, New York

<
A sheet of drawings for chairs by the Swedish designer Josef Frank (1885–1967).

Werkstätte: Gustave Siegel, Josef Hoffmann, Otto Prutscher, and Koloman Moser. Kohn hired Siegel as head designer, and Hoffmann designed geometrical Secessionist pieces for the company such as the chairs for the Purkersdorf Sanatorium and the Cabaret Fledermaus. Hoffmann's student Otto Prutscher became a lead designer for Thonet, which continued to introduce new models during the 1920s and 1930s, including examples designed by Ferdinand Kramer and Josef Frank. In 1927 Thonet marketed the chairs designed for the Weissenhof housing project by Mies van der Rohe in cantilevered tubular steel, with cane seats designed by Lilly Reich, who would later become the head of the Bauhaus weaving workshop. The Weissenhof development was probably the most architecturally prestigious enterprise of the twentieth century. Among the architects who designed buildings for it were Behrens, Le Corbusier, Poelzig, Taut, and Oud.

The major development in twentieth-century furniture design was the use of steel and other metals, and the Thonet firm became a pioneer in their use. Bentwood thus became the father of an unlikely child, tubular steel, which explains the strange similarities in shapes among classic late-nineteenth-century bentwood seats and the twentieth-century tubular steel rocking chairs created by such designers as Mies van der Rohe. Le Corbusier, describing his chaises longues as "équipement de l'habitation," expanded on the theme, as did Charlotte Perriand, Pierre Jeanneret, and the father of cantilever tubular steel, Marcel Breuer. Their creations represent the earliest examples of ergonomic chair design.

In Helsinki in the 1930s, Alvar Aalto reacted against the cold machine aesthetic of tubular steel. Birch forests abounded in Finland, and Aalto was the first to exploit the natural spring of that wood. He created numerous organic chairs and stools with bent, laminated birchwood frames, which have become classics of Modernism. Two of these are the Paimio lounge chair, Model No. 41, and a three-legged stacking stool, Model No. 60. In conjunction with Artek, a Helsinki manufacturer, Aalto produced many more chairs, armchairs, and stools. In one stool, the shaping of the leg and its socket in the seat is articulated with such refinement that it suggests a living tree.

Laminated wood, developed throughout the late 1920s and 1930s, found favor with many progressive designers of the period because of its expressive potential and its suitability for mass production. Laminated wood used for the cantilevered sections is formed from layers rather thicker than ply, the grain of each running in the same direction. This gives the wood strength, which is greatest along the length of the grain. Its springiness can be used to a greater extent than that of even the best natural timber, because weakness in the grain is braced by the successive layers. The impregnation of the timber with synthetic resins to set the material into shape also increases its strength.

Aalto's influence was wide-reaching. Following his example, around the same time in Sweden, Bruno Mathsson, the son of a cabinetmaker, created elegant "chaises" designed to be mass-produced, using solid and laminated wood. In England, Gerald Summers in the mid-1930s made an extraordinary armchair out of a single piece of plywood. The smooth surface was comfortable even without cushions, and required a low input of both labor and material. Surprisingly, despite this chair's economy, few of

>
A Nathan Lerner side chair, c. 1939. Private collection, New York

<
Two wooden side chairs by Jean Prouvé (1901–84). Collection de Beyrie, New York

these chairs were produced. In America, Breuer and Mies van der Rohe continued to explore variations on cantilevered designs, with seats and frames of molded or bent wood inspired by Aalto. The side chair designed in 1936 for the Isokon Furniture Company completed almost a full circle for Breuer, who had turned from wooden seats in 1925 to begin his revolutionary experiments with tubular steel. When he later returned to wood, his earlier preference for solid wood was supplanted by laminated wood.

Following Aalto's first success, the aviation industries in Europe and America, under the pressure of war, found new ways of bonding wood sheets using resins. The new resins allowed the sheet to be bent by electrical methods instead of steam heat, a longer process, and also led to molded plywood shapes. The structural property of the plywood was so changed that Charles Niedrinhaus and others in the United States produced models with sharp, Z-shaped profiles. Capitalizing on these developments, in

^
A pair of Zig Zag chairs by Gerrit Rietveld, c. 1932, of oak with brass fittings. Collection Barry Friedman, New York

>
A Marcel Breuer laminated wood dining chair designed for the Isokon firm. Collection Barry Friedman, New York

<
A Marcel Breuer *Latten-stuhl* ("ladder-chair") armchair, c. 1922–24. Collection Barry Friedman, New York

modern chairs 375

^
The Charles and Ray Eames LCW ("Lounge Chair Wood") side chair, c. 1945. The Eameses' landmark plywood chairs were an outgrowth of their wartime research into new and inexpensive materials. Collection Barry Friedman, New York

<
A child's chair by Charles and Ray Eames, c. 1945. Collection Gansewoort, New York

> An American desk chair by Ken Weber (1889–1963), c. 1939

California in the late 1940s Charles (1907–78) and Ray (1912–88) Eames developed a new method of bending three-dimensional plywood to create a series of seats made of untreated or color-stained birch ply. These were the first mass-produced seats using the technique for a peacetime application. They represented a new level of innovation in the manufacture of seats, an immense improvement on the technology of Aalto's Paimio chair. Rather than being bent in a simple scroll form, the wood now acquired a complex curve that permitted greater comfort in both the seat and back. The LCW chair, manufactured by the Herman Miller Furniture Company, was eminently suitable for mass production and established the Eameses as leading figures in contemporary chair design.

At about the same time in England, Ernest Race, who had worked in the aircraft industry during the war, began to produce wire and molded plywood chairs, which were enthusiastically received by visitors at the Festival of Britain in 1951. As outdoor seating for hard use, these chairs could hardly be surpassed. The fifties saw a continued interest in laminated chairs in America through the Herman Miller Furniture Company. George Nelson, Miller's director of design, created the "Pretzel" armchair, which recalls Thonet's Chair No. 9 of 1904. Another designer, Paul Goldman, followed with the Cherner chair in 1957.

The Danish designer Arne Jacobsen was awarded a Grand Prix at the 1957 Milan Triennale for his 3107 chairs. These were inexpensive, small

stacking chairs with molded plywood seats supported on a tripod steel rod or laminated wood base. First made in 1953, in 1957 they were produced wholly of molded plywood. Jacobsen's approach to the complex molding of one piece of plywood to form the seat and back was clearly influenced by the Eameses. A major French designer and architect, Jean Prouvé, worked against the prevailing trend in creating luxurious laminated seats, often resting on flat steel frames. His favorite designs, however emphasized metal tubing, and were an important forerunner of High Tech.

Even as far away as Japan, where seats were seldom used, plywood found its place. Sori Yanagi, a founder of the Japanese Industrial Design Association (JIDA), created a remarkable stool called the Butterfly, which he mass-produced at the Tendo-Mokko Company using the Eames molding technique. The Butterfly stool features an unusual construction. Two identical forms are attached symmetrically to an axis, using two screws underneath the seat and a threaded brass rod. This result is a shape reminiscent of the portals of Shinto shrines, an Asian expression that also resembles the wings of a butterfly.

Both plywood and laminated wood were used with flair by Italian designers during the fifties and sixties. Arflex of Milan was notably strong in lamination design, producing, for example, the London Chair, a large club chair built into a circular band of laminated rosewood, created in 1963 by the English designer Martin Grierson. Designers such as Cesare Mario Casati and Enzo Hybsch were also associated with Arflex, a firm that usually created seats for a wide market. Gavina, Arflex, and I. C. F. de Padova, have together produced

<
A "fauteuil Ashanti" by Philippe Starck (b. 1949). During the 1980s, Starck designed a large number of chairs with provocative names. Private collection, Paris

> A laminated cardboard "wiggle" side chair, c. 1972, by Frank Gehry (b. 1929). Private collection, New York

> An "amputee" chair by Godley-Schwan, c. 1992. Collection Neotu, Paris

> A folding chair by Dominique Freintrenie, c. 1994. Collection VIA, Paris

most of the chairs that demonstrate Italy's mastery of modern wood techniques. Other, more exclusive, designs were manufactured by Apelli & Varesio for Carlo Mollino.

The so-called king of chairs, Denmark's talented designer Hans Wegner, an apprentice of Arne Jacobsen, designed 500 chairs over the course of his long career, the most popular of which are still manufactured today. A few, such as the laminated, crisply curved and bent Shell chair that sits in his study, exist only in prototype. The Shell chair won a 1949 Museum of Modern Art competition that called for inexpensive furniture that could be made by machines, but since it would have competed with the Eames laminated lounge chair of the same period, it was never manufactured. Perhaps one day it will be, along with Wegner's other unrealized designs. Wegner has often said that "A chair is only finished when someone sits in it—and it does its job." As a reminder of this ultimate purpose, he keeps a cutout of the human spine hanging from a shelf. His work has strongly influenced young designers in his native country, where wood—carved, ply, or bent—has always been an important material for design.

The young designers Hans Sandgren Jakobsen and Nanna Ditzel are part of a group called Spring. They originated a new seat called "Tatami," a legless confection on a cushionlike disk with a ribbonlike back of folded and bent laminate. Similar backs, with seats resting on metal legs, have been designed by Andrea Banzi and marketed by Cassina. Philippe Starck, another designer, combined laminated or bentwood seats on a metal base for the famed Café Coste chair.

Today, wood, with its poetic qualities, is often used not only for the structure of a chair but to help balance the cold effect of steel. Its durability, flexibility, warmth, and low cost make it one of the primary components of chairs, even in the twenty-first century, when it can give the illusion of a return to nature, even if a domesticated one.

THE MACHINE LOOK: TUBULAR STEEL AND OTHER METAL SEATS

As we noted earlier, bentwood fathered an unlikely child: tubular steel. Both materials are well suited to mass production, and both resulted from developments in the automobile and aircraft industries. Modern chair designers often combined plywood and tubular steel; or if they created a design in one material, often switched to the other for a second version of the same chair.

Although metal campaign seats were made as early as Roman times, furniture made from steel tubing appeared only in the late nineteenth century. Steel tubing, which was light, strong, and easy to work, was first used to make hospital furniture around 1890. About 1919, automobile manufacturers began to use it to make car seats, and in 1924 it was adopted for airplane seats by the Fokker Company. Marcel Breuer began using the tubing for home furnishings with his steel club chair, which marks an aesthetic turning point in seat production, and the start of an important industry. Breuer created the first tubular steel cantilever chair for the painter Wassily Kandinsky's quarters at the Bauhaus School in Dessau in 1925. The following year, another steel tubing chair designed by the architect Mart Stam was produced by L & C Arnold; a few months later, Mies van der Rohe created Model No. MR20, a particularly refined chair of the new material, for the firm of Berliner Mettalgewerbe.

Breuer is said to have become interested in working with tubular steel after falling over the handlebars of his bicycle. He did approach a bicycle manufacturer, Adler, as a possible maker for his designs in 1925, but the management was not interested in producing furniture. Instead, the tubular steel furniture that Breuer designed for the Bauhaus refectory was made by Standard-Möbel

> The Mies van der Rohe "M5" chair. Private collection, New York

< Marcel Breuer's "Wassily" chair, c. 1925–27. The name is derived from the fact that Breuer created the chair for Wassily Kandinsky's quarters at the Dessau Bauhaus. The use of tubular steel in the chair was revolutionary, as was the way in which it was manufactured. Knoll Collection, New York

starting in 1927; later the company produced a dining chair for the Bauhaus master's apartment, and chairs for the school's auditorium. Other Breuer designs were produced by Thonet. From 1928 on, Thonet made thousands of Breuer's cantilever chairs, which soon found their way into various public places.

The Bauhaus, where Mies van der Rohe taught and Breuer studied, is now considered the most influential design school of the twentieth century, its aesthetic of simple, functional design representing, in effect, a war on nineteenth-century clutter. The school opened in 1919 in Weimar, Germany, under the direction of the architect Walter Gropius (1883–1969), with a curriculum based on the collaboration of artists and technicians for the industrial production of a wide range of goods and for re-thinking the direction of architecture. Inspired by the British Arts and Crafts Movement, the school created a new approach to the problems of industrial design by producing prototypes of articles for daily use for mass production. This aim was realized in Breuer's tubular steel chair, still one of the most popular and characteristic pieces of twentieth-century design.

In 1929 Mies van der Rohe designed what many would consider the single most important piece of industrial furniture of the twentieth century, the forged-steel-strip and leather Barcelona Chair, which, despite its apparent simplicity, requires complicated traditional (and expensive) production. Model No. MR90 was designed for the German Pavilion at the 1929 Eposición Internacional in Barcelona for the use of King Alfonso XIII and his queen at the exhibition's opening ceremonies. Almost equally well-known Mies chairs are the cantilevered Brno and Tugendhat chairs of 1930, both of which were designed for the Tugendhat house in Brno, Czechoslovakia. The former was produced in either steel-strip or tubular steel, the latter in tubular steel alone. Mies's tubular steel chair was so popular that the Belgian cartoonist Hergé used it in the 1930s as a symbol of contemporary

<
A chair used to diagnose vertigo with a test called "the labyrinth," c. 1930. Musée de l'Assistance Publique, Hôpitaux de Paris, Paris

>
A German chromed tubular-steel chair with a painted molded plywood seat and back, c. 1931, by Hans (1890–1954) and Wassili (1889–1927) Luckhardt. Collection Barry Friedman, New York

v
The Barcelona Chair ("MR90"), by Ludwig Mies van der Rohe, designed for the German Pavilion at the 1929 International Exhibition in Barcelona. Mies drew on the ancient folding stool—a traditional seat of authority in Antiquity among the Egyptians and Greeks, and the Roman senatorial *sella curulis*. Collection Barry Friedman, New York

Mies van der Rohe chairs in a room setting. Knoll Collection, New York

European civilization. In *The Blue Lotus*, a cartoon adventure novel about Hergé's popular boy reporter Tintin set in the Far East, Tintin and his friend Captain Haddock are shown seated on Mies's cantilever chairs in the Club Occidental in Shanghai.

In the late 1920s, other designers were working in tubular steel in Germany, including Mart Stam, Adolf Schneck, the firm of Heinz and Bode Rash, Heinrich Bredendieck, and Walter Gropius. During the 1930s tubular-steel chairs enjoyed wide appeal, and many copies and variations followed, which led Mart Stam to make his famous statement that he wanted "all those macaroni-like steel monsters to disappear." However, with the rise of Nazism, Germany grew inhospitable to the ideas of the Bauhaus and the men who led it, and Gropius and Mies fled to America in the early 1930s. In time, their influence would return to Europe by way of the United States. In the shorter term, Bauhaus principles exercised a significant influence on French designers.

Le Corbusier (Charles-Edouard Jeanneret; 1887–1965), a Swiss architect working in Paris, started in 1928 to design tubular seats as "équipement de l'habitation," as he called them. However, in keeping with the French taste for luxury, his seats met the demand of Parisian society for comfort, and were more luxurious than the minimalist creations of the Bauhaus. His seats, along with the designs of Charlotte Perriand and those of his cousin, Pierre Jeanneret, were made to suit a certain internal space, not for a production line. Another designer, Jean Prouvé, worked from 1926 until his death in 1984 as an architect and a designer, using prefabricated metal pieces. In 1926, Prouvé began to make architectural elements and seats out of welded and molded metal, using a

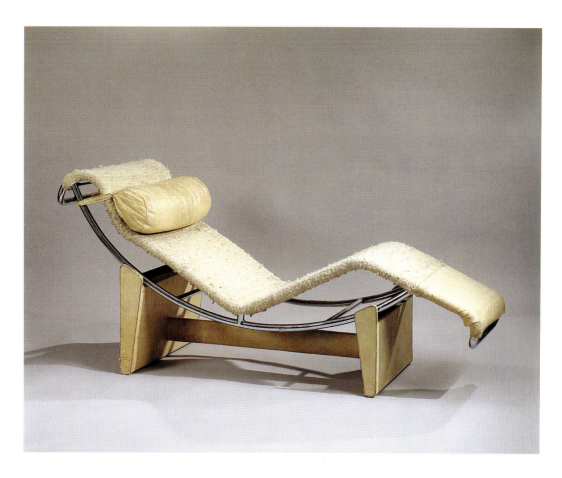

> A chaise longue by Le Corbusier, c. 1929, for Madeleine Vionnet. The first tubular-steel chair designs by the Le Corbusier studio, which appeared in 1928, were famously described as "equipment for living." Collection Barry Friedman, New York

technique employed in automobile construction at the time. Prouvé developed special structural solutions to each new problem. His chair designs bear the distinct stamp of the engineer. He said, "For me, pieces of furniture are comparable to a machine frame that is exposed to much wear and tear, and this has prompted me to design furniture with the same care, according to the laws of statics and even using the same materials." Although he designed many chairs, only a folding school chair was mass-produced.

Detractors of the new fashion were vocal. A contributor to *Decorative Art* wrote in 1931: "To construct a bed, according to the same aesthetic as a suspension bridge or to construct a house like a factory, to design a dining room as a laboratory, shows a total lack of psychology." Aldous Huxley expressed his distaste: "Personally, I very much dislike the aseptic, hospital style of furnishings. To dine off an operating table, to loll in a dentist's chair—this is not my idea of domestic bliss." Other writers, such as the French designer and writer Maurice Dufrene, a champion of Art Deco decoration, found the uniformity of the new furniture depressing: "The same chair, mechanical and tubular, is to be found in almost every country. . . . It is the anonymous, neutral, universal chair. . . . the root of Dullness." Concurrently, other designers were creating plywood, bentwood, carved wood, and slightly later, plastic seats. However, the taste for tubular pieces persisted among a large, avant-garde group.

In the United States, Walter Gropius founded a school of architecture in Chicago, and Mies van der Rohe collaborated with Hans and Florence Knoll, an association culminating in the founding of Knoll International in 1945. Many talented and progressive designers were and still are associated

A bent-chrome tubular-steel stool by René Herbst (1891–1983). Collection de Beyrie, New York

with Knoll. Harry Bertoia's innovative wire chairs of 1951 were so successful that the royalties from them allowed him to devote himself to sculpture.

The Herman Miller company, established in 1931, is one of the oldest modern chair-makers in the United States. Under the guidance of Gilbert Rhode, the firm set itself on its present course around the time the Bauhaus exiles arrived in the States. Designers were given freedom to explore, were consulted at every stage of production, and even participated in sales conferences. Owing nothing to the Barcelona chair or to Le Corbusier, yet in the same tradition, is the latest Miller line, the Cathenay seat. Designed in 1963 by George Nelson, it is too expensive for the average buyer, yet it suggests something for wider use. Using a few components in various permutations, joined by epoxy adhesive (another aircraft construction technique), it is totally revolutionary.

The 70s was the decade of plastic, glass, and High Tech, epitomized by the Omkstak chair, by the English designer Rodney Kinsman. This chair is intended for use both inside and out; its tubular-steel frame supports a pressed, sheet-steel seat and back, which are coated with epoxy for weather resistance. It is a popular classic to this day. As Kinsman noted, "It is irresponsible to design things that don't last visually. I don't believe that products should have such ephemeral form that they will be out of date long before they should be." Kinsman's philosophy was unusual in its day, and indeed, many of the plastic and glass seats of the 70s were to have a short life.

Early in the 1980s, Memphis, a group of designers based in Milan, broke the grip of streamlined design by bringing an explosion of color and new materials to chair-making, using tubular metal frames for their seats. At the launch of the first Memphis collection, the designer Ettore Sottsass wrote, "All that walking through the realms of uncertainty . . . all that talking with metaphors and utopia . . . all that getting away from it all . . . has given us a certain experience; we've become good explorers." The appearance of Memphis was a shot in the arm for the design world and for chair-making in particular. Since the early 80s, the group's playful designs have

The classic Diamond Chair, c. 1952, designed for Knoll by Harry Bertoia (1915–78). Ironically, this industrial-looking wire chair was most easily produced by hand. Bertoia, a sculptor, once said that, like sculpture, "chairs are studies in space, form, and metal." Knoll Collection, New York

A lounge designed by Florence Knoll. Knoll Collection, New York

exploded every academic convention. The primary criterion for judging a design was no longer its solution to a set of technical problems, but instead the object's capacity for communication or shock. Most of Memphis's chairs were created in small numbers, but the seat called "First" by Michele de Lucchi, one of the group's co-founders, was intended for a wide public, and indeed, sold well. The construction of this seat is a true eye-catcher, consisting of a steel tube bent to form a circle, supporting a flexible, round wooden-disk backrest and two wooden-ball armrests. The result is light, yet stable. It is an odd but colorful seat, expressing a positive attitude toward life. The antiseptic look of tubular steel was gone; the material had been, at long last, domesticated.

England's most publicized contribution to the new spirit was some experimental work forged of "found" metal pieces, sometimes combined with chipped and sandblasted glass by young designers. Among the best known are Danny Lane; Ron Arad, who specializes in hammered sheet metal pieces; and Tom Dixon, who creates poetic seats.

In the early 80s, Lane sold his seats from a stall in Camden Passage, and later in the avant-garde Crucial Gallery on London's Portobello Road. By the mid-eighties, his seats could be found at One Off, a shop owed by fellow designer Arad in Covent Garden. As their work became increasingly popular, the metal and glass boys have improved their half-art, half-design technique. Few of their chairs are industrially produced, however, and some models could be considered more art than design.

The French designer André Dubreuil's Spine chairs are in the same vein: hand-forged and very labor-intensive, they are produced in small quantities. So are the Barbares chairs created by Bonetti and Garouste; these are hand-forged with a fur seat. Another of their creations is the romantic Jour et Nuit fauteuil, featuring, at the ends of the white-painted, tubular armrests, a moon on one side and a star on the other. These are handmade, and are manufactured only in small quantities. Another unusual creation is the gleaming, lightweight, rib-mesh armchair called

<
An Italian metal high-backed chair, 1950s. Private collection, New York

modern chairs 389

> An anthropomorphic chair of tubular steel by the Italian designer Renato Basoli, c. 1955. Collection Yves Gastou, Paris

>> A rare variation on the well-known Nagasaki Chair of 1951 by the French designer Mathieu Mategot (b. 1910). This chair, made c. 1955, is of tubular steel, steel rods, and straw. Collection de Beyrie, New York

> The Techno chaise longue, c. 1954–55, by the Italian designer Oswald de Borsani (b. 1911), with a pressed and tubular steel frame and latex foam upholstery. Collection Gansewoort, New York

<

A room with DKR-2 (Dining Bikini Rod) chairs, 1951, by Charles and Ray Eames, designed for Herman Miller. Photograph: Antony Cotsifas, New York

"How High the Moon" after a Duke Ellington song, created by the Japanese designer Shiro Kuramata. The elastic mesh makes a comfortable seat, and this unexpected material transforms a classic shape into a postmodern industrial piece.

The Lockheed Lounge, by the Australian designer Mark Newson, is more anthropomorphous sculpture than functional seat. Named after the American aircraft manufacturer (a sly reference to the Eameses early experiments for the airplane industry), its body is made of fiberglass-reinforced plastic, which can be inexpensively processed. The entire surface is covered with thin-walled aluminum sheets attached with blind riveting. Ron Arad, who also worked with aluminum, became a great fan of this chair, as did the designer Philippe Starck, who developed a fascination for the piece. Starck even integrated it into the decor of the Paramount Hotel in New York, which he remodeled in 1990. While previously described designers seem to use the new technical developments of steel and metal for poetic, highly unusual seats, Starck believed in creating good design for mass production. He had a preference for aluminum, perhaps influenced by his father's work as an aircraft mechanic and inventor—if so, another influence on contemporary chairs from the aircraft industry. Starck's Louis 20 chairs feature an aluminum rear-leg and a polypropylene body, an ingenious design allowing the chairs to be stacked, used indoors or out, and produced inexpensively. Likewise, the architect William Ellis created a three-legged chair; the prototype was made of aluminum simply because it is inexpensive and easily worked.

Others, such as the Czech designer Borek Sipek, with his Sedlak chair, and the Spaniard Jorge Pensi, with his Toledo chair, created well-designed, versatile, aluminum seats affordable for a large market and easy to produce. In the early years of the twenty-first century, the cool, hospital look of tubular steel seen in the early years of the twentieth century has been replaced by a softer alternative, often made of aluminum or used in conjunction with plywood, plastic, or even upholstery. Two main tendencies seem to be emerging with these metal seats. The chairs in one group are cleverly built, light, easy to manufacture and assemble, and are aimed at a large consumption market. Those in the second group

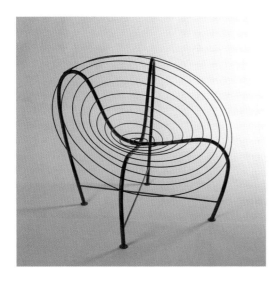

>
A Spider Chair by Godley-Schwan, c. 1989. Collection Neotu, Paris

>>
The Doctor Sonderbar Chair, by Philippe Starck, c. 1985. Collection de Beyrie, New York

<
A Martin Szekeley chaise longue. Collection Neotu, Paris

<
How High the Moon, of nickel-plated wire mesh, c. 1986/87, one of the poetic chairs by the Japanese designer Shiro Kuramata (1934–91). Collection Yves Gastou, Paris

>
A prototype for a three-legged chair by William Ellis, c. 1992, seen from the back. Private collection, New York

>>
The prototype seen from the side.

>
A painted aluminum corner chair designed c. 1991 by the minimalist artist Donald Judd (1928–94). Collection David Gilles, London

modern chairs 395

<
A leather butterfly chair. Collection Ralph Lauren

>
A Karim Rashid modular sofa. Collection Totem, New York

v
Two Karim Rashid modular chairs of tubular steel, metal, and foam, c. 1996. Collection Totem, New York

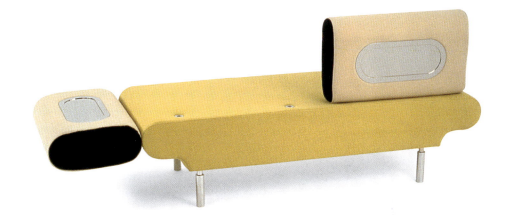

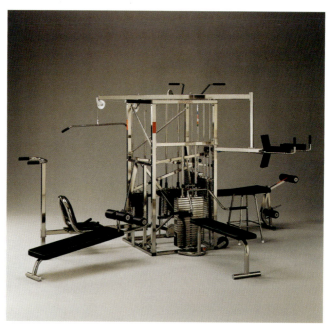

<<
The Grand Canal Chair, by Garouste & Bonetti. Collection David Gilles, London

<
The new seat for the twenty-first century: the gym. Private collection, New York

<
A large easy chair of patinated and polished stainless steel, c. 1990, in an edition of twenty, by Ron Arad (b. 1951), an Israeli active in England. Collection Barry Friedman, New York

are complicated, labor-intensive, and are made in small quantities, more as art than as design. Many avant-garde designers prefer the creative freedom that small-scale methods of production provide, establishing their own fashion; others try to combine the decorative with the functional, creating environmentally sound chairs following fashion. Both design tendencies are valid as long as the seats fulfill the sitter's needs and reflect the owner's style.

THE BIO-MORPHIC LOOK: FOAMS AND RUBBER SEATS

Along with plywood and tubular steel, one of the new materials of the twentieth century was molded plastic. Plastics are malleable, man-made substances that can be liquefied under heat and pressure and then formed into shapes. The foundation of the modern plastics industry was laid in the 1930s, with the development of the synthetic compounds polystyrene, polyvinyl chloride (PVC), acrylic, and nylon. One of the most famous examples of acrylic furniture design is the bedroom suite designed by Landislas Medgyes in the early 1940s for Helena Rubinstein, who reportedly commissioned the suite after seeing designs for her Lucite cosmetics container. In his biography of Rubinstein, Patrick O'Higgins describes his first vision of the lady herself, ensconced in her illuminated sleigh bed:

"Come in! Come in!" she summoned me impatiently with both her hands. I must have nervously examined the chair Madame pointed to, wondering if it would hold my weight, because as if reading my thought, she said: "Perfectly safe! Lucite, same stuff as our powder boxes."

Lucite was an acrylic manufactured by Dupont, however very few manufacturers were willing to produce acrylic chairs. They had to be specially ordered and made in small quantities. The designer Elsie de Wolfe used Lucite for one of her chairs in the late thirties, in a shape reminiscent of Biedermeier designs. In the late 1950s, Perspex, a transparent plastic licensed by Erwine and Estelle Laverne, was introduced, which led to the creation of the highly organic, almost invisible Buttercup and Lilly chairs, as well as the well-known Champagne dining chair. Following a similar path, Shiro Kuramata, in the late 1980s allied chemistry to poetry in his fragile-looking Miss Blanche chair, with red paper roses embedded in transparent acrylic resin.

The first plastic chairs were created by Eero Saarinen in collaboration with Charles Eames. This celebrated duo made some revolutionary prototypes for the Museum of Modern Art's "Organic Design in Home Furnishings" competition in 1940, where they won first prize for their Organic Armchair. After 1945, intensive research generated more sophisticated plastics, and production of the material increased tenfold. By 1948, Charles and Ray Eames had designed the Shell chairs for Herman Miller. These were in fiberglass, with wire-strut bases nicknamed "Eiffel Tower" and "Cat's Cradle."

Like that of tubular steel, the technology used in making Shell seats had been developed during the war for airplanes. The first 2,000 Shell armchairs were made by hand, with a metal cord embedded around the edge to reinforce it. The fabrication was plagued with problems. The rough surface of each shell had to be polished with an emery cloth. Saarinen's cast-plastic Tulip chair was also hand-molded and although it is sleekly modern, its concept was traditional. The Egg pivoting chair created by Arne Jacobsen followed

>
A French glass chair by René Coulon & Jacques Adnet, c. 1932. Collection Anne-Sophie Duval, Paris

<
The Tulip Collection by Eero Saarinen, c. 1955. Saarinen was reportedly unhappy that that these chairs could not each be cast in one piece, thinking that the aluminum stem was a betrayal of his intention to make a complete plastic chair. The use of a pedestal base, however, did satisfy his desire to "clean up the sum of legs." Knoll Collection, New York

around 1957. This was an interesting, photogenic, and comfortable seat, but the cost of its materials and its time-consuming fabrication made it more a work of art than a piece of furniture.

All of the formal innovations in chair design of the 1950s used glass fiber "mats" reinforced with resin, in which the mats were soaked. To build up sections of varying thicknesses, the resin had to be sprayed by hand. Since there was considerable handwork involved it was impossible to mechanize production sufficiently to produce these chairs inexpensively. In 1960, however, the Danish architect Verner Panton devised a new kind of plastic chair, the first injection-molded plastic seat with the seat and the base in a single piece. Its cantilevered form made it very stable.

Although chairs by Eames, Saarinen, and Panton filled the pages of design annuals in the late 1950s and early 1960s, they were to be found in very few actual homes. Early in the 1960s, however, this began to change. One reason for this was the increase in the number of young people in the population, which created an independent "youth market." The word "Pop" became a catchword for any style or sound associated with the young. The essence of Pop, as a fashion journalist observed in 1965, was an "enjoy-it-today-sling-it-tomorrow philosophy uninterested in quality and workmanship as long as the design is witty and new." Inevitably, chair design was drawn into the Pop orbit.

Pop devotees did not want to come home to a living room full of Scandinavian modern, reproduction antiques, or Victorian furniture. All the publications of the time were obsessed with young "lifestyles" (an archetypal sixties word) and "good taste" was under attack. As a writer in the London *Sunday Times* in April 1962 expressed it, "There are

^
Design drawings by Florence Knoll. Knoll Collection, New York

>
A nickel-plated steel-construction chair, with foam rubber upholstery covered with fabric, by the American designer Warren Platner (b. 1919). Platner said that "As a designer, I felt there was room for the kind of decorative, gentle, graceful kind of design that appeared in a period style like Louis XV. But it could have a more rational base instead of being applied decoration.... A classic is something that every time you look at it, you accept it as it is and you see no way of improving it." Collection Platner. Knoll Collection, New York

> Design drawings for the Umbrella Chair by Gaetano Pesce, 1992. Pesce continues to experiment with new shapes and materials. This Umbrella Chair is lightweight and collapsible, from an umbrella or a walking stick, at the push of a button. It is thus a chair suitable for any environment. Pesce Collection, New York

v The La Mamma or La Donna Chair, made of fabric-covered polyurethane foam, c. 1969, by Gaetano Pesce (b. 1939). Collection de Beyrie, New York

< Arne Jacobsen Swan Chair, 1957–58. Photograph: Anthony Cotsifas, New York

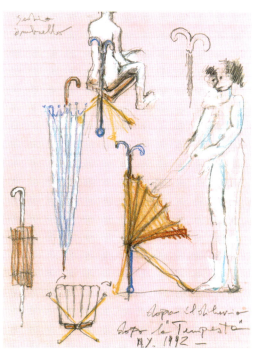

times when one longs to buy something plumb ugly and utterly unfunctional." Chairs had to be fashionable, fun, and disposable. Plastic was in vogue and the search for more sophisticated plastics continued, which led to two major developments: the use of molded polyurethane foam, and the development of injection-molding.

At the end of the sixties the introduction of polyurethane foam, made with a process developed in the automobile industry, created a sensation in chair design. Polyurethane foam suited the revolutionary spirit of the time, as a protest against gluttonous consumerism. The process was relatively simple. First, a mold was created of the desired shape (chair, sofa, or whatever). A strengthening frame, either of wood or metal, was set into the mold, and the foam was then injected in liquid form. Using this process, it was possible to make all sorts of shapes.

The lead in chair design was taken by Italian designers, who, like the Bauhaus designers, wanted to create pieces that addressed socio-cultural problems. They wanted to discourage the "fetishism of goods" that they believed characterized their time, and to meet a need for flexible living environments. In pursuit of these goals, they allied funky ideas that were often only a step away from sculpture with good design and execution. Italian manufacturers, among them Poltronova, Gavina, Sormani, and Kartell, were also willing to experiment. The result was a number of wildly humorous and mad things to sit on. Jonathan de Pass, Donato d'Urbino, and Paolo Lomazzi, for example, created the Joe chair, named after Joe DiMaggio, in the form of a giant baseball

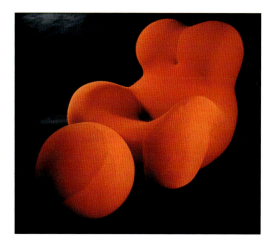

<
The painted resin Snake Chair, c. 1994, by the French artist Nikki de Saint Phalle (1930–2002), signed and numbered 7/20. Collection Loudmer, Paris

v
The Joe Chair, c. 1970, named after baseball legend Joe DiMaggio, by the Italian designers Jonathan De Pass, Donato D'Urbino, and Paolo Lomazzi. David Rago Modern Auctions, Lambertville, N.J.

<<
The Marilyn Sofa, c. 1972, by the Italian firm Studio 65. Made of stretch-fabric-covered molded polyurethane foam and named after the actress Marilyn Monroe, the sofa pays homage to Salvador Dali's earlier Mae West Sofa of 1936. Like the Allen Jones chair opposite, above, it is a quintessential Pop design. David Rago Modern Auctions, Lambertville, N.J.

> An English sculptural chair typical of Pop-Art design, c. 1969, by Allen Jones (b. 1937). Art Resource, New York

> Teodora, an armchair with a plastic laminate-veneered wood frame and a molded Perspex back, designed for Vitra by the Italian designer Ettore Sottsass (b. 1917). Collection Yves Gastou, Paris

glove, often considered an ironic comment on the numerous reissued Bauhaus chairs covered with overpriced leather. Gruppo Strum, another Italian group, came up with giant blades of grasses, called "Pratone," as an allegory of the longing for nature in the late sixties.

The English designer Roger Dean created, while still a student, the Sea Urchin chair. He wrote that his starting point was "a chair one could do anything with: one could sit in it in any position, and approach it from any direction." The chair was a dome four feet in diameter with a twelve-section polyurethane foam interior, which could shape itself around the sitter's body. It could be a recliner if approached from a high angle, or an upright chair if from a low one. When the Sea Urchin appeared in the Prototype Furniture exhibition in 1967, a critic in the *Architects' Journal* commented that "The service it provides is not so much support as symbiosis." Two English designers, Jon Wealleans and Jon Wright, made what they described as "fun furniture for children and adults," a soft PVC seat in the shape of a giant set of false teeth, a set of seats resembling pieces of a jigsaw puzzle, a soft telephone, which could be used as a chair when the receiver was removed, and a giant gym-shoe seat. The American Wendell Castle, best known for his superbly crafted wooden seats, was also inspired by teeth, creating in molded polyester a sofa and chair shaped like molars. With many of these seats, a would-be user had first to shape a place to sit within the soft form; indeed, the passivity of merely sitting on a shape created for it was portrayed as behavior typical of abhorrent consumerism. This interesting thought was characteristic of the late 1960s, and unique in the history of chair design. Malleable pieces of this period often aged badly, the material becoming brittle and worn, but transience was in keeping with the Pop aesthetic of disposability, even when the chairs were expensive unique or limited-edition pieces. It was not until the late 1960s that some types of "fun seats"—"beanbag" chairs, for example—were mass-produced, and became affordable for the younger market.

Beanbag chairs were so informal that they were not considered real seats, and so appealed to a younger clientele. The first and the most stylish was the Sacco, which was available in eight colors, designed by the Italian team of Gatti, Paolini, and Theodoro. The Sacco contained as many as twelve million plastic granules or polystyrene beads, which adjusted to the shape of the body. Many design journalists wondered at the time if it was the end of the chair in the youth culture. It was not, of course, but the Sacco and its cheaper

imitations are still popular today among the young. The same can be said of inflatable seats. Inflatable chairs, usually made of polyvinyl chloride (PVC) accorded well with the Pop ideals of youth and fashion. The Italian-designed Blow chair became an icon of 1960s popular culture and the best-known inflatable chair. It could be used either inside or out, or even in swimming pools. A puncture could be repaired with a PVC patch and glue, which were usually provided with the furniture. Although inflatable seats were novel and youthful, their shape was traditional. One journalist remarked without irony that they "blend well with Georgian proportions." The traditional forms may have helped sell the unconventional idea—a strange shape for an inflatable seat might have been too much—but the seats never lost their connotations of novelty and trendiness.

The Djinn series, made of polyurethane foam and upholstered with stretch fabric on a bent tubular steel frame, was created during the same period by a French designer, Olivier Mourgue and prominently displayed in the Stanley Kubrick movie *2001: A Space Odyssey*. The name derived from a spirit in Islamic mythology than can assume human or animal form and control men

<
Lady Bug and Turtle seats, by Beausejour Racine Roberty. Collection VIA, Paris

<<
The Fauteuil Fantome by Beausejour Racine Roberty, France. Collection VIA, Paris

<
The Noli Me Tangere Stool by the French designer Vincent Beaurin. Collection VIA, Paris

<<
The Massai Chair by the French designer Kristian Gavoille, c. 1990. Collection Neotu, Paris

<
The Zoid Sofa, by Dan Friedman. Collection Neotu, Paris

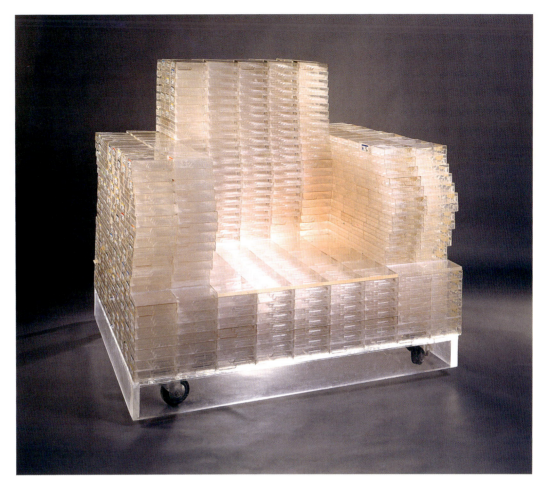

> An accumulation of acrylic paint boxes, forming a chair, by the French Pop artist Arman (Armand Fernandez; 1928–2005), c. 1988. Private collection, New York

with its supernatural powers, an example of the influence of the emerging popular interest in Eastern civilization on the decorative arts during the sixties. The Japanese designer Kazuhide Takahama, also using polyurethane foam upholstery, created the Marcel, Raymond, and Suzanne modular seating units for Dino Gavina in 1965. Modular units, another light-hearted approach to seating, can be compared to playing with Legos or dominoes. Polyurethane foam, which allowed the creation of light, easily moved seats of all shapes and sizes, was perfect for the purpose.

The Pop climate provided the incentive for a number of artists to experiment with chair design. Forms that were part functional chair and part sculptural object abounded late in the decade, some made of injection-molded polyurethane, others of molded glass fiber. A unique sheep chair made by the sculptor Lalane is one example; another was the violin chair created by the artist Arman in the 1980s. Both of these creations are, in effect, works of art, far removed from mass-production.

Injection molding improved mass production immensely. In 1954, a chemist working for the Shell Chemical Company in England synthesized polypropylene from several gases, which could be made into clear surfaces, and could be solid-colored, stain-proof, and chip-proof, with high resistance to scratching. The English designer Robin Day, capitalizing on the new material, created the immensely successful Polyprop chair in 1962. A single tooling can produce 4,000 seat-shells per week. From then on, plastic seats became affordable, and they could be marketed in large quantities. From 1963 to the present, over fourteen million Polyprop chairs have been sold in twenty-three countries. Later, in 1965, the Italian designer Joe Colombo created the first full-scale injection-molded chair, called the 4867. Ingeniously built, these popular chairs could be stacked into sets of three.

Contemporary creative spirits who believe in good design for a wide public continue to work in plastic. One example is Philippe Starck with his Cheap Chic series, including the Bubu I stool of 1991 and Dadada of 1993. In 1998 Karim Rashid managed to design an interesting, sexy chair called OH, made of polypropylene and steel tubing, which can be sold for fifty dollars. In 1999 Ron Arad introduced his Fantastic Plastic Elastic and his signed FPE chair, which are equally affordable. Only plastic chairs, produced in large quantities, can be made for such an economical price. But they can exemplify high-design work. Quality design is no longer elitist, owing to the miracle of new technology. As the metal seat was once the chair of the designer allied to the engineer, the plastic seat has become the chair of the designer allied to the chemist.

<
Squeeze-design stools and chairs. Collection Totem, New York

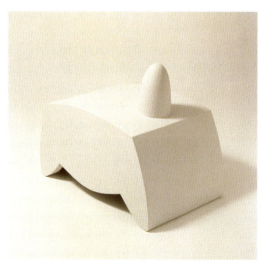

modern chairs 407

\> Design drawings for OH Chairs, by Karim Rashid

v An OH Armchair, c. 1998, by Karim Rashid. Collection Totem, New York

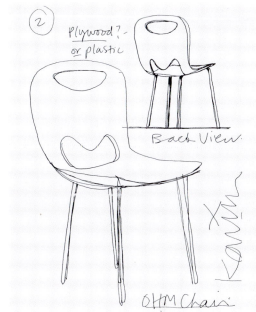

HANDICRAFT-LOOK CHAIRS

One untold story of twentieth-century design is how quickly the love affair of Modernism and technology soured for many architects, designers, and decorative artists. Many of these talented people found Modernism cold and unsatisfying, and in response created the handicraft look in furniture. Their intention was to reveal the natural wood—carved or uncarved, unpolished or hand-rubbed in natural finishes, cut in simple, functional shapes, and sometimes, complemented by ox-hide seats. Within this basic concept designers created an astonishing variety of styles.

Even the modernist Dutch designer Gerrit Rietveld (1888–1964), who was trained as a cabinetmaker, was a pioneer of the handicraft look. Early in his career, in 1918, he secured a position among the modernist vanguard with the design of an unpainted version of what would later become his famed *Roodblauwe Stoel* (Red/Blue chair). Although he had designed this chair with mass production in mind, there was no single prototype; instead there were a number of variations on it, the dimensions of which varied significantly. Indeed the early, unpainted version had been handmade in his workshop for his own use. Attached to the underside of the seat was a printed paper label that read: "When I sit down, I do not want to sit like my flesh would want me to be seated, but as my intellect or spirit would want to be seated, as if woven together." Although these lines expressed the aim of sustaining the sitter spiritually as well as physically, the sculptural qualities of the chair caused it to be considered as a work of modernist art. Around 1923, Rietveld made a painted version, with a red back, blue seat, and yellow front, which the followers of De Stijl adopted almost as a manifesto. For the first time, seats were thought of as "abstract, realistic sculptures for our future interiors." Finally, in a full reconciliation of art and the mass market, the

<
A carved-oak side chair, c. 1900, by the American designer Charles Rohlfs (1853–36). Rohlfs created unusual Arts and Crafts chairs inspired by Norwegian, Moorish, and Art Nouveau–style chairs, usually commissioned by wealthy collectors. Christie's

Italian company Cassina began manufacturing the chair in 1973.

In the 1930s, Scandinavia, with its traditional love of wood in all its forms, became a center of the handcraft look as designers rejected the cold, metal-and-glass aesthetics of International Modernism. In the years before the Second World War, the Danish designer and teacher Kaare Klint (1888–1954) established himself as the spiritual godfather of the modern Scandinavian style, stressing the need to preserve the crafts tradition and promoting wood as a more humane and inviting material than metal for chair design. In this same period, significantly, the Finnish designer Alvar Aalto began to experiment with plywood and laminated wood.

To encourage high standards, Danish furniture-makers set up the Furniture Manufacturers Quality Control Board and, as early as 1927, grouped themselves into an exhibition society called the Danish Cabinetmaker's Guild to promote quality design. In Finland, Ornamo,

\>
A valet chair by the Danish designer Hans Wegner (b. 1914). Wegner has been called "the chair-maker of chair-makers." Few other designers have consistently produced such high-quality designs. Collection Gansewoort, New York

\>\>
A copper chair, c. 1930, by Edgar Brandt. Collection Yves Gastou, Paris

\>
An unusual side chair. Robert Wilson Collection

\>\>
The Mandolin Chair by the Italian designer Piero Fornasetti (1913–88). Fornasetti's eccentric and trompe-l'oeil decoration exerted a strong influence on the Italian Anti-Design movement. Collection Gansewoort, New York

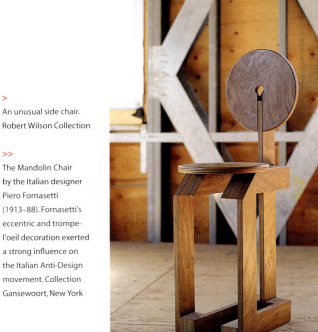

< A table with four chairs in California walnut, leather, and copper, by the American designer Garry Knox Bennett. Peter Joseph Gallery, New York

< A set of lacquered plywood and solid-wood shield-back chairs, c. 1987, by the American designer Thomas Hucker. Peter Joseph Gallery, New York

> Several views of a laminated rocking armchair by the American designer Wendell Castle (b. 1932). Castle is known for his superbly crafted wooden furniture. Peter Joseph Gallery, New York

and in Sweden, Slojdforeningen, associations of industrial designers, worked to maintain a strong image in chair design. The secret of Scandinavian success was a happy implementation of the Arts and Crafts ideal: a marriage between the interests of designer and manufacturer. In Scandinavia as a whole there was a tradition of good handmade chairs, which designers wanted to preserve. In order to do this and at the same time fulfill a growing demand for chairs, they used machines for the preliminary work, and then finished the chairs by hand. International exhibitions, including the 1954 Design in Scandinavia show in the United States and the 1956 Formes Scandinaves at the Musée des Arts Décoratifs in Paris, helped promote the handicraft look.

Among the most notable Scandinavian designers were the Swedes Carl Malmsten and Bruno Mathsson (b. 1907), both well established before World War II. Denmark's most talented designers included Borge Mogensen, Finn Juhl, and Hans J. Wegner (b. 1914), the last of whom helped bridge the gap between craftsmanship and industrial production.

Wegner's feeling for wood developed in his boyhood, when he worked as a carpenter's apprentice in Tonder, in southern Jutland. Whenever an old house was torn down, he would collect some of the seasoned timbers, which he would then carve. Later, he became famous for his perfectly crafted, handmade chairs, which often drew on traditional models. In 1949 he designed a harmonious seat known simply as "The Chair," carved in walnut and mahogany with a woven cane seat. When the editors of the American magazine *Interiors* saw it for the first time in 1950, they dubbed it "the world's most beautiful chair" and placed it on the magazine's cover. "No matter where you stand," wrote Marion Gough in *House Beautiful* in 1959, "its lyrical, fluid line seems to take on the dimension of sculpture." Wegner's chair inspired the Italian Gio Ponti (1891–1979) to create a seat made of ash with a woven cane seat, also called "The Chair."

In Wegner's hands, the English Windsor chair took on a new life as the gracious Peacock Chair of 1947. The designer strove for comfort, broadening the seat and flattening the slats of the back where they touch the shoulder blades. Wegner believes that seats should excite the senses. "Love of wood is something that all men have in common. They

V

A Conoid Bench with back, in solid walnut, c. 1974, by the Japanese-American designer George Nakashima (1905–90). Nakashima's variation on the familiar settee emphasizes how much the Shakers and the Japanese had in common with their economy of line and their understanding that simple materials are as beautiful as costly ones. Courtesy, Mira Nakashima. Photograph: George Erml

> A stacked-glass chair, c. 1986, by Danny Lane (b. 1955). Collection Yves Gastou, Paris

> Solomon's Chair, c.1988, in glass, by Danny Lane, demonstrating Lane's masterful handling of a difficult material for chairs. Collection Yves Gastou, Paris

cannot stop themselves from letting their hands stroke a piece of wood." Rather than camouflage pegs, he let them show. He buffed his chairs, or gave them a light coat of lacquer, making it easy to restore their luster.

Others who created handcraft-look chairs include the French artist Alexandre Noll (1890–1970), who in the late 1940s began to sculpt massive chairs from tree trunks, and the American designers George Nakashima (1905–90) and Wharton Esherick (1898–1970). Nakashima and Esherick represent the first generation of twentieth-century American woodworkers.

Trained as an architect, Nakashima worked in that field for some years before he began to see handcrafted furniture as his calling. In 1940, he started producing his own designs in Seattle. The classic Windsor chair, English in origin but endlessly adapted in this country, served as the basis for his famous lounge chairs. Unfortunately, Nakashima's rough-hewn wooden chairs, carefully conceived to bring out the natural grain and expressive contours of the cherry and black walnut that he favored, were caricatured in the redwood tree-stump furniture that became a 1970s cliché. Now, however, with the perspective of time, Nakashima's chairs have escaped the stigma of these crude imitations.

Throughout the 1970s the craft revival continued as a kind of protest against the modern world and its increasing industrialization, and also as a sophisticated expression of the artisan's joy in his craft. Handicraft-look chairs allow their makers to create functional pieces and at the same time express a philosophical message. The movement was strongest in the United Kingdom and the United States; its British founding father is John Makepeace, who set up a workshop in Oxfordshire in 1963 and who, in 1977, opened a school for young apprentices at Parnam House in Dorset. Makepeace juxtaposes a wide range of native and exotic woods, occasionally counterpointed by modern synthetic materials, or even hides. His example inspired a generation of young talents, instilling in them a passion for wood. Among the more distinguished practitioners of the craft in Britain are Rupert Williamson, John Coleman, and Martin Grierson.

Wharton Esherick was hailed by the designer Jack Lenor Larson as "the most important

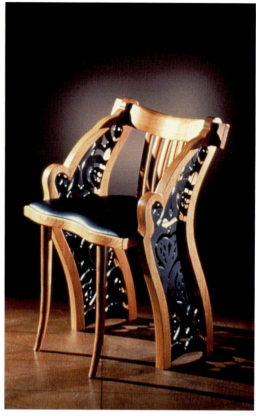

<<
The Tarred and Feathered Chair, c. 1994, by Ben Jakober. Private collection, Paris

<
An armchair by the Czech designer Boreck Sipeck (b. 1949). Collection Modern Age

<<
The Cello Chair, c. 1993, by Arman. Arman Collection, New York

<
A brass side chair in an edition of twelve, c. 1994, by Nicolas Alvis Vega. Collection David Gilles, London

furniture-maker of the twentieth century." One of his particularly fascinating chairs was a seat made in 1938 out of hammer handles. Esherick's work paved the way for the likes of Wendell Castle (b. 1932), who became the leading exponent of Arts and Crafts in America and even founded his own school for woodworking in 1980. Castle created illusory seats sculpted into forms that recall the anthropomorphic silhouettes of the Art Nouveau master Hector Guimard. Castle, along with Daniel Jackson, Bob Worth, Jere Osgood, and Bill Keyser, represent the second generation of twentieth-century American woodworkers. All are influential on chair design today.

Craft seats are a luxury, and like their counterparts produced by the Arts and Crafts Movement designers they belie the spirit that inspires them. They are often more works of art than pieces for a mass market. The notion of comfort is also of little or no importance; appearance is the primary concern. It is interesting to note how popular such seats are in the early twenty-first century, when comfort is so prized in so much other contemporary furniture. The integrity and originality of the designers have created a special place for them. Their popularity also reveals that the basic need for a special seat made of natural elements has not disappeared with modernity. Thus, handicraft seats are a valuable link to the past, as well as a step toward the future. For this reason, sophisticated collectors appreciate them, encourage the creation of new models, and collect them fervently.

> The Mid-Afternoon Chair, c. 1998, a gold-finished chair made of dildoes, by the Japanese designer Yayoi Kusama. Collection Robert Miller Gallery, New York

CONTEMPORARY UPHOLSTERY

The twentieth century saw an increase in the number of upholstered seats, owing to the growing middle class, especially in the West. Comfort became synonymous with quality of life, and lounging on a sofa became an expected part of life. Nowadays, no living room is complete without at least one couch, and the term "couch potato" entered the vocabulary of late-twentieth-century America as a reflection of common behavior.

As developing technology produced new materials for chairs throughout the modern era, chemists created new materials for upholstery, as well. Although the traditional materials of upholstery are still used—springs, slats, hair, and feathers—increasingly they are replaced by foam. Each method has its champions. The Bridgewater, considered the finest chair of the 1930s, was made by the London firm of Howard. Still available with its companion settee, the Audley, this chair is upholstered with springs, cord, hair, and wool in the traditional way. In America numerous catalogues from Calico Corners to Crate & Barrel and Pottery Barn also offer a wide range of classic sofas and chairs put together in the traditional fashion, using steel coils tied together in eight directions to create a uniform support for each frame. Springdown cushions, in various degrees of firmness, are standard on most frames. Striving for perfection, a manufacturer will use foams, feathers, hair, latex, and springs, each for the job

<
A Garouste & Bonetti armchair. Collection David Gilles, London

>
An armchair, c. 1950, by the Italian designer Carlo Graffi. Graffi worked closely with the designer Carlo Molino on several architectural projects and his exuberant designs exemplify the Turinese Baroque style. Collection Yves Gastou, Paris

>
The Marie France Armchair, by the French designer Martin Szekely. Collection Neotu, Paris

< A Garouste & Bonetti "Corbeille" (basket) Sofa. Collection Neotu, Paris

< The Kagan Sofa, 1948. Collection Gansewoort, New York

it does best, in a single chair. The New York firm of de Angelis is said to make the best—and the priciest—of sofas of this type.

The upholstery techniques developed at the end of the seventeenth century have remained the same, but have been refined with modern techniques. The new upholstery is simpler to make, and is no doubt more hygienic, but it is still doubtful that the new foams will stand up to wear with the best of traditional upholstery. After the Second World War, the use of latex or foam spread from car and airplane seats to the home, first as loose seat cushions over cable springs, and later, as rubber webbing. For the Womb Chair by Eero Saarinen, the latex-foam padding and loose cushions provided the desired comfort. Saarinen said that the design of the Womb Chair represented an "attempt to achieve psychological comfort by providing a great big, cup-like shell into which you can curl up and pull up your legs," something that women seem especially to like to do. The chair was a commercial success. Only time will tell how well its foam cushions will wear.

At first foam seemed to have everything that could be desired: replaceability, ease of cleaning, and springing that (unlike steel) would never poke through the cover. Unfortunately the cell-like structure of this upholstery breaks down under robust use and thus does not age well. Dated, also, are units of furniture that can be "played" like dominoes. In this case, the "domino" is a basic foam unit made to a size that is thought necessary for the human posterior to rest on in comfort. More playthings than serious furniture, as well, are the late-sixties single-block-of-polyurethane-foam sculptural seats created by inventive Italian designers such as Joe Colombo, Roberto Matta, and Archizoom Associati. Usually lightweight, easy to move, and multifunctional, they could often be configured in several ways—as a chaise longue, sofa, or divan—and were well suited to the informal interiors that became increasingly popular in the late 1960s. Today, contemporary designers such as Garouste and Bonetti or Kristian Gavoille, still creating avant-garde sofas, usually ally foam with feathers or even, in some instances, with springs and hair, often on wood or metal frames. The debt owed to Simon de Lobell, Louis XIV's principal *tapissier*, is immense.

> A chair called *Ceci n'est pas une brouette* ("This is not a wheelbarrow") by Philippe Starck. Private collection

INDEX

Figures in *italics* refer to illustrations.

Aalto, Alvar, 9, 269, 354, *371*, 371–372, *373*, 377, 408
abbot's chair, 63
Abildgaard, Nicolai Abraham, 258, *259*, 261, *262*, 264–265, 268
Academy of Armory (Holme), 80, 159
acanthus motifs, 81
acrylic, 131, 397
Adam, Robert, 218, 219, 224, 229–230, 233, 234, 246, 247
Adelcrantz, Carl Fredrik, 241
Adirondack chairs, 130, *130*
Adnet, Jacques, *397*
Aesthetic Movement, 304
Affleck, Thomas, *211*, 212
Afghan seat, *307*
Africa, 11, *42*, 42–49, *44*, *45*, *46*, 367
akonkromfi ("praying mantis"), 47–48
Allison, Michael, 296
aluminum, 136–137, *391*, *393*
Alvis, Nicolas, *414*
America: campaign chairs of, 115–116; Chinese influence on, 41–42; Chippendale style in, 211–212; garden chairs of, *127*, *128*, *129*, *130*, *131*; modern design in, *356*, 373–377, *376*, *377*, 385–386; Neoclassicism in, 219, *243*, 243–245, *244*, 248, 294–296; nineteenth-century designs in, 258, 265–266, 269, 303, *303*, 306, *307*, 307–309, 329, 333–334; Rococo style in, *210*, 211, 211–212; rustic furniture of, *106*, 106–108, *107*; Windsor chairs from, 95–97, *96*, *97*
Amish chairs, 131
amorino, 340
"amputee" chair, *379*
André, Jacques, 131
Androuet du Cerceau I, Jacques, 70, *70*, 75
Androuet du Cerceau, Paul, 160
Angola, 48
Angus & Co., 95
animals and animal motifs, 10, 17–18, 31, 45, *46*, 53–54, *57*, 108–110, *110*; antlers, *108*, 108–110; bears, 93, *93*, 110; buffalo, *108*; bulls, 18; crabs, *112*; crocodiles, 45; deer, 108, *109*; eagles, *111*; elephants, 45, *46*, 110, 310; giraffe, 110; horns, 108–110; horses, 110; leopards, 45; lions, 10, 18; marine life, 110–113, *112*, *113*; ostriches, *129*; panthers, 45; rhinoceros, 110; snakes, *289*; tigers, 110; tortoiseshells, 29; zebras, 110, *361*
Antigone (Sophocles), 24
Arad, Ron, 387, *396*, 406
Arbus, André, *359*
Archias, 31
architectural chairs, 183
Arflex, 378–379
Aristophanes, 26
Arman, 405, *405*
armchairs, 15, 18, 33, 36, 39, 40, 41, 49, 59, 60, 62, 70, 181. See also specific designs, e.g., OH Armchairs.
arquibanco, 64
arrow motif, *288*
Art Deco style, 353, *354*, *355*
Artek, 372
Art Furniture Movement, 304–305
Art Joven. *See* Art Nouveau.
Art Nouveau, 268, 306, 310, 341–349
Arts and Crafts Movement, 131, 303, 304, 305–308, 346, 382
Asante people, 11, 42–43, *44*, 45, *46*, 47–48, 367
asipim, 48
astronomer's chair, *292*
Aubusson tapestry, *221*, 311
Austria, 128, 213, 268, 314, 323
Avisse, Jean, *250*

Baccarat, *146*
back stools, 86
Badlam, Stephen, 219, 243
baigneuse, 340
bakermat, 102, 128
Bakst, Leon, 355
Ballets Russes, 355
balloon-backed chairs, 330–331
Bamberg, 194
bamboo, 39, *140*, *307*
banca, 65
bancos, 65
bank, *156*
bankuva, 138–139
banquets, 31
banquettes, 213, 246, *246*
Banzi, Andrea, 379
Baoule, 46
Barbares, 387

"Barbarian bed," 36–37
barber chairs, 49
Barcelona Chair, 10, 352, 382, *383*
Baringa, 47
Bari tribe, 47
baroque design, 150–174
Bashet, Marcel André, *330*
Basoli, Renato, *389*
Batavia, 142, 143, 144
bathroom chairs, 66, 189. See also chaise percée.
Baudouine, Charles, 329
Bauhaus School, 9, 347, 353, 371, 380–383, 403
Bauve, 222
Bavaria, 81, 110, 112, 170, 189, 192–193, 194, 206, 266, 277, 300, 324
Bayreuth, 194–197
beanbag chairs, 355, 403–404
Beaurin, Vincent, *404*
Beckford, William, 118
Behrens, Peter, 347–348, 371
Beitemus, 31
Belanger, François-Joseph, 218–219, 223
Belgium, 9, 62–65, 179, 341–343
Belter, John Henry, 329
benches, 23, 30, 31, *31*, 60, 62–66, *64*, *65*, 84, 93, 118, 120, *135*, *156*, 159, 213. See also settles and specific designs, e.g., chamber benches.
Bennett, Garry Knox, *410*
bentwood chairs, 131, 368–371, *369*, *371*
Bérain, Jean, *150*, 152, 157
berceuse, 339
bergère en confessional, 187
bergères, 11, 89, 103, 181, 187, *187*, 224. See also easy chairs.
Berlage, Hendrikus Petrus, 348
Berthault, Louis-Martin, 270
Bertoia, Harry, 386, *386*
Bettenfield, 22
bidet, 310
Biedermeier style, 10, 279, 310–311, *312*, *312*–*317*, *313*, *314*, *315*, *316*, *317*, 323, 369
Bijagos Archipelago, 45
Bilibin, Ivan Yakovlevitch, 305
Binderboll, Thorvald, 261
Bindesboll, Gottlieb, *263*
Bing, Siegfried, 341, 342
biomorphic look, 352, 397–406
birthing chair, *138*

bisellium, 31
Blow Chair, 136, 355, 404
Bofinger Chair, 136
Boizot, Simon-Louis, *258*
Bonetti, Mattia, 42, *387*, *396*, *416*, *418*, 419
borne, *336*, 338–339
Borsani, Oswaldo de, *389*
boss, *128*
Bosse, Abraham, *66*, *72*, *76*, 157
Boston rocker, 95
Boucher, Just-François, 223
boudeuse, 339
bouges, 55
Boulanger, Gustave Clarence Rodolphe, *268*
Boulle, André-Charles, 152, *163*, 165, *198*, *199*
bourgeois chairs, 310–341
Boutique Menuiserie (van de Passe), 168
bow chair, 98
Boyar Wedding, The (Makovsky), *65*
Brady, Matthew, 115
Brandt, Edgar, *409*
Brazil, 139–140
Brenna, Vincenzo, *242*
Breuer, Marcel, 9, 336, 352, 371, 373, *374*, *375*, *380*, 380–383
Breuer tubular seat, 352
bridal chairs, *91*
Brjullov, Alexander, 266–268
Bry, Theodore de, 70
Buddhism, 38–40
Bugatti, Carlo, *348*, 349
Burges, William, 300–302, *303*
burgomaster chair, 144
Burkina Faso, 46, *47*
Burne-Jones, Edward, 305
Butler, Thomas, 115
Buttercup chair, 397
butterfly chair, 116, *394*
Byzantine chairs, 52

Cabinet-Maker and Upholsterer's Drawing-Book, The (Sheraton), *233*, 233–234, 246–247, 248
Cabinet-Maker and Upholsterer's Guide, The (Hepplewhite), *230*, 230, 243, 246, 247, 248
cadera de sola, 165
cadiero, 90
Café Coste chair, 379
Caillon, Jean Gaspar, 180

Calamus rotang, 126, 144
Calderón de la Barca, Pedro, 156
Calpurnius Siculus, 30–31
Cameron, Charles, 219, *242*, *242*
Cameroon, 42, 44, 45, 48
camp-chairs, 115–116
canapé(s), 173–174, *174*, 214–217, 247–248. *See also* sofas.; *à confident*, 216, *217*; *à joues*, 186, *215*
caned chairs, 126, 142–144, *165*, 168–169, *169*, 183–184, 211
Canopy of State, 152
Capin, 249
Caprichos, Los (Goya), 8
caquetoire, 71
Carabin, François Rupert, *343*, 343–345
cardboard, 355, *379*
Cardinal Mazarin, of France, 76, *77*, 151
Carna Chair, 336
carpenter chairs, 90
carpenter's guilds. *See* guilds.
Carpentier, Jean Baptiste, *122*
carreau(x), 66, *67*, 153, 169. *See also* cushions.
carved chairs, 144, 225, 242
caryatid stool, 45–46
Casati, Cesare Mario, 378
cassapanca, 64, *65*, 84
Castle, Wendell, *403*, *411*, *415*
cathedra, 30–31, 60
Cathenay seat, 386
Cawthorn, James, 204
Cello Chair, *414*
Ceylon, 142
"Chair of Dagobert," 56, *56*, 114, *275*
Chairs, The (Ionesco, 1952), 8
chaise à bras, 70
chaise à l'anglaise, 225
chaise à vertugadin, 76
chaise de fileuse, 91
chaise de nourice, 90
chaise de paille, 169
chaise longues, 22, 31, 137, 173, 209, 247, 256–257, 295, 352, *389*. *See also* couches, *duchesse*, and specific designs, e.g., Techno chaise longue.
chaise percée, 171–172, 189. *See also* bathroom chair.
chaise volante, 330
chamber benches, 62
Chambers, William, 219

Champagne dining chair, 397
Charlemagne, 55
Charreau, Pierre, *358*
Charter Oak Chair, 106
chauffeuse, 91, *321*
Cheap Chic series, 406
Chekhov, Anton, 94
Cherner chair, 377
Chesterfield chair, 341
Chevigny, Claude, *224*
Chiavari chair, 330–331
children's chairs, 82, *101*, 101–103, *102*, *103*, 376
China: ancient, 32, 32–42, *33*, *34*, *35*, *36*, *37*, *39*, *40*; Ming Dynasty, 139, 144; modern, 38, 40
"Chinese Chippendale" chairs, 204
chinoiseries, 176, 180, 197, 202–206, *204*, *205*, 295
chintz slipcovers, 337
Chippendale, Thomas, 10, 42, 110, 118, 120, *120*, 176, 179, 200, 200–202, *201*, *203*, 206–209, 211–212, *212*, 217, 229–230, 234, 238, *243*, 249, 251, 298
Chokwe, 48
Church, Frederick Edwin, 305
church seating, 62, 139, 142, 159
Clark, Arundell, 368
Classical Antiquity, 176, 218
Classical Revival style, 208, 266
Clay, Henry, 332
cleanliness, 83–84
Clérisseau, 219
close stool. *See chaise percée*.
Coard, Marcel, 367
"Cobra" chair, *348*
Cochin, 57
coffre et à ciel, à, 60
Colbert, Jean-Baptiste, 151
Colini, Luigi, 103
Colombo, Joe, 406, 419
colonial chairs: of America, 74–75; outside of America, *137*, 137–147, *138*, *139*, *140*, *141*
companion chair, 340
computer chairs, 11
concrete, fibrated, 131–134
confident, 113, 214, 247, 340
confortable, 338, 339
Conoid Bench, *412*
conopée, 173–174
conversation chair, 220, 224

convertible furniture, *101*, *115*, 245
Copland, Henry, 179
Coronation of Napoleon, drawing for (David), *273*
coronation seats, 55, 57–60, *206*, 225
Corrozet, Gilles, 67–68
Cortés, Hernan, *137*
couches, 26, 31, *31*, 294. *See also* chaise longues, *duchesse*, and specific designs.
Coulon, René, *397*
country chairs, 80, 80–81, 85, 86–117, *87*, *88*, *89*
cowboy "chaise lounge," *137*
Cowper, William, 214
Crampton, Albert and Charles, 129
crapaud, 338, *339*
"creepie," 84
Cresson, Michel, 189, *190*
cross-legged seat, 41
Cubism, 353, *358*, *359*, 363, 367, 368
cult of Antiquity, 254
curule chair, *57*. *See also* sella curulis.
cushions, 19, 66, 160, 337. *See also* carreau(x).
Cuvilliés, François de, 170, 192–193, 206, 214

Dada, 353
Dagly, Gerhard, 166
damask, 77
Dangeau, Philippe de, 158
Danhauser, Josef, 109, *312*, 314–316
Dante chair, *58*, 60
Darly, 42, 208, 298
Darly, Edwards and, 42, *105*, *118*, *120*
Darmstadt art colony, 346–347
Daudet, Alphonse, 85
dauphine, 158
David, Jacques-Louis, 254, *254*, 256, 258–261, 264–265, 268, 270, *272*, 274, 286
Daw, Robert, 333
day beds, *172*, 173–174, *209*, 357
"Day Dreamer" armchair, 332
Day, Robin, 405
Dayrolles, 8
Dean, Roger, 403
De Bert Hartley, 334
deck chairs, *137*
Defoe, Daniel, 95
Delacroix, Eugène, 338
Delafosse, Jean-Charles, *191*, 223, 234
Delanois, Louis, 189, 224
Delaunay, Robert, 297, 360

Delaunay, Sonia, 297
de Lucchi, Michele, 387
Denmark, 180, 209, 240–241, *241*, 258, *258*, 259, 261, 262, *262*, *263*, 277, 355, 377–378, 379
Denon, Baron, (Dominique Vivant), 269
De Pass, Jonathan, 401, *402*
desk chair, *221*, *271*, *377*
Desky, Donald, 355
De Stijl group, 353, 367
Diamond Chair, *386*
dias, 180
Dictionnaire de l'ameublement (Havard), 68, 72, 128
diphros okladias, 23, *23*
director's chairs, 10, 60, *360*
Directory (Chippendale), 42, 120
Ditzel, Nanna, 379
divan, 338–339
Dixon, Tom, 387
Djinn series, 404–405
DKR-2 (Dining Bikini Rod) chairs, *390*
Doctor Sonderbar chair, *391*
dog's chair, 225
Donne, John, 129
double chair, 31
dowel construction, 24
dragon style, 85
Drentwett, Abraham, 152
Dresser, Christopher, 304
drum stools, 38
drunken-lord chair, *36*, 147
Dryad Works, 129
Dubreuil, André, 387
duchesse, 185, 247, *248*. *See also* chaise longues; couches.
duchesse brisée, 185, 214, 247
duchesse en bateau, 214
duchess, English, 248
Dufresne, Maurice, *354*, 355
Dufy, Raoul, 360
Dugourc, Jean Démosthène, 223, 238, 243, 282
dug-out chair, 89
Dunand, Jean, *264*, 265, *266*
Dunham Massey, 172
D'Urbino, Donato, 401, *402*
Duru, Pierre, 180
Dusch, J. A., *113*
"Dutch chairs," 86–89, 168
Dutch East India Company, 140–142, *141*, 147

Eames, Charles, 102, 134–136, 354, *376*, 377, 378, 379, *390*, 397, 398
Eames, Ray, 102, 134–136, *376*, 377, 378, 379, *390*, 397, 398
easie chairs, 167–168
Eastlake, Charles Lock, 303
easy chairs, 338, 339. *See also* bergères.
Easy Edges, 355
ébénisterie, 189
ecclesiastical thrones, 63
Edwards and Darly, 42, *105*, *118*, *120*
Egg chair, 397–398
Egypt, ancient, 9–10, *14*, 14–19, *15*, *16*, *17*, 20, 23, 26
Egyptian, neo-. *See* neo-Egyptian style.
electric chair, 9, 10
Elgin Throne (Athens), 24, *25*
Elijah, 8
Elizabethan style, 323
Ellis, Harvey, 307
Ellis, William, 391, *393*
Empire style, 208, 238, 256, 261, 266, 269, *269*–297, 313, 314
en bateau, 185
England: baroque style in, 159, 166, 167–168, 169, 200; colonial chairs of, 144, 147; country chairs of, 89, 95, 112, 115, 116; East India Company of, 140, *141*; eighteenth-century design in, 85; garden chairs of, 118–120, *120*, 126, 129; during Middle Ages, 54; modern chairs of, 377, 387; monarchy of, 53, 54, 56–57, 62, 74, 95, 155, 157, 158, 167, 168, 320; Neoclassicism in, 218, 224–225, 228, 229, *229*–234, *230*, *231*, *233*, 247, 248; nineteenth-century design in, 258, 262–265, *265*, 268, 282, 283, 286–294, *287*, *288*, *289*, *290*, *291*, *292*, *293*, *294*, *295*, 298, 299, 300–302, 304–305, 305–306, *318*, 318–321, 324, *324*, *325*, 332, 333, 336–341, *339*, 382; during Renaissance, 56–57, 60, 62, 68, 72–74; Rococo style in, 179, 181–183, 200, 200–202, *201*, 204, *204*, 206, 206–211, *207*, *209*, 212, 213, 214, 217
en gondola, 222
ergonomics, 336
escabelle, 159
Esherick, Wharton, 413–415
Estienne, Henri, 72
estrado, 155–156
Ethiopia, 48, *49*

Etruscan style, 224, 230, *254*
Evelyn, John, 169–170

fabric coverings, 116, 251, 337. See also upholstered chairs.
faldistorium, 55
faldstool. See *faudesteuil*.
Fantastici, Agnostino, 238
Fantastic Plastic Elastic, 406
fashion influencing chair styles, 9, 251, 337
faudesteuil, 55, 57–60, 114, *254*
faudestuef, 55
faun motif, *57*
fauteuil, 60, 90, 160–165, *166–167*; à la reine, *161*, 214; à oreilles, 167; bébé, *339*; canné, 183–184; confessionals, 167; de bonnes femmes, 90; de bureau, *181*, 184; de commodité, 167, 245; de malade, *182*; de marriage, 91; de veille, 167; en cabriolet, 183; en confessional, *181*; Pompadour, *339*; in Rococo style, *180*
fauteuil Ashanti, *378*
fauteuil Fantome, *404*
Fernandez, Armand, *405*
Feure, Georges de, *343*
fiddle-back chairs, 93
Finland, 85, 269, 309, 371–372
"firesides," 340
"First," 387
Fitzgerald, William C., 109–110
Flanders, 179
Flanders forms, 62–65
Fleury, Geoffroi de, 55
floral motifs, *80*, *81*
Florence, 66–67, *234*
Florida cypress chair, 131
Florio, John, 65
Flotner, Peter, *70*
"fly chair," 330
foam rubber, 355, *399*
folding chairs, 10, *35*, *36*, 38–40, *41*, 47–48, 55–56, *56*, *59*, 60, *60*, *61*, 114, 114–117, 140, 171, *335*, *360*, *379*. See also specific designs, e.g., director's chairs.
folding stools, 16, 23, *23*, 30, *32*, 36–37, 60, 157–159
Foliot, Nicolas-Quinibert, 189, 197
Folk Art Revival, 309, *310*
Follot, Paul, 360
Fontaine, Pierre-François-Léonard, 10, 256,

258, 266, 269, *270*, 272, *273*, 274, 277, 279, 282, 286, 294, 297, 316
footstools, 40, *40*, 54, 138
forms, 60, 62–65
Fornasetti, Piero, *409*
FPE chairs, 406
frailero (monk's chair), 60, 171
France: baroque style in, 150–174; colonial chairs of, 144; country chairs of, *90*, 90–91, 112; eighteenth-century designs in, 60; Imperial family of, 256, 269–270, *270*, 271–272, *272*, *273*, 274, *275*, 279; garden chairs of, 118, *120*, *121*, *122*, *126*; of Middle Ages, 54, 55, 56, *56*; modern chairs of, 355–360, *358*, *359*; monarchy of, 55, 66, 67, 68, 77, 110, 118, *121*, 150–151, 152–155, 156, 157–158, 159, 160, 166–167, 171–172, 173, 175, 183, 184, 187, 189, 213, 216, 245–246, 254, 272, *319*, 320; Neoclassicism in, 218–229, *219*, *220*, *221*, *222*, *223*, 224, *225*, *226*, *227*, 234, *234*, 247, *247*, 248, *250*, 251; nineteenth-century designs in, *254*, 269, 269–277, *270*, *271*, *272*, *273*, 274, *276*, 277, 296, 297, 298, *298*, 299, 299–300, 301, 302–303, 310, *314*, *318*, *319*, 320, *321*, 321–322, *326*, 328, *329*, 338, 339, 340, 343–345; during Renaissance, 56, *57*, 60, 66, 67–68, *70*, *71*, *72*, *77*; Revolution of, 254; Rococo style in, 170, 175–217, *176*, *177*, *181*, *182*, *184*, *185*, *190*, *216*
Frankel, Paul, 362
Frank, Jean Michel, 117, *359*, 360, 367–368
Frank, Josef, 42, 268, *370*, 371
Franque, Joseph, *274*
Freintrenie, Dominique, *379*
French Directorie style, 258
Frères, Jacob, 256–257
Freund, H. E., 261, *262*
Friedman, Dan, *404*
Friedrich, Wenzel, *108*
Füger, Heinrich Freidrich, *7*
fumeuse, 340
Furetière, Antoine de, 159
Furness, Frank, 10, 303
furniture guilds. See guilds.

Gallé, Emile, 342, *343*
Gambs, Heinrich, 266, 285, *286*
Gambs, Peter Heinrichovich, 266–268, 299, *300*

garde-meubles, 189
garden seating, 38, 80, 118–137, *120*, *121*, *126*, *127*, *132*, *133*, *134*, *135*, *136*, *137*
garde-robe. See chaise percée.
Gardner, George, 334
Garneray, Auguste, *122*
Garouste, Élisabeth, 42, 387, *396*, *416*, *418*, *419*
Gathering at the Home of Mme. Brisson (Bashet), *330*
Gaudi, Antoni, 349
Gautier, Théophile, 110
Gavoille, Kristian, *404*
Gebrüder Thonet, 369–371
Gehry, Frank, 355, *379*
Genghis Kahn's saddle, *307*
Genoa, 59, *196*
Gentleman and Cabinet-Maker's Director, The (Chippendale), 179, 200–201, *201*, 206, 208–209, 217, 230, 249, 251
George I period, *164*, 207
George II style, *200*, 206, *207*
George III style, *200*, 212, 228
Germany: country chairs of, 91, *91*, 92, 94–95, 104, 108–109, 113; modern chairs of, 9, 347, 353, 371, 380–382, *383*; Neoclassical style in, 238, *238*; nineteenth-century design in, *254*, *255*, 266, 277, 299, *299*, 312–317; during Renaissance, 72, *75*, *76*; Rococo style in, 190–197, *191*, *192*, *193*, *195*, *205*, 206, 211, 214, 238, *326*; seating etiquette in, 213; seventeenth-century design in, 166; stools of, 85
Ghana, 11, 42–43, 44, 45, 46, *46*, 49
Giacometti, Alberto, *134*
Giacometti, Diego, *134*, *136*
gilding, Neoclassical, 225
Girard, Alexander, 134
Glasgow School, 345
glass chairs, *146*, 397, *413*
Glastonbury chair, 74
Godley-Schwan, *379*, *391*
Godwin, Edward William, 304–305
Goethe, 104
Golden Stool, 45, *48*
Goldman, Paul, 377
Gold Medal, Inc., 116
gondola-shaped chairs, 272, 356
Gothic, neo-, 10, *298*, 298–303, *299*, *300*, *301*, *302*, *303*
Gothic style, 60, *62*

Goubaud, Innocent-Louis, *270*
goût grecque, 241
goût pittoresque, 176
gout stool, 246
Goya, Francisco, 8, *240*
Graffi, Carlo, *417*
graining, 83
Grand Canal Chair, 396
Grandfather chair, 340
Grandjean de Montigny, Auguste-Henri-Victor, 279
Gravelot, Hubert, 200
Gray, Eileen, 117, 267
"great chaire," 76
grecque style, à la, 219, 223
Greece, ancient, 10, 19–28, *20*, *21*, *22*, *23*, 30, 31
Greek Revival: American, 265–266; English, 262–265
Greene, William, 57
Grendey, Giles, 166, 206
Grierson, Martin, 378, *413*
griffin motif, *293*
Grimsrud, T. M., 9
Gripsholm chair, 89, 241
Gropius, Walter, 382, 384, 385
grotto chairs, 110–113, *112*, *113*
Groult, André, 364
Gruppo Strum, 403
Guatemala, *103*
Guhl, Willy, 131–134
guilds, 10, 168, 189, 190–192, 234, 242, 251, 277
Guimard, Hector, 342, *343*
Gurunsi people, *43*
Gustavian style, 219, 241, *264*
Gwere people, 48
gym equipment, 396
Gypsies, 106

Haarlemsche, 168
Haines, William, 269, *362*
Halfpenny, William, 118, 204
hall benches, *156*
Halle, Claude-Guy, *151*
handcraft-look chairs, 408–415
Hansen, Constantin, 261, *263*
Hardoy chair, 116
Hardwick, Philip, 265
Hardy, Peter J., 115
Harpy Tomb, 24
Harwood fiberboard seat, 334

Havard, H., 68, 72, 128
hedge chair, 86, *87*
Heissig, Franz, 238
heka schtool, 131
Hemba, 46
Hennequin, Philippe Auguste, *275*
Henry II style, 323
Hepplewhite, George, 214, *230*, 230–231, *231*, *232*, 233, 234, 236, 238, 241, 243, 245, 246, 247, 248
Herculaneum, 28
Herman Miller Furniture Company, 377, 386, *390*, 397
Hermès, *117*, *136*
Hervé, François, 228
Hetsch, Gustav-Fredrick, 277
Heurtaut, Nicolas, *177*, 189–190, 214
Heydt, J. W., 142
Heywood Brothers and Company, *127*, 128
hierarchy of seating, 152–155, 157–158, 169, 213
high-backed winged easy chair, 339–340
highchairs, *100*, 102
High Tech, 378
Hilker, G. C., 261
Hitchcock, Lambert, 100–101
Hoffmann, Josef, 348, 360–363, 371
Hofmann, Julius, 324
Holland, 101–102, 128, 137–138, 140–142, *141*, 147, 166, 168, *178*, 241, 279, 348. *See also* Netherlands.
"Holland chairs," 86–89, 168
Holland, Henry, 228, 262, 286, 288
Holland & Holland, 116
Holme, Randle, 80, 159
Holt, J. Lovegrove, *325*, 339
Holy Roman Empire, 190. *See also* Germany.
Homer, 24, 26
Hope, Thomas, 258, 262, 264–265, 266, 269, 288–292, *290*, *291*, *295*
Hoppenhaupt, Johann Michael, *191*, 193–194, 197, 214
Horace, 30–31
horseshoe-back armchairs, 40
Horta, Victor, 342–343
Hubbard, Elbert, 307
hu ch'uang, 36–37
Hucker, Thomas, *410*
Huet, Christophe, 202
human forms, 45–46, *47*, *389*
human surrogates, chairs as, 8
Hunt, William Holman, 296

Hunzinger, George, 95, 333–334
hwedom, 48
Hybsch, Enzo, 378

imitation antique chairs, 258–269
Ince and Mayhew, 211, 213
India, 140, *142*, *143*, 144, 147
Indiana Hickory Furniture, 131
indiscret, 340
Indonesia, 138–139, 142, 144, 147
inflatable chairs, 404
inlays and veneers, 19, *28*, *29*, *29*, 320, 334
invalid chair, *182*, *319*, 332, *333*, *333*, 341
Ionesco, Eugene, 8
Ireland, 84–85, 86, *87*, 128
Iribe, Paul, *357*
Isokon Furniture Company, *373*, *375*
Issel, Alberto, 349
Italy. *See also* specific city-states, e.g., Venice.: eighteenth-century design in, 84; garden chairs of, 128, 136; modern chairs of, 378–379; Neoclassicism in, 218, 232, 234, 234–238, *235*, *236*, *237*, *238*, 249; nineteenth-century design in, *257*, *261*, 279–281, *280*, *281*, 299, 300, 317, 327, 340, *348*, 348–349; during Renaissance, 59, 60, 64, 65, 66–67, *73*; Rococo style in, 179, *196*, *197*, 205–206, 215; seventeenth-century design in, 160–165, *162*
ivory, 19, *57*, *76*, *143*, 144, *145*
Ivory Coast, *46*, 47

Jacob-Desmalter, 274–277, *276*, *277*, 298
Jacob, Georges, 118, 218, 221, 225, 226, 226–228, *227*, 248, 254, 258, 270, 272, *272*, 276, 277
Jacobsen, Arne, 377–378, *379*, *400*
Jager, Franz, 299
Jakober, Ben, *414*
Jakobsen, Hans Sandgren, 379
James II period chairs, *155*
jamuga (side-saddle chair), 60
Japan, 304–305, 378
japanning, 166, *295*
Jardin, Nicolas Herni, 240–241
Java, 147
Jeanneret, Charles-Edouard. *See* Le Corbusier.
Jefferson, Thomas, 95–97
Jenner, Edward, 126
Jenneret, Pierre, 384
Jobain Company, 93

Joe chair, 401–403
joinery, 19, 24, 36, *54*
Jones, Allen, *403*
Jones, Inigo, 68, *75*
Jour et Nuit fauteuil, *387*
Judd, Donald, *393*
Jugendstil, 347, 348. See also Art Nouveau.
Jullian, Phillippe, 11

Kagan Sofa, *418*
kakstolle, 102
Kawaki, Kazuo, 336
Kedleston sofa, 208
Kent, William, 60, 208, 229
Kenya, 47
Kimbel, Anthony, 324
king's chair, 144
King, Thomas, 323
Kinsman, Rodney, 386
kitchen chairs, 89–90
Klint, Kaare, 137
klismos, *258*; from ancient Greece, 10, *21*, *23*, 24–26, *26*, *27*, *30*, *31*, 258; nineteenth-century, 258–260, *259*, *260*, *261*, *262*, *264*, *265*, *265*, *267*, *268*; twentieth-century, 269
kneeling, 35
Knobelsdorff, Georg von, 193
Knoll, Florence, *387*, 399
Knoll International, 116, 385–386, *386*, 399
Kohlmann, Etienne, *357*
Kohn, 370
Kramer, Ferdinand, *371*
krossie gobang, 147
Kuba people, 42, 49
Kuramata, Shiro, *355*, *391*, *392*, 397
Kusama, Yayoi, *415*

lacquer, 165–166, 264, 265, 266, 267
ladder-back chairs, 86–89
ladder-chair, *374*
Ladies in Conversation (Bosse), 66
La Donna Chair, *401*
Lady Bug seat, *404*
La Lecture (Reading) (tapestry), *53*
Lalonde, Richard de, 223, 234, *234*, *247*
La Mamma Chair, *401*
Lambert-Rucki, Jean, *264*, *265*
Lami, Eugène, *318*
lamination, 368, *371*, *372–379*
"lamphanger chairs," 40

Landi Chair, 136–137
Landi, Gaetano, *297*
Lane, Danny, 387, *413*
Lannuier, Charles-Honoré, 296
Latrobe, Benjamin, 258, 265–266, *266–267*
Latten-stuhl, *374*
Lauro, Agostino, 349
LCW (lounge chair wood), *376*, 377
leather upholstery, 77, *161*, 171, *393*
le Braalier, Jehan, 55
Le Brun, Charles, 151–152
Le Corbusier, 137, 336, 352, 353, 360, 368, 371, 384–385, *385*
Legrain, Pierre Emile, *133*, 137, 267
Leistler, Carl, 368
Leleu, Jules, 364–367
Le Moyne, François, *165*
Le Pautre, Antoine, 152
Lerner, Nathan, *373*
library armchair, *201*
Lilly chair, *397*
Linnell, John, 10, *204*, 208, 229, 230
Linnell, William, *204*, 208
lit d'alcove, 214
lit de jour, 173
lit de repos, 173, *173*
"literary machines," 340–341
Lloyd, Marshall B., 129
Lobel, Simon de, *157*, 249, 419
Lobi people, 43, 47
Locke, Matthias, 176, 179, 200
Lockheed Lounge, *391*
lolling chair, *243*, 243–245
Lomazzi, Paolo, 401, *402*
London Chair, *378*
Longhi, Pietro, 165
Loos, Adolf, 368
Louis 20, 136, *355*, 391
Louis XIV style, 7, 77, 118, *119*, 150–174
Louis XV style, *176*, 176, 179, 183, *186*, *187*, 197, 199, 202
Louis XVI style, 179, 218–251
Louise Marie de Bourbon ("*Mademoiselle de Tours*") (Mignard), *67*
"Louis Quatorze," 318
lounge chair, 136, 371, *376*, 377
Luba, 46
Lu Ban Jing, 35
Lucian, 29
Lucite, 397

Luckhardt, Hans and Wassili, *383*
Lundelius, Wilhelm, 283–285
lyre motif, 316

Machine Age style, 352, 353
Mackintosh, Charles Rennie, 42, 104–106, 342, *344*, *345*, 345–346, 348, 363
Majorelle, Louis, 342, *343*
Makepeace, John, 413
Makovsky, Konstantin, *65*
Mallet-Stevens, Roberts, *361*
Malmsten, Carl, 269, 411
Mandolin Chair, *409*
Mangbetu, 46
Mantegna, Andrea, 8
Manufacture des Gobelins, 151
Manufacture Royale des Meubles, 151–152
Manwaring, Robert, 103, 118, 208, 211, 217
marchands-tapissiers, 224, 251
Marcotte, Leon, 329
Mare, André, *356*, 360
Marie France Armchair, *417*
Marigny, marquis de, 218
Marilyn Sofa, *402*
Marot, Daniel, 151–152, *156*, *157*, *157*, *169*
Marot, Jean, 151–152
marquetry chairs, *229*
marquise, *177*, 214
marriage chairs, 91
Martha Washington chair, *243*
Martineau, Harriett, 95
Martin, Pierre Denis, *119*
Masreliez, Adrien, 180, 199
Masreliez, Louis, 262
Massai Chair, *404*
master armchair, *201*
Mategot, Mathieu, *389*
mats, 35
Mauser, F. Karl von, 213, 214
May, Samuel S., *101*
mechanical chairs, *334*
Medgyes, Landislas, 397
Medici family, *67*, *67*, 110, 151
medieval chairs, 51–77
meiguiyi, *39*
Meissonier, Juste-Aurèle, 176–179, 214, 217
Memoires d'une Bergère (Jullian), 11
Memphis group, 386–387
Men Shoveling Chairs (van der Weyden school), 8, *9*

menuisier, 189

méridienne, 357

Mésangère, Pierre Antoine Leboux de la, 277–279

Mesdach, Salomon, 68

metal furniture, 28, 29, 29, 30, 49, 56, 56, 60, 62, 124, 131, 132, 133, 371, 380–396; bronze, 136, 356; gold, 19, 53–54, 153, 415; iron, 28, 29, 29, 120, 123, 123–125, 125, 133; scrap metal, 49; sheet metal, 131; silver, 62, 143, 150, 151, 151, 152, 152, 153, 209, 225–226; stainless steel, 396; tubular steel, 11, 352, 371, 380, 380–396, 381, 382, 383, 384, 385, 386, 388, 389

Meunier, Etienne, 184

Mexico, 138, 139

Meyer, Christian, 285

Mid-Afternoon Chair, 415

Mies van der Rohe, Ludwig, 9, 10, 348, 352, 371, 373, 380, 382–384, 383, 384, 385

Mignard, Pierre, 67

Milan, 386–387

military furniture, 10, 114, 114–117, 116, 117, 177, 361

milking stools, 84, 85

Minoan civilization, 19–20

Minter brothers, 333

Miss Blanche chair, 355, 397

Mission style, 307

Mistral, Frédéric, 85

M'Kenzie, Andrew, 84

modern chairs, 352–419

Modernism, 368, 408

Modernista. See Art Nouveau.

modular units, 405

Moffat, W., 85

Molesworth, Thomas, 107, 108

Molière (Jean-Baptiste Poquelin), 159, 166, 167

Mollino, Carlo, 379, 417

Mongo, 47

Monckton Milnes, Richard, 115

monk's chair (*frailero*), 60, 171

Monreal, Julio, 155

Montferrand, Auguste Ricard de, 286

Moorish influence, 59, 139, 170–171

Mor, Antonius, 57

Moreau, 57, 254, 258

Moretti, Pascalin, 206

Morgan & Sanders, 115

Morris, William, 303, 304, 304, 305–306, 307, 308, 310, 341

mortise and tenon construction, 24, 36, 54

Moser, Koloman, 348

Mossi people, 43

mother-of-pearl, 147, 331, 354, 355

Motteville, Françoise de, 67

Mourgue, Oliver, 404–405

Mudéjar (Moorish) style, 139

Munich Werkbund, 355

musical instrument motifs, 219

musician's armchair, 184

Mycenaean furniture, 19, 20

Nadal, Jean-René, 221

Nagasaki chair, 389

Nahl, Johann August, 193

Nakashima, George, 412, 413

Naples, 317

Napoleon I, and family, 269–270, 270, 271–272, 272, 273, 274, 275, 279–280, 297

Napoleon III, and family, 321

Natural History (Pliny the Elder), 29

nebala, 46

Nelson, George, 377, 386

neo-antique seats, 261–262

Neoclassical style, 208, 218–251, 313

neo-Egyptian style, 265, 266, 269–297, 296, 297

neo-Gothic style, 10, 204, 298, 298–303, 299, 300, 301, 302, 303

neo-Louis style, 311, 318–329

neo-Pompeian style, 268

neo-Rococo, 318–320

Netherlands, 62–65, 68, 69, 70, 77, 144, 169, 179, 209. See also Holland.

Neuffforge, Jean François, 223, 234

New Book on Chinese Design (Edwards and Darly), 42

New Book on Garden Design (Edwards and Darly), 120

"new French style," 212

Newson, Mark, 391

Nicholson, Michael Angelo, 314

Niedrinhaus, Charles, 373–377

Nietzsche, Friedrich, 347

Nigeria, 42

Noli Me Tangere Stool, 404

Noll, Alexandre, 106, 413

Nordin, J.-F., 283–285

Norway, 54, 85, 309

Norwegian chair, 9

Nude Woman Resting Her Knee on a Chair (Carabin), 343

Nureyev, Rudolf, 155, 311, 313

nursing chairs, 311, 331

nylon, 397

OH Armchairs, 406, 407

Ohrmark, Eric, 262

Olbrich, Joseph Maria, 346, 346, 347

Old Hickory Chair Company, 106–108, 131

Omkstak chair, 386

opera chairs, 335

Oppenord, Gilles-Marie, 180, 214

Organic Modernism, 354

Ornamented Chair, The (Martineau), 95

osiers, 126

Osler, 146

Ottoman chair, 147

ottomane, 174, 214–216

ottomans, 322, 336, 338–339

Paimio lounge chair, 371, 377

painted decoration, 81–84, 82, 91, 91, 226

Painter of the Yale Cup (ancient Greece), 20

Palagi, Filippo Pelagio, 281, 281

Palissy, Bernard, 110

panchette, 197

Panton, Verner, 398

Paoli, Giovacchino, 232, 236

Papal State, 197

paphose, 174

papier-mâché chairs, 311, 331, 331–332

Parma, 197, 317

patent chairs, 332–336

Pauly, Signor, 113

Peacock chair, 352, 412

Peale, Charles Wilson, 203

peat, as seating material, 85

pelles à cul, 120

Pende, 48

Pennsylvania Dutch, 82, 86, 89, 93–94, 94

Pensi, Jorge, 391

Perceval, Sir John, 118

Percier, Charles, 10, 256, 258, 266, 269, 270, 272, 273, 274, 277, 279, 282, 286, 288, 292, 294, 297, 316

Pergolesi, 219

Perriand, Charlotte, 360, 384

perroquet, 171

Perspex, 397
Peru, 139
Pesce, Gaetano, 355, *401*
petits appartements, 156, 183
Philadephia, 95, 97, 98, *202*, *210*, 212, 245
Phyfe, Duncan, 294–296
Piedmont, 197, *249*
Piffetti, Pietro, 197
Pillement, Jean Baptiste, 202
pillows, 31
Pineau, Nicolas, 176, 197
Piranesi, Giovanni Battista, 218, 234, 238
plaid fabrics, 337
plastic, 11, 136, 391, 397–401; injection-molded, 398, 401, 405–406
Plateresque style, 139
platforms, 35
Platner, Warren, *399*
Plato, 24
Plautus, 30
Plexiglas, 355
pliants, 155, 157–158, *158*, 159, 213, 246
Pliny the Elder, 29, 30, 126
Pliny the Younger, 30
ployant, 60, 180
plywood, 334, 373–378, *376*
Pocock, William, 115
Poe, Edgar Allen, 311–312
pole chairs, 106
Pollux, 26
poltrona, 162
polychrome decoration, *143*
Polyprop chair, 405–406
polypropylene, 136, 405–406
polystyrene, 11, 397
polyurethane foam, 401–403, 404–405
polyvinyl chloride (PVC), 136, 397, 404
Pompadour, marquise de, 184, 218
Pompeii, 28, 30, *30*, 31
Pontremoli, *22*
Pop-Art design, 398–404, *401*, *402*, *403*, *404*, 405
Pope-Hennessy, James, 115
Poquelin, Jean-Baptiste (Molière), 159, *166*, 167
porcelain, 38
porcupine motifs, 45
Portugal, 47, 48, 89, 118, *139*, 139–140, *165*, 170–171, *179*, 209, 238–240, 327–329
Poseidon: Seated on a Throne (Füger), *7*
pouf, 338

Prairie School, 308–309
"Pratone," 403
"praying mantis," 47–48
"Pretzel" armchair, 377
Prikker, Johann Thron, 342
"primitive" art, 353
Prince of Wales chair, 339
procession chair, *183*
Protagoras (Plato), 24
Prouvé, Jean, 131, *135*, *372*, 378, 384–385
provençal chairs, 90–91
Prussia, 123–125, 166, 170, 193–194, 206, 266, 279, 323–324, 338, 341
Prutscher, Otto, 371
pseudo-archeological chairs, 254–297
Pugin, Augustus Welby Northmore, 10, 302, *302*, 303, 304
Purdy, 116

Quaker chairs, 330
Quarenghi, Giacomo, 242
Quarti, Eugenio, 349
quartz thrones, *44*
Queen Anne chair, 144, 170, 171, 212
Quinet, Jacques, *361*

Race, Ernest, 377
Raffles chair, 147
railroads, seating for, 334
Rampendahl, H. F. C., 109
Randolph, Benjamin, *202*
Rashid, Karim, *395*, 406, *407*
Rastrelli, Bartolomeo, 199, *199*
Rateau, Armand Albert, 136, *356*, 360
rattan, 126, 144
reading chairs, 11
Récamier, Madame, 9
reclining chairs, 11, *36*, 333, *333*, 334
Recueil de Décorations Intérieurs (Percier and Fontaine), 270, 277
Red and Blue Chair, 353, 408
reed, 126
Régence style, *175*, 175–176, 181, 183
Regency period, England, 90, 256, 265, *265*, 287, 288, 288–294, *289*, *290*, *291*, *292*, *293*, *294*, 295
Reich, Lily, 371
Reinach, Théodore, *27*
reine, à la, 183
Remi & Ci, 113

renaissance chairs, 51–77
Renoir, Pierre-Auguste, 8
Revett, Nicholas, 262
rib mesh, 355
Ribote de Trainquetaille, La (Mistral), 85
Richardson, Henry Hobson, 303
Riemerschmid, Richard, 129, 347, *347*, 348
Rietveld, Gerrit, 353, *374*, 408
Rigaud, Jacques, *119*
Rinaldi, Antonio, 205
Robert, Hubert ("Robert des Ruines") 225, *227*
Roberts, Thomas, 168, 173–174
Roberty, Beausejour Racine, 103, *404*
Robinson, Charles, 89
Robsjohn-Gibbons, 269
rocaille motifs, 176, 200
rocking chairs, 94, *94*–95, 99, *99*–100, *101*, *102*, 147, *315*
rocks, as seats, 23
Rococo style, 170, 175–217, 326
Roed, Joergen, 261
Roentgen, Abraham, 184–187, *192*, *193*, 238
Roentgen, David, *238*, 255, 268
Roentgen workshops, *113*
Rohlfs, Charles, 307, *408*
Roman Catholic Church, 139
Romanesque period, 60
Romantic Nationalism, 306
Rome: ancient, 9, 26, *28*, 28–32, *29*; modern, 194, 218, 246
rose motifs, 81
Ross & Co., 115
Rossetti, Dante Gabriel, 303, 305
Rossi, Carlo, 285–286, *313*
Roubo, 223
roulette, *118*, *119*
round-back chairs, 40–41
Rousseau, Jean Jacques, 104
Roux, Alexander, 303, 329
royal chairs, 18, 55, 57–60, *206*, 225. *See also* thrones.
Royère, Jean, *267*
Ruhlmann, Jacques Emile, *267*, *358*, 364
rush-seated chairs, 86–89, 89–90
Russia: baroque style in, 169–170; country chairs of, *87*, *108*, *110*, *112*, *113*, 114–115, 116; eighteenth-century design in, *82*; monarchy of, 152, 187, 199, 200, 215, 242, *242*; Neoclassicism in, 241–243, 247, *313*; nineteenth-century design in, *260*,

266–268, *284*, 285–286, 299, 300, *300*, *309*, 309–310, *314*, *316*, 317, *317*, *326*, 326–327; of Renaissance, 65, *65*; Rococo style in, 179–180, *199*, 199–200, 205, 211, 215; throne made in, 152
"Russian Jacob" chairs, 285
rustic furniture, 103–108, *104*, *105*, *106*, *107*, *118*, 125
Rustic Hickory Furniture Company, 131

Saarinen, Eero, 134, 137, 354, 397, 398, *398*
Sacco chair, 355, 403–404
Saint Edward's Chair, 54
Saint Martin's Lane style, 200, 212
Saint Phalle, Nikki de, *402*
Saint-Simon, 153, *158*, 160, 166–167, 172, 173
sanatorium chair, 9
Savonarola chair, *58*, 60
Saxony, 197
Scandinavian design, 9, 408–413
Scheffer, Henri, *319*
Schindler, Rudolph, *363*
Schinkel, Karl Friedrich, *123*, 123–125, 266, *279*, 279, 300, 330, 341
Schlott, Anton von, 194
school chairs, 101
Scotland, 84, 345
Scott, Mackay Hugh Baillie, 346
seat height, 16, 42, 53
Sea Urchin Chair, 403
sedan chair, 49
Seddon, George, *231*, 231–232
Seder, Adolf, 324, *326*
Sedlak Chair, 391
sella curulis, 10, *28*, *29*, *30*, 55. *See also* curule chair.
Sené, Jean-Baptiste-Claude, *220*, *221*, 269
Serrurier-Bovy, Gustave, 342–343
Setelstoel, 168
settee, 31, 34, 98, 125, 174, 217, *257*, 311
settles, 62–65, *65*. *See also* benches.
sexual activities, chairs for, 11, 187–189
Sezessionstil, 341, 348. *See also* Vienna Secession.
sgabello(i), 67–68, *72*, *75*
sgabello a tre piedi, 67
Shaker chairs, 89, 98–100, 103
Shakespeare, William, 7
shaving chair, 144
Shearer, Thomas, 243

Shell chair (Eames), 397
Shell chair (Wegner), 379
sheng chuang, 38–40, *41*
Sheraton, Thomas, 223–224, *233*, 233–234, 238, 241, 243, 245, 246–247, 248, 262, 264, 283
Sicily, 237
Sidoli, Alessandro, 300
Siegel, Gustave, 371
siéges courants, 225, 251
siéges meublants, 225, 251
Sika Dwa Kofi, 45
Silber & Fleming, 109
sillita de estrado, 74
sillon frailero, 171
Sipek, Borek, 391, *414*
skeleton forms, 8, *8*
slaves, as chairs, 49
slip-covers, 251, 337
slipper-chair, 311
Smith, George, 269, 288, 294, *295*, 298
smoker chair, *339*, 340
Smollet, Tobias, 95
Snake Chair, *402*
Socci, Giovanni, 281
social upheaval, chairs representing, 8, 9
sofas, 156, 173–174, *174*, 214–217, *247*, 247–248, *249*, *336*. *See also canapés*.
solium, 30
Solomon, 7, 53–54
Solomon's Chair, *413*
Song of Roland, 55
Songye, 46
sophas. *See* sofas.
Sophocles, 24
Soterictus, 31
Sottsass, Ettore, *403*
Spain, 48, 55, *59*, 60, *60*, *61*, 64, 65, 66, *74*, 82, 89, 139, 140, 155–156, 159, *165*, 167, 170–171, 180, *198*, 199, *199*, 205, 209–211, 238, 239, 240, 254, 282–283, 349
"Spanish chair," 68, *69*
sphinx motifs, 19
Spider Chair, *391*
Spine Chair, 387
spiritual power, of chairs, 42–44
Spring group, 379
squeeze-design, *406*
Sri Lanka, 138, 144–147
stabellen chairs, 92
Stahl, Ephraim, *264*

Stam, Mart, 380, 384
star chair, *129*
Starck, Philippe, 136, 355, *378*, 379, 391, *391*, 406, *418*
steam bending, 24
Stickley, Gustav, *306*, 307
Stile Florale. *See* Art Nouveau.
Stile Liberty. *See* Art Nouveau.
Stone of Scone, 54
stone seats, 24, 29, 38, 118, 120, *131*
stools, 15, 15–17, *16*, 20, *20*, 23, *23*, 28, 29, 29–30, *30*, 32, 36–38, 40, 42–43, *43*, 44–47, *45*, *46*, *47*, 60–62, 84, *85*, *86*, 138–139, 157–159, *158*, *159*, 213, 245–247, 297, 371
straw chairs, 126–130
Stuart, James "Atherian," 262
Stubbs, John, *105*
Studio 65, *402*
style étrusque, 223, 224, 228, 238
Sudan, 47
Sue, Louis, *356*, 360
Sue & Mare, *356*, 360
sultane, 250
sunduk, 65, *65*, 84
Surrealism, 353, 368
Swan Chair, *400*
Sweden: country chairs of, *85*, *88*, 89, 114; eighteenth-century design in, 81, *83*, *85*; modern design in, 372–373; monarchy of, 152, *152*, 180, 262; Neoclassicism in, 219, 225, 240, 241; nineteenth-century design in, 262, *264*, 269, 283–285, 316–317, 326; Rococo style in, 180, 199, 206
Switzerland, 92, *92*, *93*, 131–134, 136–137
swivel armchairs, *70*
Szekely, Martin, *392*, *417*

ta, 35
tabourets, 155, 157, *158*, *158*, *159*, 213
Takahama, Kazuhide, 405
Talbert, Bruce, 303
Tallement des Réaux, Gédéon, 160, 167
tamarisk, 14
Tanzania, 47, *48*
Tardieu, 57
Tarred and Feathered Chair, *414*
"Tatami," 379
Tatham, Charles Heathcote, 268, 286, 288
Techno chaise longue, *389*
Teodora, *403*

Terry, Emilio, *105*, *129*
tester (canopy), 54
tête-à-tête, *113*, 340
theater seating, 23–24, 66, *222*, *276*, *334*, *335*
Thomas, Antoine, *319*
Thonet, Michael, 94, 323, 368–370, *369*, 377, 382
three-legged chairs, 11, 16–17
3107 chairs, 377–378
Throne of St. Peter, *52*
thrones, 15, 18–19, 23, 24, 25, 30, 38–40, *41*, *42*, *43*, *44*, 46, *46*, 48, *48–49*, *52*, 52–54, *56*, 56–57, 62, *63*, *81*, 137–138, *145*, 150, *151*, *151*, *152*, 272, *272*, *273*
thronos, 23, 24
tielimu wood, *41*
Tietze, Gustav, 116
Tietz, Ferdinand, 194
Tilliard, 189
tipoy (sedan chair), 49
Toledo chair, *391*
tombs, 14, 16, 19, 35, 297
tongue and groove, 36
torture chairs, 9, *10*
tournis, à, 62
Toussaint, Carlo, 235, *236*
Trades, The: The Apothecary (Bosse), *72*
"Trafalgar" chairs, *283*, 292–294
trestle tables, 65–66
tub chairs, 128
tubular steel, 11, 352, 371, *380*, 380–396, *381*, *382*, *383*, *384*, *385*, *386*, *388*, *389*
Tulip Collection, *397*, *398*
tulip motifs, 81
Tumble, Francis, 98
turf, as seating material, 85
Turin, *238*
Turkish sofa, 338–339
turned chairs, 74
Turtle seat, *404*
Tutankhamun's tomb, 14, 16, 19, 297
"twig" chairs, metal, *132*

Ubaldini, Petruccio, 62
Umbrella Chair, *401*
upholstered chairs, 55–56, 65, *73*, *75*, 75–76, 77, *154*, *155*, 156–157, *160*, 160, *161*, *162*, *163*, 171, 248–251, 322, 336–341, *339*, 416–419

Valabrega, Vittorio, 349
van de Passe, Crispijn, *75*, 168

van der Weyden, Rogier, school of, 8, *9*
van de Velde, Henry Clement, 341–342, *342*, 347
Veerbeckt, Jacques, 184
veilleuse, 215
velvet, 77
veneers: tortoiseshells, 29
veneers and inlays, 19, *28*, 29, *29*, 320, 334. See also specific material, e.g., ivory.
Venice, 112, 113, 165, 166, 179, 183, 196, 197, 213, *353*
ventaglio, 215
Venus armchair, *113*
Verney, Mary, 74
Versailles, *150*, 151, *151*, 156, 158, *158*, 159, *163*, 165, 166–167, 169, 171–172, *174*, 183, 213, 222, 245–246
Victorian style, 11, 265
Victory Chair, *287*
Vienna, 314, 316, 323, 368–370
Vienna Cafe chair, *369*
Vienna Secession, 128, 348, 352. See also Sezessionstil.
Vierlander chair, *91*, 91
Vigée-Lebrun, Madame, 8
Viking Revival, 85
Viollet-le-Duc, Eugène-Emmanuel, 10, 302–303
vis-à-vis, 340
Vlaminck, Maurice de, 297
Voltaire, 153–155, 167, 190, 204, 214
"Voltaire" chair, 321
von Klenze, Leo, 266, *277*
von Stuck, Franz, 268
Voronikin, Andrei Nikiforovich, 285, *286*
voyelle, 181, *183*
voyeuse, 181, 220, 223–224, 340
Voysey, Charles Francis Annesley, 306
Vredemann de Vries, Hans, 70, *75*

Wagner, Otto, 348, 352
Wakefield, Cyrus, 126
Wakefield Rattan Company, 128
Walli, James, *307*
Ward, Rowland, 110, *110*
Wassily Chair, 9, *380*, 380
Watteau, Jean-Antoine, 202
Wealleans, Jon, 403
Webb, Philip, *304*, 305
Wegner, Hans, 352, *379*, 409, 411–413

Westminster Abbey, 54
Westport chairs, 130
Wetzdorf armchair, *278*
wicker chairs, 101–102, *126*, 126–130, *127*
Wiener Werkstätte, 348, 352, 363, 370–372
"wiggle" sidechair, *379*
Wilde, Oscar, 311
William and Mary chair, *165*
Wilson, Robert, *109*, *132*
Winckelmann, Johann Joachim, 218
window seats, 62
Windsor chairs, 80, 95–98, *96*, *97*, *118*, *119*
Wolf, Elsie de, 397
wood, 19, 29, 320, 334, 379; acacia, 14; beech, 29; birch, 377; box, 14–15; cedar, 14; citrus wood, 29; ebony, 15, 20, *141*, 142–144; elm, *34*; fruitwood, *89*, *261*; hickory, 131; *huanghuali*, 32, 36, *37*, *37*, *39*; mahogany, 208, 224–225, 228–229, *271*; maple, 29; plywood, 334, 373–378, *376*; rootwood, 33, *40*, *118*; rosewood, 209; satinwood, *231*, *231*; sycamore fig, 14; tree trunks, *105*; twigs and branches, 103–108, *104*, *105*, *106*, *107*; walnut, *72*; willow, 29, *126*, *306*
woodworking tools, 15
Woolsey chair, *339*
Wright, Frank Lloyd, 308–309, 345, 348, 354
Wright, Jon, 403
wrought iron, *28*, 29, *29*, 123
Würzburg, 194
Wyatt, James, *282*, 283

Xinbian Duixiangsiyan, 41
X-shaped seats, 54–55, *56*, 56–57, 316

Yanagi, Sori, 378
Yaoure, 46
Yetley, 109
yokeback chairs, 40
Youf, Jean-Baptiste, 280–281

Zaire, 42, *43*, 44, *45*, 46, *47*, 48, *49*
Zambia, *47*, 48
Zayas y Sotomayor, Maria de, 156, *159*
Zig Zag chairs, *374*
Zimba, 46
zitan wood, 32, *37*
Zocker chair, 103
Zoid Sofa, *404*
Zucchi, 219

Acknowledgments

This lengthy opus, its research spread over many years, would not have seen the light of day without the help and support of numerous friends and family members, not to mention my dynamic agent, Lois de la Haba. My deepest thanks go to friends who for years could not see a chair without thinking of me, and who helped me track down the images for the book. Among these are Wolfram Koeppe, who gave me invaluable support; Daniëlle Kisluk-Grosheide; and my dear friend Masha Nudell, all three of them at the Metropolitan Museum of Art. I also want to thank my cousin, Dominique de Courcelles, in Paris; Janic Durand at the Louvre; and my friend Jean Louis Guillemain, who once wrote to me that he was having dreams about chairs on my behalf! I wish, too, to thank my mother, who keeps clipping relevant articles about chairs from every publication she can put her hands on, and countless others, among them my close friends Tom Fallon and Nabil Nahas. A special nod also to Tim Street Porter for my portrait photograph on the jacket.

My deepest gratitude must go to my friend Joan Bernstein, who very graciously read my whole manuscript—and liked it! Many thanks also to the diligent work of my delightful and competent editor, Elaine Stainton, who made the editing work a pleasure; and to the whole team at Abrams, spearheaded by the company's terrific editor in chief, Eric Himmel. I wish to thank especially Joseph Cho and Stefanie Lew of Binocular Design for their superb work on the layout and typography, and Jane G. Searle for her meticulous oversight of the book's production.

Finally, I thank Sean, my husband, for his constant support, and Aymar, Cameron, and Valentina, who are all so happy that this book is finally finished and are brimming with suggestions for my next venture.

Florence de Dampierre

Project Manager Eric Himmel
Editor Elaine M. Stainton
Designer Binocular, New York
Production Manager Jane G. Searle

Library of Congress Cataloging-in-Publication Data

Dampierre, Florence de.
  Chairs : a history / Florence de Dampierre.
      p.   cm.
  Includes index.
  ISBN 10: 0-8109-5484-2 (hardcover)
  ISBN 13: 978-0-8109-5484-7 (hardcover)

1. Chairs—History. I. Title.

NK2715.D33 2006
749'.3209—dc22
                                2005033218

Copyright © 2006 Florence de Dampierre

Published in 2006 by Abrams, an imprint of Harry N. Abrams, Inc.

All rights reserved. No portion of this book may be reproduced, stored in a retrieval system, or transmitted in any form or by any means, mechanical, electronic, photocopying, recording, or otherwise, without written permission from the publisher.

Printed and bound in China
10 9 8 7 6 5 4 3 2 1

Frontispiece: A painting by Marie Guilhemine Benoist (1768–1826) of Pauline, Princess Borghese, c. 1808, seated in an Empire armchair. Châteaux de Versailles et de Trianon. Photograph: RMN. Arnaudet/J. Schormans

a subsidiary of La Martinière Groupe
115 West 18th Street
New York, New York 10011
www.hnabooks.com